ENCOUNTERS IN EDUCATION

ENCOUNTERS IN EDUCATION

Robert E. Fitzgibbons
Bridgewater State College

Raymond J. ZuWallack
Bridgewater State College

Harcourt Brace College Publishers

Fort Worth Philadelphia San Diego New York Orlando Austin San Antonio
Toronto Montreal London Sydney Tokyo

Publisher	Christopher P. Klein
Acquisitions Editor	Jo-Anne Weaver
Product Manager	Don Grainger
Project Editor	Louise Slominsky
Production Manager	Cynthia Young
Art Director	Melinda Welch/Lora Knox

ISBN 0-15-505140-7

Library of Congress Catalog Card Number: 97-72354

Address for Orders:
Harcourt Brace & Company
6277 Sea Harbor Drive
Orlando, FL 32887-6777
1-800-782-4479

Address for Editorial Correspondence:
Harcourt Brace College Publishers
301 Commerce Street, Suite 3700
Fort Worth, TX 76102

Web site address:
http://www.hbcollege.com

Printed in the United States of America

7 8 9 0 1 2 3 4 5 6   066   9 8 7 6 5 4 3 2 1

To
Brian
and
Joseph, David, and Joshua Ford

To
Mom, Dad, and the big white house on the hill

PREFACE

We each have been involved with teacher education for more than 20 years and generally have been disappointed with the texts that have been available for introducing prospective teachers to the challenges facing the profession. We believe that there is a need for an introductory text that deals directly with the major educational issues of the day in a manner that is both interesting and understandable to the beginning education student.

Encounters in Education is designed to meet that need. It is a book of readings dealing with the state of education in America and is intended for use in college courses such as Introduction to Education, Introduction to Teaching, Contemporary Issues in Education, and Foundations of Education. It may be used either by itself or as a supplement to a more conventional text.

One of the major problems with most books of readings on education is that students typically find them "dry" and uninteresting. Let's say it—they're boring. Both the topics and the individual selections are often stale, detached, overly academic and sometimes arcane, and frequently requiring considerable background knowledge, understanding, and a general level of sophistication that beginning students usually do not possess. We have generally avoided articles from technical education journals, since most of these are written for the scholar or the experienced teacher. This material tends to be too statistical, too abstract, and too clinically dry for the beginning student and often presents a problem for instructors when students resist doing assigned readings.

Encounters in Education, in contrast, is interesting. The selections deal with major contemporary "hot" topics. Most articles are relatively short. All articles are highly readable and provocative. They lead the student directly into the excitement and the drama of timely, central educational debates and provide the college instructor with a flexible vehicle for stimulating class discussion.

Encounters in Education provides students with relevant *background information* needed for rationally discussing the subject at hand. This includes "walk in their shoes" articles where students vicariously experience what it means to be a "real" person involved in a politically charged educational situation. For example, in H. G. Bissinger's article, "We're All Racists Now," the reader experiences the burned out, jaded, inner-city teacher. The second type of background article is the "hard-core, data-driven essay," where readers are presented with manageable empirical evidence upon which they can formulate intelligent judgments. One of these is David Berliner's article, "Mythology and the American System of Education," where they are presented with clear data concerning IQ scores as they relate to the question of whether today's American public school students are more or less intelligent than those of previous generations. *Encounters in Education* contains background information of both types of articles on virtually every controversial issue in contemporary education.

Among books in the field, *Encounters in Education* is unique. There is no other introductory education text that contains the range and number of provocative selections from such well-written, lively publications as *The Atlantic Monthly, U.S. News & World Report, Psychology Today, Time, Science, The Progressive, The Washington Monthly, The Brookings Review,* and *Vital Speeches of the Day. Encounters in Education* contains readings from all of these sources along with direct, timely articles from some of the nation's leading newspapers: *The Atlanta Journal & Atlanta Constitution, The Boston Globe, The Chicago Tribune, The Christian Science Monitor, The Los Angeles Times, The New York Times, USA Today, The Wall Street Journal,* and *The Washington Post.* And there are engaging selections from distinctly educational publications: *Children Today, The College Board Review, The Education Digest, Education Week, Educational Leadership, NEA Today, Phi Delta Kappan, Teachers College Record, The Delta Kappa Gamma Bulletin, The Journal of Black Studies, The Mathematics Teacher,* and *Thrust for Educational Leadership.*

While many education texts possess a decidedly ideological slant, *Encounters in Education* employs an informal pro–con format. Its function is to assist students in developing a more comprehensive understanding of the diversity of opinions, and often blatantly clashing ideologies, surrounding contemporary educational issues while at the same time adding to the readability of the text. Moreover, the "take no prisoners" quality of many of these selections provides the instructor with a natural motivational tool to promote genuine student involvement.

The organizational structure of the book naturally leads the reader into the critical educational debates of the day. Part one, *Background,* considers four major core factors outside of the school that obviously affect what goes on in the school. These external factors are *family, gender, religion,* and *race.* Part two, *Equality,* explores a range of controversial areas involving the school as an arena for social engineering—*compensatory education, bilingual education, multicultural education, detracking,* and *inclusion.* These concern what actually goes on, and what should go on, inside the school, in light of the background factors examined in part one. What is done inside the school naturally leads to a consideration of the issues identified in part three, *Quality.* A chapter on *achievement* examines the issue of just how well the schools are doing in actually meeting traditional academic objectives. This chapter is followed by a consideration of current, radically divergent proposals for *future* directions for American schools. First, from the liberal point of view, the debates over *outcome-based education and portfolio assessment* are investigated.

Then, from the conservative side, the issues of *standards and school choice* are examined.

We wish to thank Jo-Anne Weaver, senior acquisitions editor, for her faith in this project and her early recognition that our proposal for *Encounters in Education* was indeed unique in format, scope, and readability and that the book would be a significant contribution to students' better understanding of critical educational issues. Our thanks also go to Louise Slominsky, project editor, for her consummate professionalism. With patience and gentle prodding, she shepherded the text through all the various stages of the production process. She has contributed significantly to making this a better book.

Finally, we thank our wives, Barbara and Linda, for their unfailing encouragement and support.

CONTENTS

Chapter 6
BILINGUAL EDUCATION   196

Chapter 7
MULTICULTURAL EDUCATION   220

Chapter 8
DETRACKING   246

Chapter 9
INCLUSION   275

PART THREE
Quality   305

Chapter 10
ACHIEVEMENT   307

Chapter 11
OUTCOME-BASED EDUCATION AND PORTFOLIOS   348

Chapter 12
STANDARDS AND SCHOOL CHOICE   **375**

ENCOUNTERS IN EDUCATION

PART ONE

Background

Chapter 1

FAMILY

INTRODUCTION

There appears to be something terribly wrong with American education. Politicians, columnists, television commentators, and radio talk-show hosts and their callers have been quick to fault schools, in general, and teachers and students, in particular, for what they perceive as a precipitous decline in quality. They charge that education in the United States has become academically and morally "second-rate." They maintain that students—if not all, then certainly a large number—graduating from high school do not possess the fundamental skills of an educated person: They cannot write coherently; they cannot read with understanding; they cannot do simple mathematics; and they cannot reason cogently. Not only are they deficient in these basic skills, but, the critics argue, students' lack of knowledge is abysmal: They do not know history; they do not know geography; they do not know science; and significantly, they do not even know their own country's Constitution. And with regard to their behavioral characteristics, the perception is often that most young people are ill-mannered, many are prone to violence, and growing numbers tend to take drugs and engage in promiscuous sexual activity.

Even though there is a high level of agreement that there are problems with American education, there is far less agreement about exactly what the problems are, their causes, and what corrective steps should be taken. One common diagnosis places the locus of many of these ills not in the school but in the family. Many see the "breakdown of the family unit" as the root cause of much of what is wrong with American education today.

Is there one best way for a family to be organized? Is a two-parent family inherently better than a single-parent family? What is the import, if any, of divorce on children and particularly on their academic achievement? What values should parents instill in their children? What responsibility do parents themselves, as opposed to the state, have for the education of their children?

Do we have any hard, scientific evidence that family structure has specific educational effects on children? Why is it that one "study" indicates that the family has certain educational effects and another "study" indicates just the opposite? How would a study have to be designed and conducted in order to confirm to a high degree that family factors have specific educational effects?

Windows on Children's Worlds
Indira A. R. Lakshmanan

William Teleau stares as a cluster of his fifth-grade classmates gleefully jostle each other onto a school bus, bound for an afterschool children's choir. For a long moment, his hand-me-down sneakers seem frozen to the concrete schoolyard. Downcast, he turns and jogs away, head bowed.

For his clear, soprano voice and eagerness to participate, William was chosen for a prestigious choir that draws children from all over Boston and its suburbs. But with no one available to fetch him from choir, William is homeward bound for an afternoon of solitude instead.

Some 20 miles from William's home in Mattapan, Kim Griffis flies through the door of her Marshfield home from her Girl Scout troop meeting. She speeds through her homework, plays Nintendo with her brother and sister, then surfs through 50 cable channels, past music videos and sports shows, CNN and movies. Quickly bored, she opts instead for a CD-ROM computer art program for kids.

Journeying through a typical day in each of their lives, these two fifth-graders offer a window onto what it is to be a child in the 1990s, whether city or suburban.

William and Kim's lives are light-years away from their parents' childhoods. Both see less of their mothers, who work full-time, but the second incomes mean they live more comfortably than their parents did. Through school and television, both know more about drugs, sex and violence and how to avoid them—topics that weren't discussed within earshot of youngsters a few decades ago. But their childhoods are also different in a subtler, just as important way: how they play.

William spends his afternoons alone—a virtual prisoner in his home. His parents work, and are too fearful of the gunfire they sometimes hear in the neighborhood to let him play outside unsupervised.

"Our children, when they go out to recess, they don't know how to play with each other. We have to teach them to throw a ball, play with other kids,"

SOURCE: *The Boston Globe*, June 5, 1995, pp. 1; 6–7. Reprinted courtesy of *The Boston Globe*.

says William's principal, Cheryl Fontes of the Charles Taylor Elementary School in Mattapan. "Their neighborhoods are dangerous and their parents are afraid, so the minute they get in the house, they're in."

Likewise, Kim's life in Marshfield is different from the casual childhoods her parents remember from their summers growing up there. Her afternoons are scheduled, her social life organized and her leisure time filled more with Nintendo, cable television and computer games than with spontaneous stickball, tag and board games her parents shared with neighborhood pals.

"The freedom of being outdoors," Kim's mother sighs. "When I was growing up, as long as my homework was done, it didn't matter what I did as long as I was home for dinner. Everything is arranged now—I call the mother, the mother calls me."

In school and home life, both fifth-graders convey volumes about what has changed for children in just a single generation.

Good Morning America blares as Kim prints out a school report on the home computer for her older sister on a recent Tuesday morning. As in countless other families, the computer revolution is happening so fast that the technological savvy of younger siblings often eclipses that of the older ones. Kim's mother darts around organizing everybody while blow-drying her hair. Joanne Griffis must have everyone ready by 8 A.M. to get Kim to band practice before school and still make it to her job in Boston by 9. Everyone's got to stay on schedule. Her husband has left already for his 7 A.M. start as a naval technician in Boston.

"Is your room squared away, T. J.?" Griffis calls out to Kim's younger brother over the din of the dryer, the computer printer and the TV.

"Yup," comes the reply from beneath the brown bowl haircut.

"Is your bed made?"

"Yup."

"Did you put your report in your folder?"

"Nope."

"So do that," Griffis directs. "Are you guys buying or bringing lunch today?"

Kim scans the school menu and extends her hand for a dollar. Kim's mother grins; that means she won't have to make lunch.

Griffis works as the customer service manager at National Braille Press in Boston's Back Bay—an hour's commute each way. She took the job before the family moved to the Marshfield home she partly inherited three years ago. The family needed her income, but the schedule was crazy. She would watch the clock until the school bus arrived; drive an hour to work, and tear home in the evening to relieve a babysitter before cooking and collapsing, too tired to do much more than put the kids to bed.

"I finally said to my boss, 'This is too difficult. What if I worked a couple days at home?'" Griffis recalls.

So Griffis, with the help of a computer printer and extra phone line, now works two days a week of her full-time job at home—one of 18 percent of mothers with school-age children working part of the week at home, according to the Census.

Kim "wouldn't be able to do Girl Scouts or softball or other activities if I couldn't drive her," Griffis says. "Some people say it makes kids more independent, freer thinkers, stronger to be alone, but I say they have plenty of time for that when they're 18."

The doorbell rings, and it's a friend of Kim's who needs a ride to band practice. Kim grabs her saxophone, the kids pile into the Plymouth Voyager, and promptly at 8, they're off.

Brief Moments Together for Mother and Son

At 7 A.M. sharp on a recent Thursday, William's mother shakes him awake on his cot in the second-floor hallway.

William's family—his mother and stepfather, brother and grandparents— moved to this grey clapboard home on Brockton Street two years ago from another part of Mattapan. It was a step up, to a roomy, free-standing two-story set far back from the street, in a safer neighborhood. But with only two bedrooms for the extended family, William sleeps in the hall and his older brother sleeps in the basement.

School doesn't start for two hours, but William's mother, Paula Thermo, is already running late for her first job of the day, as a home health aide.

To make ends meet, Thermo, 41, must work five days a week, from 8 A.M. to midnight in three patients' homes. She leaves right after waking William, and often doesn't see him again until the next morning. On weekends, she works half days.

As a result, William's childhood is striking in several respects. He spends hours on end alone. The 10-year-old cooks his own breakfasts, and when his grandmother is ill, his own dinners. In a typical week, he sees his mother for about 90 minutes over the course of five days.

This groggy moment of half-consciousness when she rouses William is one of their few times together. When she can, she stops at home for an hour between her second and third jobs to nap, gobble some dinner and see her son. But by then, her half closed eyes are too tired to focus on much.

So in the morning, she strokes his face and tells him to do all his work in school. She reminds him to take a bath, eat breakfast and clean his teeth, and squeezes toothpaste onto his brush so he won't forget. William wraps her in a tight hug and clambers out of bed as she rushes out the door.

William pads into the kitchen, expertly spreads margarine in a weathered pan, cracks eggs, adds cheese and slips some bread in the toaster. "My mother taught me how to cook since I was 7," he declares proudly. "Rice, eggs, macaroni, spaghetti, tacos. So when I grow up, I'll know how to make my own food."

After eating breakfast alone, William packs his books and reads while waiting for his grandfather to drive him to school.

A clock radio blares from his grandparents' bedroom, and the old man eases down the stairs sleepily, telling William in Creole it's time to go to school.

In the playground of the Taylor School, William races to his friend Jonathan and grasps him in a playful head-lock. These moments in the schoolyard are his few with his friends: there's no one to take him to their homes after school, and like most of his classmates, he isn't allowed to walk alone on city streets.

His school is considered fairly typical of public elementary schools in Boston, both in what he is taught and the condition of the school.

William's antiquated school building is so jam-packed with students that every room is full. "We have no gym, no cafeteria, no auditorium, no art room, no music room, no conference room, no counseling room," sighs principal Fontes. "Every single space, even closets, are utilized." A Boston Public Schools spokesman calls the overcrowding at the Taylor School "typical" of the city's public elementary schools.

One result of the overcrowding is that the students never leave their classrooms except to go [to] the bathroom; they even eat lunch at their desks. They don't have gym or computer class either; that was last semester.

Half of the students at William's school are poor. One in five of his schoolmates speaks English as a second language. And despite years of explosive efforts to desegregate the Boston schools, William's exposure to classmates of other races is limited; of 21 students in the class, 19 are black and two white. William sits at a table of five boys; all but one speak Creole at home.

William's mother loves the school. It is, she notes, clean and safe and has a principal who encourages her staff to act as surrogate parents during the school day.

William eagerly makes his way to his basement classroom. But his face falls when he sees he has a substitute teacher again—for the fifth week in a row.

Substitute Emily McNeal motions to the board, where she has written a definition of the Peace Corps. She asks the children if they would want to commit two years of their lives to help a foreign country. One Haitian child says she wants to help Haiti.

The students then read aloud, and McNeal talks about classics and asks the class if they know any Greek myths.

The replies: "Mona Lisa," "Michelangelo," "Donatello."

McNeal shakes her head in amazement. "You guys are fifth-graders and you don't know any myths? We'll do a unit on Greek, Roman and Norse myths." For now, it's on to math.

William's favorite subjects are math and science. He gets As and Bs and wants to be a doctor. But he struggles with the decimal problems today, and is too shy to raise his hand for help. Later at home, he will do his homework alone—with no one available, to help him through the tough parts.

At 12:45 P.M., William, like almost every student in the class, gets a free lunch of a small dry cheeseburger, chocolate milk, fruit cocktail and a cookie. The children eat in enforced silence at their desks, chided by an aide when they chatter.

After lunch, it's time for a spelling test. William listens with rapt concentration to the words—cork, soar, flare.

At day's end, they've earned recess: They finally get to play.

■ ■ ■

School's Challenges Fill Up the Hours

Kim's day at Gov. Winslow Elementary School passes fast and furiously. Every moment is packed with activity, challenges, a parade of praising teachers, quizzes and reviews. For all the widespread complaining about public schools today, Kim's parents say they are pleased with the education she's getting, and so does she.

As in William's school, racial diversity is nearly nonexistent. Kim's school is 98 percent white, just like the town. While half of the children in William's city school are poor, 12 percent of the students in Kim's school are.

Homeroom teacher Jerry Morris tells his 24 students that they will get to use the classroom computer for their history reports if they've been unable to use a computer at home. One-third of his students, Morris estimates, use computers at home—a level of techno-literacy their parents wouldn't have dreamed of as children.

Morris then leads the class in spelling baseball, with words like "baggage" and "superlative." After recess, and lunch in the cafeteria with a dozen friends from other classes, it's time for math. Morris calls out an unfamiliar sequence of numbers from an advanced worksheet they are using to practice for math team competitions.

"It's the Fibonacci Sequence," Kim's classmate Eliot calls out excitedly. "I saw it on a PBS math show!"

A few kids groan and roll their eyes, but all of them listen attentively as Eliot explains how the sequence works.

Morris teaches them to calculate interest, and talks about mortgages, car loans and mutual funds.

After history class, Morris leads the students in a debate on moral and legal issues in current events. Last week it was whether sea lions should be killed because they're eating salmon; today it's whether a Houston basketball player was justified in hitting a fan who mocked his wife's stillborn baby.

Morris, who has been teaching in Marshfield for 25 years, says, "Ten years ago, only half of my students had seen a PG movie; today, almost every kid in class has seen an R-rated movie. The good is they have additional knowledge—but the bad is that they may not be able to handle that knowledge."

The bell rings the end of the day at 2:45. But Kim has a busy afternoon of Girl Scouts and drama ahead, since her mom has arranged her schedule to pick her up today.

But once at home, technology dominates Kim's afterschool hours. She finishes her homework and heads off to play *Final Fantasy 3,* a Nintendo game full of demons and death. The noise of slashing and shooting is deafening. Then it is back to TV, an endless array of cable channels. "There's nothing on," Kim announces, before heading to the computer and a CD-ROM that allows kids to "paint" hundreds of pictures on screen.

Computers and television often fill her afternoons in a way that roaming outside with next-door buddies and playing pick-up games filled her mother's childhood. Suburban sprawl means Kim's friends live too far away to walk or bike to visit them.

Kim's grandparents built this three-bedroom ranch house as a summer retreat for their seven children in 1962, when there were only two other homes on the street. The family knew everyone. Today, they don't know the next-door neighbors.

Kim's mother thinks the CD-ROM games are a terrific innovation, but laments the passing of a time when playing outside was more spontaneous and inside was more creative.

"We could go out for 10 minutes and have 25 kids together for a kickball game," Griffis, 39, recalls. They spent summers in this home with no TV, entertaining themselves with board games, a record player, paperbacks and tag. "I see kids playing outside in the schoolyard today, but it's always structured."

Griffis' kids know about AIDS and date rape from *90210* and other TV shows. And they know about violence from real life; the Marshfield middle school student killed last year while he and a friend played with a gun was a neighbor.

But while the world has changed a lot since her parents were kids, some things have stayed the same: Kim, a self-assured A student who wants to be a journalist, says her biggest concern is popularity.

With both parents at work, William's afternoon drips by with the tempo of a leaky faucet. His grandfather works evenings and leaves for work after picking William up from school. His brother is preoccupied with finding a job. His grandmother is weak and spends much of her time in bed. In the hours before his stepfather comes home, there is no one to talk to, no one to play with, no one to listen to.

William's principal says he is one of the lucky ones of the children she knows: With two strict and loving parents, plus grandparents at home, all preaching good values and a work ethic, his prospects are probably brighter than those of most children at her school, she says.

But the demands on him as a child on his own after school can be hard.

After an hour of calculating and erasing his math homework and rereading a dog-eared library book, William heads for the kitchen.

The spicy scent of Haitian food hangs like a canopy in the air, but since his grandmother, who usually cooks, is sick, William fends for himself today. He boils two hot dogs, smothers them in ketchup, and makes a bologna and cheese sandwich.

At 5:50, his stepfather's car pulls up, and William runs to the back door to greet him. William hugs him and doesn't let go, dragging along behind as Renaud Mirville laughs and makes his way in.

Mirville strokes William's head proudly. "I think someday, with his intelligence, life will be good for him if he continues with school," Mirville, 55, says. "Everything we tell him to do, he does. He's the best kid. If our situation were better, we'd give him everything he needs. If he wants a bicycle, we don't have the opportunity to give him the best one."

Mirville, who has been living with William's family for five years, was trained as an accountant, and worked for years as the manager of a pizza parlor. When the pipes there burst early this year, he was out of a job. He hasn't been able to find regular work since. So he leaves early every morning and spends the day with a notary friend, helping him do people's taxes for money. He plans to apply for a small business loan, and dreams of opening his own pizza store.

At 6:10, William's mother arrives, plants a tired kiss on Mirville's forehead and her son's cheek and collapses, exhausted, into a chair. She got dinner from a Burger King drive-thru on the way home, but has only 15 minutes until she must leave for her night job at a home in Revere.

Thermo strokes William's head and declares that life is easier for her sons than it was for her back in Haiti, the poorest country in the Western Hemisphere.

"These kids are privileged, they get what they want," she says. She went to school for longer hours and lived on a farm with no telephone or television. William's life seems more carefree to her. Her only chance for higher education was junior college here a few years ago. She hopes William will get into university and says she'll take on another job to pay for it.

But Thermo worries about random violence and drugs in Boston that didn't exist in her own childhood in Haiti. "They grow up too fast here. Some kids in the U.S. don't listen to their parents." To make sure William learns the right values, she has a Bible teacher come to the house every weekend.

William's afternoons alone strike his mother as a necessity, but not a hardship. "I try to keep him as safe as I can. There's a phone if he wants to call his friends to talk."

She regrets he can't go to choir because she can't pick him up, but she's too proud to ask for help. "It's hard to raise a kid when you're struggling to survive," she says. "I just want him to be happy."

William's music teacher recently learned he didn't have a ride home from choir, so she arranged for another mother to shuttle him home every week. Smiling radiantly when he heard he'd finally have something to do after school, William took out his sheet music and has been practicing at home ever since.

Dan Quayle Was Right
Barbara Dafoe Whitehead

Three Seventies Assumptions

As it first took shape in the 1970s, the optimistic view of family change rested on three bold new assumptions. At that time, because the emergence of the changes in family life was so recent, there was little hard evidence to confirm or dispute these assumptions. But this was an expansive moment in American life.

The first assumption was an economic one: that a woman could now afford to be a mother without also being a wife. There were ample grounds for believing this. Women's work-force participation had been gradually increasing in the postwar period, and by the beginning of the 1970s women were a strong presence in the workplace. What's more, even though there was still a substantial wage gap between men and women, women had made considerable progress in a relatively short time toward better-paying jobs and greater employment opportunities. More women than ever before could aspire to serious careers as business executives, doctors, lawyers, airline pilots, and politicians. This circumstance, combined with the increased availability of child care, meant that women could take on the responsibilities of a breadwinner, perhaps even a sole breadwinner. This was particularly true for middle-class women. According to a highly regarded 1977 study by the Carnegie Council on Children, "The greater availability of jobs for women means that more middle-class children today survive their parents' divorce without a catastrophic plunge into poverty."

Feminists, who had long argued that the path to greater equality for women lay in the world of work outside the home, endorsed this assumption. In fact, for many, economic independence was a stepping-stone toward freedom from both men and marriage. As women began to earn their own money, they were less dependent on men or marriage, and marriage diminished in importance. In Gloria Steinem's memorable words, "A woman without a man is like a fish without a bicycle."

This assumption also gained momentum as the meaning of work changed for women. Increasingly, work had an expressive as well as an economic dimension: being a working mother not only gave you an income but also made you more interesting and fulfilled than a stay-at-home mother. Consequently, the optimistic economic scenario was driven by a cultural imperative. Women would achieve financial independence because, culturally as well as economically, it was the right thing to do.

The second assumption was that family disruption would not cause lasting harm to children and could actually enrich their lives. *Creative Divorce: A New*

SOURCE: *The Atlantic Monthly,* April 1993, pp. 60–84. Reprinted with permission of the author. Copyright © 1993 Barbara Dafoe Whitehead, as first published in *The Atlantic Monthly.*

Opportunity for Personal Growth, a popular book of the seventies, spoke confidently to this point: "Children can survive any family crisis without permanent damage—and grow as human beings in the process. . . ." Moreover, single-parent and stepparent families created a more extensive kinship network than the nuclear family. This network would envelop children in a web of warm and supportive relationships. "Belonging to a stepfamily means there are more people in your life," a children's book published in 1982 notes. "More sisters and brothers, including the step ones. More people you think of as grandparents and aunts and uncles. More cousins. More neighbors and friends. . . . Getting to know and like so many people (and having them like you) is one of the best parts of what being in a stepfamily. . . is all about."

The third assumption was that the new diversity in family structure would make America a better place. Just as the nation has been strengthened by the diversity of its ethnic and racial groups, so it would be strengthened by diverse family forms. The emergence of these brave new families was but the latest chapter in the saga of American pluralism.

Another version of the diversity argument stated that the real problem was not family disruption itself but the stigma still attached to these emergent family forms. This lingering stigma placed children at psychological risk, making them feel ashamed or different; as the ranks of single-parent and stepparent families grew, children would feel normal and good about themselves.

These assumptions continue to be appealing, because they accord with strongly held American beliefs in social progress. Americans see progress in the expansion of individual opportunities for choice, freedom, and self-expression. Moreover, Americans identify progress with growing tolerance of diversity. Over the past half century, the pollster Daniel Yankelovich writes, the United States has steadily grown more open-minded and accepting of groups that were previously perceived as alien, untrustworthy, or unsuitable for public leadership or social esteem. One such group is the burgeoning number of single-parent and stepparent families.

The Education of Sara McLanahan

In 1981 Sara McLanahan, now a sociologist at Princeton University's Woodrow Wilson School, read a three-part series by Ken Auletta in *The New Yorker.* Later published as a book titled *The Underclass,* the series presented a vivid portrait of the drug addicts, welfare mothers, and school dropouts who took part in an education and training program in New York City. Many were the children of single mothers, and it was Auletta's clear implication that single-mother families were contributing to the growth of an underclass. McLanahan was taken aback by this notion. "It struck me as strange that he would be viewing single mothers at that level of pathology."

"I'd gone to graduate school in the days when the politically correct argument was that single-parent families were just another alternative family form, and it was fine," McLanahan explains, as she recalls the state of social-scientific thinking in the 1970s. Several empirical studies that were then current supported an optimistic view of family change. (They used tiny samples, however, and did not track the well-being of children over time.)

One, *All Our Kin,* by Carol Stack, was required reading for thousands of university students. It said that single mothers had strengths that had gone undetected and unappreciated by earlier researchers. The single-mother family, it suggested, is an economically resourceful and socially embedded institution. In the late 1970s McLanahan wrote a similar study that looked at a small sample of white single mothers and how they coped. "So I was very much of that tradition."

By the early 1980s, however, nearly two decades had passed since the changes in family life had begun. During the intervening years a fuller body of empirical research had emerged: studies that used large samples, or followed families through time, or did both. Moreover, several of the studies offered a child's-eye view of family disruption. The National Survey on Children, conducted by the psychologist Nicholas Zill, had set out in 1976 to track a large sample of children aged seven to eleven. It also interviewed the children's parents and teachers. It surveyed its subjects again in 1981 and 1987. By the time of its third round of interviews the eleven-year-olds of 1976 were the twenty-two-year-olds of 1987. The California Children of Divorce Study, directed by Judith Wallerstein, a clinical psychologist, had also been going on for a decade. E. Mavis Hetherington, of the University of Virginia, was conducting a similar study of children from both intact and divorced families. For the first time it was possible to test the optimistic view against a large and longitudinal body of evidence.

It was to this body of evidence that Sara McLanahan turned. When she did, she found little to support the optimistic view of single motherhood. On the contrary. When she published her findings with Irwin Garfinkel in a 1986 book, *Single Mothers and Their Children,* her portrait of single motherhood proved to be as troubling in its own way as Auletta's.

One of the leading assumptions of the time was that single motherhood was economically viable. Even if single mothers did face economic trials, they wouldn't face them for long, it was argued, because they wouldn't remain single for long: single motherhood would be a brief phase of three to five years, followed by marriage. Single mothers would be economically resilient: if they experienced setbacks, they would recover quickly. It was also said that single mothers would be supported by informal networks of family, friends, neighbors, and other single mothers. As McLanahan shows in her study, the evidence demolishes all these claims.

For the vast majority of single mothers, the economic spectrum turns out to be narrow, running between precarious and desperate. Half the single mothers in the United States live below the poverty line. (Currently, one out of ten married couples with children is poor.) Many others live on the edge of poverty. Even single mothers who are far from poor are likely to experience persistent economic insecurity. Divorce almost always brings a decline in the standard of living for the mother and children.

Moreover, the poverty experienced by single mothers is no more brief than it is mild. A significant number of all single mothers never marry or remarry. Those who do, do so only after spending roughly six years, on average, as single parents. For black mothers the duration is much longer. Only 33 percent of African-American mothers had remarried within ten years of separation. Consequently, single motherhood is hardly a fleeting event for the mother, and it is likely to occupy a third of the child's childhood. Even the notion that single mothers are knit together in economically supportive networks is not borne out by the evidence. On the contrary, single parenthood forces many women to be on the move, in search of cheaper housing and better jobs. This need-driven restless mobility makes it more difficult for them to sustain supportive ties to family and friends, let alone other single mothers.

Single-mother families are vulnerable not just to poverty but to a particularly debilitating form of poverty: welfare dependency. The dependency takes two forms: First, single mothers, particularly unwed mothers, stay on welfare longer than other welfare recipients. Of those never-married mothers who receive welfare benefits, almost 40 percent remain on the rolls for ten years or longer. Second, welfare dependency tends to be passed on from one generation to the next. McLanahan says, "Evidence on intergenerational poverty indicates that, indeed, offspring from [single-mother] families are far more likely to be poor and to form mother-only families than are offspring who live with two parents most of their pre-adult life." Nor is the intergenerational impact of single motherhood limited to African-Americans, as many people seem to believe. Among white families, daughters of single parents are 53 percent more likely to marry as teenagers, 111 percent more likely to have children as teenagers, 164 percent more likely to have a premarital birth, and 92 percent more likely to dissolve their own marriages. All these intergenerational consequences of single motherhood increase the likelihood of chronic welfare dependency.

McLanahan cites three reasons why single-mother families are so vulnerable economically. For one thing, their earnings are low. Second, unless the mothers are widowed, they don't receive public subsidies large enough to lift them out of poverty. And finally, they do not get much support from family members—especially the fathers of their children. In 1982 single white mothers received an average of $1,246 in alimony and child support, black mothers an average of $322. Such payments accounted for about 10 percent of the income of single white mothers and for about 3.5 percent of the income of single black mothers. These amounts were dramatically smaller than the income of the father in a two-parent family and also smaller than the income from a second earner in a two-parent family. Roughly 60 percent of single white mothers and 80 percent of single black mothers received no support at all.

Until the mid-1980s, when stricter standards were put in place, child-support awards were only about half to two-thirds what the current guidelines require. Accordingly, there is often a big difference in the living standards of divorced fathers and of divorced mothers with children. After divorce the average annual income of mothers and children is $13,500 for whites and $9,000 for nonwhites, as compared with $25,000 for white nonresident fathers and $13,600 for nonwhite nonresident fathers. Moreover, since child-support awards account for a smaller portion of the income of a high-earning father, the drop in living standards can be especially sharp for mothers who were married to upper-level managers and professionals.

Unwed mothers are unlikely to be awarded any child support at all, partly because the paternity of their children may not have been established. According to one recent study, only 20 percent of unmarried mothers receive child support.

Even if single mothers escape poverty, economic uncertainty remains a condition of life. Divorce brings a reduction in income and standard of living for the vast majority of single mothers. One study, for example, found that income for mothers and children declines on average about 30 percent, while fathers experience a 10 to 15 percent increase in income in the year following a separation. Things get even more difficult when fathers fail to meet their child-support obligations. As a result, many divorced mothers experience a wearing uncertainty about the family budget: whether the check will come in or not; whether new sneakers can be bought this month or not; whether the electric bill will be paid on time or not. Uncertainty about money triggers other kinds of uncertainty. Mothers and children often have to move to cheaper housing after a divorce. One study shows that about 38 percent of divorced mothers and their children move during the first year after a divorce. Even several years later the rate of moves for single mothers is about a third higher than the rate for two-parent families. It is also common for a mother to change her job or increase her working hours or both following a divorce. Even the composition of the household is likely to change, with other adults, such as boyfriends or babysitters, moving in and out.

All this uncertainty can be devastating to children. Anyone who knows children knows that they are deeply conservative creatures. They like things to stay the same. So pronounced is this tendency that certain children have been known to request the same peanut-butter-and-jelly sandwich for lunch for years on end. Children are particularly set in their ways when it comes to family, friends, neighborhoods, and schools. Yet when a family breaks up, all these things may change. The novelist Pat Conroy has observed that "each divorce is the death of a small civilization." No one feels this more acutely than children.

Sara McLanahan's investigation and others like it have helped to establish a broad consensus on the economic impact of family disruption on children. Most social scientists now agree that single motherhood is an important and growing cause of poverty, and that children suffer as a result. (They continue to argue, however, about the relationship between family structure and such economic factors as income inequality, the loss of jobs in the inner city, and the growth of low-wage jobs.) By the mid-1980s, however, it was clear that the problem of family disruption was not confined to the urban underclass, nor was its sole impact economic. Divorce and out-of-wedlock childbirth were affecting middle- and upper-class children, and these more privileged children were suffering negative consequences as well. It appeared that the problems associated with family breakup were far deeper and far more widespread than anyone had previously imagined.

The Missing Father

Judith Wallerstein is one of the pioneers in research on the long-term psychological impact of family disruption on children. The California Children of Divorce Study, which she directs, remains the most enduring study of the long-term effects of divorce on children and their parents. Moreover, it represents the best-known effort to look at the impact of divorce on middle-class children. The California children entered the study without pathological family histories. Before divorce they lived in stable, protected homes. And although some of the children did experience economic insecurity as the result of divorce, they were generally free from the most severe forms of poverty associated with family breakup. Thus the study and the resulting book (which Wallerstein wrote with Sandra Blakeslee), *Second Chances: Men, Women, and Children a Decade After Divorce* (1989), provide new insight into the consequences of divorce which are not associated with extreme forms of economic or emotional deprivation.

When, in 1971, Wallerstein and her colleagues set out to conduct clinical interviews with 131 children from the San Francisco area, they thought they were embarking on a short-term study. Most experts believed that divorce was like a bad cold. There was a phase of acute discomfort, and then a short recovery phase. According to the conventional wisdom, kids would be back on their feet in no time at all. Yet when Wallerstein met these children for a second interview more than a year later, she was amazed to discover that there had been no miraculous recovery. In fact, the children seemed to be doing worse.

The news that children did not "get over" divorce was not particularly welcome at the time. Wallerstein recalls, "We got angry letters from therapists, parents, and lawyers saying we were undoubtedly wrong. They said children are really much better off being released from an unhappy marriage. Divorce, they said, is a liberating experience." One of the main results of the California study was to overturn this optimistic view. In Wallerstein's cautionary words, "Divorce is deceptive. Legally it is a single event, but psychologically it is a chain—sometimes a never-ending chain—of events, relocations, and radically shifting relationships strung through time, a process that forever changes the lives of the people involved."

Five years after divorce more than a third of the children experienced moderate or severe depression. At ten years a significant number of the now young men and women appeared to be troubled, drifting, and underachieving. At fifteen years many of the thirtyish adults were struggling to establish strong love relationships of their own. In short, far from recovering from their parents' divorce, a significant percentage of these grownups were still suffering from its effects. In fact, according to Wallerstein, the long-term effects of divorce emerge at a time when young adults are trying to make their own decisions about love, marriage, and family. Not all children in the study suffered negative consequences. But Wallerstein's research presents a sobering picture of divorce. "The child of divorce faces many additional psychological burdens in addition to the normative tasks of growing up," she says.

Divorce not only makes it more difficult for young adults to establish new relationships. It also weakens the oldest primary relationship: that between parent and child. According to Wallerstein, "Parent–child relationships are permanently altered by divorce in ways that our society has not anticipated." Not only do children experience a loss of parental attention at the onset of divorce, but they soon find that at every stage of their development their parents are not available in the same way they once were. "In a reasonably happy intact family," Wallerstein observes, "the child gravitates first to one parent and then to the other, using skills and attributes from each in climbing the developmental ladder." In a divorced family, children find it "harder to find the needed parent at needed times." This may help explain why very young children suffer the most as the result of family disruption. Their opportunities to engage in this kind of ongoing process are the most truncated and compromised.

The father–child bond is severely, often irreparably, damaged in disrupted families. In a situation without historical precedent, an astonishing and disheartening number of American fathers are failing to provide financial support to their children. Often, more than the father's support check is missing. Increasingly, children are bereft of any contact with their fathers. According to the National Survey of Children, in disrupted families only one child in six, on average, saw his or her father as often as once a week in the past year. Close to half did not see their father at all in the past year. As time goes on, contact becomes even more infrequent. Ten years after a marriage breaks up, more than two thirds of children report not having seen their father for a year. Not surprisingly, when asked to name the "adults you look up to and admire," only 20 percent of children in single-parent families named their father, as compared with 52 percent of children in two-parent families. A favorite complaint among Baby Boom Americans is that their fathers were emotionally remote guys who worked hard, came home at night to eat supper, and didn't have much to say to or do with the kids. But the current generation has a far worse father problem: many of their fathers are vanishing entirely.

Even for fathers who maintain regular contact, the pattern of father–child relationships changes. The sociologists Andrew Cherlin and Frank Furstenberg, who have studied broken families, write that the fathers behave more like other relatives than like parents. Rather than helping with homework or carrying out a project with their children, nonresidential fathers are likely to take the kids shopping, to the movies, or out to dinner. Instead of providing steady advice and guidance, divorced fathers become "treat" dads.

Apparently—and paradoxically—it is the visiting relationship itself, rather than the frequency of visits, that is the real source of the problem. According to Wallerstein, the few children in the California study who reported visiting with their fathers once or twice a week over a ten-year period still felt rejected. The need to schedule a special time to be with the child, the repeated leave-takings, and the lack of connection to the child's regular, daily schedule leaves many fathers adrift, frustrated, and confused. Wallerstein calls the visiting father a parent without portfolio.

The deterioration in father–child bonds is most severe among children who experience divorce at an early age, according to a recent study. Nearly three quarters of the respondents, now young men and women, report having poor relationships with their fathers. Close to half have received psychological help, nearly a third have dropped out of high school, and about a quarter report having experienced high levels of problem behavior or emotional distress by the time they became young adults.

Long-Term Effects

Since most children live with their mothers after divorce, one might expect that the mother–child bond would remain unaltered and might even be strengthened. Yet research shows that the mother–child bond is also weakened as the result of divorce. Only half of the children who were close to their mothers before a divorce remained equally close after the divorce. Boys, particularly, had difficulties with their mothers. Moreover, mother–child relationships deteriorated over time. Whereas teenagers in disrupted families were no more likely than teenagers in intact families to report poor relationships with their mothers, 30 percent of young adults from disrupted families have poor relationships with their mothers, as compared with 16 percent of young adults from intact families. Mother–daughter relationships often deteriorate as the daughter reaches young adulthood. The only group in society that derives any benefit from these weakened parent–child ties is the therapeutic community. Young adults from disrupted families are nearly twice as likely as those from intact families to receive psychological help.

Some social scientists have criticized Judith Wallerstein's research because her study is based on a small clinical sample and does not include a control group of children from intact families. However, other studies generally support and strengthen her findings. Nicholas Zill has found similar long-term effects on children of divorce, reporting that "effects of marital discord and family disruption are visible twelve to twenty-two years later in poor relationships with parents, high levels of problem behavior, and an increased likelihood of dropping out of high school and receiving psychological help." Moreover, Zill's research also found signs of distress in young women who seemed relatively well adjusted in middle childhood and adolescence. Girls in single-parent families are also at much greater risk for precocious sexuality, teenage marriage, teenage pregnancy, nonmarital birth, and divorce than are girls in two-parent families.

Zill's research shows that family disruption strongly affects school achievement as well. Children in disrupted families are nearly twice as likely as those in intact families to drop out of high school; among children who do drop out, those from disrupted families are less likely eventually to earn a diploma or a GED. Boys are at greater risk for dropping out than girls, and are also more likely to exhibit aggressive, acting-out behaviors. Other research confirms these findings. According to a study by the National Association of Elementary School Principals, 33 percent of two-parent elementary school students are ranked as high achievers, as compared with 17 percent of single-parent students. The children in single-parent families are also more likely to be truant or late or to have disciplinary action taken against them. Even after controlling for race, income, and religion, scholars find significant differences in educational attainment between children who grow up in intact families and children who do not. In his 1992 study *America's Smallest School: The Family,* Paul Barton shows that the proportion of two-parent families varies widely from state to state and is related to variations in academic achievement. North Dakota, for example, scores highest on the math-proficiency test and second highest on the two-parent-family scale. The District of Columbia is second lowest on the math test and lowest in the nation on the two-parent-family scale.

Zill notes that "while coming from a disrupted family significantly increases a young adult's risks of experiencing social, emotional or academic difficulties, it does not foreordain such difficulties. The majority of young people from disrupted families have successfully completed high school, do not currently display high levels of emotional distress or problem behavior, and enjoy reasonable relationships with their mothers." Nevertheless, a majority of these young adults do show maladjustment in their relationships with their fathers.

These findings underscore the importance of both a mother and a father in fostering the emotional well-being of children. Obviously, not all children in two-parent families are free from emotional turmoil, but few are burdened with the troubles that accompany family breakup. Moreover, as the sociologist Amitai Etzioni explains in a new book, *The Spirit of Community,* two parents in an intact family make up what might be called a mutually supportive education coalition. When both parents are present, they can play different, even contradictory, roles. One parent may goad the child to achieve, while the other may encourage the child to take time out to daydream or toss a football around. One may emphasize taking intellectual risks, while the other may insist on following the teacher's guidelines. At the same time, the parents regularly exchange information about the child's school problems and achievements, and have a sense of the overall educational mission. However, Etzioni writes:

> The sequence of divorce followed by a succession of boy or girlfriends, a second marriage, and frequently another divorce and another turnover of partners often means a repeatedly disrupted educational coalition. Each change in participants involves a change in the educational agenda for the child. Each new partner cannot be expected to pick up the previous one's educational post and program. . . . As a result, changes in parenting partners mean, at best, a deep disruption in a child's education, though of course several disruptions cut deeper into the effectiveness of the educational coalition than just one.

The Bad News About Stepparents

Perhaps the most striking, and potentially disturbing, new research has to do with children in stepparent families. Until quite recently the optimistic assumption was that children saw their lives improve when they became part of a stepfamily. When Nicholas Zill and his colleagues began to study the effects of remarriage on children, their working hypothesis was that stepparent families would make up for the shortcomings of the single-parent family. Clearly, most children are better off economically when they are able to share in the income of two adults. When a second adult joins the household, there may be a reduction in the time and work pressures on the single parent.

The research overturns this optimistic assumption, however. In general the evidence suggests that remarriage neither reproduces nor restores the intact family structure, even when it brings more income and a second adult into the household. Quite the contrary. Indeed, children living with stepparents appear to be even more disadvantaged than children living in a stable single-parent family. Other difficulties seem to offset the advantages of extra income and an extra pair of hands. However much our modern sympathies reject the fairy-tale portrait of stepparents, the latest research confirms that the old stories are anthropologically quite accurate. Stepfamilies disrupt established loyalties, create new uncertainties, provoke deep anxieties, and sometimes threaten a child's physical safety as well as emotional security.

Parents and children have dramatically different interests in and expectations for a new marriage. For a single parent, remarriage brings new commitments, the hope of enduring love and happiness, and relief from stress and loneliness. For a child, the same event often provokes confused feelings of sadness, anger, and rejection. Nearly half the children in Wallerstein's study said they felt left out in their stepfamilies. The National Commission on Children, a bipartisan group headed by Senator John D. Rockefeller, of West Virginia, reported that children from stepfamilies were more likely to say they often felt lonely or blue than children from either single-parent or intact families. Children in stepfamilies were the most likely to report that they wanted more time with their mothers. When mothers remarry, daughters tend to have a harder time adjusting than sons. Evidently, boys often respond positively to a male presence in the household, while girls who have established close ties to their mother in a single-parent family often see the stepfather as a rival and an intruder. According to one study, boys in remarried families are less likely to drop out of school than boys in single-parent families, while the opposite is true for girls.

A large percentage of children do not even consider stepparents to be part of their families, according to the National Survey on Children. The NSC asked children, "When you think of your family, who do you include?" Only 10 percent of the children failed to mention a biological parent, but a third left out a stepparent. Even children who rarely saw their noncustodial parents almost always named them as family members. The weak sense of attachment is mutual. When parents were asked the same question, only one percent failed to mention a biological child, while 15 percent left out a stepchild. In the same study stepparents with both natural children and stepchildren said that it was harder for them to love their stepchildren than their biological children and that their children would have been better off if they had grown up with two biological parents.

One of the most severe risks associated with stepparent–child ties is the risk of sexual abuse. As Judith Wallerstein explains, "The presence of a step-father can raise the difficult issue of a thinner incest barrier." The incest taboo is strongly reinforced, Wallerstein says, by knowledge of paternity and by the experience of caring for a child since birth. A stepfather enters the family with-out either credential and plays a sexual role as the mother's husband. As a re-sult, stepfathers can pose a sexual risk to the children, especially to daughters. According to a study by the Canadian researchers Martin Daly and Margo Wil-son, preschool children in stepfamilies are forty times as likely as children in in-tact families to suffer physical or sexual abuse. (Most of the sexual abuse was committed by a third party, such as a neighbor, a stepfather's male friend, or an-other nonrelative.) Stepfathers discriminate in their abuse: they are far more likely to assault nonbiological children than their own natural children.

Sexual abuse represents the most extreme threat to children's well-being. Stepfamilies also seem less likely to make the kind of ordinary investments in the children that other families do. Although it is true that the stepfamily house-hold has a higher income than the single-parent household, it does not follow that the additional income is reliably available to the children. To begin with, children's claim on stepparents' resources is shaky. Stepparents are not legally required to support stepchildren, so their financial support of these children is entirely voluntary. Moreover, since stepfamilies are far more likely to break up than intact families, particularly in the first five years, there is always the risk— far greater than the risk of unemployment in an intact family—that the second income will vanish with another divorce. The financial commitment to a child's education appears weaker in stepparent families, perhaps because the steppar-ent believes that the responsibility for educating the child rests with the bio-logical parent.

Similarly, studies suggest that even though they may have the time, the par-ents in stepfamilies do not invest as much of it in their children as the parents in intact families or even single parents do. A 1991 survey by the National Com-mission on Children showed that the parents in stepfamilies were less likely to be involved in a child's school life, including involvement in extracurricular ac-tivities, than either intact-family parents or single parents. They were the least likely to report being involved in such time-consuming activities as coaching a child's team, accompanying class trips, or helping with school projects. Ac-cording to McLanahan's research, children in stepparent families report lower educational aspirations on the part of their parents and lower levels of parental involvement with schoolwork. In short, it appears that family income and the number of adults in the household are not the only factors affecting children's well-being.

■ ■ ■

Poverty, Crime, Education

Family disruption would be a serious problem even if it affected only individual children and families. But its impact is far broader. Indeed, it is not an exaggeration to characterize it as a central cause of many of our most vexing social problems. Consider three problems that most Americans believe rank among the nation's pressing concerns: poverty, crime, and declining school performance.

More than half of the increase in child poverty in the 1980s is attributable to changes in family structure according to David Eggebeen and Daniel Lichter, of Pennsylvania State University. In fact, if family structure in the United States had remained relatively constant since 1960, the rate of child poverty would be a third lower than it is today. This does not bode well for the future. With more than half of today's children likely to live in single-parent families, poverty and associated welfare costs threaten to become even heavier burdens on the nation.

Crime in American cities has increased dramatically and grown more violent over recent decades. Much of this can be attributed to the rise in disrupted families. Nationally, more than 70 percent of all juveniles in state reform institutions come from fatherless homes. A number of scholarly studies find that even after the groups of subjects are controlled for income, boys from single-mother homes are significantly more likely than others to commit crimes and to wind up in the juvenile justice, court, and penitentiary systems. One such study summarizes the relationship between crime and one-parent families in this way: "The relationship is so strong that controlling for family configuration erases the relationship between race and crime and between low income and crime. This conclusion shows up time and again in the literature." The nation's mayors, as well as police officers, social workers, probation officers, and court officials, consistently point to family breakup as the most important source of rising rates of crime.

Terrible as poverty and crime are, they tend to be concentrated in inner cities and isolated from the everyday experience of many Americans. The same cannot be said of the problem of declining school performance. Nowhere has the impact of family breakup been more profound or widespread than in the nation's public schools. There is a strong consensus that the schools are failing in their historic mission to prepare every American child to be a good worker and a good citizen. And nearly everyone agrees that the schools must undergo dramatic reform in order to reach that goal. In pursuit of that goal, moreover, we have suffered no shortage of bright ideas or pilot projects or bold experiments in school reform. But there is little evidence that measures such as curricular reform, school-based management, and school choice will address, let alone solve, the biggest problem schools face: the rising number of children who come from disrupted families.

The great educational tragedy of our time is that many American children are failing in school not because they are intellectually or physically impaired but because they are emotionally incapacitated. In schools across the nation principals report a dramatic rise in the aggressive, acting-out behavior characteristic of children, especially boys, who are living in single-parent families. The discipline problems in today's suburban schools—assaults on teachers, unprovoked attacks on other students, screaming outbursts in class—outstrip the problems that were evident in the toughest city schools a generation ago. Moreover, teachers find many children emotionally distracted, so upset and preoccupied by the explosive drama of their own family lives that they are unable to concentrate on such mundane matters as multiplication tables.

In response, many schools have turned to therapeutic remediation. A growing proportion of many school budgets is devoted to counseling and other psychological services. The curriculum is becoming more therapeutic: children are taking courses in self-esteem, conflict resolution, and aggression management. Parental advisory groups are conscientiously debating alternative approaches to traditional school discipline, ranging from teacher training in mediation to the introduction of metal detectors and security guards in the schools. Schools are increasingly becoming emergency rooms of the emotions, devoted not only to developing minds but also to repairing hearts. As a result, the mission of the school, along with the culture of the classroom, is slowly changing. What we are seeing, largely as a result of the new burdens of family disruption, is the psychologization of American education.

Taken together, the research presents a powerful challenge to the prevailing view of family change as social progress. Not a single one of the assumptions underlying that view can be sustained against the empirical evidence. Single-parent families are not able to do well economically on a mother's income. In fact, most teeter on the economic brink, and many fall into poverty and welfare dependency. Growing up in a disrupted family does not enrich a child's life or expand the number of adults committed to the child's well-being. In fact, disrupted families threaten the psychological well-being of children and diminish the investment of adult time and money in them. Family diversity in the form of increasing numbers of single-parent and stepparent families does not strengthen the social fabric. It dramatically weakens and undermines society, placing new burdens on schools, courts, prisons, and the welfare system. These new families are not an improvement on the nuclear family, nor are they even just as good, whether you look at outcomes for children or outcomes for society as a whole. In short, far from representing social progress, family change represents a stunning example of social regress.

■ ■ ■

Our Fractured Sense of Family
Mike Barnicle

"Seven out of twenty-nine," she said, the words sounding like a hammer pounding a nail. "That's how many kids in my little girl's fourth-grade class last year came from homes with two parents. Seven out of twenty-nine, that's all."

"There was us, me and my husband. Five Vietnamese families and one white couple. The other twenty-two children, there was either no mother, no father or it was your DSS situation: foster home. And nobody thinks there's anything wrong with that. We get so we think that's a normal situation."

She was outside Purity Supreme in Fields Corner. It was the day after a local 4-year-old got hit by a bullet fired from a gun held by another of these young sport shooters who strip whole neighborhoods of any sense of sanity or safety because they are so self-involved they grind along with no respect for anything or anyone, including themselves.

"You ask me, that's a bigger danger than guns," the woman was saying. "All these children growing up, not knowing what it's like to have a mother and father home at the same time. That's a huge problem. You can have all the wonderful teachers in the world but if it isn't happening at home, it just isn't happening.

"Kids got to see their folks going out to work every day. They got to know their folks is going to be there for them at night. It's crazy to expect school or the police to be the parent. Crazy.

■ ■ ■

"Everybody always talks about kids with guns," she said. "A kid gets shot and it's all over TV all night long and in the papers and everything like it's a real big deal, and it is. I don't mean to say it isn't. But do you know what's worse than kids with guns? Do you know why people like me and my husband think about moving out of the city for the first time ever?

"It's the kids that urinate in your hallway every night. It's the kids that sell crack and heroin outside your building all day. It's the kids that steal your child's bike off the sidewalk. It's the kids that are drinking and swearing at midnight. That stuff makes you want to pack up and go.

"And you look at these boys and girls and you know, you just know, half of 'em living in places where nobody cares what they're doing, what they're up to or who they're with. There's hardly any more families left around here. By family I mean what I just told you: Here's mummy. Here's daddy and here's the little kids. You know, a normal family."

Certainly, the fractured sense of family in this country has more than a little to do with the deterioration of proper values. An empty apartment cannot point

---

SOURCE: *The Boston Globe,* August 31, 1995, p. 25. Reprinted courtesy of *The Boston Globe.*

out what is right, wrong or expected, and schools, already collapsing beneath the burden of simply having to educate children, are asked to proceed to the next, nearly impossible step: instill values too.

So we end up on the verge of being surrounded by a brand new minority, perhaps a majority: young people with no idea of what it's like to live in a house containing two parents willing to help guide them past some of life's obstacles. Young people tossed into the world like fresh bait, forced to become old before their time merely to survive.

And who cares? The culture moves at such a furious pace we are content to simply hang on to the rail, and take care of ourselves and those around us without noting the impact of social explosions like divorce, teen-age pregnancy or poor, single-parent households where the adult is afraid of the child.

■ ■ ■

Sure, whenever a child is killed, scalded, abandoned, put out for prostitution or up for sale, we keel over, lapse into a shocked, momentary coma. Yet, once the wave of anguish passes there is debris to deal with and it includes a lost generation of sometimes rudderless children looking for a definition of right and wrong in a world where their problems are too often beyond teachers, beyond any additional public money and, increasingly, beyond help too.

Punished for the Sins of the Children
John Leo

In a burst of mostly patronizing publicity from the national media, the small town of Silverton, Ore., and the Oregon state legislature have moved to hold parents responsible for offenses committed by their children.

"Both stigmatize parents with their assumption that a child's misbehavior results from a failure of parental supervision," clucked a page 1 *New York Times* report. And the reporter for public TV's *MacNeil/Lehrer Newshour* explained that Silverton's belief that parents are responsible for children up to age 18 is "a homespun philosophy from a homespun town." (Translation: We are dealing here with a town full of rubes.)

What the reporter seemed to think was some sort of rural aberration is actually part of a fast-growing national trend. Hundreds of exasperated communities,

SOURCE: *U.S. News & World Report,* June 12, 1995, p. 18. Copyright © 1995, *U.S. News & World Report.* Reprinted with permission.

large and small, are holding parents responsible for curfew violations, graffiti damage and crimes by their children. Often they impose fines or community service and sometimes require attendance at basic classes on how to parent.

Many changes in welfare plans also make parents responsible for their children's attendance at school, and in some public housing, a parent can be evicted if a child is found to be dealing drugs out of the family apartment.

In some cases, these laws are popping up in basically stable, but apprehensive, communities. By big-city standards, the level of vandalism and youth crime in Silverton seems quite low. And in the dozens of Chicago-area communities that now have parental responsibility laws, the targets seem to be illegal teen drinking parties and drunken driving. In these cases, the tactic is chiefly to embarrass well-off parents into taking charge.

"Call It Quits"   In devastated urban areas, however, the practical and ethical problems are very different. It can look as though poor mothers are being punished for the sins of children they can't control. Patricia Holdaway, the first parent charged under the curfew law of Roanoke, Va., said: "I went through so much with these kids. I'm just ready to call it quits." Her 16-year-old son, arrested at 5 A.M. for his fifth curfew violation and for driving without a license, said, "I just left. It's not her fault. She shouldn't be held responsible. I know right from wrong."

Roanoke's policy is a reasonable one—it wants to work with at-risk youngsters and keep things out of court, if possible. It wants to establish the principle that parents should supervise a youngster in trouble. But in this case, the policy led to a $100 fine and a 10-day jail sentence for a woman who already agreed with the principle of parental responsibility but couldn't enforce it. She is appealing the conviction.

Very few parental responsibility laws allow jail terms. But given the stresses on the poor, many of them single mothers, even mandatory community service or $100 fines can be very punitive. That's why parental responsibility laws catch so many of us leaning both ways, pro and con. Are these laws attempts to reassert reasonable civic expectations about parenting, or are they desperate attempts to use the coercive force of the state to solve a cultural problem?

"When a culture is in free fall, as ours is, and our nonlegal institutions are falling apart, there's a temptation to move in with laws and government," said David Blankenhorn, president of the Institute for American Values. And the laws work best with parents who are already in control and merely need a wake-up call; they work poorly, or not at all, when the no-parenting ethic is ingrained or passed on from one generation to the next.

Still many communities are so besieged that something must be tried. It's hard to keep kids off the streets during early morning hours when gangs are roaming if parents don't cooperate. And the detachment of many parents from the fate of their young is a crucial problem—many don't even bother to go down to a police station to collect an arrested son or daughter.

"These laws are signs that the antibodies are starting to kick in," said Roger Conner, head of the American Alliance for Rights and Responsibilities. "But they have to be regarded as experiments. We have to find out what works, what encourages responsibility without resorting to draconian penalties." Conner thinks the Silverton ordinance is too strong—it allows a fine for a first offense, requires parental responsibility to age 18, and has been applied to cover teens caught smoking.

The statewide Oregon measure, which has passed the legislature and has to be signed into law by the governor, is more carefully constructed. The law covers responsibility for children up to age 15—a way of recognizing that older teens are much harder to deal with and sometimes beyond parental control. The first offense draws only a warning. The second time a parent faces mandatory attendance at a parenting class. Only after a third offense is a fine likely, and even then not if a parent can show reasonable efforts to control the child. The offense is civil, not criminal, and parents cannot be jailed.

With feedback from the community, these laws can be adjusted depending on results and a changing social consensus. Let the experiments continue.

The Way We Weren't Can't Help Today's Kids
Stephanie Coontz

The revival of the family values crusade poses serious dangers for people who sincerely want to improve the lives of American children. Beneath the claim that the "breakdown of the family" causes all our social ills lies a simplistic analysis of how traditional family forms and gender roles used to operate, of where contemporary family problems originate, and of what parents should do to raise healthy children in the 1990s.

Modern Americans are both unrealistic and untraditional in expecting families to go it alone economically. Emotionally, too, it was never a traditional expectation that the family should be the only place to meet everyone's needs. Only in the 1950s did large numbers of Americans begin to identify the nuclear family as the main source of childhood socialization and the center of all personal happiness.

SOURCE: *Education Digest*, September 1995, pp. 9–13. Reprinted from *The Education Digest*, September 1995, Ann Arbor, Michigan.

During the Great Depression and World War II, millions of Americans doubled up in housing or moved in with parents, and millions more were parted from spouse and children. Murder rates in the 1930s were higher than in the 1980s. Marriage rates reached an all-time high in 1946, but, by 1948, one in three new marriages ended in divorce. Relief after World War II gave way to deep anxieties about the Bomb, while Senator Joseph McCarthy led a witch hunt into people's political associations. Having the wrong friend at the wrong time could lose a job or destroy a reputation.

In these circumstances, community institutions, extended families, and same-sex peer groups began to lose their luster. The nuclear family began to seem a welcome refuge, a potential oasis of security, if marriage could be made more stable. Amid the extraordinary consumerism unleashed by the postwar economic boom, the prospects seemed bright for finding new comforts, both material and emotional, in the home.

An unprecedented emotional and spatial rearrangement of family life occurred in the 1950s, as everyone from family therapists to real estate agents, from automobile advertisers to movie script writers, urged young couples to move away from parents and kin and cut ties with old networks of friends and neighbors who might compete for emotional attention. The new ideal was to wean couples away from traditional extra-familial networks, encouraging them to focus all energies and find all gratifications within the home.

Did Father Know Best?

At the time, everyone knew that the families on television did not represent the way it was, but the way many hoped it *might* be. Sitcoms were testimonials and how-to lessons for a new way of organizing gender and age roles. Buy these ranch houses, appliances, and new child-rearing ideals; relate to your spouse like this; organize your dinner like that—and you too can have harmonious families in which father knows best, mother is never bored, and teenagers are always eager to hear parental wisdom.

If the decade of the 1950s was the "heyday" of the nuclear family, it was also a historical aberration. At the end of the 1940s, for the first time in 100 years, the average age of marriage and parenthood fell, the proportion of marriages ending in divorce dropped, and the birth rate "approached that of India." The percentage of women remaining childless reached an all-time low, while timing and spacing of childbearing became far more compressed, so young women were likely to have two or more children in diapers at the same time, without an older sibling to help.

Also for the first time in 100 years, the educational gap between middle-class women and men increased, while the employment gap between noncollegebound male and female teens peaked. These demographic changes (in contrast to gradual opposite trends since the early twentieth century) increased dependence of young women on marriage. All these innovations lasted about 10 years. By 1958, the older, long-term trends began to reassert themselves.

Fluke or not, say the "new traditionalists," the 1950s stand as a model for what family values can accomplish. But history does not support such a scenario.

In the 1950s, 30 percent of American children lived in poverty (more than today), as did nearly half of married African American couples. Many "traditional" families were hardly idyllic, as thousands of survivors of alcoholic dysfunction, abuse, battering, or incest can testify. Women and blacks were denied fundamental economic, educational, and legal rights. One reason people worried less in the 1950s was that few of these problems made the nightly news. They were taken for granted or systematically covered up.

The existence of racist mobs and of McCarthyite witch hunts contradicts the image of 1950s serenity. Yet for most people, these realities did not overshadow personal commitments and neighborhood solidarities because socioeconomic trends fostered stability. Rising expectations of economic improvement softened social conflict.

Poverty was falling, the gap between rich and poor was narrowing, and there was a sense of shared sacrifices in the past and shared fortunes in the future. Young people had little reason to opt out of the social contract, as they could look forward to living better than their parents, if they played by the rules. Those rules did not include saying no to sex, because young people could afford to get married early. The teen birth rate peaked in 1957 and has not been equaled since.

But the social stability of the 1950s was less a result of its family forms or values than of its unique socioeconomic and political climate. High rates of unionization, heavy corporate investment in manufacturing, and generous government assistance (public works projects, veterans' benefits, student loans, housing subsidies) gave young families a tremendous economic jump start, created paths out of poverty, and led to unprecedented increases in real wages. Today, both conservatives and liberals tend to forget how much family values and effective child rearing depend on a supportive economic and social environment.

To evaluate family change over the past three decades and help families make the best choices in new situations, we must understand that people's "lifestyle choices" and family transitions are not the *foremost* causes of such problems as poverty, crime, educational failure, and personal dysfunction.

There is no great mystery about what it takes to help a troubled child or family. In study after study, two things stand out for kids who make it against the odds.

First Is Second

The first is access to a second chance to succeed at something failed at before—going back to school, being helped to pass a class (not being passed through it), getting a chance to correct a wrong and make it right (as opposed to being punished or excused for it), receiving concrete aid and an opportunity to reciprocate it. The second factor is intervention of just one caring person from *outside* the family to get involved in the child's life. The combination of high standards and concrete help to achieve them is what works.

Both at societal and interpersonal levels, we can provide such second chances and outside interventions. The Big Lie of the 1990s is that nothing except the family works. In fact, history shows that government programs can be very effective. The low point of child poverty and the high point of child health came not in 1964, after 14 years of unprecedented family stability, but in 1973, after a few short years of the Great Society programs so many people now denigrate. No sooner were the programs cut, in the second half of the 1970s, than the positive trends for children began to be reversed. Failures of government agencies, such as Child Protective Services, came only after their caseloads were multiplied. Several local studies show a good success rate for those agencies in their early years.

In December 1994, RAND Corporation researchers found that, from 1975 to 1990, minority students made much faster gains than whites on the National Assessment of Educational Progress—largely due to government programs aimed at poor students. In 1990, however, the performance gap between the highest and lowest-achieving students began to widen for the first time. Such academic polarization is not surprising given the socioeconomic polarization that has been accelerating since 1986.

Respecting Strengths

Schools, social programs, and caring individuals can compensate for stressful environments and troubled families. And they do not have to do everything at once. The reduction of *any* risk factor can make the difference between success and failure. When you read the life histories of impoverished children, the first thing that strikes you is the obstacles they face, but the second is how small the difference between success and failure can be, while a third is how important it is to respect the strengths and knowledge that *do* exist in those communities.

Local organizers are much more effective than outsiders in identifying problems. James Comer has shown that it is possible to involve impoverished parents in their local schools. The Judson Center in Newark, New Jersey, trains and pays women on welfare to rear two or three emotionally or physically damaged children. Fellow teens are especially effective at helping peers reduce alcohol and drug abuse; training students who are the objects of prejudice so they can tutor those who might feel superior goes a lot further than lectures about tolerance in overcoming bias and stereotypes.

We also know what doesn't work: fragmentation of services, red tape, denial of flexibility and judgment calls to frontline workers, lack of preventive intervention, destroying successful programs by asking them to take on ever-new problems and multiplying their caseloads, paying entrepreneurial "experts" to identify "dysfunctions" of families instead of learning what their real needs and resources are, funding new career paths for bureaucrats or consultants rather than hiring people to provide concrete help to families trying to cope with daily challenges, and overestimating what people can do without investment in infra-structure and ongoing support networks.

Not all programs that work are immediately cost-effective. There is no cheap way to make sure people succeed at *real* tasks and reach *meaningful* goals. Still, we have the resources to do so. The United States spends well over a *trillion* dollars a year on programs including ad campaigns for American corporations, subsidies to agricultural landowners, and military hardware. It would have cost $5,138 per family to lift every American family out of poverty in 1989, less than we spent in 43 days on the Persian Gulf War. For new funding, we could pick up $100 billion a year just by taxing the 1 percent of richest Americans at the rates they paid in the 1960s.

Character Counts

But money isn't the real problem. The question that gets lost in the debate over how to build individual character and family values is whether we as a society have the "character" to make hard decisions about priorities and the "strong values" to defer immediate gratification for long-range aspirations. When we pose the issue this way, immediate costs of investment in the future pale beside the long-run costs of failing to invest. The Children at Risk Project, providing intensive interventions for selected poor children in six cities, costs $4,000 per child per year, against more than $20,000 a year to keep a youth in prison. Consequences of child poverty cost America $36 billion a year.

Most Americans are open to these arguments, even after the politicians' 20-year campaign to reverse our nation's commitment to children and social justice. Although those who crusade for family values have managed to turn welfare into a dirty word, they have not wiped out Americans' sense of fairness. The task is to help people look behind the slogans of political demagogues, so they can rediscover their hope for the future and their commitment to making it better.

Stable communities and economics are the bedrock of stable families. It makes more sense to spend our time and energy building such communities than it does to spend it grading families by how well they stand up to pressures of the late twentieth century.

Children today are a precious and threatened resource. They make up only 26 percent of the population, and they are the poorest of any age group in the nation. Yet it is these children who will grow up to appreciate the work we leave behind, to provide for the elderly (us!), to contribute to the Social Security fund on which we all depend. Either that, or they will *not* do any of these things. It is up to all of as, not just parents, to decide which it will be, because we are all affected by the way these children turn out.

We cannot return to "traditional" family forms and expectations that were at least partly mythical in the first place. To help our children move successfully into the twenty-first century, we need to stop organizing our institutions and values around the notion that every family can—or should—have one adult totally available at work and another totally available at home. We have to adjust economic programs, schools, work policies, expectations of family life, and moral reasoning to the realities of family diversity and the challenges of global transformation. The new family values crusade, no matter how sincere the motives of its participants, points us backward rather than forward.

Remaking Schools to Fit Families of the Twenty-First Century
Richard Weizel

The regular school day had ended and a group of fifth graders sat in a circle on the floor and talked about what it was like to be the youngest, oldest, middle or only child in their families.

Down the hall a group of preschoolers watched a video while they waited for their parents to pick them up, and upstairs in the gymnasium some pupils played basketball, while others took part in arts and crafts in a nearby classroom.

These were among the activities taking place on a recent afternoon at the Rogers School in Stamford—one of eight community resource centers in Connecticut that have implemented a concept known as the School of the 21st Century—created by the cofounder and former director of the national Head Start program, Dr. Edward Zigler.

"Our main goal is to utilize the school building to its fullest capacity to provide programs for our pupils and the community, not only during typical schoolday hours, but before and after school and on weekends," the executive director of the Rogers School Community Center Organization, Christina Ramaglou, said.

"We believe this is what school should be doing: not only educating pupils but also working hard to become a valuable resource that is available to the entire community," Ms. Ramaglou said.

A Collaborative Effort

The school's principal, Mary Jennings, said that several social service and child care agencies are involved in programs at the school. "It's a collaborative effort that allows us to make the school more than just a place for academic learning," she said. "It's a place where families can come to learn about child care, where working parents can leave their preschoolers in a safe and nurturing environment and where we can also provide quality education for our students."

SOURCE: *The New York Times*, February 13, 1994, Sec. 13; pp. 1; 23. Reprinted with permission from *The New York Times*.

In the mid-80's, Dr. Zigler, the director of the Bush Center in Child Development and Social Policy at Yale University, and another Yale professor, Dr. Matia Finn-Stevenson, came up with the idea of school-supervised, comprehensive programs for children that would take place before and after the regular school day.

Since its inception in 1987, school districts in 10 states have developed the program in nearly 250 schools. The concept combines traditional education with comprehensive family support services such as child care training for young mothers as well as adult education in the schools on weekends.

"This is the wave of the future, the direction schools absolutely must take if we are to insure that our children are getting the proper care and education at an early age," Dr. Zigler said. "As a society we have been avoiding the issue of day care for 20 years—with 70 percent of day care centers being poor in quality—and the problem is now so immense that we've had to find some very creative solutions. I think the School of the 21st Century is one of them."

1,500 Schools by 2000

Dr. Finn-Stevenson, associate director of the Bush Center and national project director of the School of the 21st Century, said she expects schools in every state to be utilizing the concept—in nearly 1,500 schools—by 2000.

"We're developing strategies right now about how we can insure quality even as the concept grows around the country," she said. "This is a vitally important approach to education that will be helping more and more families to solve their child day care needs."

The General Assembly provided financial support in 1988 for three schools to implement the concept in schools in Killingly, Hartford and North Branford, and since then five more have followed, the program manager for the State Education Department's family resource centers, Paul Vivian, said.

Mr. Vivian said Connecticut was one of three states, of 44 that applied, to be awarded a $4.5-million grant over three years by the Federal Department of Health and Human Services for a School of the 21st Century program. He said the grant would make it possible for each existing school to receive up to $187,000 annually over the three-year period, and for new schools developing the concept to receive up to $125,000 a year.

"We're most proud of the fact that the program has grown here in Connecticut in spite of the major budget problems we've had the past few years," Mr. Vivian said. "These schools are successfully showing how to meet the multifaceted needs of their particular communities."

Mr. Vivian said the aspect he liked most about the concept is how it brings together children and families from diverse ethnic and economic backgrounds. "These schools are for the poor, the middle class and the wealthy," Mr. Vivian said. "I've witnessed wealthy parents talking to poor parents and finding out that their children are not all that different. It's really helping to break down barriers that have been extremely difficult to break down in the past."

Bringing down those barriers is one of the major goals at the 6–6 Interdistrict Magnet School in Bridgeport, which opened in September for 45 preschoolers. Grades one through six will be phased in over the next two years. Open from 6 A.M. to 6 P.M., hence the 6–6 in the name, the school has brought together more than 40 preschoolers from four suburban towns and Bridgeport.

Reducing Racial Isolation

"In our first year we believe we are already accomplishing our mission to reduce racial isolation and provide a good education for children in the city and surrounding suburbs," the school's director, Anne Alpert, said. "We're trying to instill an individual pride in every child about their own culture, but at the same time teaching them to appreciate and respect the backgrounds and cultures of others."

Parents at the school say the idea is working well. "I watched the children playing a game called red light, green light in school one day and my son was saying it in Spanish," Mark Williams of Stratford, whose 3-year-old son Kenzie attends the school, said. "At home, out of the blue, he will just start using Spanish words, and I think that's great. He's really learning about other cultures at a very early age."

The Rogers School in Stamford became a School of the 21st Century in 1991, using a combination of state money and sliding-scale fees to provide a full range of year-round education and family support services during a 7 A.M. to 7 P.M. school day.

Staying Out of Trouble

Programs like Positive Youth Development, which works to help children stay out of trouble and in the classroom, are conducted after normal school hours.

During a recent session at school, a group of fifth graders expressed how it felt to be the youngest, oldest or only child in their families. One girl said she fantasized about being an only child because "my brothers are always bothering me."

Another girl said that being the youngest was the most difficult: "You always have to go to bed so early."

The group's teacher, Ruth Haendler, gently pointed out that all had their advantages and drawbacks.

Afterward, Ms. Haendler said the program was among those working well as part of the School of the 21st Century concept. "Being able to work with these pupils in a relaxed setting after school hours is helping them enormously," she said. "I really believe it is preventing some of them from slipping through the cracks of the system."

Easing Burdens, Easing Minds

Working parents said the family resource centers have also greatly eased their burden, as well as easing their minds. "It's wonderful because I can leave my two boys at the school from 7:30 in the morning until the late afternoon and go to my job knowing they [are] in a safe place where they are being kept busy," Gloria Valle, whose children are at the Rogers School in Stamford, said. "Before coming here, my younger son, who is now 4, had a baby-sitter and watched TV every day. Now, he loves going to school because he says he has so much fun."

Most of the family resource centers throughout the state have also implemented a program called Families in Training, that helps young mothers and expectant parents to cope with issues pertaining to early childhood. Parents attend support groups conducted in the schools, as well as having parent aide visits in the home.

"It reduces the isolation that mothers feel sometimes when they're at home with the baby or babies," an administrator for the family resource center in North Branford, Susan Moss, said. "What we try to do is develop self-esteem in both the child and parent by empowering the mother with as much early childhood information and as much support as possible. Young mothers learn to deal with all facets of their child's development and that prevents a lot of problems later on."

Rene Haddad, who has been attending the Families in Training program at the Charter Oaks School's family resource center in West Hartford, said she has been delighted with the program since she moved to Connecticut from Ohio two and a half years ago. "When we first moved here," she said, "I didn't know anybody and it was really great to have this program because I was having some behavior problems with my oldest son after he found out he was going to have a younger sibling.

"It was so helpful having a group of mothers I could share that with, and my parent aide helped me to give my son the support he needed to get through the experience of suddenly having a younger brother."

Linda Fosco, the director of the family resource center at Killingly Memorial School (the state's first School of the 21st Century), said the concept would become even more crucial by the end of the decade and the century.

"When you look at local, state and national trends of what families will look like in the year 2000—such as the growing number of working and single mothers and families with two full-time working parents—there is going to be an increasingly greater need to coordinate and collaborate services for children and families in the schools," Ms. Fosco said. "Well, we're doing it here in Connecticut already . . . we've got a really good head start."

Chapter 2

GENDER

INTRODUCTION

In 1992, the American Association of University Women released a report claiming rampant gender discrimination in American schools. Immediately, it was one of the hottest topics going. It was highlighted on the news programs of major television networks, reported prominently in major newspapers, and was *the* topic of conversation on virtually all of the radio talk shows.

Indeed, a "gender divide" was perhaps most dramatically apparent on the talk shows. Typically, women told stories of remembered instances of bias or discrimination in school; men almost unanimously felt that girls were no worse off than boys. The attacks and counter-attacks were acrimonious and often personal. Feminists versus "white males," liberals versus conservatives, the "politically correct" crowd versus the "tell it like it is" crowd—they all had something to say on the issue. Preconceived philosophical positions, gender identification, and personal anecdote, rather than scientific evidence, seemed to govern the debate. Details of the AAUW's report were quoted when they seemed to benefit a particular side and were dismissed when they did not.

Among all the pros and cons, the comments of one high school senior girl stood out. A talk show host had just expressed her support for some of the AAUW's charges of gender bias against girls and women. But the senior complained, "No way. That report is crazy and I think it's unfair to my teachers to say that they are anything but fair to *both* boys and girls." After a pause, she continued. "To think of it, it's the *girls* who mostly sit up front in math class, not the boys. It's the *girls* who mostly answer the teacher's questions. It's the *guys* who bluff because they didn't finish their homework."

Is systematic gender discrimination against girls and women in schools *actually a fact* as the AAUW report claims—or is it mostly myth surrounded and clouded by ideology? Indeed, could it be true, as some others have claimed recently, that gender discrimination affects *boys* more significantly than girls? Or, is it the case that the whole "gender issue" is a red herring that distracts from the main issue of how to improve the quality of American education for *all* students?

More fundamentally, we need to ask: What *precisely* is gender discrimination? And then, given a precise definition of gender discrimination, why is it wrong?

Researchers Study Years of Tests, See Gender Differences in Aptitude
Anita Srikameswaran

An examination of 32 years of tests given to thousands of boys and girls across the nation may provide insight into how the sexes develop skills that lead to careers.

Males dominated females by a 7 - 1 ratio at the highest levels in science test scores but also outnumbered them at the lowest levels in reading and writing skills.

Females' scores tended to cluster in the middle on all measures of ability, according to researchers at the University of Chicago.

Such disparities may mean that girls are less likely to choose careers in science and may not be encouraged by their mentors and families if they do, said Dr. Larry Hedges, professor of education at the U. of C. and lead researcher in the study, which appears in this week's edition of the journal *Science.*

"It is a profound difference," said Hedges of the results. "As a society, we've made efforts to achieve greater gender equity, but the numbers suggest we are going to have to do a much better job to recruit women into the sciences."

In some science and vocational aptitude tests, no girls fell in the top 4 percent. On the other hand, Hedges said, boys may need assistance in enhancing their reading comprehension and writing skills.

Boys not only scored lower on average than girls but were over-represented at the bottom of the scale, prompting concern that individuals "with such poor literacy skills will have difficulty finding employment in an information-driven economy," Hedges said.

As the study noted: "The data imply that males are, on average, at a rather profound disadvantage in the performance of these basic skills."

The six large national surveys were administered between 1960 and 1992 and studied different groups.

Some tested abilities in 15-year-olds both in school and among those who had dropped out—and sophomore and senior students in both public and private high schools.

Other exams tested 8th grade students initially and again four years later.

Tests included the National Longitudinal Study of Youth, the National Assessment of Educational Progress and the Armed Services Vocational Aptitude Battery.

The U. of C. team re-examined the data looking specifically for sex differences in average scores, distribution and the number of boys and girls in the top and bottom 10 percent.

"By using data from national studies, we can be quite confident that the results would apply to the whole country," Hedges said. "That's a significant advantage of this study—most of the others have been done on a small scale."

Hedges also found small differences between the sexes in other areas of intellectual ability.

Girls did slightly better in tests of reading comprehension, speed of perception and in associative memory—a measure of learning and memory—but boys did a bit better in social studies and math.

The largest difference in terms of average score occurred in vocational aptitude scales. "Boys did much better in stereotypically male areas: mechanical reasoning, electronics information and auto and shop information," Hedges said.

However, this was probably due to experience, he speculated. "The differences have a lot to do with socialization and opportunity. Girls are still less likely to work on the car with their fathers."

The tests were intended to measure developed abilities rather than innate potential alone.

"It would be a mistake to take them as a measure of biologically dictated aptitude," Hedges cautioned.

The Last Word on Gender Differences
Susan Baxter

Once upon a time, men were men, women were women, and anyone who rocked the boat got eaten by sharks. Men walked tall, lords of everything they surveyed—including women. It was the natural order of things; any gibbon could tell you that. The truth was that women weren't really necessary at all,

SOURCE: *Psychology Today,* March 1994, pp. 50–53; 85–86. Reprinted with permission from *Psychology Today Magazine.* Copyright © 1994, Sussex Publishers, Inc.

even for reproduction, since the mighty sperm carried the blueprint for life. Women were mere biological incubators. Which may explain why the 17th-century scientist, Antonie van Leeuwenhoek, the first person to see bacteria under a microscope, also saw "exceedingly minute forms of men with arms, heads, and legs" inside sperm.

Well, *in vitro veritas,* as they used to say.

Fast forward to a time of fax machines and heart transplants, when real men change diapers and real women carry guns. A time when it's not always easy to pinpoint what traits are strictly male or female. Norms change quickly, and one decade's meat is another's high-cholesterol poison. So, today, how should we differentiate between sex (innate, physiological) and gender (socialized, learned) differences?

Or, perhaps a better question is: Should we even be discussing it at all?

There are three kinds of lies, said Mark Twain: lies, damn lies, and statistics. And however gingerly one steps through the minefield that is the study of biological sex differences, one cannot help but be struck by all kinds of intellectual and statistical rubbish.

Take the case of the AGS girls:

Some 40 years ago, before we knew that acronyms and pharmacology could be hazardous to our health, some pregnant women were given the synthetic steroid progestin. Which led, in turn, to some female fetuses receiving, *in utero,* a dose of androgens (male hormones, chiefly testosterone). Unremarkable in itself (drugs causing side effects, what a revolutionary concept!), these girls were born with adrenogenital syndrome (AGS)—meaning they had masculinized genitalia requiring surgical correction.

Enter Doreen Kimura, a 30-year veteran of neuropsychology, whom *Scientific American* dubbed "perhaps the world's authority" on sex differences. "There are less obvious aspects of female/maleness [other than physical height and weight] such as aggressiveness, nurturance, and intellectual style or ability." The reason, she says, lies in the one piece of genetic equipment men and women don't share: the sex chromosome. More precisely, she claims that prenatal hormones so affect the developing fetus that "from the start, environment is acting on differently wired brains in girls and boys."

Emphasis on the *pre*natal, boys and girls. As for the AGS girls, the fact that they behaved more "tomboyish and aggressive than their unaffected sisters," says Kimura, provides "compelling" evidence that hormones do, in fact, seal your sexual fate.

Uh, hold on, let's backtrack here. *Tomboyish??* Now there's a word that zips us back a quick century or two. For a long time, as you'll no doubt recall, femininity was just another word for delicacy, modesty, gentleness—and weakness. Of course, constricting clothes and corsets can work wonders at ensuring compliance. Heck, even when I was a kid, little girls couldn't wear pants to school—and I've got the scabby knees to prove it. So how did the retrogressive term "tomboyish," a social value judgment if ever I heard one, become part of scientific "proof"?

In addition, in "objective" observations of these girls at play, psychologists noted that they preferred rough-and-tumble play and opted for "typically masculine toys — for example, they played with cars for the same amount of time normal boys did." Well, as a matter of fact, I was the nerdiest bookworm that ever lived, and I've *always* preferred cars to babies. Anyway, scads of studies show that girls happily play with trucks, trains, or any other boy toys, provided no boys are around to stop them.

Still, language aside, what about these girls, "normal" except for that brief exposure to male hormones? Must mean something. You bet your bronzed baby booties it does. These girls were not normal at all, not unless you consider a tiny penis and scrotum normal for a girl. Goodness knows what effect this extreme genital ambiguity had on them — and their parents.

In a different case study, in a freak accident, a baby boy's penis was burned off during what was supposed to be a routine circumcision by electrocautery. After some agonizing soul-searching, the parents decided to authorize sex-change surgery to turn him into a her. (Wait for it, it gets weirder.) Amazingly, this boy had an identical twin brother, which made it possible to compare two genetically identical individuals raised as a boy and a girl. (Never mind the fact that the boy's hormone-producing testes were removed — remember we're talking about *prenatal* influences here.)

The upshot? Except for some tomboyish tendencies (sorry), our hero became the perfect little girl, the very picture of adorable femininity. She even asked for a doll house for Christmas, versus the toy garage her brother had wanted.

Such dramatics aren't necessary to show how differently we treat boys and girls. In a British study, the same baby was dressed alternately as a boy or girl. As a girl, the baby was held and cooed at: "Aren't you pretty?" The "boy" on the other hand, was not held, encouraged to explore, cheered on. Which reminds Barbara Ehrenreich, biologist, author, and essayist, of something that happened when her son was around two years old: "He had long, blond hair, and a waitress came up to us and said, 'Oh, she's so cute. What a sweetie,' and so on. And I said, 'Well, he's actually a boy.' The waitress, without missing a beat, said, 'Tough little guy, huh?'"

Now you or I might look at all this and take it as a front-row seat at the Nature/Nurture Open; still, there are those, such as Kimura, who don't buy it. "The conventional wisdom has been that behavioral differences between the sexes are learned," she says. But they are really "stamped into our brains before birth." Early hormonal events, she says, have a "lifelong, *irreversible* effect on behavior." What behavior? "Men are more accurate in tests of target-directed motor skills [discus throwers take note]. Women tend to be better at rapidly identifying matching items [like socks from a dryer?], a skill called perceptual speed. They have greater verbal fluency and are faster at certain precision manual tasks, such as placing pegs in designated holes on a board [something I know I've always been proud of]."

Like Kimura, the list of differences is precise, authoritative, firm. But is it suspect? Aside from the language of researchers, isn't the datum itself contradictory, depending on one's vantage point?

As I researched this topic, I found that various people I talked to argued for significant innate sex differences, just like Kimura. Parents in particular repeatedly insisted (eyes raised heavenward) that boys run around more, talk less, are more destructive, while girls chatter, are more biddable and cuddly. "And I treat my kids exactly the same," they all say.

Short of accusing one's friends of lying, all one can do is wonder. If little Johnny showed a predilection for pink hair ribbons or nail polish, wouldn't these same gender-blind parents gently but firmly dissuade him? And if little Kathy ladles mud soup out of a tiny dish and pretends she's Mommy, isn't she just the cutest thing? While I absolve the parents of any malice, I agree with anthropologist Stephen Jay Gould, who remarked that theories are most successful when they let us believe that our "social prejudices are scientific facts after all."

In the wacky world of sex versus gender differences, the demarcation lines are as clear as any Yugoslavian border, particularly in these enlightened, polarized times: You're either a politically correct stooge unwilling to accept that biology is destiny or you're a strong-minded scientist, studying hormones or the hypothalamus. In which context, incidentally, aforesaid strong-minded scientist can ramble on about his or her own personal experiences and call it empirical evidence.

Take this 1991 *Time* magazine cover, for instance: "Scientists are discovering that gender differences have as much to do with the biology of the brain as the way we are raised." Inside, however, University of Chicago psychologist Jerre Levy relates how watching her 15-month-old daughter *convinced* her of the genetic base for behavior: "I had dressed her in her nightie and she came into the room with this saucy little walk, cocking her head, blinking her eyes, especially at the men. You never saw such flirtation in your life."

Pardon me? A 15-month-old? Flirting? Ah, let's project complex adult erotic feelings onto a small child, why don't we? Kimura doesn't hesitate to use herself as backup, either, describing her use of landmarks to find her car in a crowded parking lot as being "stereotypically female" behavior. Interesting that if you or I use personal experience, it's anecdote. But not here.

Throughout all of this, I can't help noticing how pathetically meager is the range of attributions for female behavior. If girls play with cars, they're ersatz boys. They aren't attracted to cars because the automobile represents freedom, power, status, speed.

Even more infuriating is how sex-difference research always manages to denigrate women. Ten years ago, for instance, Camilla Benbow and Julian Stanley analyzed 10,000 SAT scores, whereupon they announced to the world that males are "inherently" superior at math. The world was clearly impressed. "Do males have a math gene?" wondered *Newsweek*. (Good old math gene. Wonder if there's a sense of humor gene, too?) Benbow herself even remarked that "many women can't bring themselves to accept the sexual difference in aptitude. But the difference in math is a fact."

(The best riposte I heard to this was Jane Pauley's, on the *Today* show. Does this mean, Pauley sweetly asked two male biodeterminist guests, that men who can't do math aren't "real men"?)

Call me curmudgeonly, but last I heard, SATs measured learning, not innate ability. And recently, the questions themselves have come under fire for their gender bias. For instance, 27 percent more boys than girls correctly answered a question based on basketball scores. And when an analogy began "Mercenary is to soldier as. . . ," boys outscored girls by 16 percent. (I guess Barbie just never found the right outfit for the French Foreign Legion.)

In fact, what the SATs need, quipped *Glamour,* are questions like, "Donna's chemistry teacher calls on boys 75 percent of the time. If there are twice as many boys as girls in the class, what is the chance that Donna will become a famous scientist?"

Slim. Because whether Donna knows it or not, girls' scholastic performance nosedives at puberty. (Gee, I wonder why that could be? *Hormones?*) "Unless nature selected for smart girls and dumb women, something goes very wrong at the middle-school level," writes Barbara Ehrenreich. Maybe it's teachers who call on and encourage boys more. Or maybe it's the high-school politics that equate good grades with terminal geekdom. Even more important than teachers, though, is girls' growing realization that straight A's aren't necessarily the fastest way to point B (for boyfriend).

"Males [still] tend to prefer females who make them feel stronger and smarter," says Ehrenreich. "Any girl who's bright enough to solve a quadratic equation is smart enough to bat her eyelashes and pretend she can't."

Psychologist Janet Hyde of the University of Wisconsin recalls discussing her SAT scores with colleague Marcia Linn after the Benbow and Stanley study. "Here we were, sitting and talking to each other and trying to figure out why we aren't good at math," she laughs. "Marcia got an 800 on the SAT and I got a 780." Hyde's interest is not incidental: to examine gender differences in mathematics performance, she analyzed results from more than *three million* subjects. The conclusion? "Approximately 51.5 percent of females score above the mean for the general population versus 48.5 percent of men. Thus, the overall-effect size is so small that it indicates little practical significance."

Even more interesting, what differences there were have declined over the years. "Women's hormones haven't changed in the last 20 years, but we found that the magnitude of the gender differences declined," says Hyde. Verbal ability? Gone. Spatial ability? Gone, except for three-dimensional rotation, where boys still do better. (Boys play a lot more games that involve throwing balls through three-dimensional space.) "And if a phenomenon can disappear, how could it have been biologically correct?"

In any event, intellectual *similarities* between women and men far outweigh the differences. Yet while biology is no longer an acceptable reason for barring women from higher education, the innate-difference argument is still used to rationalize why female engineers, architects, or brain surgeons are rare. "Boys don't go into nursing," says Kimura, "because they're less nurturing than girls." Oh, are we talking about Florence Nightingale here? Because nursing happens to be one of the most violent professions—after police work and taxi driving. Shouldn't men, physically stronger, be the more natural candidates?

"Everything starts as mystique and ends up as politics," someone once scrawled on a wall in Paris. And politics is exactly what the sex-difference debate is about. Not the politically correct "Who's the victim!" game we're so fond of these days ("Pick me, I'm a woman!" "No, me, I'm a straight white male"), but a subtler divide that rationalizes history and obscures rationality. The smug empiricists of neuroscience are telling me that, as a female, my genetic lot is inferior. Doomed by my DNA, I must be nurturing (I am. So what? So are all the men I know); bad at math (wrong); useless with maps (okay, I confess, I prefer landmarks); good at precision tasks (lousy at them—no patience).

On the flip side, the implication is that those wonderful fathers I know (like my own) are some sort of evolutionary anomaly. That men of letters (like Yeats, who luckily didn't realize he shouldn't excel at verbal tasks) are somehow lacking as real men. And that men who hate cars and like babies are pseudo-females.

To give researchers such as Kimura their mathematical due, they make no claims about the individual. "If you're guessing on the basis of a person being a woman what her abilities are going to be, you're going to do a very poor job," Kimura says. "When I study sex differences, I feel like I'm studying human variation. It's important to make that distinction."

But how many people reading *Newsweek* do make that distinction? Especially when Kimura herself makes vast, sweeping generalizations about how boys shouldn't be nurses or girls engineers. Hyde reports (with some heat) that after the girls-can't-do-math flurry, psychologist Jackie Eccles, in a longitudinal study, found that mothers who had read the news reports subsequently had lower expectations of their daughters' math competence than before.

Differences, alas, make headlines. "A no-result isn't news," says Ehrenreich. "But a result showing any kind of teensy-weensy intellectual or behavioral difference is."

Again, part of the problem lies in the language, this time of statistics. Words like "significant" or "average" mean something very different to the average (see what I mean?) person than they do to those versed in the study of raw data. Then there's experimenter bias, crude tests, even nonverbal nuances. For instance, psychologist Robert Rosenthal observed that more than 70 percent of male experimenters smiled when they gave instructions to female subjects; only 12 percent smiled at males. "It may be heartening to know that chivalry is not dead," Rosenthal said. "But it's disconcerting [*vis-à-vis*] methodology."

Nevertheless, simply substituting environmental determinism won't work, either. Our brains have around one million billion neural connections; if you started counting them now, you'd finish in 32 million years (and by then you'd have evolved into a higher being with more important things to worry about). And the operative word here is *individual*. Even within one culture, one society, there is immense variability, enormous complexity.

If there are neuropsychological sex differences, clearly, we don't know what they are or what causes them. Perhaps to the point, whatever differences have been tallied in the past are gone, or are disappearing rapidly. In the end, there may be subtle differences, but don't bet any real money on these ever predicting who'll be the better nurse or engineer.

Because however much we yearn for simple truths, there aren't any here.

Bias Against Girls Is Found Rife in Schools, With Lasting Damage
Susan Chira

School is still a place of unequal opportunity, where girls face discrimination from teachers, textbooks, tests and their male classmates, according to a report being released today that examined virtually all major studies on girls and education.

Girls and boys start school roughly equal in skills and confidence, but girls trail by the end of high school, said the study, "How Schools Shortchange Women: The A.A.U.W. Report," commissioned by the American Association of University Women Educational Foundation.

"This latest report presents the truth behind another myth—that boys and girls receive equal education," said Alice McKee, president of the A.A.U.W. Educational Foundation, in the report's foreword. "The wealth of statistical evidence must convince even the most skeptical that gender bias in our schools is shortchanging girls—and compromising our country."

The Specifics of Bias

The A.A.U.W. foundation calls the report one of the most comprehensive of its kind ever undertaken. Researchers at the Wellesley College Center for Research on Women examined more than 1,000 publications about girls and education, including hundreds of research studies. From the material, most of it from the 1980's, the researchers drew a number of conclusions.

- Teachers pay less attention to girls.
- Girls still lag in mathematics and science scores, and even those who do well in those subjects tend not to choose math and science careers.
- Reports of sexual harassment of girls by boys are increasing.
- Some tests remain biased against girls, hurting their chances of scholarships and getting into college.

SOURCE: *The New York Times,* February 12, 1992, pp. A1; A23. Reprinted with permission from *The New York Times.*

- Textbooks still ignore or stereotype women, and girls learn almost nothing about many of their most pressing problems, like sexual abuse, discrimination and depression.

The report does acknowledge that girls generally get better grades than boys, but it argues that, when all their experiences are examined, girls are still shortchanged. The United States Department of Education says that 61.6 percent of the girls who graduated from high school in 1989 were enrolled in college that fall, compared with 57.6 percent of the boys.

"This is truly a wake-up call to the nation's education and policy leaders, parents, administrators and guidance counselors that unless we pay attention to girls' needs today, we will find out 15 years from now that there is still a glass ceiling," said Anne Bryant, executive director of the association. The report addressed the experiences of girls in public schools from preschool through high school. The report makes 40 recommendations, including training teachers and changing teaching methods to meet girls' needs, encouraging girls in mathematics and science, toughening school policies against sexual harassment and placing girls' problems on the agenda of education reformers.

While the individual research programs that the report synthesized have been published previously, together they paint a damning picture of girls' lives in school. The findings, many educators said, will surprise many teachers and administrators and could help them. "I think this is dynamite stuff," said Keith Geiger, president of the National Education Association, the country's largest teachers union. He said the research "makes the point very clearly that there are many subtle and unknown things teachers do in the classroom" that hurt girls.

Both he and David Imig, executive director of the American Association of Colleges for Teacher Education, said they planned to distribute the report to their members to help teachers learn how to treat girls more fairly.

In one of the best-known studies cited in the report, Myra and David Sadker observed teachers over three years and found that most teachers called on boys more often than girls, offered boys more detailed and constructive criticism, and allowed boys to shout out answers but reprimanded girls for doing so.

Although there is very little research on the experience of black girls in school, one study did find that when black girls tried to approach teachers, teachers tended to rebuff them and paid more attention to white girls.

Girls May Be Ignored

These and other examples of bias have held girls back in math and science, the report argues. Two recent studies found that many science teachers, and some mathematics teachers, tended to ignore girls in favor of boys.

Boys not only continue to score higher than girls on science standardized tests, but the gap may be widening, the report found. Moreover, even those girls who did well in science and mathematics tended not to pursue careers in those fields. Studies of girls who continued to study science after high school showed that encouragement of teachers was crucial in their decisions.

Researchers cited in the report also found that girls had less confidence in their math abilities than boys did, and that as their confidence diminished, so did their performance.

But the report also offered some good news: the gap between boys' and girls' mathematics scores is narrowing, according to a review of standardized test results. The report pointed to the success of special programs in math and science for girls in the summer or after school as one way to bolster girls' confidence and interest.

Tests Still Fall Short

Yet the report cautioned about over-relying on standardized test scores which it found underestimated girls' performances, particularly in mathematics and science. The report found that girls' grades are far higher than their standardized test scores, and said that while many test developers have worked to eliminate obviously biased test questions, instances of bias remain. For that reason, the report said, tests should be given less weight in determining scholarships and college admissions.

Teachers who want to help girls in the classroom can draw on a range of techniques that researchers have found effective. One such approach is "cooperative learning," in which students study in groups rather than being pitted against one another. Because several studies show that girls often learn better in single-sex environments, the report also suggests creating all-girl work groups within mixed classrooms. Researchers also recommend that teachers eliminate sexist language, strive for a congenial classroom atmosphere and videotape themselves teaching to monitor their behavior toward girls.

Girls in school are also enduring increasing sexual harassment from their male classmates, but many teachers tolerate such behavior, the report said. But these and other problems central to many young girls' lives—like sexual abuse, sexism in society, sex education or depression—are rarely discussed in the classroom, the report said.

Some of these problems actually contribute to girls' dropping out of high school, the report said. Despite widespread perceptions, less than half of girls drop out because they are pregnant. Many are asked to take on too many family responsibilities at home—something that more active discussion of female roles and sexism might equip women to resist, the report suggests. Those teen-agers who are pregnant often find that schools discourage their return, or are not flexible enough to help them graduate.

In a widely discussed study issued last year, the A.A.U.W. reported that girls' self-esteem drops markedly, even faster than that of boys, as they approach adolescence. Although the writers of this report say no research has been done to document a cause-and-effect connection they speculate that a sexist curriculum may be one reason.

"Students sit in classrooms that, day in, day out, deliver the message that women's lives count for less than men's," the report said. Only one of 10 books most commonly assigned in high school English classes was written by a woman, and while many textbooks have added more material on women, there is still too little, the report argues.

■ ■ ■

Gender Balance: Lessons From Girls in Science and Mathematics
Ann Pollina

Are we emphasizing the right issues when we talk about gender in the mathematics, science, and technology classroom? We are and we aren't.

The need for equitable treatment of girls and women is beyond dispute: Women are still greatly underrepresented in fields like physical sciences, engineering, and technology. As a matter of simple justice, there should be no field of academic inquiry closed to women.

The economic necessity argument is valid as well, particularly as women make up a greater share of our work force. And if we are to remain competitive in a world market, U.S. women must be well trained in mathematical, scientific, and technological fields.

But as important as these issues are, we cannot allow them to overshadow a third critical argument: the characteristic approaches that many girls and women bring to learning and scientific inquiry are vital to science and to science education.

Feminizing Scientific Inquiry

Too often in the past, we have focused on girls as if they were the problem. If not enough girls took math and science, we asked, "What is wrong with them, and how do we fix them?" How do we make them more aggressive, more analytical, more competitive, tougher, so that they will survive in these disciplines? For years, we gave girls what researchers at Smith College have called courses in remedial masculinity. Then we wonder why many girls lack self-esteem.

Instead of trying to change the way our female students approach mathematics, science, and technology, we need to study the ways they *do* learn. We

SOURCE: *Educational Leadership, 53,* no.1, (September 1995): pp. 30-33. Reprinted with permission of the Association for Supervision and Curriculum Development. Copyright © 1995 by ASCD. All rights reserved.

need far more than a grudging willingness to change our pedagogy to simply accommodate learning styles. We must be willing to learn from them. Even more important, we must come to believe that the messages they have for us are of real value.

The work of a number of women scientists demonstrates how profoundly a woman's perspective can enrich and enliven scientific study. The unusual insights of Barbara McClintock, for example, opened a new window through which to view the study of genetics. In 1983, McClintock won the Nobel Prize for her discovery that genes can rearrange themselves on a chromosome. The direction of her research was informed by a "feeling for the organism" (Keller 1983).

Jane Goodall and Diane Fossey, who revolutionized the understanding of primate behavior, did not hypothesize and then corroborate by observing a group of apes. Instead, they took a relational approach and focused on a single ape, tracing that primate's interactions. Their work has become a model for wildlife observation.

These women's formation of questions and approaches to problems represented a new way of looking at science: They introduced feelings and relationships into the discipline.

Ten Tips From Girls' Schools

How do we begin to learn lessons from girls in the classroom? The collective wisdom of teachers from girls' schools can provide educators with insight into the learning styles of girls. Believing girls' schools to be an untapped resource in our country's efforts to find ways to inspire young women to study mathematics, science, and technology, the National Coalition of Girls' Schools has sponsored three symposiums in these fields. Two were held at Wellesley College, in June 1991 and 1995; and a third in conjunction with the Dudley Wright Center at Tufts University in March 1993. Each brought together educators from public, independent, single-sex, and coeducational schools to examine research and proven strategies for teaching girls in the classroom.

Here are some of the messages from these workshops that I use in my high school classroom at Westover, an all-girls school in Connecticut.

1. Connect mathematics, science, and technology to the real world. My students remind me how much richer mathematics is when we do not divorce it from its history, its philosophical underpinnings, and its functions. Connecting my subject to the lives of real people and the good of the world is a powerful hook for girls.

Some specific exercises:

Collect examples of decorative borders from different cultures. My geometry students study transformation and isometry using these.

Establish links with other disciplines. Both the calculus and the European history classes at my school spend some time looking at the powerful effect

Newton's laws of motion had on the thinking of the Enlightenment, and we share presentations between classes.

Divide a class into groups and ask them what sort of mathematics a prehistoric hunter–gatherer clan might need to survive. You will have a wonderful discussion about the nature of mathematics.

2. Choose metaphors carefully, and have students develop their own. For years we have asked girls to *tackle* problems and master concepts using metaphors and real-world problems more closely tied to boys' life experiences. We have taught fractions using batting averages and presented parabolas as paths of missiles and rockets. Presenting images of mathematics and science that are comfortable and meaningful for girls is more than a sign of our current preoccupation with political correctness.

In my classes, I often ask students to create their own metaphors. A teacher may gain valuable insights into students' own perceptions of learning style by asking questions such as:

"If math were a food, for me it would be _____ because _____ ."

My favorite response to this question was from a ninth grader entering Algebra 1:

> If mathematics were a food, for me it would be a sandwich because sometimes I like what's on a sandwich and sometimes I don't. When there's too much stuff on a sandwich, I can't fit it in my mouth.

After reading this, I knew what that student needed in a math classroom. This exercise is the kind of "window on students' thinking" that the National Council of Teachers of Mathematics speaks of in its *Teaching Standards* (Leiva 1993–1995). Dorothy Buerk, who teaches mathematics education at Ithaca College, has developed a wealth of these exercises (Buerk 1985).

3. Foster an atmosphere of true collaboration. Collaborative learning has become the classroom panacea of the '90s. Although a collaborative environment *is* attractive to many girls, pulling desks into a circle does not assure a collaborative, noncompetitive experience. Small groups work for girls if all members are taught to listen and are responsible for one another's learning. Some teachers insist that a true group project is one that no single group member can complete without the group's help.

4. Encourage girls to act as experts. When the teacher is the touchstone for all knowledge and answers, students rarely exhibit self-confidence. Only when the group is responsible for verifying its own logic and when students critique their own work and that of their peers do they begin to see themselves as scientists. The technique of the teacher refusing to act as an expert has been used successfully for over a decade in the Summer Math program at Mount

Holyoke College. The program is designed for high school girls to address under-representation of women in mathematics-based fields.

5. *Give girls the opportunity to be in control of technology.*   The issue of the expert is also a critical one in technology. Both boys and girls need to recognize the masculine cast of the computer industry. Taking any computer magazine and comparing the numbers of men and women pictured or mentioned in advertisements will stimulate a good class discussion.

At Westover, the computer room is staffed and serviced by students, usually from our Women in Science and Engineering (WISE) program. These girls are responsible for basic repairs, for teaching software, and for dealing with data emergencies. At times they teach the required computer literacy course. Girls need to see other girls in control of technology. In coed settings, an all-girls computer club may allow girls to develop more computer expertise.

6. *Portray technology as a way to solve problems as well as a plaything.*   Girls use computers differently than do boys. Few girls will play with a computer just because its there; most often girls use it as a tool, not a toy, and they need to see its relevance to their lives. One way to encourage girls to play on the computer is to emphasize the networking and communication capability. Single-use work stations can be isolating; pairing girls creates a comfortable atmosphere and stimulates discussion.

When asked to create a dream machine, girls want to create things that can help make our lives better. Cornelia Brunner and Margaret Honey of the Center for Children and Technology have crafted a variety of exercises to explore technological imagination (Brunner and Honey 1990).

7. *Capitalize on girls' verbal strengths.*   Strong writers and good readers—both girls and boys—have valuable tools at their disposal. Yet, often, we are not creative enough in teaching them how to use those tools to their advantage in a mathematics or science classroom.

At the Coalition of Girls' Schools' symposiums cited earlier, teachers presented a wealth of situations in which they used writing. Students were encouraged to express the logic behind their solutions in essay or picture form. Proofs might be essays and well-constructed arguments with a minimum of mathematical notation.

My calculus students keep journals in which they reflect on their experiences in the course, comment on their progress, and set goals for themselves. Two possible journal questions:

> You died while doing your physics homework. Write your physics obituary.

> You are a spider on the wall of your room observing you doing your mathematics homework. What do you see?

8. *Experiment with testing and evaluation.*   Assessment methods must reflect the research suggesting that girls do not think in linear right/wrong categories. Multiple-choice testing that requires forced choices or contains out-of-context questions and topics unrelated to real-world experiments make no use of girls' ability to synthesize, make connections, and use their practical intelligence. The work of Maryellen Harmon and her colleagues at Boston College's Center for the Study of Testing, Evaluation, and Educational Policy suggests that, for this reason, such assessments inhibit science education reform (Madaus et al. 1992).

Alternate strategies that do work well for girls include *embedded assessments*—activities in which students, usually working in groups, perform experiments, discover patterns, and arrive at hypotheses. A teacher circulates and observes student performance to evaluate them. Another form of assessment is the *circus,* where stations with reflection questions or experiments are set up around a room. Students go from station to station and are evaluated on the quality of their investigation at each.

9. Give frequent feedback, and keep expectations high.   Because girls still may not expect to do well in mathematics and science, they tend to need more encouragement than do boys. The role of the teacher in praising students and verbalizing expectations is critical. Teachers at the girls' schools' forums found it vital to provide frequent feedback in the form of homework checks, quizzes, and comments thereby reinforcing students' belief in their control of the material. Many said they use this strategy to develop the kind of self-reliance that all students need to survive in an inquiry-based classroom.

10. Experiment with note-taking techniques.   Girls are dutiful learners. They can get so absorbed in taking down every note and diagram that they are too preoccupied to take part in discussions. Teachers at the symposiums suggested a variety of techniques to counter this tendency, ranging from the "no note taking allowed" classroom to handing out copies of lecture notes or having them available on the computer. My algebra and geometry students take notes on reading material before coming to class. Most teachers at the symposiums included some standard note-taking situations so that students could learn this important skill.

Single-Gender Versus Coed Settings

The number of single-gender experiments in schools from New Hampshire to California bears witness to our interest in equity and our willingness to change. Those experiments are also steeped in controversy, and for good reason. If the purpose of such experiments is to divide girls from boys because girls can't compete in a "real" mathematics or science classroom, then our experiments, by conveying this message to girls, can do infinite harm. But if we begin these experiments believing that our female students have something to teach us, then what goes on in such a classroom can be more subtle and powerful than the absence of boys: it can be the empowerment of girls.

A recent, well-publicized experiment at the Illinois Mathematics and Science Academy in Aurora illustrates this point dramatically. In 1993, the academy, an experimental, residential school serving gifted and talented students, offered an all-girls' section on mechanics as part of a year-long calculus-based physics course. David Workman, the physics teacher involved, did not simply import his usual classroom methods, but was willing to learn from the young women. He found some approaches successful—collaborative processes, hands-on experimentation, connection of abstract concepts with practical application—and he made these the cornerstone of his class. Then—and this is most vital—he tried to import these methods into his coed setting.

Workman made it clear to the girls that there was nothing wrong with the way they related to physics or to the physical world. His powerful message:

> I'm not just doing these things because you are incapable of learning physics
> the "right way"; I am using the teaching methods that appeal to you because
> they are valid and important methods of scientific inquiry.

A report on the experimental section (Dagenais et al. 1994) showed it mirrored much of the atmosphere of all-girls' classrooms that other academy teachers describe: a spirit of co-learning, with both teacher and students feeling free to ask questions, admit mistakes, take risks, express confusion, and so on; a profound sense of responsibility for one's own learning and that of others; and a special rapport between and among the teacher and the students.

He Said, She Said

Workman's initial efforts to replicate this collaborative atmosphere in his coeducational classes [were] foiled: many boys tended to blurt out answers to questions posed to the class as a whole, with predictable results. The other students were suddenly diverted from collective problem solving and inquiry to an explain-the-answer-to-me mode. "In this environment," said Workman, "all except the boldest and fastest hesitate to be open, ask questions, and take risks."

To get around this problem, Workman has his students write down answers rather than speak them. Then, moving from table to table, he confirms whether an answer is right or whether the student or group of students needs to work through the problem again.

These difficulties notwithstanding, the single-gender experiment has already helped to level the playing field. Last year, for example, girls performed on a par with their male peers (in prior years their performance declined relative to boys' as the semester went on); more girls enrolled in and successfully completed the year-long physics course than ever before; and girls in the single-gender section gained more self-confidence than did those in coeducational sections.

Workman and his colleagues plan to further analyze the results of the experiment. "We're going to take what we learned and think harder about how we can preserve the strengths of both male and female modes of learning in mixed classes in order to benefit everyone," he said. In single-gender class experiments, the culture that surrounds a class is as vital as teaching itself. If we are willing to stop trying to change girls and ready to let a feminine approach to science inform our pedagogy, we may see some exciting results for boys and girls and for science and technology.

REFERENCES

Brunner, C., and M. Honey. (1990). "Hampton Hills Gazette—An Instrument for Evaluating Technological Imagination." New York: Center for Children and Technology.

Buerk, D. (1985). "The Voices of Women Making Meaning in Mathematics." *Journal of Education* 167:3.

Dagenais, R., E. Moyer, D. Musial, M. Sloan, L. Torp, and D. Workman. (December 1994). "The Calculus-Based Physics Exploratory Study Summary Report." Aurora: Illinois Mathematics and Science Academy.

Keller, E. F. (1983). *A Feeling for the Organism.* New York: W. H. Freeman and Co.

Leiva, M. A., series ed. (1993–1995). *Curriculum and Evaluation Standards for School Mathematics.* Reston, Va.: The National Council of Teachers of Mathematics.

Madaus, G. F., M. M. West, M. C. Harmon, R. G. Lomax, and K. A. Viator. (1992). *The Influence of Testing on Teaching Math and Science in Grades 4–12.* Boston: Center for the Study of Testing, Evaluation, and Educational Policy, Boston College.

An Equation for Equality: Same-Sex Classes Target Girls' Math, Science Skills
Marilou Tousignant

It is 8:55 A.M. in Sue Nuckolls's second-period algebra class, and the 13 eighth-graders are quickly taking their seats. In two minutes, Nuckolls has them teamed up in groups of three and four, reviewing their homework.

"I think your general mistake is in how you multiplied," says one student, helping a puzzled classmate.

One hour later, it's third-period algebra, and 12 students fill the room.

This class is more boisterous, even jumpy. Four students immediately seek Nuckolls's attention because they have no pencils. She keeps spares that dangle from long strings the students loop around their necks, badges of forgetfulness.

SOURCE: *The Washington Post,* March 15, 1994, pp. A1; A10. Copyright © 1994, *The Washington Post.* Reprinted with permission.

Each pupil is sent to the board, to work alone on the same problems that the previous class handled in teams.

The two approaches are as different as the two classes: The first has all girls, the second all boys.

It is not a fluke in scheduling. Administrators at St. Stephen's and St. Agnes, private Episcopal school in Alexandria, have deliberately separated by sex all their math and science classes, including honors courses, for grades, seven and eight. The intent is to focus on the different learning styles of girls and boys, school officials say, and to raise girls' self-confidence in two subjects where they have traditionally lagged.

Research has shown that girls prefer cooperative learning while boys tend to be more competitive and individualistic. "The girls are much more interested in how you got that answer, while with the boys, they cut to the chase: 'If you got what I got, fine, let's move on,'" said Nuckolls, who exposes her students to both learning styles.

A few public schools across the country—none so far in the Washington area—have joined the nascent movement toward single-sex math and science classes. So far, the constitutionality of the courses for public schools has not been challenged.

The approach is not without its critics, who say it demeans girls by telling them they require special handling and cannot hold their own against boys. But that's not the way they see it at St. Stephen's and St. Agnes.

Carlos Hernandorena, 14, said he is more comfortable in his all-boy classes because "there's no pressure" to perform or show off. And Courtenay Burley, 13, said she likes the time apart because girls are more patient, while guys are "'C'mon, let's go.' If you ask a question, the guys will voice the fact that they think you're stupid."

"All the research shows that sixth grade is where girls' confidence begins to erode," said Joan Holden, head of the school. Adds Nuckolls: "If we can get them to the point where they're not afraid to ask a question, not afraid to express their ideas, then they're off to a good start."

This is the third year that the coeducational school has divided math and science classes by sex. Before that, St. Stephen's and St. Agnes were separate schools and did not mix boys and girls at all in the middle and upper grades. Administrators say they will monitor girls in the single-sex classes during the next several years to see how many take higher-level math and science classes in high school.

■ ■ ■

But is segregating the sexes the answer? No, at least not in public schools, said Sara Mandelbaum, head of the womens' rights project for the American Civil Liberties Union. "The way to remedy the inequities in a coed classroom is to educate teachers, not to take the girls out."

Chris Mikles, who teaches two algebra classes for girls at Ventura High School in California, agrees that the long-term solution lies in educating teachers.

But she says that for now, giving the girls their own course is getting them "back on par for all the discrimination they've had."

And Charlotte McElroy, principal at Ventura's Anacapa Middle School, which is experimenting with single-sex math, said some of her girls "are feeling real success for the first time in their lives."

While there may be academic gains for girls in single-sex instruction, some educators worry there could be societal losses. "We have to help young men understand that women are able and competent partners in math and science, and that happens in coed classes," said Geoffrey Jones, principal at Thomas Jefferson High School for Science and Technology in Annandale.

An informal survey last year at the magnet school, which is 44 percent female, found girls overwhelmingly opposed to separate classes.

"I need the guys to push me. I get a lot of strength and fire from them," said Sara Rab, 17. She added, though, that in one of her classes "there are eight girls behind me, and I never hear their voices. It's always the guys. . . . The girls never raise their hands."

Rab and three female classmates said they consciously limit the number of questions they ask in some classes. But they felt it had more to do with their unease with the subject matter than with their male peers. "I've always dominated or been intimidated by my intelligence, not my gender," said Kerry O'Shea, 18.

Locally, St. Stephen's and St. Agnes appears to be the only coeducational school with single-sex courses. Public school officials in the Washington area say that single-sex classrooms would pose legal problems and that they are focusing their efforts instead on teacher training.

"I remember what it was like being a girl in school," said Susan Rudy of Springfield, who accompanied her 10-year-old daughter to a workshop on sexual equity held recently at a Fairfax County school. "You just sort of were in a haze of hormones, and you assumed that nothing you said or did was very smart. So you just sat quietly at the edge of the room. . . . My daughter is at an age where that starts kicking in, the low self-esteem, and I wanted to find out what we can do."

One fifth-grader who attended said she sometimes doesn't bother to raise her hand in class. "I figure what's the point, because she's going to call on the boys anyhow," she said of her teacher.

Two years ago, the staff at Thomas Jefferson High School began a gender awareness seminar for sophomore girls. Now, for the first time, a majority of senior girls are taking the most difficult calculus course, and boys far outnumber girls in advanced placement biology, once considered a class favored by girls.

While they wouldn't want to be in all-girls classes themselves, Rab and her classmates all said they knew girls who would benefit.

O'Shea described one friend "who in a lot of ways has given up. She would never in a million years want to appear more intelligent than a guy."

Math Class Separates Girls From Boys
Kate Zernike

PRESQUE ISLE, Maine—Amy Roy would rather have died than ask a question in front of the boys in math class.

Instead, she'd look up the method in the textbook. Hope somehow that she'd "get it." Ask her father. Anything to avoid that "How can you be so stupid?" look from the boys.

She didn't learn anything last year.

This year, Roy's C's have shot up to A's. If the 14-year-old has a question, she raises her hand. To her own surprise, she finds she can do all the problems. And wants to do more.

There are no boys in Amy Roy's math class anymore.

Seven years ago, alarmed by an enormous gap between girls' and boys' scores on standardized math tests, the public high school in this depressed farming community unintentionally started a national trend by becoming the first to offer an all-girls' math class.

A high school generation later, the results are stunning: the gap in scores has shrunk to 16 points from a high of 129. Enrollment in calculus and advanced math classes has tripled. Girls who used to think they were math idiots are now in college planning engineering and science careers.

"When guys used to shout out the answer, I'd say 'I'm so stupid,'" said Heather Beaulieu, who took the class last year and is now in a mixed geometry class. "Now, I say, 'No, you're wrong, and I know the right answer.'"

But the newly won confidence of girls like Beaulieu hasn't shielded same-sex classes from criticism. Some feminists say that they create a "pink ghetto" in which girls feel they need special treatment to succeed.

Federal officials say they may violate laws forbidding sex discrimination in publicly funded schools although they dropped a complaint here when Presque Isle High School agreed to change its course name from "All-Girls' Algebra I" to "Algebra I with an Emphasis on Women's Contributions in Mathematics."

Despite the concerns, the classes are spreading. Public schools in Ventura, Calif., and Manassas, Va., offer all-girl math classes. The Pacific Rim Charter School, opening in Boston next year, plans to offer them. And a New Jersey school district is testing single-sex classes in all subjects.

What sparked the national interest in the math gap was the 1992 publication of a study by the American Association of University Women. In it, the same girls who had said they were good in math in fourth grade said they weren't by the time they were in eighth grade.

Their test scores slipped with their confidence, with a 50-point gap between boys and girls on the SAT and a 37-point gap on the Math Achievement

SOURCE: *The Boston Globe,* April 2, 1996, pp. 1; 16. Reprinted courtesy of *The Boston Globe.*

Test. Ultimately, the study showed that girls are less likely to go on to careers that require math—careers that also pay high.

Presque Isle was three years ahead of that research when it began considering the classes in the spring of 1989. While educators here knew nothing of the national gap, they did see the school's results on the Maine Educational Assessment.

In eighth grade, the average math gap between girls and boys was 14 points, on a test scored from 100 to 400. By 11th grade, that gap was an average 72 points, and one year was 129 points.

When the school surveyed girls to learn why they might be freezing in math, two answers came up again and again: They didn't want to look stupid in front of the boys; but they didn't want to look too smart, either.

The school also looked at research suggesting that girls and boys learn differently. While boys see class as a competition—shouting out the answer, right or wrong—girls tend to consider all options and work together to find the right answer.

During a recent mixed class of ninth graders, teacher Lisa Charette drilled the students with brain teasers. The boys shot back answers, rapid-fire. Tianna Morrison, 15, raised her hand, then, seeing the boys' hands, dropped hers. Eventually, she did manage to get a question in—the lone one from a girl.

Over in the all-girls' algebra class, ninth grader Abby Culberson walked in, sat down, and raised her hand. "I don't know how to shade," she told teacher Donna Lisnik, pulling out a sheet of paper with a parabola on it.

As the girls worked on word problems, those who found the solution first leaned over desks to help the ones still solving.

"You can ask a girl to help you, but if you ask a guy they'd be like, 'What?'" said 14-year-old Nicole Madore. "They don't want to take the time."

Girls who took the class in past years even seem to raise the energy level around them. They stride confidently down the halls, laugh freely and speak their minds—loudly. Seeing how much they learn when they assert themselves, teachers said, the girls continue doing so once they are back in mixed classes.

"You realize that if you want to learn, you have to ask questions," said sophomore Hillary Trainer.

The number of schools following Presque Isle's lead nationwide is unknown. David Sadker, whose "Failing at Fairness" documented disparities in how girls and boys are treated in classrooms, said schools in at least a dozen states have all-girls' classes. But they hold them quietly, he said, concerned about violating Title IX, the law banning sex discrimination in public schools. That concern made schools in Portsmouth, N.H., reject a proposal for the classes.

There are also philosophical objections, even among women who have devoted their careers to promoting equity for schoolgirls.

Susan McGee Bailey, co-author of the 1992 study and director of the Wellesley College Center for Research on Women, said she fears that all-girls' classes unintentionally perpetuate the stereotype that girls can't do well in math.

"It's giving up to say, 'The only way we can make things equal is by sticking them in their own class,'" she said.

Dick DuRost, the principal at Presque Isle, acknowledged that some female teachers at the school had the same criticism.

But Lisnik, who oversees both mixed classes and the all-girls' class, said even teachers who try to treat boys and girls the same often fail. "In spite of what I do, there are times when I let the guys take over," she said.

Lisnik also cautioned that schools can't simply stick girls in separate classes. They have to change the way they teach them, with more group work to reflect girls' learning style.

To avoid violating antidiscrimination laws, schools must leave the classes open to boys though schools nationally say none have asked to take them. The girls, all ninth graders, are assigned randomly, or they can request to be included. Parents can pull students out, but none has.

The real proof, Lisnik argued, is in improved test scores—and in the girls themselves.

Andrea Kenney, who took the class four years ago, said she found herself defending it in a women's studies class at the University of Maine earlier this year.

"If I hadn't taken that class," she told her classmates, "there's no way I would have the guts to stand here and defend it."

The Flight From Science and Reason
Christina Hoff Sommers

New Jersey sponsors the "New Jersey Project." Its goal is to "transform" the curriculum in higher education to make it more multicultural and "inclusive." The project circulates a "guideline" cautioning that "much previous scholarship has offered a white, male, Eurocentric, heterosexist, and elite view of 'reality.'" Citing the words of feminist historian of science Elizabeth Fee, the guideline explains how male scientists exploit nature the way a violent man exploits a helpless woman: "Nature was female, and knowledge was created as an act of aggression—a passive nature had to be interrogated, unclothed, penetrated, and compelled by man to reveal her secrets."

The document is striking because it emanates from an official government agency. But it is the kind of attack that has been routinely leveled at science by multiculturalists, radical environmentalists, feminist theorists and others on the cultural left for the past several years. One example from academia is a 1986

SOURCE: *The Wall Street Journal,* July 10, 1995, p. A14. Reprinted with permission of *The Wall Street Journal.* Copyright © 1995 Dow Jones & Company, Inc. All rights reserved.

convocation address delivered by Donald Harward, then vice president of academic affairs at the College of Wooster in Ohio. Mr. Harward informed the students that "there is no objectivity even in science," and put them in the know by telling them that "learning and teaching have less to do with truth, reality, and objectivity than we had assumed." He has since gone on to become president of Bates College in Maine.

An Active Defense

Until quite recently, professional scientists studiously avoided reacting to these sort of "critiques." Fortunately, some are beginning to realize that "anti-science" is a serious threat that calls for an active defense. Last month, under the auspices of the New York Academy of Sciences, University of Virginia biologist Paul Gross and Rutgers mathematician Norman Levitt helped organize "The Flight from Science and Reason," a high-level conference of more than 200 scientists, physicians and humanists who met "to consider the contemporary flight from reason and its associated anti-science."

The distinguished panelists, who included Harvard economist Henry Rosovsky and Nobel Laureate Dudley Herschbach, explored "fashionable irrationalisms," and examined "the threats, or the damage already done, to public understanding. . . and considered practical possibilities for effective responses."

In one damage report Prof. Gerald Holton, physicist and historian of science at Harvard University, described how the Smithsonian Institution blindsided the American Chemical Society (ACS). It was a more telling example of self-righteous politics at the Smithsonian than even the notorious Enola Gay exhibit.

In 1989, the ACS commissioned the Smithsonian Museum of American History to design a permanent exhibit on "Science in American Life." The ACS scientists naturally expected an exhibit celebrating the triumphs of 20th century American science and did not imagine that this needed to be spelled out in the contract. But five years and $5 million later, what the scientists got was an exhibition that presented American science as a series [of] moral debacles and environmental catastrophes: Hiroshima and Nagasaki, Silent Spring, Love Canal, Three Mile Island, and the explosion of the space shuttle. The ACS was not opposed to showing undesirable effects of science and technology. But by highlighting failures and horrors, the Smithsonian exhibit took an overwhelmingly negative view of American scientific achievement.

Head curator Arthur Molella was unmoved by the ACS's complaint that the exhibit lacked balance. As he told *Science* magazine, "The purpose wasn't to do something about the triumphs of science." The curators defended their presentation as if theirs was the only principled stand: "We know it is important to preserve the integrity of the Smithsonian."

American pre-eminence in science and high technology is one major reason why the 20th century will go down in history as the American century. So it is astonishing, as well as dismaying, that our cultural custodians feel morally impelled to impugn American science and to shut their eyes to how it has dramatically improved human life. Negotiations between the scientists and the Smithsonian are still continuing, but a happy ending is far from certain.

Martin Lewis, a geographer and environmentalist at Duke University, informed the conference that "hostility to science, coupled with misgivings about reason, is the norm among a sizable and influential group of academics devoted to the study of. . . environmental philosophy." Western philosophy and science are seen as "irredeemably flawed," says Mr. Lewis, "while the rest of the world is pictured as having existed in a state of near ecological bliss." He reports a particular hostility to the founders of modern science—Galileo, Bacon, Newton, Descartes—who are seen as "eco-villains."

Resentment against "Eurocentric" thinkers reaches deep into the past. Prof. Mary Lefkowitz, a classicist from Wellesley College, told of Afrocentric scholars accusing Aristotle of stealing the ideas for which he is best known from the library of Alexandria. Putting aside the question of how white Aristotle was or how black the Egyptians were, Ms. Lefkowitz reminded the audience that the library was not even built until after Aristotle's death.

By rejecting objective scholarship, the ideologues license themselves to write history as they wish. Rene Denfeld reported on the feminist scholars (most notably UCLA archaeologist Marija Gimbutas) who postulate a Women's Golden Age claiming that Stone Age Europe was the site of a harmonious, peaceful, egalitarian society that worshipped "The Great Goddess." This civilization was purportedly destroyed between 4000 and 3500 B.C. by violent, male-god worshipping Indo-European invaders on horseback—"herstory" with no basis in fact.

The flight from reason can lead to an embrace of the occult. More than one participant noted that many students now graduate from college knowing little or nothing about math or science, thus creating a void into which "flow negative and bizarre views." Philosopher Paul Kurtz complained that there was very little scientific opposition to the "literally thousands of books. . . written about psychic healing, therapeutic touch, levitation, channeling, firewalking, poltergeists, etc., claiming wondrous powers." A surprising number of educated Americans claim to be communing with angels.

A clear consensus emerged at the conference: Scientists must now speak up against these and other popular manifestations of irrationalism. In particular, many panelists urged official scientific organizations to recognize, and play an active role in combating, the "flight from reason" in our cultural institutions.

Many aggressively antirational, antiscience projects are kept afloat by prestigious private foundations. But government is just as culpable. The Department of Education, particularly its Fund for the Improvement of Post Secondary Education (FIPSE), actively supports irrationalist education projects. FIPSE backed *Women's Ways of Knowing,* an influential book that impugns "male ways of knowing" as excessively concerned with logic and hard data, and "valorizes" something called "connected knowing," a compassionate style of cognition women are supposed to be especially good at.

The National Science Foundation has done nothing to counter the anti-science movement; nor has the American Association for the Advancement of Science. To the contrary, the NSF is sponsoring a faculty development project that runs seminars and workshops on the doctrines of prominent anti-science feminist epistemologists.

Perhaps there is a place for romantic rebellion against reason and objectivity, but that place is not the Department of Education, nor the National Science Foundation, nor university administrations (which are duty bound to promote respect for reason in the students under their care); nor is it in educational projects paid for by the taxpayers of New Jersey.

A Time Bomb

Oxford biologist Richard Dawkins was recently asked his opinion of the fashionable, politically correct "Gaia Hypothesis," according to which the Earth is a single nurturing, living organism. He replied, "The idea is not dangerous or distressing except to academic scientists who value the truth." Mr. Dawkins, like many scientists, underestimates the danger.

Harvard's Prof. Holton has noted that parascience and pseudo-science "become a time bomb waiting to explode" when incorporated into political movements. According to the "Flight From Science" conference participants, the anti-science bombs have already done damage, with great potential for further harm. A scandalously inadequate system of science education and diminished public regard for clear thinking and objective truth are just the early casualties.

Flirting or Hurting
Stefanie Weiss

A boy in Amy's sophomore English class wouldn't leave her alone. Nearly every day in class he made obscene remarks to her, poked her, and laughed when she got mad.

One day, he told Amy, "I just dissected a frog, and I'm going to give the frog's [sexual organ] to you."

"It made me feel really disgusted and discouraged," explains Amy, now a senior at the same high school in western Massachusetts. "I felt helpless because I didn't know who to turn to."

SOURCE: *NEA Today,* April 1994, pp. 4–6. Reprinted with permission of *NEA Today* and the author.

Amy confided in a girlfriend. "She said, 'Ignore him. He's a pain, but what can you do? You'll be a baby if you tell.'"

But Amy couldn't ignore him. Her grades were slipping. "I couldn't concentrate. All I could think about was what he was going to do and say next. It made me not want to go to class—and English is one of my favorite subjects."

Amy told her teacher about the harassment. The teacher moved Amy to the next row. "That made me feel like *I* was in the wrong," Amy says now.

The final resolution: school ended. Amy, normally an *A* student, pulled a *C* in English. And that was that.

At the time, Amy didn't call what was happening to her "sexual harassment." Like generations of girls before her, Amy toughed it out. But girls today don't have to. They have the law on their side.

"Sexual harassment is a part of the daily fabric of school life," says Nan Stein, director of the Sexual Harassment in Schools project at the Wellesley (Massachusetts) College Center for Research on Women. "It's so embedded and so accepted, most adults see it as inevitable."

According to two national surveys conducted last year, the vast majority of teenage girls—and boys—say they've been the targets of sexual harassment at school (see "Hostile Hallways" box on p. 63).

The most common incidents, according to kids, involve sexual comments and gestures, touching, pinching, and grabbing. Also typical are bra-snapping, skirt-flipping, and drawer-dropping.

Such behavior becomes sexual harassment, most agree, when it is unwelcome, unwanted, and interferes with a student's right to equal educational opportunity. And that's when it becomes illegal under Title IX of the Educational Amendments of 1972.

Though the law's 22 years old, attention to the issue is relatively new. "The Anita Hill/Clarence Thomas hearings raised the nation's consciousness, and we now have an administration that believes this is a problem," explains Ellen Vargyas, senior counsel at the National Women's Law Center in Washington, D.C.

Still, she adds, it was a 1992 Supreme Court ruling that brought the issue home. In *Franklin v. Gwinnett County Public Schools,* the Court ruled that students can sue recipients of federal funding (schools or school districts) for sexual harassment claims. And they can win "compensatory damages"—in a word, *money.*

"Now it's clear," Vargyas says. "Schools need to take complaints seriously. They need to have rules and accessible procedures for handling them. And they need to take corrective action."

If they don't, warns Nan Stein, "get ready for the depositions."

Many school districts and NEA members aren't waiting for the lawyers. They're acting now.

Those with successful programs seem to agree on a few key points: Kids learn best from other kids. Kids need to be involved in designing accessible policies and procedures to deal with complaints.

HOSTILE HALLWAYS

Two national surveys released in 1993 show that students find sexual harassment in school a widespread and serious problem.

A Harris poll sponsored by the American Association of University Women reached 1,600 public school students in grades 8–11. Key findings:

- Four out of 5 students—85 percent of girls and 76 percent of boys—report that they have been the target of some form of sexual harassment during their school lives.
- Two-thirds of students have been the targets of sexual comments, jokes, looks, or gestures.
- More than half of the students report having been touched, grabbed, or pinched in a sexual way at school.
- One in 10 students say they have been forced to do something sexual at school other than kissing.
- Of those reporting harassment, 66 percent say it took place in the halls; 55 percent say it took place in the classroom.

A survey by *Seventeen* magazine brought 4,300 responses from girls in grades 2–12. An analysis of 2,000 responses showed a similar percentage of girls reporting sexual harassment in school, with little difference by type of school attended or by racial or ethnic background.

As Rhode Island guidance counselor Maureen Tessier says, "We want this to be a student issue. None of our mindsets matches those of 15- or 16-year-olds." With that in mind, here's what's going on in a few places around the country.

- Acting out—on stage—is a popular way students choose to educate each other about sexual harassment. In southwestern Wisconsin, more than 6,000 students over the past three years have seen "Alice in Sexual Assault Land," a 45-minute play about everything from sexual harassment to date rape.

  With advice and assistance from NEA teacher-member Laurel Hoeth, the play—full of characters from children's literature—was written and is regularly performed by Stevens Point High School students.

  After each performance, the play's actors meet in small groups with students to discuss key messages. The most important goal, says Hoeth, "is to get students comfortable enough to talk about the issues."

■ Also on stage are students at Ponaganset High School in North Scituate, Rhode Island. With a nudge from principal Richard Oswald and some help from NEA members, students there are putting on skits for the rest of the school.

In one, explains senior Jaime LaPorte, "a boy treats four girls at their lockers in the same way, but they all react differently." The point: sexual harassment is in the eye of the beholder.

The students are also involved in creating a more accessible policy for dealing with sexual harassment complaints. Their proposed policy encourages targets to go to harassers—with or without a student advocate or school employee—and ask that the offensive behavior be stopped. Students follow-up with a written note, which they keep a copy of.

■ At Framingham High School in Massachusetts, consumer and family studies teacher Ellen Makynen is one of 46 teachers to pilot test *Flirting or Hurting?*—a soon-to-be-released NEA Human and Civil Rights curriculum on sexual harassment for students in grades 6–12.

Makynen, who teaches seniors, was surprised at students' interest in the material. "They were very serious about it. They listened to each other and were quite genuine in their responses."

For most students, Makynen explains, there were revelations. "It's quite a moment for kids when they realize that sexual harassment is against the law, and that it can stop if they want it to."

The curriculum has been so popular with students—and parents— that Makynen says school staff will try to offer the unit to others at the high school and to middle school students as well.

The NEA curriculum will be available nationally soon. . . .

■ Just outside the Twin Cities in Minnesota, middle school health education teacher Rosemary Fink is in her second year of teaching a brief unit on sexual harassment to eighth graders.

"It's been very well received," Fink says. "The girls say, 'Thanks for telling us we can say no.' And the boys say, 'I'm glad we were told what's unacceptable. We never knew it wasn't right.'"

Teaching the curriculum brought back memories, Fink says. "We're talking about the same behaviors I remember as a kid. There was a certain hall girls just didn't walk down. But I grew up when you just took it or ignored it."

Times have changed—and so has Fink. "A few years ago, when I saw kids standing in the hall eyeing a girl walking by, I was just as uncomfortable as the girl they were eyeing, but I didn't do anything. Now, I'll step in.

"As teachers," Fink notes, "We have to retrain ourselves, too."

Student-to-Student Sexual Harassment
Perry A. Zirkel

In response to a nationwide survey sponsored by the American Association of University Women, 85% of girls and 76% of boys reported having experienced sexual harassment while attending public school. Although approximately 20% of these students reported victimization by a teacher or other school employee, almost 80% pointed to other students as the harassers.

Filing a complaint with the Office for Civil Rights (OCR) is one avenue of relief and carries with it the threat to the alleged offender of losing federal funds, but the remedy is usually limited to a directive to put a proper policy and procedures in place. State law proceedings offer the possibility of more potent relief, such as teacher termination or even monetary damages, but the instances of such results have been rare. A more appealing alternative is to turn to the relatively uniform and potentially broad avenue of federal legislation and the Constitution. Two recent trial court decisions[1] illustrate the odds of obtaining judicial relief in the form of monetary damages as a result of taking this federal route.

The Petaluma Case

Jane Doe was a junior high student in the Petaluma City School District in Sonoma County, California. Throughout seventh and eighth grades she was allegedly sexually harassed by other students.

In the fall of 1990, when she was in the seventh grade, two boys said to her, "I hear you have a hot dog in your pants." A week or so later another student told her that a rumor was spreading around the school about her having a hot dog in her pants. Within a few days she reported the specifics to the guidance counselor, told him she was upset, and asked him to stop the harassment. He did nothing. When students continued to make such comments, she went to him approximately every other week during the rest of the semester, but he said that all he could do would be to warn them. He did not tell her that the vice principal was the school's Title IX coordinator and would be the appropriate person to handle the situation, nor did he apprise her of the Title IX grievance procedure.

Toward the end of the semester, Jane's father and mother spoke to the counselor about the comments and rumors. He said that he was taking care of the problem and that, knowing how students of that age tended to go through rapid phases, he expected the comments to cease in a short time. When her father told him that one or more girls had threatened to fight with Jane because

Source: *Phi Delta Kappan*, April 1995, pp. 648–650. Reprinted with permission of *Phi Delta Kappan* and the author.

she had reported their harassment, the counselor assured him that he had taken care of the matter. Nevertheless, the harassment continued.

In the early months of 1991, two other students made a comment to Jane in English class about her having a hot dog in her pants. She reported the matter to the counselor, who called the boys into his office and warned them. When Jane's father followed up with the counselor, he responded that he had warned them but that, essentially, "boys will be boys."

When Jane also complained to the counselor about female students making hot dog comments, he advised her that girls could not sexually harass other girls. Further, he told her that, since there were so many students calling her "hot dog," warning all of them would be futile. He did bring in groups of girls and told Jane to work it out with them. Although they promised to stop the harassment, it did not cease.

During the rest of the spring semester, Jane complained to the counselor about five times a month. She reported being called a "hot-dog bitch," "slut," and "hoe" by girls trying to get her into a fight. The counselor said that he could not stop them because of their free speech rights. When she reported that boys were similarly engaged in such harassment, he continued to do nothing more than assure her mother that he was keeping an eye out for Jane.

The comments and threats continued both on and off the school grounds during the summer. Within the first few weeks of eighth grade they reached a daily level. Jane reported the incidents to the counselor on a weekly basis, per his instructions. She got a reputation as a tattletale. Going to school became increasingly difficult for Jane. The counselor's response to repeated calls from her mother and father was that sooner or later the students would mature and cease. He never mentioned the Title IX coordinator or the grievance procedure.

On 21 January 1992, a student slapped Jane and was suspended for two days. A month later, a classmate named Dan stood up in English class and said, "This question is for Jane. Did you have sex with a hot dog?" The entire class laughed. The teacher made Dan apologize, but Jane ran out in tears. Vice principal Noll, who was the Title IX coordinator, told Jane that this incident was the first she had heard of Jane's sexual harassment. On Jane's mother's insistence, Mrs. Noll suspended Dan for two days. Meanwhile, students had written so much graffiti about Jane in the bathroom that she stopped using it.

In late February, Jane's father met with the principal, the vice principal, and the counselor to insist that something be done. The principal advised him that Mrs. Noll was the school's Title IX coordinator. Mrs. Noll stated that she had not been informed of the ongoing harassment. When Jane's father asked the counselor why he had not informed Mrs. Noll, he responded that he "didn't feel it was important."

Soon thereafter, two boys taunted Jane with hot dog comments, and Mrs. Noll suspended them for two days. A few days later, a girl assaulted Jane, but a school employee intervened and took Jane to Mrs. Noll. On being called, Jane's mother came to school and insisted on a transfer.

When she was transferred to another junior high, however, Jane continued to be the target of harassment. As a result, her parents felt they had no choice but to move her to a private school. Jane also underwent medical and psychological treatment.

Her parents filed suit in federal court against the school district for monetary damages, including Jane's private-school tuition and the costs of medical and psychological treatment. The primary basis of their suit was Title IX of the Education Amendments of 1972, which prohibits sexual discrimination by school districts and other entities that receive federal funds. For this purpose, they relied to a significant extent on *Franklin v. Gwinnett County Public Schools*, an employee/student sexual harassment case in which the U.S. Supreme Court ruled that money damages are available in Title IX suits.[2] As an additional basis, they claimed that the school district, principal, and counselor had violated Jane's "liberty" or substantive due process rights under the 14th Amendment.

The Monroe Case

LaShonda D. was a fifth-grade student in the Monroe County School District in Georgia. Allegedly beginning in early 1993, LaShonda's classmate G. F. sexually harassed her. He repeatedly made vulgar comments to her, such as "I want to get in bed with you" and "I want to feel your boobs," and also tried to touch her breasts and crotch. After the first two incidents, LaShonda told her classroom teacher about the problem. Her mother followed up with a telephone call, in which the teacher assured her that she had notified the principal.

On February 3, while in gym class, G. F. placed a doorstop in his pants and behaved in a sexually suggestive manner toward LaShonda. She reported this third incident to her gym teacher.

On February 10 and March 1, G. F. again engaged in harassing behavior, which LaShonda reported to her teachers. It was not until late March, however, after continued complaints, that her classroom teacher allowed LaShonda to change her assigned seat, which was next to G. F. Moreover, when she and other girls who had been harassed by G. F. asked the teacher if they could go as a group to the principal's office, she did not allow them to do so.

In early April, G. F. rubbed his body against LaShonda in a suggestive manner. Once again she informed her teacher.

In mid-May, LaShonda complained to her mother that she did not know how much longer she could tolerate G. F.'s behavior. When Mrs. D. contacted the principal, he said he would "threaten the boy a little bit harder." He also asked her why LaShonda "was the only one complaining." Mrs. D. then called the superintendent to complain about both G. F. and the principal.

Mrs. D. filed suit in federal court against the school district for monetary damages, claiming that the board's failure to institute a policy concerning student-to-student sexual harassment caused LaShonda's mental health to deteriorate and her academic grades to decline. She based her claim not only on Title IX but also on substantive due process rights under the 14th Amendment.

The Judicial Results

In the Petaluma case, the federal district court dismissed Jane Doe's Title IX damages claim, with permission to amend and refile the complaint, because she had failed to allege that the school district had engaged in intentional discrimination.[3] Intentional discrimination in cases of student-to-student sexual harassment, the court clarified, means more than negligence, which consists of the district's knowing or having reason to know of the hostile environment and failing to take reasonable steps to end it. The court even more strongly disposed of Jane's constitutional claim, dismissing it, without permission to amend, in favor of the school district and the principal, thus allowing the claim to proceed only against the school counselor. The school district was immune under the 11th Amendment, and the principal, unlike the counselor, lacked knowledge of the alleged harassment.

In the Monroe case, the court disposed of the constitutional claim even more conclusively.[4] Citing a 1989 Supreme Court decision[5] and its lower court progeny, the federal district court reasoned that public school authorities have no constitutional duty to protect students from private persons, such as other students, as opposed to school employees. With regard to the Title IX claim, the court recognized and rejected the Petaluma ruling. Instead, the court dismissed the Title IX claim in relation to the principal and the superintendent, reasoning that liability under the statute extends only to federally funded institutions, not to their individual employees. Similarly, the court dismissed the Title IX claim in relation to the school district; LaShonda had not alleged that the board or its employees had any role in causing or conducting the harassment.

The proceedings, however, have not ended in either case. The Petaluma decision is on appeal to the Ninth Circuit with regard to the guidance counselor's possible liability, and, because Doe's attorney is amending her complaint to allege intentional discrimination, the trial is also pending against the school district. LaShonda's mother has similarly appealed the Monroe decision to the 11th Circuit.

Although student-to-student sexual harassment is a serious problem, the legal remedies are not commensurately potent, at least to date. Forceful orders are obtainable. For example, in Petaluma, the OCR had previously found a Title IX violation and ordered appropriate actions based on the negligence standard (know or had reason to know). State law avenues, such as teacher termination proceedings and tort suits, vary from one jurisdiction to another but have generally resulted in limited success. Finally, the federal highways of Title IX and the Constitution have thus far proved to be a much more narrow, winding, and uphill route for those seeking monetary damages for student-to-student harassment than for those seeking monetary damages for employee-to-student sexual harassment.[6]

Perhaps the solution ultimately lies in better education of district employees and students.[7] In the meantime, employee attitudes that "boys will be boys," that such behavior is protected free speech unless accompanied by an assault, and that girls cannot commit sexual harassment are, as these two cases amply illustrate, not coincidentally connected to a hostile and harmful atmosphere among students.

NOTES

1. Because each court decision arose in relation to a motion for dismissal, which is prior to the formal fact-finding stage of the trial, the allegations are treated here as true, for the limited purpose of understanding the relevant law.
2. 112 S. Ct. 1028 (1992). See, for example, Perry A. Zirkel, "Damages for Sexual Harassment," *Phi Delta Kappan,* June 1992, pp. 812-13.
3. *Doe v. Petaluma City Sch. Dist.,* 830 F. Supp. 1560 (N.D. Cal. 1993). I obtained supplementary information via telephone interviews on 23 January 1995 with Rose Fua and Larry Frierson, attorneys for the student plaintiff and the school defendants respectively.
4. *Aurelia D. v. Monroe County Bd. of Educ.,* 862 F. Supp. 363 (M.D. Ga. 1994).
5. *DeShaney v. Winnebago County Dep't of Social Serv.,* 489 U.S. 189 (1989). See, for example, Perry A. Zirkel, "Poor Joshua," *Phi Delta Kappan,* June 1989, pp. 828-29.
6. For a more detailed analysis see, for example, Gail Sorenson, "Peer Sexual Harassment: Remedies and Guidelines Under Federal Law," *West's Education Law Reporter,* September 1994, pp. 1-18. For a more recent court decision, which focused on an athletic hazing incident and reflected a similarly restrictive judicial attitude, see *Seamons v. Snow,* 864 F. Supp. 1111 (Utah 1994).
7. See, for example, Robert Shoop and Debra Edwards, *How to Stop Sexual Harassment in Our Schools: A Handbook and Curriculum Guide* (Needham Heights, Mass.: Allyn & Bacon, 1994); and Robert Shoop and Jack Hayhow, *Sexual Harassment in Our Schools: What Parents and Teachers Need to Know to Spot It and Stop It* (Needham Heights, Mass.: Allyn & Bacon, 1994).

The War on Boys
Fiona Houston

Of all the political battlefields where large social disputes might be fought, none has the ecological fragility of the American schoolyard. For decades—and especially since the 1950s—religious fundamentalists have sought to create a political

---

SOURCE: Reprinted with permission of the author.

environment in the public schools congenial to its sectarian goals. Parents, quite rightly, have tried to protect their children from proselytizing and from being forced to conform to a biased set of social values.

But then the forces of "progressive" activism began seeking what the religious right had wanted so badly for so long—namely the chance to use boys and girls as political pawns in a program of morally inspired social engineering. The difference between fundamentalist Christians and the feminist-educational activists, however, is that the Christian right has only God on its side, while the politically correct have ABC, CNN, *The New York Times, The Washington Post,* the American Association of University Women, and the United States Congress.

It isn't even close.

The Senate has just passed an important package of education legislation that will change forever the political landscape of America's schools. Collectively, this legislation is called the Women's Equity in Education Act (WEEA), and it gives the force of law to such abstract notions as "gender sensitivity" and "self-esteem." Under the new law, millions of dollars will be spent in elementary and secondary schools to promote programs that seem to be concerned with improving girls' school experiences, but which carry an unmistakable message that says boys are predators and girls are victims. Backers claim the legislation is needed to stem the erosion of self-esteem in adolescent girls, a "crisis" revealed in a series of reports sponsored by the American Association of University Women (AAUW).

As federal legislation goes, the WEEA package is not a huge budgetary item. What it does do, however, is open a Pandora's box of politically motivated expansions, facilitations, enforcements and entitlements, the federally funded fertilizers required to make small government programs grow into big ones. It also does little to help solve the crushing problems overtaking America's boys [see "Blackboard Bungle," p. 73].

Because of its low profile, the bill has quickly sailed through Congress. No hard questions have been put to its sponsors; no skeptical analysis of the bill has appeared in the national press. There has been no grassroots activism calling into question the central assumptions underlying the legislation. Only one book, Clark University professor Christina Hoff Sommers' *Who Stole Feminism?,* has appeared that challenges the bill's backers, and Sommers has been pilloried for her trouble. When parents inquire, they're told it's a matter of simple justice for the girls of America. "The [WEEA] legislation," Congresswoman Patricia Schroeder reassured the nation, "will help make schools an environment where girls are nurtured and respected, where they can learn that their lives are valuable. . . ."

WEEA also gives "gender feminists" influence over individual students. How? Like this:

- Under WEEA, a growing army of gender-equity trainers will put boys through retraining to learn how to treat girls better. . . , while teachers will be instructed in "gender sensitive teaching techniques" to make sure they teach in accordance with "effective equity training models."

- The Department of Education will spend $5 million to appoint a federal Special Assistant of Gender Equity. In addition to monitoring kids' behavior patterns, this office will develop model curricula, textbooks and software "free of gender stereotyping and bias."
- A rewording of the Elementary and Secondary Education Act will allow millions of dollars in federal funds to be used for gender-equity training, and it will expand the definition of "effective schools" to include an "environment free from sexual harassment and abuse." Public schools failing to take these new instructions into consideration are unlikely to receive federal funding provided under the Elementary and Secondary Education Act.

Now, a reasonable parent might look at the "crisis" in teenage girls' self-esteem and agree that, since the beginning of time, girls' self-image has indeed changed in adolescence. And a careful reporter might have read the AAUW report carefully enough to see that the group scoring highest in self-esteem is black boys, thus casting some doubt on the relationship between self-esteem and educational success. And an unbiased observer might look at the outcome of public schooling, see the unprecedented levels of success reached by young women, see that more women than ever—and far more women than men—are attending college, and conclude the public educational system appears to be treating the country's schoolgirls pretty well already. So why is Congress spending millions of dollars to fix something that, at least for girls, not only isn't broken, but seems to be working just fine?

The politicizing of public education is a textbook example of how special-interest groups can manipulate good will in order to achieve a very specific partisan goal. All it took was the creation and promotion of a plausible story, one easy to pass off as fact. The story was the Myth of the Suffering Schoolgirl.

In 1990, the venerable AAUW, under the influence of a new generation of leaders such as Anne Bryant, Sharon Schuster and Alice McKee, moved out of the mainstream of academic tradition and into the forefront of radical-academic feminism and began pursuing an aggressively strident agenda. In 1992 McKee outlined her vision for the AAUW's Educational Foundation, which she saw as "exploring new frontiers of research on critical issues" in order to help "shape society's agenda for women and girls." One of the AAUW's new gurus, Peggy McIntosh, of the Wellesley Center for Research on Women, for example, described boys as "winner-killers" and worried about the dangers of having both nuclear weapons and "white males" together on the same planet at the same time.

One of the first orders of business for the new AAUW was to hire Greenberg-Lake, a Washington-area polling firm, to compile data that could be used to show irrefutable evidence of pervasive gender bias in our nation's schools. In the report-generating business, this is called "advocacy research," in which the remarkably flexible tools of social science—surveys, polls and the like—are used to create "scientific evidence" to support an already established view. In 1991, the AAUW released a report, "Shortchanging Girls, Shortchanging America," in which the claims of tumbling esteem among adolescent schoolgirls were first advanced. "Girls are being left out and left behind in school," AAUW president Sharon Schuster said at the time. "America cannot compete with only half its team on the field."

The report became the first in a coordinated series of related studies, each based on the study that preceded it and each based on findings that were subsequently shown to be misleading. All were nevertheless reported uncritically by the press. This successful media campaign was accompanied by intensive lobbying of supportive members of Congress, already under assault by feminist-activists over the Clarence Thomas–Anita Hill hearings and Senator Bob Packwood's gropings. "They are all terrified," summed up one top-level congressional researcher.

As the Myth of the Suffering Schoolgirl blossomed in the hot spotlight of media attention—"Little girls lose their self-esteem," *The New York Times* grimly reported—a number of unsupported fictions came to be accepted, as fact:

- Increasingly, girls are victims of harassment and abuse. This finding was the centerpiece of the AAUW's 1993 *Hostile Hallways* report. Feminist researchers had discovered that "85 percent of all girls surveyed report being sexually harassed." How were these numbers created? The AAUW was able to verify an "epidemic" of harassment by simply lumping together a huge range of teenage behavior—everything from "sexual looks" to "sexual assault," for example—and defining it all as "sexual harassment." Perhaps that's why researchers were also able to claim that "76 percent of boys" were harassment victims, too.
- An insensitive educational establishment unconsciously caters to boys at the expense of girls.
- Girls are discouraged from aspiring to professional and managerial careers and instead are being "marginalized" by ongoing educational unfairness.
- Girls are victims of bad teaching habits and unfair testing procedures.

Thus, in a relatively short time, the Myth of the Suffering Schoolgirl has become part of the nation's pop-political consciousness. With the passage of the AAUW's gender-equity legislation, the feminist myth that girls are victims of public education, that teachers are habitually sexist and that boys are villains will be institutionalized, perhaps forever. As a result, overstretched public schools will be required to spend precious education dollars dealing with "gender-equity issues" instead of teaching boys and girls how to read, write, add and subtract.

Blackboard Bungle
Diane Ravitch

Every national magazine has repeated the same terrible story: Teachers consistently show favoritism to boys; girls are suffering a crisis of self-esteem; the hopes and dreams of girls are regularly shattered by the discriminatory treatment they receive from their teachers in the public schools.

The trouble is, none of it is true. In fact, the real story—arguably the biggest, most underreported education story of our time—has been the successful conquest of American education by girls and women. Consider:

- *Collegiate success.* Fewer boys than girls are going to college. This year, 55 percent of all collegiate undergraduates are women. Women are 59 percent of all master's degree candidates and now constitute the majority of all graduate and professional students in American higher education.
- *Higher hopes.* Surveys conducted by the U.S. Department of Education—and by independent researchers—agree that women and girls have higher aspirations than their male counterparts. Eighth-grade girls are *twice as likely* as boys to aspire to a professional, business or managerial career. Young women who are high-school seniors and college freshmen also have higher aspirations for education and professions than their male peers.
- *Stronger scores.* In elementary and high schools, girls have marginally lower scores than boys on national tests in math and science. But they have substantially higher scores than boys in reading and writing.
- *Boys lose.* Eighth-grade boys are 50 percent more likely to be held back a grade than girls, and in high school, two-thirds of special-education students are boys. In 1990, among 15- to 24-year-olds, men were four times more likely to be victims of a homicide than women, and six times more likely to kill themselves.

It's difficult to slow a journalistic phenomenon when it is in full cry. But sooner or later, the facts will prevail over the myth. One hopes.

SOURCE: Reprinted with permission of the author.

"Alarming Facts" About Boys, Girls
Jeff Jacoby

Look out, patriarchy, here comes Sally Kerans.

The state representative from Danvers, unnerved by the widespread op-pression of girls in society, is going after the male hegemony that conspires to keep females down. She kicked off her crusade last week with legislation to cre-ate a government commission on the status of girls, testifying before a legisla-tive committee on the "critical situation" and the "alarming facts" that make such a commission essential.

"There is a gap in the treatment of girls and boys in Massachusetts today," Kerans told the committee. There is "unequal treatment of girls by schools and all sectors of society."

Apparently the poor dears are getting clobbered in the gender war. They "receive significantly less attention from classroom teachers," says Kerans. They are "less likely. . . to pursue the study of math and science." They face an "increase in the number of sexual harassment incidents by boys." They suffer a "documented loss of self-esteem. . . that is twice that of boys."

So brutally are girls repressed in our phallo-centric commonwealth that many of them simply give up the fight. "The most dramatic fact" of all, Kerans intoned last week, is that "girls have twice the suicide and school dropout rates as boys."

That *is* dramatic. Fortunately for the girls of America, it is also wrong. Wildly wrong. Virtually every syllable of Kerans' testimony, it turns out, is de-monstrably false. Casey Stengel used to say, "You could look it up." Sally Kerans clearly didn't.

Start with dropout rates. It is boys, not girls, who drop out more frequently. Between 1988 and 1990, according to the government's annual compilation of education statistics, 7.2 percent of boys—but just 6.5 percent of girls—dropped out of school before reaching 10th grade.

Not only are girls more likely to graduate, they tend to start school earlier and to fall behind less often. (In 1992, 14 percent of male students had been held back one or more grades. Females: 9 percent.) Girls are far less likely to be in special education or to need remedial math when they get to college. And they *do* get to college—not only in greater numbers than boys (55 percent of college students are female, and most academic degrees go to women), but more quickly (64 percent of girls matriculate right after high school vs. 59 per-cent of boys).

Girls get less attention from their teachers? That's a modern myth peddled by the Wellesley College Center for Research on Women, a hot-house of femi-

---

SOURCE: *The Boston Globe,* February 6, 1996, p. 15. Reprinted courtesy of *The Boston Globe.*

nist zealotry. In its 1992 report "How Schools Shortchange Girls," the center declared that "boys in elementary and middle school called out answers eight times more often than girls. When boys called out, teachers listened. But when girls called out, they were told to 'raise your hand.'"

But the Wellesley report was a fraud. In her acclaimed 1994 book *Who Stole Feminism?* Christina Hoff Sommers proved it was based on bogus research, imaginary data, or falsified studies. The business about boys getting called on more often in class, for instance, was a bald distortion. Consider what the original source actually said:

> Boys, particularly low-achieving boys, receive eight to 19 times as many reprimands as do their female classmates. . . . When both girls and boys are misbehaving equally, boys will receive more frequent discipline.

Equally phony is the alarum about massive sexual harassment of schoolgirls. This, too, stems from a report by the Wellesley Center—one based on a tear-out questionnaire published in *Seventeen*, a girl's magazine. *Seventeen* has 1.9 million subscribers, of whom 4,200—0.2 percent—sent in the questionnaire. On the strength of that response, the Wellesley Center warned that for "thousands of adolescent girls, school may be teaching more about oppression than freedom." As Sommers notes, this was exactly the polling methodology *Literary Digest* used in 1936 to forecast Alf Landon's landslide victory over FDR.

Not one of Kerans' "facts" stands up to scrutiny.

Girls avoid math and science? In fact, according to the National Center for Education Statistics, more girls than boys study geometry, algebra II, biology and chemistry.

The self-esteem gap? Nonexistent, according to most scholars of adolescent psychology. The only evidence for it is a discredited study by an advocacy group, the American Association of University Women. So spurious are its findings that no other experts have replicated them.

Suicide? The disparity between boys and girls in this tragic category is indeed, as Kerans says, "dramatic." But it isn't girls who are dying by their own hands. In 1992, according to the Centers for Disease Control, 5,007 young people killed themselves. More than 85 percent—4,276—were boys.

More boys dropping out, more boys flunking, more boys in special ed, more boys needing remedial math, more boys not entering college, more boys facing discipline, more boys dying. A legislator concerned more with children than with feminist ax-grinding would be investigating the question of why *boys* are in such trouble. Sally Kerans—career rating from the National Organization for Women: 100 percent—is not such a legislator.

Chapter 3

RELIGION

INTRODUCTION

It's like something that might be staged as a high school debate—an assigned topic to be argued in a civics class. But the ideological war being waged in the backrooms—and often the "frontrooms"—of many school boards and legislatures across America is real. At stake ultimately is the role, the place, and the function of religion in establishing policies for the public schools. The battles concerning religion, however, are usually not undertaken on a grand scale, but rather are focused on more limited issues.

Sex education is one. Many parents feel that current sex education curricula are a calculated attempt to undermine their children's religious beliefs and their rights as parents. They believe the school should complement—not *subvert*—the values they teach at home. Yet when they attempt to get school administrators or school boards to accommodate them, they claim they are often met with silence. Or worse, they maintain, they are made to feel that there is something wrong with *them* for being religious. The message they hear is that governmental authorities, and not they, know what is best for their children.

Today, many of these parents are fighting back. More and more are running for election to their local school boards, and in some instances are seeking higher office. If those political bodies will not be responsive to them, they will take them over and control the school and its curriculum.

With sex education, these parents are fighting a rearguard action; with creationism, they are on the attack. In various ways, attempts are being made to institute creationism as a *part* of the science curriculum. Essentially, their argument is that since the Darwinian theory of evolution has not yet been proven with certainty, it is just one more *theory* among others concerning the creation of human beings. Consequently, there must be room for creationism in the curriculum as something to be taught alongside evolution.

What role, if any, should people's religious beliefs play in the formation of school policy? Is it right for the public schools to teach children anything that directly contradicts their religious beliefs?

Lamontagne Backs Teaching Creation Theory
Clare Kittredge

MERRIMACK—The chairman of the state Board of Education said last week that he endorses teaching the Biblical theory of creation alongside evolution in public school science class. His remarks come as the Merrimack School Board prepares to reject the idea tomorrow—at least temporarily.

"To the extent that there is legitimate scientific inquiry into the theory of creationism, school districts should be open to presenting both in science class," said Ovide Lamontagne, whose board sets education policy for the state.

Lamontagne said he does not "literally" believe that the world was created in six days with God resting on the seventh. "For me, that's a religious question. . . . As I understand it, reputable scientists are looking into the origins of man along the theme of spontaneous creation by a supreme being, so I think it's fair game to present it in science class."

A proposal by Merrimack pastor Paul Norwalt to teach creationism along with evolution in Merrimack public school science classes seems headed for defeat tomorrow after a storm of controversy in this high tech, southern New Hampshire border town of 22,000. But some say the proposal could be back as soon as this summer, for a social studies or philosophy class.

Creationism—or creation science, as some call it—is based on the premise that all human beings can trace their ancestry to Adam and Eve in the Garden of Eden.

Advocates say they have new scientific evidence to prove them right, but opponents say creationists are pushing bad science and bad law.

So explosive is the issue here that Chris Ager, chairman of the Merrimack School Board, predicts his board will take no action on a creationism proposal that is on the board's agenda tomorrow.

"I will not vote to include creationism in our science curriculum," Ager said. The chairman, who blames disgruntled liberals and the media for whipping up hysteria on the issue, said creationism is taught in several other New Hampshire public school districts. He would not say where. "It's just not a priority for us to tackle at this time. Do I believe in creation? That's another question."

Despite Ager's assurances, school board member Brenda Grady said that the creationism issue is not really dead in Merrimack.

"I have no doubt it will resurface. The media has been made to think this issue is going to die, but I think that's a hoax," said Grady, a Nashua high school biology and zoology teacher. "It's sad. We are in 1995. We will soon be in a new

---

SOURCE: *The Boston Globe*, February 5, 1995, Sec. NH; p. 1. Reprinted with permission of the author.

century. This should be a renaissance of technology and scientific thought. It's the Dark Ages instead."

As for this week's highly publicized visit by Duane Gish, co-founder of the California Institute for Creation Research and a leading guru on creationism, to the Merrimack High School cafeteria, Ager said "I think it's great. We're allowing the presenting of ideas. That's what America is all about."

But a Washington civil rights group, People for the American Way, says Gish's institute is a "fundamentalist Christian graduate school" that "distorts the language of science in order to advance religious doctrine into public school classrooms."

Seventy years ago, a young science teacher in a small southern Bible Belt town was arrested for teaching Darwin's theory of evolution in science class. The "Scopes Monkey Trial" pitted new science against established faith and a Tennessee law outlawing the teaching of evolution. Teacher John Scopes' victory on appeal was considered a milestone for education.

Seven decades later, debate over creationism in Merrimack has provoked similar passions. But this time, advocates of creationism complain that "evolution is in the driver's seat."

As Norwalt sees it, creationism is based on the "supernatural order of all things." Norwalt, the leading proponent of creationism in Merrimack, said this means "intelligence is God-given like Rush Limbaugh says, intelligence is on loan from God."

Creationism also involves "a net basic decrease in complexity over time," meaning that "everything is winding down, the sun is getting smaller, the Earth is turning slower, that means it's all going to come to an end," said Norwalt, pastor of the Merrimack Baptist Temple.

Another principle of creationism is that Earth history is dominated by catastrophic events, Norwalt said. The recent earthquake in Kobe, Japan, was "the convulsions of the Earth under judgement by God," he said. "What's left from the catastrophe of The Flood has produced these conditions around the world."

Creationism is the second bombshell involving religion and the public schools to hit this affluent community since its liberal school board was swept out of office last May and replaced by conservatives.

Soon after the election, the new board was engulfed in controversy when one of its new members was accused of being a "stealth candidate" for the religious right. Shelly Uscinski denied the charge, but later went on an all-expenses-paid trip to speak to the Christian Coalition's annual meeting in Washington. Uscinski then proposed a "moment of silence" in Merrimack public schools. Opponents attacked it as school prayer in disguise. Approved last fall, the silent moment has since spread to several other New Hampshire communities.

Norwalt said he first approached School Board chairman Ager last fall with the idea of inserting creationism into the science curriculum.

On Jan. 17, he asked the School Board to amend the science curriculum to remove items dealing with evolution, replace existing textbooks with books not teaching evolution as fact, and have public school teachers teach both creationism and evolution in science classes.

Tomorrow, Norwalt will ask the School Board to refer his proposal to a committee for study.

"The creation model says the world and all its creatures were formed by a creator with a plan, but the evolutionary model says everything began in chaos," Norwalt said. "The ramifications of the evolutionary model leave us with a society that is confused. The creation model leaves us under an all-knowing God who declares an absolute law and brings order to society," Norwalt said.

All this is controversial fare for locals who want religion kept out of public schools.

"It's ludicrous to think that creationism is appropriate for the science curriculum," said Rosemarie Rung, whose children attend Merrimack schools. "They cut money for computers and yet they're considering creationism."

Grady said teaching creationism in public school science class is illegal. "It's impossible to strip down the creationism arguments from its Biblical reference. Once you take away the Bible there is no creationism issue," Grady said.

So divisive is the issue that several hundred townspeople packed a recent School Board meeting amid a mob of national media.

"Complete nausea and total disgust is too weak a phrase to describe my displeasure," Merrimack High graduate and substitute teacher Tim Rourke said at the meeting. The Union Leader of Manchester has kept up a steady drumbeat of editorials on creationism, arguing that "It's Science vs. Science," not simply religion vs. science.

People for the American Way has threatened a lawsuit if the School Board goes ahead with creationism in science class.

And the Roman Catholic Diocese of Manchester got involved, pointing out in a recent newsletter that Catholic schools are unfettered by debate over the role of religion in public schools and are free to teach both religion and evolution.

One disgruntled School Board member recently remarked that Merrimack is starting to look more like a Bible Belt town than a bustling Golden Triangle commuter town.

"This used to be a progressive town 50 miles north of Boston," Chuck Mower said. "Now we're just a Gooberville in Arkansas."

The "C" Word Is Back: Creationism
Carol Chmelynski

Evolution has long been a key topic in public school science classes. But can teachers also discuss the biblical theory of creation as an alternative to evolution? Can they discuss "evidence against evolution"? These are questions school

SOURCE: *Education Digest,* November 1994, pp. 14–17. Reprinted with permission from *The Education Digest,* Ann Arbor, Michigan.

boards soon might face as proponents of "creation science" renew efforts to get their viewpoint into the public school curriculum.

Most states require public schools to teach evolution, and schools cannot be banned from teaching it, says Eugenie C. Scott, executive director of the National Center for Science Education, Inc. (NCSE), based in Berkeley, California. She maintains that "teaching biology without evolution is like teaching chemistry without the periodic table of elements."

But, says Scott, "from kindergarten through high school, public school teachers face pressure to teach creation science or 'evidence against evolution,' or at least downplay evolution. Our caseload at NCSE has been steadily increasing over the last six years."

The key ruling on whether creationism has a place in U.S. public schools was issued by the U.S. Supreme Court in 1987 when it ruled that creationism is a religious idea and its teaching violates the First Amendment clause that prohibits state establishment of religion.

Decades ago, some states passed laws barring evolution from the curriculum because it conflicted with the biblical account of creation. In the Scopes "Monkey Trial" in 1927, the Tennessee Supreme Court upheld such a law, prohibiting the teaching of any theory that denies the Genesis version of creation or suggests "that man has descended from a lower order of animals."

In 1968, however, the U.S. Supreme Court struck down an anti-evolution statute in Arkansas under the establishment of religion clause. In *Epperson v. Arkansas,* the court reasoned that evolution is science, not a secular religion, and a state cannot restrict student access to such information simply to satisfy religious preferences.

Proponents of creationism now challenge evolution as advancing a secular faith, and their more recent efforts have focused on securing laws that require equal emphasis on the biblical account of creation whenever evolution is taught in the public schools. By the late 1970s, "equal time" laws were under consideration in at least 26 state legislatures. Arkansas and Louisiana passed such laws, which were legally challenged and declared unconstitutional.

Religious Idea

In 1987, the Louisiana case reached the Supreme Court, which proclaimed in *Edwards v. Aguillard* that creationism is inherently a religious idea. The teaching of creationism thus represents a state advocacy of religion, violating the establishment clause of the First Amendment to the Constitution, the court ruled.

It reasoned that the "equal time" law actually inhibited teachers' discretion to incorporate scientific theories about the origin of humanity into the curriculum. However, it also states: "[T]eaching a variety of scientific theories about the origin of humankind to schoolchildren might be validly done with the clear secular intent of enhancing the effectiveness of science instruction."

Today, Bob Walsh, chairman of the International Conference on Creationism, says, "The problem with the whole origin debate is that neither creationism nor evolution satisfies all the phenomena of science—that it be observable, repeatable, testable, and falsifiable. No one alive has observed [evolution]. No one can test it, and we certainly can't repeat it. If creationism is not allowed to be taught in science class, neither should evolution. Evolution is just as much religious as creationism."

John Peloza, a California biology teacher who believes in creationism, sued the Capistrano (California) Unified School District in 1991 for forcing him to teach evolution, which he calls "a secular religious view of the world's creation."

The U.S. 9th Circuit Court of Appeals disagreed, ruling that evolution was not a religious belief, and that Peloza must teach evolution to his students even though it goes against his religious beliefs.

The court also said school officials could direct Peloza to stop teaching students about Christianity during the school day, saying that Peloza's right to speak freely about his beliefs was less important than the students' right to be free from religious influence while at school.

The appeals court has, on its own initiative, opted to reconsider at least portions of this decision, says school district attorney David Larsen. "This could mean that the three-judge 9th Circuit panel will make very small changes or that the case could be considered by an 11-judge panel." He estimates the district's cost to fight the case could be as high as $100,000.

A similar case involving the Moon Area School District in Pittsburgh could cost the district more than $200,000, says school attorney Lee Price. Last March, a guest lecturer at Moon Senior High School spoke to all biology classes about creation science and presented what he considered scientific evidence in support of creationism.

To the ACLU

The next day, students in one class were asked to write down which theory they believed and why. Some parents objected and went to the American Civil Liberties Union (ACLU), which has sued the Moon Area School District, charging it with violating the First Amendment prohibition against state establishment of religion.

Price says, "the principal okayed it from a scientific perspective. My problem is that some kids are saying that the guest lecturer taught creationism as a religious belief. The ACLU maintains that if it can't be scientifically proven, it should not be presented in a science course. The ACLU truly believes that school boards are being taken over by the religious right. If the parents came to the school district, the problem could have been resolved very quickly and amicably. Instead, they went straight to the ACLU."

Notes Scott: "It is okay to talk about any religious explanation for the world, but if you advocate it, you are violating the establishment clause of the First Amendment. Teachers are not allowed to sneak creation science into science class."

Scott warns educators to be on the lookout for the following "euphemisms for creationism that avoid the 'C' word":

- Some creationists urge teachers to teach evolution in class but also to present "evidence against evolution." Says Scott, "Scientists don't argue over whether evolution occurred, though there is debate over how it occurred. To scientists, there are no arguments against evolution."
- "Intelligent design" theory was popularized by the Foundation for Thought and Ethics, a Texas-based organization that supports creationism. The foundation published *Of Pandas and People* in 1989 as a supplement to high school biology texts. The book suggests the presence of an omniscient, supernatural "designer" whose existence can neither be confirmed nor denied scientifically. According to Scott, "the term obviously suggests divine creation, although the authors deny that the intelligence is necessarily supernatural."
- The "abrupt appearance" theory says all life appeared suddenly, without intermediate, ancestral forms. "This theory hides its religiosity by saying we don't know what caused it," Scott says.

Creationists' biggest victory so far was in Vista, California, where Christian activists have a majority on the school board. In August 1993, the Vista school board adopted a controversial policy that states, "No theory of science shall be taught dogmatically and no student shall be compelled to believe or accept any theory presented in the curriculum."

Furthermore, "To enhance scientific exploration and dialogue, scientific evidence that challenges any theory in science should be presented," it says, and "discussions of divine creation, ultimate purposes, or ultimate causes are included at appropriate times in the history–social sciences and/or English–language arts curricula."

Some residents of Vista, concerned about the growing conservative, Christian presence among Vista school leaders, asked People for the American Way (PAW), a civil liberties group, to analyze the constitutional questions raised by the creationism policy. Of particular concern was one board member's statement that the policy puts creationism "on an equal footing with evolution."

PAW called the equal footing view "incorrect as a matter of law." PAW believes "the policy can be interpreted and implemented [to] reaffirm current district policy and the Constitution."

But if it "is instead interpreted to direct or authorize teachers to teach creationism in science class, to discuss nonobjectively divine creation or similar subjects in any class, or in any way to advocate or teach religion rather than simply teaching about religion where relevant to the curriculum, the policy would violate the First Amendment and subject the school district to liability."

According to the National School Boards Association (NSBA), the courts clearly have ruled against the creationists. State laws requiring that creationism be taught in the science classroom have been found unconstitutional, says NBA General Council [member] August W. Steinhilber. "It's a resolved issue because the Supreme Court has already spoken to the issue in *Edwards v. Aguillard.*"

Says Scott, "Contrary to some creationists' beliefs, evolution is no more antireligious than long division. But if teachers cave in to pressures to clutter science classes with nonscientific theories or to avoid teaching evolution completely, that is a threat to science."

Scott quotes geneticist Theodosius Dobzhansky: "Nothing in biology makes sense except in the light of evolution." Without it, she says, "students will learn nonsensical biology, a pile of sundry facts unconnected by an organized theory."

Darwinian Struggle—Instead of Evolution, a Textbook Proposes "Intelligent Design"
Erik Larson

BEAUMONT, Texas—During a conference on science teaching here, Charles Swift, a burly biology teacher from Lubbock, pauses at a booth to examine an unfamiliar textbook. When told it presents "another look" at evolution, he grows wary, asking: "Is this creationism?"

"No," the display's attendant says. "It's 'intelligent-design theory.'"

Resolving to keep an open mind, Mr. Swift orders a copy for a free one-month review. But he is a bit miffed. "To have him look me straight in the eye and say it's not creationism. . . ," he says. "If I read this and I find out it *is* creationism, boom their stock is going to go way down."

The book is *Of Pandas and People,* and it is either an unflinching scientific look at flaws in evolutionary theory or the advance wedge of a new effort to return old-time religion to U.S. schools. Attacks on evolution have occurred often since the so-called Monkey Trial of John Scopes in 1925. But this book, published by the Foundation for Thought and Ethics in Richardson, Texas, uses a new tactic: It leaves religion out of the argument, jettisoning such incendiary terms as God, creation and Creator.

Citing a Mission

Instead, the authors deploy accepted scientific laws to argue that the world is too complex to be explained by Charles Darwin's mindless natural forces. Therefore, they reason, an "intelligent agent" must have sat at the drafting table. But the book stops short of identifying this agent.

"We're just saying, 'Let's open the doors and let people look at both sides,'" says Dean Anderson, the publisher's director of marketing and the man who spoke with Mr. Swift, the biology teacher.

Not so, says Delos B. McKown, a philosophy professor at Alabama's Auburn University. "The purpose is to get God into public education without using the word G-O-D."

The book's mission, he and other critics assert, is to sneak creationism past a 1987 Supreme Court decision barring public schools from teaching creation science but allowing teachers to present scientifically valid alternatives to evolution. The court defined creation science as a religious belief rooted in the biblical story of Genesis. These critics worry that *Pandas* could resurrect creationism in many communities where religious conservatives hold sway.

"Hidden Agenda"

When the book faced review by Alabama's school textbook committee in 1990 its backers presented a petition with 11,800 signatures endorsing intelligent design. Two months ago, scores of residents of Louisville, Ohio (pop. 7,800) attended a town meeting where they voted 121–2 to urge the school board to adopt the book as a supplementary biology text.

"This is the 'stealth' book," says Raymond Vasvari, a Cleveland attorney working with the American Civil Liberties Union to oppose creationism in Louisville's schools. "You have a very cleverly drafted document that has an agenda, but doesn't speak its agenda."

How wide an acceptance *Pandas* has achieved is difficult to gauge. Jon Buell, the foundation's founder and president, says that there are 22,500 copies in print and that teachers and curriculum buyers in 48 states have bought the book. Fifteen school districts have ordered quantities large enough to indicate classroom use, he says. He declines to identify them for fear of embroiling them in controversy.

Winning Converts

The book has won some allies with impeccable academic credentials, if not necessarily in biology. Phillip E. Johnson, a University of California, Berkeley, law professor and staunch defender of intelligent-design theory, calls the book a pioneering effort to challenge evolutionary doctrine. "What we need," he says, "is honest nondogmatic science education that is as honest about what evolutionary biologists don't know as what they do know."

Another prominent defender is Robert Kaita, a leading physicist at Princeton University's fusion lab. The foundation flew him to the Beaumont teachers' conference to deliver a talk titled, "Princeton University's Nuclear Fusion Breakthrough, Plus Personal Views on Intelligent Design." He calls intelligent-design theory "something that seems to be eminently reasonable."

The foundation also likes to tout the book's two principal authors and their past work on mainstream scientific textbooks. One writer is Dean Kenyon, a tenured biology professor at San Francisco State University, who in 1969 shared authorship of a clearly evolutionist text on the origin of life but now incorporates intelligent design into his lectures on evolution.

Religion had little to do with his own conversion, Mr. Kenyon says. Rather, he says, he became impressed with the lack of scientific data supporting crucial evolutionary concepts such as the notion that natural forces created the complex codes embedded in genes. "I'm not trying to deceive anyone here," he says. "I'm trying to suggest that we can look at the information about origins several different ways."

His co-author is Percival Davis, a professor of life science at Hillsborough Community College in Tampa, Fla. A biographical sketch in the book identifies him as a co-author of *Biology,* a mainstream college text with more than a million copies in print, published by the Saunders College Publishing unit of Harcourt General Inc. in New York.

"Deeply Disturbed"

But Elizabeth Widdicombe, publisher of Saunders, says Mr. Davis was listed as a co-author on only one edition of *Biology,* for revising several chapters. Mr. Davis's name was dropped in 1990 after three professors in Illinois alerted the company to his creationist bent. In a letter to the professors, Ms. Widdicombe wrote, "We at Saunders are deeply disturbed by our association, even through a past author, with a pseudoscientific text like *Of Pandas and People.*"

The biography omitted another book Mr. Davis co-wrote, *Case for Creation,* published by an arm of the Moody Bible Institute, Chicago. Of *Pandas,* he says: "Of course my motives were religious. There's no question about it."

In building a case for intelligent design, Messrs. Kenyon and Davis attack the underpinnings of evolution. They argue, for example, that chemicals floating in the primordial soup would have been unlikely to combine in ways necessary to produce life. They also attack what they see as the absence of fossil evidence for evolution. If Darwin had been right, they argue, museums today would be chock full of fossils representing "transitional forms" of creatures that bridged the wide gaps between species. They write that intelligent design "fits well with the empirical data, with the fact that fully formed organisms appear all at once, separated by distinct gaps."

Evolutionists acknowledge that major gaps exist, but they also argue that some transitional forms have been found—just not in the kind of smooth progression Darwin postulated. They contend, too, that fossils representing intermediate species may simply never have formed, or perhaps have yet to be uncovered. Arguing over whether evolution took place, says Eugenie Scott, director of the National Center for Science Education in Berkeley, Calif., "is like arguing whether the earth is spherical." But scientists still "fight like cats and dogs" over exactly *how* it occurs, she says. She accuses *Pandas* of disguising religion as science, "and quite frankly, that's offensive to people who prize honesty."

At the Beaumont science-teaching conference, the Foundation for Thought and Ethics gave visitors packets containing assurances that *Pandas* in no way embodied the biblical story of creation and was thus perfectly legal to use in public schools. A look at the path the book followed to production, however, suggests that its promoters may have nurtured a less-than-secular agenda.

Genesis on Campus

Before launching the foundation in 1980, Mr. Buell had worked full time in Christian campus ministries, including the Campus Crusade for Christ. Mr. Anderson, who joined the foundation as marketing director in May, met Mr. Buell when he, too, was working for Campus Crusade.

Mr. Buell, 54 years old, had high hopes for *Pandas.* During his search for a company to actually produce the book, he sent a pitch to a Boston firm in which he projected revenue of over $6.5 million in five years based upon "modest expectations for the market." At the time, the high court hadn't barred creation science from public schools. If the court allows such teaching, Mr. Buell wrote, "then you can throw out these projections, the nation-wide market would be explosive!"

In a December 1988 fund-raising letter to "friends" of the foundation, he announced that Haughton Publishing Co., a tiny press in Mesquite, Texas, would manufacture the book. Contributors, he promised, would receive as a gift an enameled box with a panda on the lid. "In your home," Mr. Buell wrote, "it will become a pleasant reminder to pray for our work."

The first edition of *Pandas* came out in late 1989; a refined second edition was released last year. To market the books, Mr. Buell first tried a head-on approach, pitching the book as a supplemental text to state and local boards that approve school books in Idaho and Alabama. Idaho rejected the book. In Alabama it ignited a firestorm, and the state chapter of Phyllis Schlafly's conservative Eagle Forum charged to its defense. The chapter previously hadn't taken a position on any book, says Eunie Smith, its president. "But in this instance, we thought it was so important that the children be given something other than just the evolutionist view of life's origins."

The publisher imported scientists from Yale, Brandeis and Princeton to testify in favor of intelligent-design theory, among them Princeton's Dr. Kaita. "That precious man!" exclaims Mrs. Smith.

When a negative vote seemed inevitable, however, the foundation withdrew the book. "It was our first time out of the gate," says Mr. Buell. "We realized we were dealing with politics, not scholarship at all."

He changed tactics, promoting *Pandas* through grass-roots channels directly to biology teachers. "Biology teachers are generally easy to contact, available for a meeting on short notice and receptive," he wrote in another letter to supporters. "If you would like to be a part of this 'quiet army,' please let us know right away." Those choosing not to enlist he said, "may wish to support those who do by their prayers."

The troops got material support as well, including a video of testimonials by scientists and a script for pitching the book to small groups. To counter objections that *Pandas* would bring religion into the classroom, the foundation suggested a response: "I agree that personal beliefs should not be taught in science classrooms but intelligent design is not a personal belief; it is accepted science, a view that is held by many highly qualified scientists."

But even Mr. Johnson, the Berkeley law professor, says a bit more candor about the nature of the designer might be in order. "You're playing Hamlet without Hamlet if you don't say something about that," he says. He exonerates the authors, however. "The fact is they're working against enormous prejudice here, and enormous bigotry. And they're trying to put it in terms that the courts and science will allow to exist."

Mr. Anderson, the marketing director, says he wasn't trying to deceive Lubbock's Mr. Swift when he denied *Pandas* was creationist—he was just applying the Supreme Court's definition of creation science. He himself believes in "a Creator with a capital C" and that God is indeed the designer. But, he says, "that is really up to the reader of the book to make that connection."

Joan Kendall, education chairwoman of Eagle Forum's Alabama chapter, agrees that the designer could be anyone—or anything, for that matter.

With rich Southern inflection, she quips, "Somebody else might think it was a giant turtle."

Creationism: Alabama Cracks Open the Door
Constance Holden

Science educators are nervously awaiting the selection of school textbooks in Alabama later this year. Their fear: Guidelines for science teaching adopted by the state board of education last month may open the door to the teaching of creationism in that state. The guidelines, which apply to textbooks for kindergarten through 12th grade, emphasize that evolution is only a "theory."

The board will select textbooks incorporating these guidelines in September, for use throughout Alabama's public schools, and members of the Alabama Academy of Sciences are fearing the worst. Under the current course guidelines, adopted at the last go-round in 1988, evolution is not "qualified," and creationism is not mentioned, says geologist Scott Brande of the University of Alabama, Birmingham. But the new guidelines specify that "explanations of the origins of life and major groups of plants and animals, including humans, shall be treated as theory and not as fact."

Other changes, according to Brande and Tuskegee University biologist John Fransden, chair of the Alabama Academy of Sciences' Committee on Science and Public Policy, include small revisions such as adding horseshoe crabs—

SOURCE: *Science*, April 7, 1995, p. 33. Reprinted with permission. Copyright © 1995 American Association for the Advancement of Science.

which, like the creationists' version of humans, haven't changed over time—to a discussion about fossils.

Indeed, Fransden notes, evolution foes "have succeeded in removing all the wording" that could hinder state approval of creationist texts. The scientists worry in particular that a book explaining "intelligent design" that was rejected in the past, called *Of Pandas and People,* may be back in the running.

Molleen Matsumura of the National Center for Science Education, a group in El Cerrito, California, that monitors anti-evolution trends, fears that other states may follow suit. Alabama, she says, is not the only place where creationism appears to be "picking up steam." In Louisiana, for example, school authorities at one parish recently instructed teachers to read a disclaimer to students before any discussion of evolution.

In Tennessee, a Move for Genesis
The Associated Press

NASHVILLE—The state where John Scopes was tried and convicted in 1925 for teaching evolution wants again to restrict what students can be told about human origins.

The Tennessee Senate is considering legislation to fire any teacher who presents evolution as fact. The bill was expected to pass during last night's session but instead was sent back to committee for study of six proposed amendments.

The amendments included one that would have protected teachers who wanted to teach the biblical version of creation along with evolution. Another changed the wording to say a teacher "could" be fired instead of "shall" be fired.

The bill had been expected to pass despite an attorney general's opinion it violates the constitutional separation of church and state. Republican state Sen. Keith Jordan said he moved to send the bill back to the Education Committee in hopes of figuring out a way to make it constitutional.

"We cannot constitutionally tell what is to be taught, particularly when there are religious underpinnings," Jordan said.

"This is a trilogy that is making this state a comedy," said Sen. Steve Cohen, a Memphis Democrat.

The sponsor of the evolution bill is Sen. Tommy Burks, whose home district is 45 miles northwest of Dayton, site of the 1925 Scopes "monkey trial." He said he introduced the bill because constituents told him evolution was being taught as fact in Tennessee schools. He did not name the schools.

SOURCE: *The Boston Globe,* March 5, 1996, p. 3. Reprinted with permission of The Associated Press.

Gov. Don Sundquist, a Republican, has not said what he will do if the bill reaches his desk.

The bill is more lenient than the law under which Scopes, a substitute biology teacher, was convicted and fined $100.

That law prohibited teaching "any theory that denies the story of the Divine Creation of man as taught in the Bible, and to teach again that man has descended from a lower order of animals."

"Teachers will be afraid to teach anything about evolution," so students will miss a portion of their basic science curriculum, said Wesley Roberts, an ecology teacher at Nashville's Hillwood High.

Rethinking Indoctrination
Warren A. Nord

Consider a Christian academy that requires students to study fundamentalist theology for 12 years but requires no course work in science (though scientific beliefs are occasionally mentioned in history textbooks, which are, of course, written by fundamentalist theologians). Biology recapitulates the first chapter of Genesis, history begins with Adam and Eve, and morality is essentially a matter of the Ten Commandments and the Beatitudes. Needless to say, the academy's teachers are not themselves required to have done any coursework in science—and few have.

Would students in such an academy be indoctrinated? I expect most of us would answer affirmatively. Would it make any difference, in answering this question, if parents supplemented their children's education by teaching them science or if they watched *Nova* on television? I take it this would make no difference: The academy cannot be acquitted of the charge of indoctrination because parents compensate for its shortcomings.

Now consider a public school that requires students to study science, social science, and secular ways of making sense of the world for 12 years but requires no coursework in religion (though religious beliefs are occasionally mentioned in history textbooks, which are, of course, written by social scientists). Neo-Darwinian accounts of evolution are taught in biology classes, Adam and Eve have been replaced in the cast of characters by various prehistoric anthropoids, and students learn either that morality is culture-relative or that it is essentially a matter of self-actualization. Needless to say, the school's teachers are not required to have done any coursework in religion—and few have.

SOURCE: *Education Week, 14,* no. 35, (May 24, 1995): pp. 36; 44. Reprinted with permission of the author and *Education Week*.

Would students in such a school be indoctrinated? Would it make any difference, in answering this question, if parents supplemented their children's schooling by taking them to church or synagogue?

Students are indoctrinated, I suggest, when they are socialized to accept, uncritically, some culturally contested way of understanding the world rather than another. They are educated when they have some significant understanding of the alternatives and sufficient distance on them so that they can think critically about them.

But if this is what indoctrination is, then public schools come close—perilously close—to indoctrinating students by socializing them to accept, uncritically, secular over religious ways of making sense of the world.

After all, public schools teach students to see nature as purposeless and devoid of sacred qualities. They take no note of the claim basic to all Western religion, that God's hand shapes the structure of history. Psychology and home economics replace the immortal soul with the temporal self. Economics classes teach students that they are self-interested utility maximizers. Students learn to value the goods of this world, not those of the world to come. Indeed, they can learn whatever they need to know about whatever they study without learning anything about religion. Education relegates religion to irrelevance.

Religious alternatives—conservative *and* liberal—to the conventional social wisdom of public schooling go unspoken and unconsidered.

It is sometimes argued that because religion is a matter of faith it is not a fit matter for education. Science and social science, by contrast, are grounded in reason—and hence are the stuff of good education.

But, of course, this too-simple distinction begs all the important questions. If some religious folk believe because of blind faith, most do not. Arguably, the mainstream claim of all religious traditions is that religion is *reasonable*—not in any narrowly scientific sense, of course, but then why let science define reason? Similarly, many theologians argue that science is itself grounded in faith of a kind. And then there are, nowadays, many secular postmodernists who argue that science must dispense with its claims to Truth and admit that it simply provides yet another set of meta-narratives, no better or worse (in any "objective" sense) than others.

That is, there are many ways of defining reason and faith. Typically, educators assume one highly controversial set of definitions—those provided by modern science and social science—and then convey them uncritically to students. Now it may strike the reader as implausible that students can be indoctrinated to accept science—for surely science depends on the critical use of evidence and public reason to test its claims. But no matter how scrupulous science and social science are about evidence and rationality *within* their governing frameworks, if the philosophical assumptions that define those frameworks are not themselves held up for critical scrutiny and compared with alternatives (such as those drawn from religions) then, on at least the meaning of the word, they are accepted as a matter of faith—and students who are taught to accept them uncritically will have been indoctrinated.

The astronomer Arthur Eddington once told a parable about a fisherman who had for many years used a net with a three-inch mesh. After never catching any fish shorter than three inches he concluded that there were no such fish in the ocean.

Needless to say, the kind of conceptual net we use determines what we catch. Public schools provide students with a conceptual net constructed almost entirely from scientific method. And when we teach students to think in entirely secular, scientific ways about history, nature, psychology, morality, and society, it should come as no surprise that after 12 years they conclude that there are no religious fish to [be] found in the sea. Or if there are, one must accept their presence as a matter of faith.

Consider miracles, for example.

Scientific method requires that knowledge-claims be (scientifically) testable and that experiments be replicable, the governing assumption being that reality is lawlike.

Not surprisingly, this approach rules miracles out of the picture *a priori*—for the evidence for miracles is often a matter of religious experience (rather than the kind of "hard" data measurable by scientific instruments) and it is not likely to be replicable. While we might put nature on the rack to make her divulge her secrets, as Francis Bacon once recommended, we cannot force God to replicate miracles.

But for Western religion, reality has the structure of a story, and there are singular events—miracles, if you will—by means of which God moves the story along. Miracles fit into a different pattern of intelligibility than that provided by modern science. Indeed, what may be irrational to believe given scientific method and universal laws of nature might be rational to believe from within a religious world view given the unfolding story and the religious power of the experience.

Public education does not indoctrinate students by attacking religion or promoting a militant secularism. Instead, it removes the awareness of religious possibilities; it makes religious accounts of the world seem implausible, even inconceivable. It fails to provide students with the intellectual and emotional resources that would enable them to take religion seriously.

It is not enough to teach students something of the role of religion in history. Students must learn something about contemporary religious ways of thinking about virtually all aspects of life. They should learn something of religious ways of making sense of history, religious accounts of justice and the economic world, religious views of nature (including creationism and theistic accounts of evolution), and religious interpretations of morality and human nature.

Indeed, religion is sufficiently important and complicated to require that students take at least one religion course taught by teachers certified in religious studies. (The claim, frequently made, that there is not now time in the school day to do this is revealing: The fact that we typically require 12 years of mathematics for college-bound students and no religion demonstrates just how parochially secular we are.)

I want to be clear that I make this argument not because I'm a religious fundamentalist (a possibility which may have occurred to some readers). Far from it.

A liberal education should provide students with some understanding of the major points of view on the most important matters of human experience. To ignore religion is to be profoundly illiberal.

My argument is both liberal and secular.

Indeed, *political* liberals should be particularly concerned to include religion in the discussion, for it is part of our agenda to give voice to disenfranchised subcultures, and no subculture (well, hardly any subculture) is more thoroughly disenfranchised, more without voice, in contemporary public education than are religious subcultures.

This is also the *constitutionally* liberal view. As the liberal majority on the U.S. Supreme Court has interpreted the establishment clause over the last 50 years, it requires public schools to be *neutral* between religion and nonreligion. (This is, in large part, what the Court means by a "wall of separation.") But public schools are now anything but neutral. They uncritically promote secular over religious ways of making sense of the world. It is not open to schools to *promote* or *practice* religion, of course; but they must treat it neutrally, taking it seriously—just as they do the secular alternatives.

Finally, my argument is a secular argument. I make no claims for including religion in the curriculum because some variation on it gives us the truth. Maybe, maybe not. It should be included because it is important, and because not including it makes public education a matter of indoctrination—secular indoctrination. Any good secular liberal should be in favor of requiring students to study a good deal more religion than they now do.

Suit Challenges Religious Practices in Alabama Districts
Mark Walsh

An assistant principal in Alabama filed a federal lawsuit last week challenging classroom prayers, Bible distribution, and other religious practices he contends his school district has long condoned in violation of the U.S. Constitution.

Michael Chandler, the assistant principal at Valley Head High School, sued the DeKalb County school district after years of complaining about such practices as prayers before graduation ceremonies and football games, classroom distribution of Gideon Bibles, and classroom prayers, his lawyers said.

Source: *Education Week, 15,* no. 20, (February 7, 1996): p. 3. Reprinted with permission from *Education Week.*

Mr. Chandler and his son, who attends a school in the 7,285-student De-Kalb County system—as well as another plaintiff identified as Jane Doe and her daughter—are being represented by the American Civil Liberties Union of Alabama and Americans United for Separation of Church and State, a Washington-based advocacy group.

The lawsuit, filed Feb. 1 in U.S. District Court in Montgomery, also challenges a 1993 state law that authorizes student-initiated prayers at "compulsory or noncompulsory" student assemblies, graduation ceremonies, and athletic contests. The suit says the law and the challenged practices violate the First Amendment's prohibition against government establishment of religion.

Alabama was one of several states to consider or adopt such a law after the U.S. Supreme Court in 1993 declined to disturb a lower-court ruling that endorsed student-led, nonsectarian graduation prayers.

Just last month, however, a federal appeals court struck down a Mississippi law that is nearly identical to Alabama's. The ruling by the U.S. Court of Appeals for the 5th Circuit said the Mississippi law "tells students that the state wants them to pray."

The 5th Circuit's ruling does not cover Alabama.

The new suit also comes as the U.S. House of Representatives is weighing measures that would amend the Constitution to provide stronger guarantees of student religious expression in public schools.

The Talladega, Ala., city school board is also named as a defendant in the suit, which cites the inclusion of prayers at the 1995 graduation ceremony at Talladega High School, where Ms. Doe's daughter is a student.

The bulk of the lawsuit, however, challenges practices in the DeKalb County district, where "organized religion just pervades the school day," Steven Green, Mr. Chandler's lawyer with Americans United, maintained.

"Any chance there is for religion at a school-sponsored event, it seems to occur" in the district, he said in an interview.

For example, Mr. Chandler contends that his son's 6th-grade teacher last year solicited students to pray at the front of the class or to read from the Bible. Prayers at high school football games and graduation ceremonies are commonplace, the suit alleges, and they are led not just by students but also by clergy members.

The suit also cites a compulsory 1994 ceremony for a drug education program during which, it says, an elementary school student read from the Bible and a similar ceremony at Valley Head High School where a minister was invited to lead prayers. Prayers are a regular part of 4-H meetings, pep rallies, and other student assemblies, the suit contends. The suit also alleges that school distribution of Bibles by Gideons International occurs frequently in the DeKalb district.

Mr. Chandler contends in the suit that when he objected to prayers in his son's classroom, Superintendent Weldon Parrish told him that "prayer in schools did not hurt anything and might do some good."

Mr. Parrish said late last week that he had not seen the suit and could not comment on specific incidents.

"Our policy here is that our schools are in compliance with state and federal rules and regulations," the superintendent said. "The district is not doing anything that was not authorized by the 1993 state law," he said.

Praying for Sanity in Schools
John Leo

There are two ways of looking at the call for a school-prayer amendment to the Constitution.

1. The radical religious right, angry at the modern world and contemptuous of the Constitution, is trying to subvert church–state separation and take over the public schools. This is the conventional view of the American Civil Liberties Union and its easily alarmed ally, People for the American Way.
2. It is a predictable, explosive reaction to the vast hostility toward religion that has steadily permeated the schools since the Supreme Court struck down school prayer in 1962. Egged on by the ACLU, with its "customary crabbed view of religious speech" (Nat Hentoff's memorable phrase), the school establishment has refused to make any reasonable and constitutional accommodation to the feelings of religious parents.

My vote is for Explanation 2.

The Constitution's clause prohibiting the establishment of religion does not require government, or public schools, to become adversaries of religion. But the need to avoid endorsing religion has mutated into an unmistakable antagonism.

The almost obsessive attempt to stamp out any religious utterance in or around public schools is now routine. Principals try to make an alarming church–state issue out of teachers who discuss religion with one another on their lunch hours, students who gather at the flagpole for voluntary preschool prayer, and children's drawings or show-and-tell items that contain religious references. A suit against a St. Louis public school alleged that a fourth grader was ridiculed and placed in three-day detention for bowing his head and whispering a private prayer before lunch in the school cafeteria. Another suit charged that school officials ordered an 11-year-old Oklahoma girl not to use her recess time to pray and discuss religion with classmates.

SOURCE: *U.S. News & World Report*, November 28, 1994, p. 38. Copyright © 1994, *U.S. News & World Report*. Reprinted with permission.

ACLU on the Wrong Side   The senior class president at a Douglasville, Ga., high school was ordered not to give the traditional farewell address to classmates because he could not be relied on to leave religion out of his speech. He presumably could have turned the occasion into a rally for Jeffrey Dahmer or called for the violent overthrow of the state of Georgia without attracting any censors, but a suspected reference to God was enough to shut him up. Where is the ACLU when you need it? Answer: in its usual place, on the wrong side. Ultimately, sanity prevailed and the student was allowed to give his speech.

Fearing ACLU litigation, even soft secularists in the school bureaucracy have been converted into grim zealots determined to root out anything that looks faintly religious. They have done everything but arrest kindergartners for bringing in coins saying "In God We Trust." Christmas trees, an ancient pre-Christian Teutonic custom, are being banned in some schools, and so is Santa Claus, who is approximately as religious as Frosty and Rudolph and just about as threatening to church–state separation.

A clear indicator of the pointless hostility is the long, shameful battle to prohibit students from forming after-class religious discussion groups. As columnist Jeff Greenfield writes, "It took years of litigation and political pressure before young Christians were given the same legal rights as the 4-H club, the glee club, the stamp collectors club and the gay youth of America."

The campaign against a moment of silence is even more debased. The ACLU is the best known group willing to insist that 60 seconds of silence establishes a religion, perhaps its most tortured reading of the Constitution. Behind it, of course, lie fears that not all students will use the time for praiseworthy secular thought or salacious musings. Some may actually pray!

Though the growing hostility to religion in public schools is clear, the need for a school-prayer amendment is not. Official school prayer would dishonor our tradition of church–state separation. As a practical matter, it would tie up for many years energies desperately needed on other fronts. And even success would look bleak: a watered-down, generic set of prayers that would be litigated for a decade and have little impact on the social and moral decline they are supposed to arrest.

A better goal would be to push for the moment of silence and relief from the day-to-day antireligious pressures on the schools. A minute of reflection before the school day is perfectly appropriate in a culture that has always believed in the moral, character-forming aspect of schooling. Nobody outside the ACLU should feel threatened that students are invited to take stock of their lives and think about where they are going, even if this results in some ethical or (gasp!) religious thoughts not shared by all.

And we should note that the school-prayer issue is surely a symbolic struggle as well as a literal one. A lot of parents have lost confidence in the school system and the new values that have overtaken it. Gil Sewall, head of the American Textbook Council, says: "They see the schools accommodating a lax secular age, and they don't like it. They want something with more soul and character." Instead of railing against these parents, the elite in this country might take the time to find out what alarms them about the culture of our schools and how these concerns might be met.

The Failure of Sex Education
Barbara Dafoe Whitehead

Amid rising concern about the hazards of teenage sex, health and school leaders are calling for an expanded effort to teach sex education in the schools. At the moment the favored approach is called comprehensive sex education. The nation's highest-ranking health officer, Surgeon General Joycelyn Elders, has endorsed this approach as the chief way to reduce unwed childbearing and sexually transmitted diseases (STDs) among teenagers. The pillars of the health and school establishments, including the National Association of School Psychologists, the American Medical Association, the National School Boards Association, and the Society for Adolescent Medicine, support this approach. So do a growing number of state legislatures. Over the past decade seventeen states have adopted mandates to teach comprehensive sex education, and thirty more support it.

Sex education in the schools is not new, of course, but never before has it attempted to expose children to so much so soon. Comprehensive sex education includes much more than a movie about menstruation and a class or two in human reproduction. It begins in kindergarten and continues into high school. It sweeps across disciplines, taking up the biology of reproduction, the psychology of relationships, the sociology of the family, and the sexology of masturbation and massage. It seeks not simply to reduce health risks to teenagers but also to build self-esteem, prevent sexual abuse, promote respect for all kinds of families, and make little boys more nurturant and little girls more assertive. As Dr. Elders explains, comprehensive sex education is not just about giving children a "plumbing lesson."

This approach is appealing for several reasons. First, it reaches the vast majority of American schoolchildren, through the public school system. Second, it is inexpensive. Principals have to do little more than buy a sex-education curriculum and enroll the coach or home-economics teacher in a training workshop, and their school has a sex-education program. Third, to panicky parents, worried about their ability to protect their children from AIDS and other STDs,

SOURCE: *The Atlantic Monthly,* October 1994, pp. 55–80. Reprinted with permission of the author. Copyright © 1994 Barbara Dafoe Whitehead, as first published in *The Atlantic Monthly.*

comprehensive sex education offers a reassuring message: The schools will teach your children how to protect themselves.

Nonetheless, comprehensive sex education has provoked vigorous opposition, both at the grass roots and especially in the organized ranks of the religious right. Its critics argue that when it comes to teaching children about sex, the public schools should convey one message only: abstinence. In response, sex educators point to the statistics. Face facts, they say. A growing number of teenagers are engaging in sex and suffering its harmful consequences. It's foolish, if not irresponsible, to deny that reality. If more teenagers are sexually active, why deprive them of the information they need to avoid early pregnancy and disease? What's more, why insist on a standard of conduct for teenagers that adults themselves no longer honor or obey? As usual, the Surgeon General states the basic proposition memorably: "Everybody in the world is opposed to sex outside of marriage, and yet everybody does it. I'm saying, 'Get real.'"

This rhetoric is politically shrewd. It is smart to identify sex education with realism, honesty, and sexual freedom. (Its opponents are thereby unrealistic, hypocritical, and sexually unliberated.) Similarly, it is advantageous to link the sex-education campaign with the struggle against religious fundamentalism and, more generally, with opposition to religious argument in public life. When the issue is cast in Scopes trial terms, it appears that an approach to sex education based in science will triumph over one rooted in blind faith.

But the sex educators' rhetoric is double-edged. As credentialed professionals, trained in the health and pedagogical sciences, advocates for a "reality-based" approach must at some point submit to reality tests. Their claims raise the inevitable question: How realistic is their approach to solving the problems associated with teenage sex? Or, to be more specific: What is the evidence that comprehensive sex education can achieve its stated goals? Does comprehensive sex education respond to the real-life circumstances of teenagers today? Does the new sex pedagogy take into account the realities of teenage sex in the 1990s?

The New Jersey Model

A few months ago I set out to answer these questions by venturing into a state with a long and strong commitment to comprehensive sex education. Few states have worked harder or longer than New Jersey to bring sexual enlightenment to schoolchildren. In 1980 the state adopted one of the nation's first mandates for comprehensive sex education—or family-life education, as it is called there—and it was the very first to require sex education for children in the primary grades. Its pioneering efforts have earned New Jersey the equivalent of a five-star rating from the Sex Information and Education Council of the U.S. (SIECUS), a national advocacy organization that promotes comprehensive sex education.

Virtually every public school student in New Jersey receives sex education (the average is twenty-four hours a year), and some school children, like those in the Irvington public schools, have an early and full immersion. Overall, teachers are trained and experienced, averaging close to ten years of teaching a family-life curriculum.

■ ■ ■

The Philosophy of Sex Education

Susan Wilson runs the [New Jersey Network for Family Life] from her handsome gated home in Princeton. (The Network is officially headquartered at Rutgers.) Wilson, who has been an indefatigable crusader for comprehensive sex education for more than a decade, helped to write and pass the state mandate in the late 1970s, while she was a member of the State Board of Education. A few years later she took over as the head of the Network. With a budget of about $200,000 this year, mostly from foundations and the state government, Wilson and her small staff publish a newsletter, testify at hearings, train teachers, develop sex-education materials, fight efforts to overturn the mandate, and perform the scores of other duties required in their advocacy work. But Wilson's single most important task, which she clearly enjoys, is traveling up and down the state making the case for comprehensive sex education.

Because the case that she makes represents today's comprehensive sex-education orthodoxy, it deserves close attention. It has several tenets. First, children are "sexual from birth." Like many sex educators, Wilson rejects the classic notion that a latency period occurs between the ages of about six and twelve, when children are sexually quiescent. "Ever since I've gotten into this field, the opponents have used that argument to frighten policymakers," she says. "But there is a body of developmental knowledge that says this is not true." And, according to Wilson, it is not simply that children are born sexual or that their sexuality is constantly unfolding. It is also that sexuality is much broader than most imagine: "You are not just being sexual by having intercourse. You are being sexual when you throw your arms around your grandpa and give him a hug." Second, children are sexually miseducated. Unlike Europeans, who learn about sex as matter-of-factly as they learn about brushing their teeth, American children grow up sexually absurd—caught between opposing but equally distorted views of sex. One kind of distortion comes from parents. Instead of affirming the child's sexuality, parents convey the message that sex is harmful, shameful, or sinful. Or, out of a misguided protectiveness, they cling to the notion of childhood innocence and fail to provide timely or accurate information about sex. The second kind of distortion comes from those who would make sex into a commodity. While parents withhold information, the media and the marketplace spew sexual misinformation. It is this peculiar American combination of repressiveness and permissiveness that leads to sexual wrong thinking and poor sexual decision-making, and thus to high rates of teenage pregnancy and STDs.

Third, if miseducation is the problem, then sex education is the solution. Since parents are failing miserably at the task, it is time to turn the job over to the schools. Schools occupy a safe middle ground between Mom and MTV.

They are places where "trusted adults" can teach children how to protect themselves against the hazards of sex and sexual abuse.

Moreover, unlike homes, schools do not burden children with moral strictures. As Wilson explains, schools can resolve the "conflict between morality and reality" by offering unbiased statements of fact. Here, for example, is how a teacher might handle the subject of masturbation in a factually accurate way: "Some people think it is okay to masturbate and some people think it is not okay to masturbate, but most people think that no harm comes to you if you masturbate." Consequently, when it comes to sex, schools rather than homes offer a haven in the heartless world.

A fourth and defining tenet is that sex education must begin in the earliest grades. Like math or reading, comprehensive sex education takes a "building blocks" approach that moves from basic facts to more sophisticated concepts, from simple skills to more complex competencies. Just as it would be unthinkable to withhold math education until the sixth grade, so, too, is it unwise to delay the introduction of sex education until the eighth grade.

In the beginning, before there is sex, there is sex literacy. Just as boys and girls learn their number facts in the first grade, they acquire the basic sex vocabulary, starting with the proper names for genitalia and progressing toward an understanding of masturbation, intercourse, and contraception. As they gain fluency and ease in talking about sexual matters, students become more comfortable with their own sexuality and more skillful in communicating their feelings and desires. Boys and girls can chat with one another about sex, and children can confide in adults without embarrassment.

Early sex education readies grade school children for the onslaught of puberty. By the time they reach adolescence, they are cognitively as well as biologically primed for sex. Moreover, with early sex training, teenagers are much more likely to engage in what Wilson and her colleagues consider responsible sexual conduct: abstinence, noncoital sex, or coitus with a condom. Since abstinence will not lead to pregnancy or STDs, and noncoital and protected sex are not likely to do so, comprehensive sex education will help to reduce the incidence of these problems among teenagers.

This is the philosophy of comprehensive sex education. But how to translate it into lessons for little children? Although the state mandate allowed school districts to shop around for a suitable curriculum, at first not much was available for primary schoolers. Most teachers had to improvise a curriculum or adapt higher grade-level texts to the early grades. What was missing was a standard text: a Dick and Jane reader for the Michaels and Ashleys of the post-sexual-revolution generation.

Family Life

Rutgers University Press seized the opportunity. With a growing number of states adopting comprehensive sex-education mandates, and with the 595 school districts of New Jersey seeking to meet their state mandate, the market for a sex primer looked promising. The press set out to fill that market niche. It assembled a small, sympathetic advisory panel, including Susan Wilson, and then hired Barbara Sprung, an independent consultant from New York City, to write its pathbreaking sex-education text.

A graduate of Sarah Lawrence and the Bank Street College of Education, Barbara Sprung spent eight years as an elementary school teacher before she embarked on a second career as a diversity-education specialist. During the 1970s and the 1980s, working first for a feminist organization and then for her own organization, Educational Equity Concepts, Sprung produced books, teachers' guides, and other materials based on a "nonsexist, multicultural, disability-sensitive, early childhood approach." The Rutgers project was her first venture into sex education.

With her advisers, she came up with *Learning About Family Life,* a "textbook package" described in the Rutgers University Press marketing brochure as a "pioneering" approach to family-life education for school children in kindergarten through third grade. The textbook also carries a pioneering price tag—$250 a package. As befits a fundamental text, the curriculum sets forth its guiding principles: "Sexuality is a part of daily living, as essential to normal functioning as mathematics and reading." And as befits a primer, it offers the sex basics. Here is a representative sampling:

> *On female genitalia:* "The vulva is the area enclosing three parts: a vagina, the opening you urinate from, and a clitoris. . . . Clitoris is a small sensitive part that only girls have, and it sometimes makes you feel good."

> *On sexual intercourse:* "To have sex, the man and woman lie very close to each other so that their bodies are touching. Usually it happens in bed, and they don't have any clothes on. Together the woman and man place the man's penis inside the woman's vagina, and while they are loving each other, many sperm come from the testicles into the man's penis. After awhile, the sperm come through the little hole at the end of the man's penis, and they swim up the vagina and meet the egg in the fallopian tube."

> *On masturbation:* "Grown-ups sometimes forget to tell children that touching can also give people pleasure, especially when someone you love touches you. And you can give yourself pleasure, too, and that's okay. When you touch your own genitals, it's called masturbating."

> *On sex:* "When you are older, you can decide if you want to have sex. Most people do, because they like it and it's a very important way of showing that we love someone."

These sex facts are presented in a particularly captivating form. Unlike standard sex-education curricula, which are about as exciting to read as an IRS Form 1040, *Learning About Family Life* tells a story. The text follows a fictional class of primary school children and their teachers, Ms. Ruiz and Mr. Martin, as they experience a series of family events during the course of the school year. The teachers and children are characters in a continuing saga, full of drama and incident. Primary school teachers tell Sprung that children eagerly ask, "When are we going to talk about those kids in Class 203 again?" Little wonder. This is sex education packaged as *Sesame Street.*

Like *Sesame Street, Learning About Family Life* deals with the social and family issues of the day. During the year Classroom 203 encounters the following events: Ms. Ruiz's pregnancy and childbirth, the death of Mr. Martin's father, the drug arrest of Martine's cousin, the birth of a child to Joseph's teenage sister, the arrival of Natan's grandmother from Russia, Sarah's trip to see her divorced father, and the visit of Seth's HIV-infected uncle. These events and others, presented in forty-three vignettes, provide an occasion for straight talk about genitalia, sexual intercourse, pregnancy and childbirth, HIV and AIDS, masturbation, sexual abuse, physical disability, drug abuse, death, divorce, grandparents, and all kinds of families.

As they read about Classroom 203, children acquire a scientific sex vocabulary. "Adults in the children's families probably don't use accurate terms like anus and buttocks," the teachers' resource guide warns. "You, as the teacher, are the best role model for creating comfort." Indeed, the teacher is to insist on replacing even words that are perfectly apt for a six-year-old's vocabulary with more-scientific terms. In a lesson on pregnancy, Brian talks about how his mother's tummy felt when the baby was growing inside. Ms. Ruiz says, "I know we are used to saying *baby* and *tummy.* But *fetus* and *uterus* are more accurate words." And when it comes to a hot issue like masturbation, a teacher's cool command of the facts is crucial: "Masturbation is a topic that is viewed negatively in many families, based on long-standing cultural and religious teachings. Assure parents that your approach will be low keyed and will stress privacy, but also make it clear that you will not perpetuate myths that can mar children's healthy sexual development." Teachers must also debunk the myth that masturbation is only for boys. Girls must be granted equal time to ask masturbation questions.

If girls need nudging in the sex department, boys need coaxing in the emotions department. Indeed, one of the strongest themes in the text is the problematic nature of boys. Boys are emotionally clogged, unable to cry or to express feelings. And little boys may enter grade school with the idea that such sex-related matters as pregnancy, childbearing, and baby care are only for girls. Therefore *Learning About Family Life* enlists boys in nurturing and "feelings" activities. These may be difficult for boys who come from macho backgrounds. But here again the school provides a cultural haven. If the lessons in nurturing conflict with a boy's family or cultural teachings, the teachers' manual advises, the teacher should say, "In school, talking about feelings is a part of learning."

In early sex education feelings talk and sex talk are closely related for good reason: little schoolchildren do not have the capacity to understand big adult issues directly. But many are now exposed to big adult issues at an early age, and so it is necessary to find routes to understanding. Early sex education thus turns to affective pathways and to a therapeutic pedagogy.

Stuff Happens

According to its publishers, *Learning About Family Life* provides a realistic slice of contemporary family life. Nonetheless, it is a highly selective slice. There is a vignette designed to expose children to an "amicable divorce." But there is no corresponding vignette to give children a picture of an amicable, much less a long-lasting, marriage. (Susan Wilson believes that you "can't beat kids all over the head" with marriage.) There is a story about sex as a way to show love, but no story about commitment as a way to show love. There is an effort to give children positive messages about expressing sexuality, but no effort to give children positive messages about the advantages of not expressing sexuality before they are grown. And this family world is only thinly populated by men: Ms. Ruiz is a well-defined character in the story; the male teacher, Mr. Martin, is more of a bit player, taking center stage in one story to talk about masturbation and in another to cry. There are grandmothers but no grandfathers. A brand-new father makes a cameo appearance to show off his nurturing skills, but the only other father is divorced and a plane ride away.

Here is the dilemma: *Learning About Family Life* is caught between two competing tendencies. On the one hand, it works hard to reflect the real-life family circumstances of many children. It deals with some hard-edged issues: sexual abuse, unwed teenage motherhood, drug dealing, and divorce. On the other hand, it takes a deeply sentimental view of these gritty realities. Consider, for example, the story "Joseph Is an Uncle":

Joseph's seventeen-year-old sister has a new baby. She is not married. The baby's father is gone. Joseph's parents are mad and sad at the same time. His sister is tired and out of sorts. Yet things work out. The family rallies round. An aunt takes care of the baby during the day. Joseph's sister returns to school. Joseph shows the photograph of his new nephew to his best friend, but he doesn't want anyone else to know about his sister's baby. His friend encourages him to show the photo to Mr. Martin and Ms. Ruiz.

Of all the sex tales, Joseph's story merits the closest attention. Early sex education, after all, purports to help children avoid the fate of Joseph's teenage sister. So what are we to make of this story? First, though illegitimacy is not treated cavalierly, it is depicted as a family crisis that is quickly resolved, because all the folks pitch in. Apparently there are no longer term consequences for Joseph's sister or his little nephew—such as poverty, welfare dependency, or diminished school and job prospects. Second, in a curriculum designed to teach personal responsibility, the text misses an opportunity to do so. Unwed teenage parenthood is not an affliction visited on people like hurricanes or drought, yet that is the message of the story. Among the families in Classroom 203 stuff happens.

Finally, think about the baby's father. Joseph's sister's boyfriend has sex as an expression of love, exactly as the sex primer describes, but then he takes off. Though *Learning About Family Life* has stern messages for boys about caring and sharing, it ducks the basic question of male responsibility. A seven-year-old boy listening to this story might well conclude that illegitimacy is a girls' topic.

As it turns out, then, early sex education is not straight talk at all but a series of object lessons. And these are offered not so much with a nose for the facts as with an eye to the sex educators' philosophy. *Learning About Family Life* is no less didactic in its views on family life than Dick and Jane. To be sure, a truly fact-based approach would have to deal with some hard truths. For example, it would have to say that unwed teenage parenthood carries grave consequences for teenagers and their babies; that not all families are equally capable of caring for children; and that absent long-term commitment, responsibility, and sacrifice, love does not conquer all. Since some children grow up in broken or unwed teenage families, there is an understandable concern that children not feel stigmatized by such facts. Yet such tender concern raises a tough question: If the classroom is the source of unbiased factual information, how can the problems of illegitimacy and broken families be dealt with without touching on the key facts in the matter?

The Pedagogy of Sex Education

In the middle grades sex education takes a more technical turn. At eleven and twelve many young people are approaching the threshold of puberty while others are already in full pubertal flower. (Today the average age of menarche is twelve and a half.) Now, as hormones kick in, children are ready to express themselves sexually. Thus the focus of sex education shifts from sex literacy to building sexual skills. This is when students must acquire the knowledge and technical skills to manage their emerging sexuality.

Sex-education advocates agree that abstaining from sex is the best way to avoid STDs and early pregnancy. But they reject an approach that is limited to teaching abstinence. First, they say, abstinence-based teaching ignores the growing number of adolescents who are already sexually active at age twelve or thirteen. One Trenton schoolteacher said to me, "How can I teach abstinence when there are three pregnant girls sitting in my eighth-grade class?" Second, abstinence overlooks the fact that, as Susan Wilson explains, "it is developmentally appropriate for teenagers to learn to give and receive pleasure."

Consequently, the New Jersey sex-education advocates call for teaching middle-schoolers about condoms, abortion, and the advantages of "protected" sex. But given the risks to teenagers, they are not crazy about sexual intercourse either. Indeed, Wilson says, Americans are fixated on "this narrow little thing called intercourse." The alternative is a broad thing called noncoital sex or, in the argot of advocates, "sexual expression without risk."

Noncoital sex includes a range of behaviors, from deep kissing to masturbation to mutual masturbation to full body massage. Since none of these involves intercourse, sex educators see them as ways for teenagers to explore their sexuality without harm or penalty. And from a broader public health perspective, risk-free sexual expression has great potential. According to the Rutgers education professor William Firestone, who conducted a study of sex-education teaching in New Jersey for the Network for Family Life Education, noncoital sex offers "real opportunities to reduce dangers to many teens who engage in sexual behavior, despite recommendations for abstinence." Yet as Firestone's survey research shows, many teachers shrink from this approach. Wilson says, "We hardly ever talk to teens about necking and petting and admiring your body and maybe massage."

As Wilson points out, noncoital sex is most practicable when teenagers can communicate with each other. "A lot of people think that once you start down the road to sex, you can't stop, and that's the problem. But I think that by talking about these things and by role playing, you give kids control and you give them the language to say 'That's enough—I don't want any more. I don't want to have intercourse.'"

Since safe petting and good talking go together, middle school students need to continue to practice their communication skills. But in teaching these skills teachers cannot rely on old-fashioned didactic methods. Middle school students are still short-term thinkers, reckless in deed. Therefore sex education in middle school does not yet enter the realm of thinking and ideas but remains lodged instead in the realm of what one teacher calls "feelings and values."

"Hello, Vulva"

I attended a teacher-training conference sponsored by the Network for Family Life Education to get acquainted with the way sex is taught. In New Jersey, as in other states with mandates for comprehensive sex education, such one-day workshops are a mainstay of teacher training. For a small investment of time and money—a day out of the classroom and $35—teachers learn the latest in sex-education theory and practice. On the day I attended, the crowd was made up of physical-education, home-economics, and health teachers with a scattering of elementary school nurses as well. Almost all were women.

Deborah Roffman, an independent sex-education consultant from Maryland who teaches in several private middle and high schools, was the keynote speaker. (Like Roffman, most of the trainers at this conference came to it from the world of advocates, family planners, and private consultants. Only one teaches in the public schools.) She was an engaging speaker with the timing and phrasing of a good comedian. (*Teacher in audience:* "What do you say when a student asks you to define 'blow job'?" *Roffman:* "You say it is oral sex." Pause. *Roffman again:* "But what if the student's next question is 'Does that mean you talk while you screw?'") To kick off the conference, Roffman gave a rousing talk, urging teachers to adopt bolder teaching methods. I was curious to see what she had in mind, so I attended her workshop.

She began the workshop session with these instructions: "Turn to the person next to you. Make eye contact. Say 'Hello, penis.' Shake hands and return the greeting: 'Hello, vulva.'" This warmup exercise underscores a central idea in sex pedagogy: for teachers no less than for students, talking about sex provokes anxiety and embarrassment. Such embarrassment stands in the way of good communication, and good communication is crucial to responsible sexual conduct.

So is emotional literacy. To become more emotionally articulate, middle schoolers engage in a series of feelings exercises. The purpose is to help students "normalize" and share common growing-up experiences. Roffman handed out a list of sample questions: "What is the worst thing your parents could find out about a child of theirs who is your age?" "Have you ever experienced the death of someone close to you?" "What is a way in which your parents are 'overprotective'?" In the middle schools as in the elementary schools, there is a continuing effort to break down boys' emotional reserve. Encourage your students to sit boy–girl, Roffman suggests, and ask the biggest boy in the class the first feelings question.

The Consortium for Educational Equity, at Rutgers, offers a similar set of feelings-and-values exercises in a sex curriculum designed for seventh- and eighth-graders. Some are sentence-completion exercises. In one, seventh-graders are asked to complete the sentence "If someone loves me, they. . ." and then elsewhere to "compare their ideas [about love] to [Eric] Fromm's and [Leo] Buscaglia's material on love." In another, students are to "write a positive self-statement. . .—'I am strong'. . . 'I am happy'. . ."—and then discuss the "impact of positive self-statements on feelings of self-esteem."

Other exercises draw on more therapeutic methods, such as role-playing and small-group work. There are gender reversal exercises, in which girls and boys each play the role of the opposite sex. In small groups students may brainstorm about ways to deal with an unwanted pregnancy or come up with a list of their expectations of nonmarital sex.

Some of the gender-reversal exercises sound like birthday-party games. In one exercise, called the Fish-Bowl, girls are seated in a circle in which there is one empty chair. Boys form a circle around the girls. Girls talk about what they like and dislike about boys. If one of the boys wishes to speak, he sits in the empty chair in the girls' circle. After a time the boys repeat the exercise, with the girls in the outer circle.

Because of its intimate subject matter, the feelings-and-values classroom institutes a new code of classroom conduct. There are confidentiality rules. Roffman's middle school students are told that nothing said in sex-education class goes out of the class without students' express permission. In discussions middle schoolers must protect the privacy of individuals who are not class members; except for classmates', no names may be used. Another rule is that any student who does not want to answer a question may pass. In some classes students agree to use only "I" statements, rather than "you" statements, in order to express their thoughts more positively.

In therapeutically oriented classrooms, moreover, the teacher assumes the role of confidant and peer. Like students, teachers are encouraged to share personal experiences. An idea book for New Jersey teachers, published by the

Network, tells the inspirational story of a high school teacher who talks to his class about his vasectomy and how he feels about it. Yet although they are advised to share experiences, teachers are not to impose their opinions, even when it comes to arguably the most important question: "What is the right time to begin having sex?" The teacher is encouraged to turn the question back to the students: "How would you begin to make that decision?"

Sex educators defend this approach with the language of empowerment. Students, they say, must acquire the knowledge and skills to answer these questions for themselves. After all, grown-ups aren't around to supervise teenagers every minute of the day. Teachers can't follow students home, and working parents can't check up on teenagers who are home alone. Why not invest teenagers with the power to make wise choices on their own?

Reality Tests

On its face, this new therapeutic sex pedagogy does not seem all that therapeutic or all that new. Teenage girls have enjoyed self-inventory tests at least as long as *Seventeen* magazine has been around. And there's nothing particularly revolutionary about small-group discussions of feelings and values. This, after all, is why teenagers invented the slumber party.

But on second glance there is something radically new about comprehensive sex education. As both a philosophy and a pedagogy, it is rooted in a deeply technocratic understanding of teenage sexuality. It assumes that once teenagers acquire a formal body of sex knowledge and skills, along with the proper contraceptive technology, they will be able to govern their own sexual behavior responsibly. In brief, what comprehensive sex education envisions is a regime of teenage sexual self-rule.

The sex educators offer their technocratic approach as an alternative to what they see as a failed effort to regulate teenage sexuality through social norms and religious values. Face facts. In a climate of sexual freedom the old standard of sexual conduct for teenagers—a standard separate from adult sexual standards—is breaking down. Increasingly teenagers are playing by the same sexual rules as adults. Therefore, why withhold from adolescents the information and technologies that are available to adults?

To be sure, sex educators have a point. Traditional sexual morality, along with the old codes of social conduct, is demonstrably less effective today than it once was in governing teenage sexual conduct. But although moral standards can exist even in the midst of a breakdown of morality, a technocratic view cannot be sustained if the techniques fizzle. Thus comprehensive sex education stands or falls on the proven effectiveness of its techniques.

For a variety of reasons the body of research on sex-education programs is not as rich and robust as we might wish. However, the available evidence suggests that we must be skeptical of the technocratic approach. First, comprehensive sex education places its faith in the power of knowledge to change behavior. Yet the evidence overwhelmingly suggests that sexual knowledge is only weakly related to teenage sexual behavior. The researcher Douglas Kirby, of ETR Associates, a nonprofit health-education firm in Santa Cruz, California, has been studying sex-education programs for more than a decade. During the 1980s he conducted a major study of the effectiveness of sex-education programs for the Department of Health, Education and Welfare, and he has since completed a review for the Centers for Disease Control of all published research on school-based sex-education programs designed to reduce the risks of unprotected sex. His research shows that students who take sex education do know more about such matters as menstruation, intercourse, contraception, pregnancy, and sexually transmitted diseases than students who do not. (Thanks to federal funding for AIDS education in the schools, students tend to be very knowledgeable about the sources and prevention of HIV infection.)

But more accurate knowledge does not have a measurable impact on sexual behavior. As it is typically taught, sex education has little effect on teenagers' decisions to engage in or postpone sex. Nor, according to Kirby, do knowledge-based sex-education programs significantly reduce teenage pregnancy. And although teenagers who learn about contraception may be more likely to use it, their contraceptive practices tend to be irregular and therefore ultimately unreliable.

Comprehensive sex education assumes that knowledge acquired at earlier ages will influence behavior. Yet the empirical evidence suggests that younger teenagers, especially, are unlikely to act on what they know. An analysis of a Planned Parenthood survey concludes that a "knowledgeable thirteen-year-old is no more likely to use contraceptives than is an uninformed thirteen-year-old." As Kirby puts it, "Ignorance is not the solution, but knowledge is not enough."

If knowledge isn't enough, what about knowledge combined with communication skills? Sex education does appear to diminish teenagers' shyness about discussing sexual matters. One study shows that girls who have had sex education may be more likely to talk about sex with their parents than those who have not. Since talking with their mothers about sex may help some girls avoid pregnancy, this is a mildly positive effect. There does not seem to be a parallel effect for boys, however.

Overall, parent–child communication is far less important in influencing sexual behavior than parental discipline and supervision. One study, based on teenagers' own reports of levels of parental control, shows that teenagers with moderately strict parents had the lowest level of sexual activity, whereas teens with very strict parents had higher levels, and those with very permissive parents had the highest levels. Moreover, there is a strong empirical relationship between diminished parental supervision and early sexual activity.

In boy–girl communication, girls say that they want help in rejecting boys' sexual overtures. In a survey taken in the mid 1980s, 1,000 teenage girls aged sixteen and younger were asked to select from a list of more than twenty sex-related topics those areas where they would like more information and help. The girls were most likely to say they wanted more information on how to say no without hurting boys' feelings. This is especially noteworthy given that all the girls in the survey were sexually active, and some were mothers.

Beyond "no," better communication about sex does not seem to contribute to higher levels of sexual responsibility. To be sure, there has been little research into this aspect of teenage sexuality. But even absent research, there is good reason to be skeptical of the claim. If free and easy sex talk were a key determinant of sexual behavior, then we might expect the trends to look very different. It would be our tongue-tied grandparents who had high rates of illegitimacy and STDs, not today's franker and looser-lipped teenagers.

■ ■ ■

Sexuality Education Works: Here's Proof
Linda A. Berne and Barbara K. Huberman

School leaders need to make good decisions about sexuality education, decisions based on reliable and valid information. Yet, the time it takes to work through the research in this single area is prohibitive for most administrators. Consequently, we present here the 17 arguments most frequently put forth by groups that oppose comprehensive sexuality education, and we examine the scientific literature to determine the validity of their arguments.

The first four arguments concern the effectiveness of abstinence instruction, including specific programs that have been studied under controlled conditions. Next, we take up concerns about intimate sexual behavior, including the effectiveness of condoms and contraceptives. Finally, we deal with abortion as a resolution to unintended pregnancy.

Myth 1: Abstinence-until-marriage curricula work.   In 1981, the American Family Life Act was passed, creating Title XX funds. The intent was to establish a variety of abstinence-based sexuality education programs and to test their results in delaying sexual intercourse among teens. In five studies of the three major abstinence-until-marriage programs, students who had taken part in the programs one to two years earlier showed no significant gains in maintenance of abstinence over a control group not exposed to a program. The three programs investigated were *Sex Respect, Success Express,* and *An Alternative National Curriculum on Responsibility (AANCHOR).*

Myth 2: Abstinence-plus curricula with skills development, followed by lessons about contraception, give students a "mixed message" and encourage sexual behavior.   In studies of seven abstinence-plus programs that were followed by lessons on contraception, students surveyed one and

SOURCE: *Education Digest*, February 1996, pp. 25–29. Reprinted with permission from *The Education Digest*, Ann Arbor, Michigan.

two years after the program *maintained abstinent behaviors longer than a control group.* Among the successful programs were these three: *Postponing Sexual Involvement, Reducing the Risk,* and *Skills for Life.* Two new programs in this category, *Be Proud! Be Responsible!* and *Get Real About AIDS,* have also proved effective.

Myth 3: Researchers from the Institute for Research and Evaluation in Utah have shown that* Sex Respect *works.   While behavior research on *Sex Respect* was completed in 1989 and 1991, to date, the researchers have not submitted their studies for peer review or publication in professional journals. The report to the Office of Adolescent Pregnancy Programs (OAPP), which administered the Title XX funds, showed that *Sex Respect* made no significant and lasting differences in attitudes or behaviors after one and two years. In a new study, submitted in 1991, the researchers claimed a slight behavioral difference in favor of the *Sex Respect* group, but the OAPP reported that the research methods were flawed and that such conclusions could not be reached on the basis of the data analysis.

Myth 4:* TEEN AID *is a highly successful abstinence until-marriage curriculum; in San Marcos, California, teen pregnancy was reduced by 86 percent when* TEEN AID *was taught.   To date, the *TEEN AID* curriculum has not been investigated in a scientific study for behavioral effect. The "San Marcos miracle" has not been substantiated by scientifically collected data or by the counselors at the school. Advocates and detractors have described the benefits and drawbacks of *TEEN AID* and *Sex Respect.* Both programs are involved in litigation in several states.

Myth 5: Sex education encourages students to become sexually active at younger ages.   The World Health Organization recently reviewed 35 controlled studies of sexuality education programs in the United States and Europe and found that in no cases did students who took part in the programs initiate sexual intercourse at an earlier age than students in the control groups exposed to no programs. One 1984 retrospective recall study found that girls who took a sex education course were "slightly more likely" to have had intercourse at ages 15 and 16, but the authors reported the factor "weaker than virtually every other variable found to have a significant relationship with first intercourse at these ages."

Myth 6: Teaching students about contraception causes students to initiate sexual activity.   Studies show that American teenagers initiate sexual intercourse and have unprotected sex for between six and 18 months or longer before they seek contraception. They typically seek contraception because of a pregnancy or a pregnancy scare.

Myth 7: Teaching students about contraception increases the likelihood that they will become pregnant.   There is evidence to the contrary. European educators include contraception in family-life education throughout the middle and high school grades. In a 36-country study, it was found that, while girls in the United States initiated first sexual intercourse at the same ages and with the same frequencies as European girls, the rates of pregnancies were two to seven times higher among U.S. girls.

Myth 8: Because contraceptives fail so frequently, we should teach teenagers to abstain from sex.   While teen sexual behavior has increased significantly over the past two decades, the rate of *pregnancy* among 15- to 19-year-olds has declined by 19 percent, due to more effective use of contraceptives. The overall *number* of pregnancies among 15- to 19-year-olds has risen 23 percent since 1972, because of the large increase in the numbers of sexually active young people. With more effective contraceptive instruction and the introduction of Norplant and Depoprovera (which are as effective as vasectomy but completely reversible), teen pregnancy levels could be significantly reduced in the United States, as they have been in other industrialized countries.

Myth 9: Contraceptives do not protect against AIDS and sexually transmitted diseases (STDs).   Other than total abstinence from risky behaviors, only condoms can provide significant protection against STDs. If teens choose not to abstain, it is recommended that the male always use a condom and that the female use a reliable method of contraception until they are ready to parent a child and if they are determined to be free of STDs.

Myth 10: Condoms have a failure rate of 12 percent to 40 percent.   The failures of condoms can be attributed mostly to the people using them rather than to the product. For instance, some people who claim that they use condoms for contraception don't use them every time, put them on after they have had intercourse but prior to ejaculation, don't hold onto them during withdrawal, or use petroleum-based lubricants that dissolve the latex. The lack of knowledge about how to use a condom effectively and the lack of motivation to use one every time mean that condoms fail much more often than they otherwise would.

The Centers for Disease Control and Prevention, the National Institutes of Health, and the Food and Drug Administration have issued a joint report on condoms that sets the failure rate at less than 2 percent for consistent and correct condom use. For comparison, one might ask how often people who intend to practice abstinence fail and thereby expose themselves and their partners to the risks of unprotected sex.

Myth 11: Condoms break frequently.   The quality of condoms does vary. Triple-dipped latex condoms that are less than two months old and treated with nonoxynol 9 are considered the most reliable. In an eight-country study of condom breakage, an average of 4 percent of the participants experienced breakage over a year's time (range, zero percent to 13 percent). Interviews with those who said that condoms broke indicated that many users had damaged condoms by stretching or inflating them before they put them on, had reused them, had used petroleum-based lubricants, had cut them with fingernails, and so on.

Myth 12: Condoms do not prevent HIV from passing through the latex. There is some evidence that the pores in certain condoms are larger than HIV, the virus that causes AIDS. However, in laboratory studies, nondefective latex condoms have been 100 percent effective in stopping the passage of HIV, according to the Centers for Disease Control and Prevention.

Myth 13: Condoms are not effective in preventing the transmission of HIV. An eight-country study of condom failures among couples in which one partner had HIV and the other did not reported that "no uninfected partner acquired HIV from an infected partner with consistent use of condoms in approximately 15,000 acts of intercourse." However, the rate of infection in couples who used condoms *inconsistently* was reported to be 4.8 percent. No transmission rates are available for couples who did not use condoms at all.

Myth 14: Contraceptives like the pill, Norplant, and the intrauterine device (IUD) are dangerous and unsafe. Most contraceptives have side effects that vary in severity. However, mortality studies of contraceptives show that using contraception is four times safer than becoming pregnant and having a baby. The oral contraceptive, in fact, is much safer for younger women than for older women.

Myth 15: Abortion is a dangerous procedure. Studies of complications arising from abortion indicate that legal abortion is seven to 25 times safer than becoming pregnant and having a baby, and comparative mortality statistics show that legal abortion is safer than playing football, driving a car, or using a tampon.

Myth 16: Abortion prevents a young woman from having a baby in the future. Multiple abortions may indeed jeopardize subsequent pregnancies. However, studies show that infertility, miscarriage, low-birth-weight babies, and other conditions were no more prevalent among women who had had an abortion than among those who had not.

Myth 17: Abortion causes mental anguish and psychiatric problems. Former Surgeon General C. Everett Koop's report on abortion found inconclusive evidence to consider abortion a physical or mental health problem. Small numbers of women do experience post-abortion stress syndrome, but the American Psychological Association concluded that abortion brings women so much mental relief and there is so little evidence of psychiatric problems following abortion that abortion does not cause more psychiatric problems than unwanted pregnancy.

This discussion has sought to bring credible scientific information to the argument over whether schools should provide comprehensive or abstinence-only sexuality education to students. Most experts believe that comprehensive sexuality education, taught within the framework of health education, is the most effective strategy.

The Division of Adolescent and School Health of the Centers for Disease Control and Prevention has recently established a system (called RESEARCH to CLASSROOM) for evaluating school curricula and encouraging the dissemination of those found to have a positive behavioral impact. Evaluation, program, and teaching experts work together to evaluate materials, update and revise them for classroom use, and then support teacher training and technical assistance through the comprehensive school health training network. The training network works with state departments of public instruction.

A program is deemed successful if it brings about one or more of the following results: delaying initiation of sexual intercourse, decreasing the frequency of unprotected intercourse, and increasing condom use. Three curricula have qualified thus far: *Reducing the Risk, Get Real About AIDS,* and *Be Proud! Be Responsible!*

While there is encouraging news about sexuality education, helping youths adopt risk-reducing behaviors, and the effectiveness of various preventive strategies when used correctly, the moral and ethical implications posed by those who argue on both sides of these issues are legitimate and need to be addressed. Therein lies the special responsibility of the family (as the primary sex educator of children) and of religious institutions to put human sexuality into context.

However, it is certainly the school's role, even its moral obligation, to meet the needs of learners. The research justifies making recommendations for accurate and age-appropriate information, for skills development, and for instruction designed to motivate young people to protect their health and the well-being of others.

Forum on Gay Issues in Schools Draws Ire
Patricia Nealon

CAMBRIDGE—A handful of protesters holding signs proclaiming their membership in Mothers Against Pedophilia milled around outside a regional conference of gay, lesbian and straight teachers yesterday at Cambridge Rindge and Latin School. As about 400 teachers and 75 high school students from across New England attended workshops on subjects ranging from Homophobia 101 to Exploring Gay and Lesbian History in Elementary School, eight protesters stood on a sidewalk nearby.

SOURCE: *The Boston Globe,* April 28, 1996, p. 37. Reprinted courtesy of *The Boston Globe.*

Ed Beucler, a black-and-white sign tucked under one arm, accused the school of subverting the values of parents like him, who believe that sex is wrong outside of marriage.

"I am very angry about teachers thinking that they can bring in their own personal political agenda and teach it to our children," said Beucler, a member of the Christian Coalition. "It is wrong."

Beucler, whose son is a freshman at Rindge and Latin, objected to an assembly held at the school in the fall as part of a national Coming Out Day. "During that rally, children were encouraged to go out and sexually experiment," he said.

Al Ferreira, a gay Rindge and Latin teacher who founded a group for gay and lesbian students, called the assertion "a lie."

Ferreira, who serves on a state task force on training future teachers to be more sensitive to homosexual students, said the protesters had been invited to attend the workshops but declined.

The annual coming out program, he said, included presentations by parents and students and was completely voluntary, with about half the school's 2,000 students attending.

Megan McGuire, co-president of the senior class, grew up in a gay household with two lesbian mothers and spoke of her experience at the assembly last fall. "It's not a sexual thing that we're talking about," she said. "It's about prejudice." But for Precious Nails of Mattapan, the subject shouldn't be mentioned at all in school. "I have a 3-year-old son and I don't want him to learn what is going on in the gay and lesbian life," Nails said. "I grew up, I didn't have to learn it and I feel like I turned out fine."

Chapter 4

RACE

INTRODUCTION

In what some called "the trial of the century," the football star, actor, and sports commentator, O. J. Simpson, was found not guilty of the charge that he had murdered his former wife and her friend. Television networks had their cameras ready in locations around the nation in order that they might record people's spontaneous reactions when the verdict was announced. And capture them they did.

However uncomfortable it may have been, one conclusion was inescapable: There was a marked correlation between race and perception of justice in the comments. Many whites were angry and typically thought that the jury, which was predominantly black, "let him off because he was black." And then there was the image of black students at Howard University clapping and cheering the not guilty verdict. To them, the judgment was just and the race of the jurors was not a significant factor. Emotional reactions were running high on both sides of the decision. In the aftermath of the Simpson verdict, some observers have concluded that the racial divide in America has increased.

Emotion often clouds vision and good judgment. And when it comes to discussing education, not much is more emotional than the topic of race. Yet if we are to make significant progress in improving the quality of education for *all* children, emotion must not overrule reason as we make our judgments and formulate our school policies. What, if anything, can the schools do to ameliorate what many consider to be America's most pressing social problem—race relations? What role, if any, should race play in making educational decisions?

We're All Racists Now
H. G. Bissinger

When first spied off the thick spine of the Eisenhower Expressway, Proviso West High School suggests all the ingredients of a stable place. Its low-slung beige brick, undulating for acre after acre over the fairways and greens of the old golf course in Hillside, Ill., makes it seem more like a corporate campus than a suburban high school. Its location, nestled in a comfortable patch between a cemetery, a shopping mall and a movie theater, gives it the feel of a sanctuary sealed off from the monotone of Chicago's western suburbs, with their endless strip malls and four-lane highways and fast-food restaurants. In the strong early morning light, when the school parking lot is empty of the rattle of cars, and students have not yet begun to congregate outside the metal doors waiting to be let in, there is something truly monumental about Proviso West, a place built in the helter-skelter suburban-boomtown days of the 1950's—and built to endure.

Inside the school there is the feel of a place where taxpayers' money was well spent—a kind of mini-Pentagon, with more than half a million square feet. Adjacent to the main complex is the high canopy of the field house with its fast track surfaces. There is the gym with row after row of rising bleachers, and the sparkling indoor pool where a swimmer pulls smooth, fine strokes that barely break the water.

The grounds, at first glance, are just as lovely: well-kept wooden benches, an outdoor stage, the Senior Circle courtyard so filled with the chirping of birds that it sounds rigged—all the shrubbery impeccably manicured and flat topped. In one corner of Senior Circle there is an elegant sundial that was donated by the class of 1963. Near the sundial is a stone bench donated by the class of 1962 with an inscription that says, "The Future Belongs to Those Who Prepare for It."

Proviso West, and its sister school Proviso East, form what is known as Proviso Township High Schools District 209. Ten communities feed into the district, all of them in the near-western suburbs of Chicago, with populations ranging from 4,000 to 27,000. Beginning in the 1950's, many of them boomed from tiny villages into thriving, healthy communities. Some, like Bellwood, had their roots among the working class. Others, like Hillside and Westchester, were bedroom communities where median incomes and housing prices ranked among the top 35 percent of all Chicago suburbs. During this growth spurt they were also distinguished by something else—they were almost totally white. Of the communities feeding into the schools, only one, Maywood, had any black population to speak of in 1960. The others all had black populations of less than 1 percent.

It was in this era that Proviso (pronounced pro-VEYE-zo) West was spawned. Built in the late 1950's with a $6.75 million bond issue, it was more than a

SOURCE: *The New York Times Magazine,* May 29, 1994, pp. 27–33; 43; 50; 53–54; 56. Reprinted with permission from *The New York Times.*

school: it was a symbol. At the dedication ceremonies on Nov. 16, 1958, the words of the American educator James Bryant Conant were invoked: "Our purpose is to cultivate in the largest number of our future citizens an appreciation of both the responsibilities and the benefits which come to them because they are American and free."

Later on, at the punch-and-cookie tours arranged by volunteers, several thousand people came to admire the place their tax dollars had built. And what a place it was, with floor-to-ceiling glass and sweeping curves and airy space, with touches like the tiled outdoor mall that could be used for student dances and the mosaic mural of Sioux Indian themes that arched its way along the western facade. The Chicago newspapers heralded the school's opening.

Thirty-six years later, those touches have become almost invisible. The mural is still there, but the blue of its tile is faded, almost lusterless. Students have been discouraged from using the Senior Circle since someone set fire to the shrubbery there a few years ago. Once-white curtains now spill out of the windows like dirty handkerchiefs hanging out of pockets. On a bulletin board in the social studies office, a teacher has posted a chart from *Mad* magazine showing that, one way or another, for today's students all academic roads lead to the same thing anyway—a job flipping burgers at McDonald's.

Over the past decade, Proviso West has experienced a dizzying degree of demographic and socioeconomic change. In the 1990–91 academic year, 11 percent of the students were from low-income families. This year, the figure has almost doubled, to 19 percent. In 1973–74, the school, with roughly 4,500 students, was less than 1 percent black and Asian, nearly 2 percent Latino and 98 percent white. Now, 20 years later, there are only 2,300 students, of whom roughly 56 percent are black, 22 percent Latino, 18 percent white and the balance Asian.

Between 1970 and 1990, the population of the township shrank nearly 12 percent, to 152,000. Pockets of middle-class comfort became increasingly harder to find. Factories and companies that had once prospered there shut their doors. Looming over these unhappy developments was rampant white flight: as the black population more than tripled, the white population plummeted. Whites are still the predominant racial group in Proviso Township, but in the past two decades their numbers have fallen 40 percent.

Some whites who went to Proviso West in the 1970's would never, ever send their children there. They say the best thing to do would be to close it and sell it off to a big corporation. They describe it as a "jail" and complain about how the place is killing their property values. When asked to think of ways to improve the educational environment of the school they come up with ideas like metal detectors and hall sweeps with K-9 police tracking dogs.

"I would say with metal detectors, I would feel a little bit better," says one parent, Annette LoBello. "You never know who's going to come in a car and get you with an AK-47." (School officials say there has been only one shooting incident on Proviso West property in the history of the school.) As for the K-9 dogs, LoBello sees the idea as a plus for everybody. "So bring the dogs in. If nothing's happening then what's the worry?"

LoBello has decided that her two children, both of whom are not even 10 yet, will not go to Proviso West. But the whole issue of public education is still very much on her mind. She served as the coordinator of Citizens United for Better Education, a movement founded by several Westchester residents in 1992 to explore the possibility of "de-annexing" their town from the Proviso high-school district. The idea was to join a neighboring district that had appreciably better American College Testing (A.C.T.) scores, that sent more students to college and that, like Westchester, was more than 90 percent white. The effort failed, but LoBello, a reservations agent for Southwest Airlines, is now working with the group on another plan in which Westchester and perhaps one or two other communities would separate from Proviso West and create their own school district.

Thomas Winkler, a lawyer from Westchester who is among those studying the new district idea, explains the impetus behind it: the needs of students from Westchester are simply no longer compatible with the needs of other Proviso West students. "You're just getting a very different student coming out of the Westchester elementary and middle schools, a much brighter student," says Winkler.

Blacks believe such assertions are unfair and insulting. Many students from Westchester may come to Proviso West better prepared to do the work, they say, but that does not make them inherently smarter than the school's other pupils. Wylmarie Sykes, a professor at Malcolm X College in Chicago and the current president of District 209's school board, says: "There are some Westchester students who do well and some who do less so. You have high-achieving students of all races and economic backgrounds."

As proof, she points to her four children, who graduated from Proviso East and went on to academic success at M.I.T., Georgetown and West Point. She acknowledges that there are students at both Proviso East and Proviso West who are suffering academically but maintains that their problems are often the fault of the schools serving them.

Teaching must become more innovative, the school day must be lengthened, the community must pass property tax referendums for urgently needed improvements in instruction. "I think all kids can learn everything that we have to teach," she says. "The same things that the honors kids are taught can be learned by all kids."

"It's not that your child is better than my child," says Janice Bennett, whose daughter, Charise, ranks in the top 10 percent of the junior class at Proviso West. "It's only color that separates the two."

But that separation is becoming wider all the time. Proviso West is an example of the painful drama of race that is being played out in many communities. A kind of negative synergy is at work. Whites respond to integration by abandoning their communities the moment blacks move in. Blacks, seeking suburban refuge from the crime and chaos of the city just as whites did 20 years earlier, move, only to find themselves still isolated.

It's Friday, and to Bill Paterson, a Proviso West social studies teacher, it's been a long week. The inspiration doesn't come so easily anymore, and it is on days like this, when he feels tired, just wanting to go home, that the VCR comes in so handy. It's the second video of the week for his sociology classes. The first was a *20/20* segment on an exorcism conducted by a Roman Catholic priest, and Paterson felt obliged to warn that the material, in which the subject of the exorcism screams and speaks in tongues and has to be tied to a chair, might be too scary to watch. Roughly 10 minutes into the film now being watched, the process of human reproduction is shown. Paterson hasn't said much so far, but the image of sperm meeting egg causes him to speak up.

"How many people know about this from personal experience?" he asks the class, which is made up of juniors and seniors and is mostly minority. "We got any fathers in here? Any mothers?" Some of the students laugh embarass-edly, but then, this is Mr. Paterson, or Mr. P. as his students call him, and Mr. P. often jokes.

With the film playing, Paterson continues his line of questioning, whispering to a female student, "We got anyone pregnant in here?" She turns her head and looks at him almost quizzically, as if tying to figure out what on earth such a question has to do with sociology class. She says nothing, hoping to dismiss the whole thing with a little laugh, but he doesn't let up. "Come on, you'd know."

There are days, particularly with his junior honors class, when Paterson is an electric teacher. In trying to explain the theories behind the French Revolu-tion, for example, he used to ask students to consider what it would be like if there were a revolution at Proviso West. He then assigned each of his students roles, producing a lively, spirited debate. He doesn't do much of that anymore, and he explains why: "I have run into problems now that I have a lot of black kids. They won't shut up."

Over the past 20 years, the school's academic performance has faltered. Some teachers say that students in general no longer have a thirst for learning. They're drowning in the immediacy of the cable age and the video age and are sadly incapable of viewing their future beyond the next 24 hours. These teachers also say that, given the changing economic landscape, it's difficult to blame students. It must be hard, they say, for a Proviso West student to walk across the frontage road to the mall and see empty storefront windows, or to hear sto-ries from older friends who have come back home with their hard-earned col-lege degrees and can't find jobs that will pay the rent, much less repay the tuition loans. "It breaks my heart when I think about what they're going to be in 10 years," says Ann Rebello, a social studies teacher, of her students.

Rebello is also acutely aware of the assumptions that are made about Pro-viso West students purely on the basis of their color. Upon hearing that she had taken a job at a school that was more than 80 percent minority, acquaintances immediately assumed she was "in a bad school with bad kids." They kept telling her that the only way to survive would be with toughness and rigidity. But when she got to Proviso West last fall as a new teacher, Rebello found students who were open, yearning for attention. "You don't have to be tough to teach here," she says.

Paterson, who is 53 and started at the school in 1971 when it was virtually all white, sees the place very differently. In relating what he believes is the inevitable decline of Proviso West into an underclass school, he stresses the socioeconomic changes that have transformed the township over the past 20 years but also focuses on one racial group—the blacks. His outspokenness has made him something of a patron saint among some white students. "There are some days I come in, I don't want to see anyone black," he says. "I've had it."

Paterson cites the behavior of blacks in the hallways between classes ("The conduct of some of these black males is incredibly immature—the yelling, the screaming, the way they hit girls"). He talks about the time three blacks came into his class and started beating up one of his black students with a bat. (As it happened, none of the three attended the school.) He tells stories of white students who have dropped out because they couldn't stand being with blacks ("You know, Mr. P., I'm sitting in an English IV Academic class, and I'm sitting here with these black kids who can't even write a complete sentence"). He also tells the story of a former teacher, now retired, who moved to a small coastal island so he would never have to see another black face.

"I wish I could leave this year," says Paterson. "There are days I come here when I can hardly face it. I have to force myself."

■ ■ ■

Contrary to Proviso West's reputation for violence and turmoil, often fostered by people who have never set foot inside during school hours, the place is orderly and quiet. The curriculum, in the best tradition of public education, is expansive and egalitarian, offering courses ranging from the vocational to the college level. The students, rich and poor, black, Latino and white, say it is still possible to get a good education.

It is true that A.C.T. scores at Proviso West are below those of surrounding suburban districts. It is true that the number of students who go on to four-year colleges is not as high as in those districts. But it's also true that many Proviso students have come from the difficult streets of Chicago, and that even within their new communities the temptations of drugs and gangs may still be present. Many also come from families so troubled that just getting to school is a major accomplishment.

"We are at one of the most complex times in the history of this district," says Thomas Jandris, Proviso West's principal. When he came to the school in 1992, he saw a place that confirmed that first-glance impression off the Eisenhower Expressway—a classic and beautiful suburban school. "The facade was calm," he says. But once he got inside, it didn't take very long to realize something else entirely: "The undertow was incredible." Jandris found a place beset by an overwhelming flatness, as if nearly everyone who worked there had just about given up and accepted as a *fait accompli* the downward cycle of the school. The attitude toward students, he felt, was symbolized by the lack of doors on the bathroom entrances, even on the stalls inside.

"It's not very elegantly stated," says Jandris. "It sounds very simple, but education and the best interests of students have grown far apart." And for the past two years he has worked to bridge this gap. He put doors back on the bathrooms.

He abolished the requirement for students to wear IDs around their necks like dog tags. At the same time, he has been tough, instituting a strict new attendance policy.

But he also knows that the road to recovery for Proviso West is long, and he speaks bluntly about two issues that make change so elusive. One is the conduct of the school board that for 20 years, during the most pivotal time in the history of the Proviso district, fretted excessively over maintenance contracts and patronage hiring and not enough over the educational needs of its students. The other issue that concerns Jandris may ultimately pose far more of a challenge. "The bigotry is the same as it's been for 10,000 years of humanity," he says. "It's based on ignorance and fear. It is alive and well in Proviso Township in very insidious ways."

Whites may not be sending their children to Proviso West in significant numbers anymore, but they still exert enormous influence over both Proviso West and Proviso East. The high-school district is still predominantly white and has a very high proportion of elderly residents. It doesn't take much imagination to wonder how white voters respond when asked to approve property-tax rate hikes so spending can be increased at its two predominantly minority high schools.

Since 1969, there have been three referendums asking voters to approve increases in the property tax rate for Proviso Township High School District 209's education fund, and each has been defeated. Schools ask taxpayers for more money all the time, but in the Proviso district the need is double-edged: to maintain the current quality of education and also to afford better instruction for the students at both high schools who are considered at risk. The percentage coming into Proviso West with serious learning problems continues to grow, and administrators say that as many as 25 percent of all students at the school are "at risk" academically. "You want to stretch and prepare and help get ready those students who are clearly not ready now," says Dale Crawford, the district's assistant superintendent for curriculum and instruction. "They need more attention. The resources they need are significantly more than for the kid who is O.K."

Financial relief seems unlikely, however, either at the local or state level. School financing proposals are often talked about in the state capital, Springfield, but the net result of the impassioned rhetoric, says Peter Parrillo, Proviso Township High Schools' business manager, has been loss. State educational aid has declined from 12 percent of the district budget in 1984 to about 7 percent for the fiscal year that ends in June. "I have always been appalled at the way in which the state of Illinois, and the local officials of Cook County, have prostituted education in this state," says Parrillo, who is retiring this year and feels free to speak his mind.

If the State Legislature does nothing, and local taxpayers do nothing, the only other choice is obvious. Curriculum gets cut to the bone, extracurricular activities get cut to the bone, troubled students continue to founder and the very mission of Proviso West, to provide comprehensive education for everyone, becomes impossible to sustain. It turns into the educational equivalent of a public housing project. Those with the greatest needs stay because they have no other place to go; those with the greatest means flee farther west to other suburbs, or to the parochial and private schools that ring Proviso West like buzzards.

"You do a slash-and-burn cut," says James Boyd, school board member. "Then the remaining ones who do care are going to leave."

In the meantime, some of those who work in the district continue to fight the good fight. A new superintendent was hired for the district in 1992 after a national search. New principals were put in place at Proviso West and Proviso East. The school board has been revamped. A carefully written mission statement has been distributed in the hope of creating unity and a strong sense of purpose.

Patricia Berent doesn't have a problem with educational credos. In her experience as a teacher at Proviso West since 1969, she has seen them come and go. On paper they sound wonderful, sometimes inspirational. But in her third-floor classroom during first period, they seem as vapid as the poster on the wall of Bo Jackson with a book in his hands. Most of the students in her remedial English class are freshmen who, though not typical of the majority of Proviso West students, read at the third-grade to the fifth-grade level, causing Berent to wonder what, if anything, they were taught before they got here. "It's too late to make these kids academically prepared for college," says Berent. "It's almost too late for them to be at a maturity level to get a good job." A girl sucks on a lollipop. A boy examines his finger.

Today, Berent's class and another remedial English class are working together. The assignment is to take a statement by a noted black figure and explain the essence of its meaning. Two gleaming banks of Macintosh computers flank the walls. The students sit down before them. There is the familiar whir and click of floppy disk into disk drive. Some just stare at the screen. Some play, piling up data window after window on the gleaming screen like thick layers of paint, to the point where they can no longer find the file they were working on in the first place. Some write a sentence, maybe two, before becoming absolutely locked up, frozen, shifting from side to side, calling for the teacher because they need help, desperately need help.

"Miss Berent. . . Hey, Miss Berent. . . ."

She works the room diligently, poking and prodding and nurturing and negotiating, moving back and forth from Macintosh to Macintosh. She knows the children are trying, and she is trying. Slowly, bit by bit, words appear on the screens:

The pepel from wen Martin Luther King Jr. Lived did not wrly get along. Martin Luther King wanted wigth and blck people.

Dr. Martin Luther King Jr. Brogth the word to me and some of my friends to. That if a person do a job, be the best they can be, so Iam. By cutting hair and putting S cure in pepole hair. Like the other day, when I was looking at TV the door bell rung, and my little brother answer it. It was three boys with some mast up hair comeing into my house. So I cut there hair, because they need it. And they were happy.

Violence in America is very bad. I saw a let of bad things in my life, once I saw
a boy get shot at a fair where I lived at it was about three people got shot that
night. One time I saw this man get beat so bad that he was crying blood.

Alexis Wallace has that look on her face, eyes blazing, mouth slightly open,
and she's walking through the aisles between desks on one of her patented
search-and-destroy missions. Weren't they listening at the very beginning of the
semester when she told them that Shakespeare's *Julius Caesar* was one of her
all-time favorites? Did they think she was joking? If they did, they won't be laughing now. And she knows who the slackers are. She knows who read Act I last
night and who did not, who is for real and who thinks they can fake their way
through a question by pleading that it was too hard to understand and, Come
on, Mrs. Wallace, how were we supposed to figure out all that crazy language,
"thou" this and "yore" that? Why do they think she gave the quiz at the beginning of class, and why do they think she immediately graded it and then read
the scores aloud, one by one, in a very, very loud voice: "Fifty!" "Twenty!" "Fifty!"
    "I did not say your scores to embarrass you. I said your scores to moti-
vate you."
    And now she is off through the classroom, and no one is safe, not even the
girl at the back who has taken her pacifier out of its little plastic holder and is
fervently sucking on it. "I want to make sure that you're getting it," she says almost sweetly. "There is no shame. We're all learning." Her students in the class,
sophomores in a college preparatory curriculum, aren't falling for it; and one
thing is for sure: none of the students have their heads resting on their desks so
they can take a little nap. In some classes you can do that and no one messes with
you. But not in Mrs. Wallace's class.
    She finds her primary victim. It is Keith. She reads a passage from *Julius
Caesar,* Act I, Scene II: "Why, there was a crown offered him: and being offered
him, he put it by with the back of his hand, thus; and then the people fell a-
shouting."
    She asks Keith to explain. He says nothing. She repeats the passage, her
voice even louder, so that pretty much everyone on all three floors of the school
can hear it. He tries to say he doesn't understand it, but she cuts him off mid-
sentence. She won't tolerate that excuse, because she knows what he can do
when he does the homework, reads the study guides and adheres to the New
Year's resolution that Wallace set for the class at the beginning of the semester.
Positive Mental Attitude, P.M.A.
    "You're not an imbecile. You're supposed to have an I.Q. over 10!"
    She reads another passage and once again there is the same silence.
    "Are you trying? Are you *trying?* No!"
    He still pleads ignorance, but it doesn't register. After all, he failed the quiz
miserably, and that tells her it isn't a matter of aptitude but a matter of motivation and self-confidence.
    "I am trying to open up the passage between the two ears," she says. She
eases off after that, the fire and brimstone replaced with familial warmth, and
after class, students rush up to her calling her "Mother," and she calls them

"Baby." Ten years from now, few of the students in this class may remember a line of *Julius Caesar*. But she is pretty sure none of them will forget the experience of having been taught it. Her teaching philosophy derives from something Frederick Douglass once said: "If nothing is expected of a man, he finds that expectation hard to contradict."

"We have some teachers who say these kids can't learn and don't know this and don't know that," says Wallace. "I think some teachers use as an excuse, 'This is Proviso,' and they don't have to perform."

■ ■ ■

The day after the debacle of *Julius Caesar,* Act I, Wallace gives a quiz on Act II. The failure rate is high again, and she is not pleased, not pleased at all. Her mouth is pursed, as if she just tasted something sour, and she isn't interested in excuses, not interested in who had to do what after school. When the bell rings and students gather up their books, Wallace's eyes get that heat-seeking glare.

"Sit down! This is my time. I'm talking!"

There will be a quiz on Act III. The scores will be read aloud so everyone knows exactly where they stand. And those who fail. . . .

■ ■ ■

"O.K., the day of reckoning is here," she says the next day as she begins to read the results, somber and quiet, as if it's really her own day of reckoning. "Seventy." "Eighty." "One hundred." "Eighty." "Eighty." "Ninety." "Ninety." All but one of the students have passed. But Wallace still has something to say to the class.

"Give yourselves a hand."

The brightest students in the school are in a double-period honors course for juniors called American Studies. Entrance is based on strict academic requirements, and the reading list is an educator's dream. The racial makeup of the students in the course is almost the opposite of the makeup of the school. Of the 52 students, only 7 are black and 4 Latino.

Most of the other students appear to take comfort in the honors courses. They like the intellectual challenge and also seem to relish any situation at school in which they are in the majority. As one student put it, her process for picking senior-year elective courses has as much to do with racial makeup as it does with course content. The more blacks there are in a course, the less inclined she is to take it: "I'm thinking, 'A lot of blacks in this class, a lot of blacks in this class, a lot of blacks in this class. . . .'"

Six of the students in American Studies are eager to say how they feel about going to school here. They feel that what they have to say is crucial to understanding the school. They also feel that as members of the school's white minority, they often go unheard. They are involved in extracurricular activities. They do well in school. They all want to go to college, and they all have ambitions to become lawyers and doctors and business executives. Most of them live in Westchester, where they saw almost no blacks and did not even have a single black teacher at their grammar schools.

As the six students begin to describe the school they seem a little like children attacking a piñata. "It's like going to hell here," says one. "I get pushed, and because I'm white I can't say anything because there's too many of 'em. I'll get my butt kicked."

"They think they can touch you, they think they can do anything to you."

"I cannot stand the race. I'll never date anyone who isn't white."

"They're always saying 'slave' this and 'slave' that. Sorry, I don't know a slave. I never owned a slave. I'm sick of them throwing it in our face."

When asked to describe a typical black, one of the students responds this way: "Ignorant, rude, loud."

"Ignorant and scum, a lot of poverty, self-righteous, you owe me that, you owe me this, gimme, gimme, gimme," says another.

One student brings up a scene in *2001: A Space Odyssey* when a group of apes goes out of control: "In a typical day in the hallways, that's what it looks like here." Others laugh and nod their heads approvingly. They think it's a good description. They like it.

Despite this atmosphere, they agree that they have gotten a strong education at Proviso West. They also have a potential solution for fixing the school's problems: remove the predominantly black town of Bellwood from the school's attendance boundaries. Or, if that won't work, remove almost exclusively white Westchester from the attendance boundaries and let its students go someplace else. As they talk about it, it sounds almost like a liberation movement in an occupied territory. They sound just like their parents.

On another day, the seven blacks enrolled in American Studies file into an empty classroom to speak their minds. They, too, are honors students. They, too, plan to go to college. They, too, have ambitions to be lawyers and doctors and businessmen, and they all come from Bellwood, the place the white students would dump from the attendance boundaries. They say they're acutely aware of a double standard that exists for them among whites, the expectation that they can't do the work. At the beginning of the year it was made clear to the American Studies class that those who could not keep up would be asked to leave. That standard is one of the reasons the course is so good. "Everybody looked at us," says Charise Bennett. Four students were asked to leave during the school year, all of them white. And when a cheating scandal broke out, it was among white students.

When they talk about whites, it isn't with bitterness but with frustration, almost amusement. Of the seven, only one says that the experience of being at Proviso West has made her feel more prejudiced against whites. They laugh about the way whites insist on talking to them in what they think is "black dialect"—the way they say "What's up" and "Hey, girl." They also laugh at the way whites, when they go on field trips, stare out the window of the bus and exclaim over graffiti, as if they had never seen it before. The whites strike them as being insulted and utterly unaware of the larger world outside their communities.

These black students also talk about the way other black students often treat them, about how they're accused of being "nerds" and "sellouts" because they are on the honors track. "Why are you in a class with all the white kids?" they are asked. "Why are you using a white man's book?" Steven Freeman Jr., the one black male in American Studies, gets such comments routinely. "They are shocked that a black male can read," he says. "They expect me to take the book and throw it in my locker." He described the following interplay between teacher and student as being typical:

"Excuse me, I'm just trying to wake you up so you can pay attention."

"Well, I'm going back to sleep because you ain't sayin' nothing."

Because of the expectations that many white (and black) students have of them, these seven students exist almost entirely in their own world. "We're not accepted by the white people because they think we're not smart enough," says Loura Banks. "We're not accepted by black people because they think we're too smart. So we just hang with each other."

But they continue to believe in the school, and they are committed to it, and so are many of their parents. Loura Banks's father, Leo, is a member of the school board. Charise Bennett's mother, Janice, is so involved in her daughter's education that teachers, if they believe in self-preservation, should just run when they see her, for as Janice Bennett puts it, "If something happens to my child, someone's in trouble."

Because of all the rumors of violence swirling around Proviso West, Janice Bennett sent her daughter to a parochial school her freshman year. But the atmosphere there, which included fights during chapel, wasn't what she expected from any school, much less one that was costing her $4,000 a year. So Charise went to Proviso West, where she has excelled, has been challenged and is said by some teachers to be the smartest student in the school. Her mother, a supervisor with AT&T nearby in Oak Brook, is aware that her daughter is perceived as being something of an anomaly at the school, but it doesn't bother her a whole lot as long as Charise continues to get a good education.

"She hasn't sold out to Whitey," says Janice Bennett. "She's sold out to her mama, who will kick her butt." Through her daughter, she is also aware of how many white students are disgruntled and want to leave. But she knows the survival of Proviso West depends on their staying, not because they're any smarter than her daughter, but because of the political and economic clout they carry. "If all the white children choose to leave," she says, "and it's just Hispanics and blacks, the quality of the school will go down."

■ ■ ■

It's the end of another day at Proviso West, and for Dennis Bobbe, a social studies teacher, it's not a moment too soon. He came to the school in 1966 when it was at its apex, filled with those seemingly timeless shows of spirit, the pep rallies, the sock hops, the earnest debates over war and peace. Now, it's nobody's school, all the spirit sucked dry. He finds nothing remarkable about Proviso West at all, except, perhaps, for the pathos. "They're actively resisting learning," he says of his students. "They just don't want to learn. It's not fun. It's too much effort." He pauses, and then takes a turn inward.

"Maybe it's me."

He knows they're bored to tears. He knows what their ability to analyze or do something in-depth is. He knows what the pop culture effects of television and music are, "the bing-bang-boom," as he calls it.

"I can't compete."

He caters to them, minimizing the complexity of the material and the amount. He tries to be an entertainer, even though that contradicts his whole persona—beard, soft voice, pudgy body. "Kids come in asking for a routine. A vaudeville show. Abbott and Costello. Who's on first?" He talks about United States history and he sees the glaze set in their eyes. He could lecture naked. He could lecture upside down. He could not lecture at all. Would they even notice? He's getting too old, too entrenched to grope for meaningful answers. "I am near the end of my career."

Yet he wonders what happened to the notion of the American public school as a sacred place, a vital place, a place unlike any other in the world. "What was it that peeled away? What was it that was lost?"

It is a gray, late-winter day as he teaches his seventh-period class. He has pulled down a map depicting the boundary changes in Europe during World War I. Over another blackboard hangs a pithy statement that reads, "Not Preparing! Is Preparing Not to Pass." As Bobbe talks about the war, he tries to engage everyone, including those who have their heads on their desks.

"Who is Herbert Hoover?" he asks.

"The vacuum guy?" asks one student.

"Overall, there were 10 million killed in the military in World War I," says Bobbe.

A girl yawns.

He tells them that Woodrow Wilson had once been the president of Princeton University.

"What do you mean, while he was president?" asks a student.

"No, before," says Bobbe.

He introduces Wilson's 14 points. He introduces some of the post-World War I European leaders: Clemenceau, Lloyd George.

"Boy George?" says a student.

"All right, we'll stop here. Monday, I won't be here. We'll have a movie."

The bell rings and the students shuffle out of class.

There are two narrow windows in Bobbe's classroom. From them you can see a thin line of students leaving the building. They walk past the drab wheat colors of the baseball field and the brown concrete of the football stadium. Some gather in clumps outside the tall metal gates of the school at the bus stop. Others walk past the mall, where so many stores are closed.

Maybe it's the way they seem so anonymous and swallowed up in their jackets, with those oversize hoods and long hemlines. Maybe it's just the grayness and chill of the ceaseless midwestern winter. But from Bobbe's narrow windows, as they walk slowly away, for a moment, just a brief moment before they disappear, they look as if they just finished a day shift at the factory instead of a day at school.

Do Teachers Punish According to Race?
Jon D. Hull

In the basement of Dater Junior High, just next to the boiler room and marked off by thick prison bars, school officials have crafted a fate worse than algebra class. Teachers at the school, part of the Cincinnati, Ohio, public school district, simply call it "the dungeon." Students have more descriptive—if unprintable—names for the small windowless cell. Though the prison bars are just painted on the cinder-block entrance, the punishment is real. Delinquent students must remain in the room—absolutely quiet—all day, even eating at their desks. "It's so hot and so boring," moans a seventh grader named Lance, 12, serving day two of a three-day sentence for tardiness. His pencil is worn to the nub from writing "I will follow school rules" 200 times. (The record is 500.) "This place is just terrible."

The dungeon is the center of a debate over not the effectiveness of pedagogic hard labor but the race of the punished and the race of the punishers. Black students are twice as likely to end up in the dungeon as white students; in fact, black students are twice as likely to end up disciplined throughout the entire Cincinnati public school system. It is a particularly awkward statistic for a school district mired in a 20-year-old desegregation suit. So awkward, in fact, that the board of education has agreed to an explosive remedy: if the judge concurs, the Cincinnati public schools (CPS) will soon start tracking the race of the teacher as well as the student in each discipline case. More important, those statistics will be factored into the teacher evaluation. Though the board insists that it is simply gathering relevant information to understand the racial disparity, teachers are receiving a far different message. "We're very worried," says art teacher John Rodak. "Do we have to start thinking about race now every time we discipline a student?"

Many teachers and administrators say, often barely above a whisper, that black students are much more trouble prone. Superintendent J. Michael Brandt, who is white, says that in some circumstances, "blacks tend to be more boisterous." John Concannon, a white attorney for the district, blames a "complicated mix of reasons," including the possibility that "some black males are more physical."

But twice as boisterous and twice as physical as white students? "That's ridiculous," says attorney Trudy Rauh, who represents parents and students in the bias suit against CPS that began in 1974. Eager to end the costly suit, the school board last fall acceded to the plaintiffs' demand for racial data to be collected on teachers as part of a broad new plan to hold them more accountable for students' behavior. The settlement warned that "staff members who are

---

deficient in student-behavior management will not be retained in their positions if they fail to improve."

And what exactly does this mean? teachers ask. [*sic*] Are white teachers deficient if they spend more time disciplining blacks than whites? What if black teachers discipline a disproportionate number of whites—or a high number of blacks, for that matter? And if the intention is to eliminate the racial disparity, will that be achieved by disciplining blacks less or whites more?

School officials insist that the racial data are just one small element in a comprehensive plan to help Cincinnati teachers deal with discipline problems. "It is a time-honored method of enforcing civil rights laws to keep statistics," says William Taylor, another attorney for the plaintiffs. "There is no reason to believe that the information will be misused." Brandt says, "an administrator needs good info." He has a point. Even assuming that teachers are justified in sending twice as many blacks as whites to the assistant principal—nationwide, black students are disciplined in disproportionate numbers—what about the teacher who disciplines five or even six times as many black students? Shouldn't administrators be able to identify such egregious examples of racial bias? Moreover, Superintendent Brandt says, offending teachers—meaning those instructors whose racial-discipline patterns are grossly out of whack with those of their colleagues—will first be offered counseling to improve their management skills.

The national teachers' union warns that the proposed settlement will lead to discipline quotas. "It will have a chilling effect," predicts Albert Shanker, president of the American Federation of Teachers. "Basically, teachers will throw in the towel and say, 'Why should I get into trouble?'" He compares the proposal to requiring police to make racially balanced arrests. Kathy Nemann, a seventh-grade history teacher at Crest Hills Middle School in north Cincinnati, agrees. "Teachers will simply stop referring students for discipline," she says. "They'll handle the problem in the classroom"—at the expense of all students. Donald Mooney Jr., attorney for the Cincinnati Federation of Teachers, says, "Whether you call it p.c. or whatever, it is still a form of intimidation. Teachers are worried that they are now going to have to balance their discipline referrals by race rather than calling it the way they see it. It'll be like, 'If this week I've disciplined three black students, then next week I'd better find three whites.'"

Many teachers feel overwhelmed by classroom chaos. Last month the CPS started using metal detectors in the schools. "Kids are just more aggressive now," says teacher Arthur Leahr. "You're always nervous because you wonder if the kid might have a gun." The union says teachers started to lose control in 1988, when the district abolished corporal punishment while directing administrators to reduce suspensions. "Before long, the students were running the schools," complains Tom Mooney, Don's brother and president of the Cincinnati teachers' union.

In 1991 the union pushed the CPS to impose a tough new discipline policy, which included mandatory suspension for fighting, forgery, fraud and profanity. Suspensions promptly jumped 77%. In the 1991-92 school year, more than 10,000 students—20% of the total enrollment—were suspended from school.

Many parents were infuriated, complaining, correctly, that the new policies only increased the racial discipline gap. Concedes Brandt: "We had people being suspended for looking at someone the wrong way."

Pressured by parents, the district changed course again last fall and enacted a progressive code, which offers more options short of suspension, including in-school detention. Yet the nettlesome racial disparity persists, along with the smoldering debate over whether black students are getting fair treatment. Indeed, the 1974 case that is at the root of the controversy was supposedly settled 10 years ago when the Cincinnati board of education agreed to a laundry list of remedies to desegregate the schools. But there was one caveat: After seven years, the courts would review compliance. In 1991 a judge found that the schools remained deficient in three areas, including discipline, and ordered a study, which confirmed that black males were twice as likely to be suspended. Thus the controversy and the CPS offer of statistical monitoring.

A court decision on the proposed settlement is expected within weeks. Will the ruling finally put an end [to] decades of acrimonious legal wrangling? Perhaps some of it—but not all. If the settlement is approved, the teachers' union has threatened to sue.

Talking the Talk
Lynn Schnaiberg

"What's a Homie?" Anthony Jackson asks his 5th-grade class at the 99th Street Accelerated School in Los Angeles, a series of low-rise beige stucco buildings and cement playgrounds enveloped by a tall metal fence, perched on the outskirts of the tough Watts neighborhood.

"A friend," his students answer in unison.

"What are some situations where you might want to translate into mainstream American English?" Jackson prompts. Hands fly up in his predominantly Hispanic and African-American classroom.

"At a job interview."

"In a meeting."

"In church."

"When you're trying to rent a house."

Jackson is taking his students through a skit they wrote called "homies on the phone" as part of a pilot program in the Los Angeles Unified School District

Source: *Education Week, 13,* no. 36, (June 1, 1994): pp. 26–29. Reprinted with permission from *Education Week.*

designed to teach African-American students standard English as a second language. The program is being implemented in 24 elementary schools where African-Americans make up at least half of the school's enrollment.

The skit setting: three boys lounging at home on the phone with each other, deciding if they want to go to the Raiders' football game.

GREGG: "Me an' Marcus talkin' 'bout goin' to the Raiders game. You down?"
LAMAR: "Yeah. When you comin' to get me?"
GREGG: "Well, Marcus gone call Ticket Masters and get tickets now, so dey be on will call. Then we be dere in about 40 minutes."

Marcus then calls Ticket Master and says: "Yes, I would like to order three tickets to the Raiders game this afternoon. And I'd like to charge the cost to my American Express card. . . ."

"Why do we need to speak mainstream American English?" Jackson asks after the students have read their parts.

"You might have a better chance of doing what you do."

"So they can understand you better."

The "Cash Language"

The nation's second-largest school system, enrolling more than 630,000 students, has tackled the exquisitely sensitive issue of language use in school. The subject goes beyond questions of grammar and syntax into issues of race, class, cultural identity, and teachers' attitudes and expectations.

While the Los Angeles program's tenets may seem radical to some, it is one of few efforts in the country that explicitly confront the issue as a possible means of boosting the academic achievement of black students, particularly those who live in segregated, and often linguistically isolated, neighborhoods.

Spurred by pressure from African-American parents who wanted their children to get a piece of the district's growing bilingual-education pie and by a 1989 report that called for a language-development plan for students not covered by the district's bilingual master plan, the "language development program for African-American students" was born in 1990.

It is now in its second year of implementation under the district's division of bilingual education and language acquisition and has a $1.8 million annual budget. The program does not receive federal bilingual-education funds.

Although the district has no data on whether the program is helping raise students' grades or reading-test scores, a wealth of anecdotal evidence from teachers and students suggests that the program strategies are making some inroads.

The tenor of the debate over "black English"—now termed "African-American vernacular English," "African-American language," or "ebonics"—has changed since the 1970's, when some linguists and educators rejected the teaching of standard English as a form of cultural oppression.

Today, there is more general acceptance of standard English as the "cash language"—the one students must acquire to gain access to higher education and the job market.

Given that awareness, many educators are concerned that some African-American students are not mastering standard English, oral or written. One such educator is Willie Hamilton, the principal of Webster Academy, a public elementary school in Oakland, Calif., whose enrollment is 80 percent black.

Hamilton recently gave 62 black students in his school a state-approved language-proficiency test normally used to determine eligibility for bilingual-education or English-as-a-second-language classes. The results: Only four tested as fully English proficient. A total of 26 were deemed non-English speaking.

And while many teachers and administrators say that the current system—a standard language-arts curriculum—is not working for many of these students, there is almost no agreement on what should take its place or be added to it.

Meanwhile, most teachers are left alone in their own classrooms to grapple with how to handle the language that as many as 80 percent of African-American students speak at home.

Creating a Bridge

Norma LeMoine, the director of the language-development program for African-American students, moved with her family from Austin, Tex., to Los Angeles when she was entering 7th grade. She had attended largely segregated schools in Texas, where she spoke what she calls African-American language, though she had "some facility" in standard English.

She showed up at her new school without a transcript because her family's move had been sudden. The counselors at the front desk asked her what courses she had taken in Texas. She started explaining in her "best African-American language": "Algebra one, Spanish one. . . ." But she never got beyond that. Hearing her pronunciation, the counselor looked at some of the other adults there and signed her up for remedial courses.

In college, her papers came back strewn with red marks because she used the language she grew up speaking. As an adjunct professor, she shuddered when she heard her colleagues speculating about how "those minority kids" ever got into the university, since they couldn't write.

"The language issue became one of the biggest in my school experience," she recalls. "Nobody explained to me why what I was doing was wrong, just that it was wrong. Those experiences left their mark on me."

The Los Angeles program has sent nearly 1,000 teachers and 600 paraprofessionals—mostly non-African-American—through various seminars, courses, workshops, and conferences on language and cultural issues.

The program touches 20,000 of the district's 94,000 black students, and works with parents to help them become more familiar with standard English.

Apart from arming teachers with a list of structural differences between standard English and the vernacular, there is no prepackaged curriculum. Teachers are given strategies for getting students to distinguish between "African-American language" and "mainstream American English" and suggestions on how to discuss when it's appropriate to use each.

The program's stated goal is to insure that students master standard English so that they can switch between the two languages. But it is also to combat the negative association many teachers have with the way their African-American students speak, which can lead to lowered expectations and send students off to special-education classes, LeMoine says.

The reason many black students are not using standard English is that "they don't know what to do to change their 'bad' English, and we don't know what to tell them to do it," LeMoine says. "You can sit and tell me all day that it's 'desk' instead of 'des,' but if you don't understand that what I'm saying is a result of a different linguistic rule, how can you ever change it? That's why just correcting a student doesn't work."

LeMoine, a speech pathologist, makes it clear that there are two things the program is not doing: one, eradicating the home language; two, "teaching" black English. It does, however, encourage students and parents to use the language at home and encourage teachers to use it as a "bridge" to teach standard English.

Such a bridge is necessary because, while the differences between the dialect and standard English can be subtle, LeMoine believes that what many students are speaking is a language whose structure is distinct from English—an argument hotly contested by many linguists.

Next year, LeMoine plans to use a language-proficiency test specifically targeted to African-American students, developed over the past three years by the Center for the Study of Evaluation at the University of California at Los Angeles, to gauge how well they speak and write standard English after participating in the program.

Both the state and the Los Angeles district itself have had programs with similar goals in place; the district's dates to 1978. Clearly, educators there think that these strategies hold some promise of moving away from what the district's 1989 report called the "institutionalized racism" embedded in the cavernous gaps that remain between white and African-American children's success in school.

Apparently, many other districts agree: LeMoine has been asked to speak at countless conferences across the country, and districts such as San Diego and Portland, Ore., have requested her materials and guidance in developing similar programs for their own minority students.

African Roots

Anthony Jackson, who studied political science at U.C.L.A., grew up six minutes from the school where he teaches today. Although he recently moved out, "I view this as my community," he says of the neighborhood, whose streets are lined with scraggly palm trees and small one-story stucco homes with security bars on the windows.

His grandmother still chastises him for using words like "stuff" because it's not "proper English." He views as partly generational the debate over whether the way many of his African-American students talk is a language distinct from English.

"The old guard may never accept those words on a piece of paper" because it legitimizes a means of communication that older people view as poor English, he says, pointing to a shelf full of books that include the dialect.

Clearly, his students are confused at times about what exactly African-American language is, because often it is so similar to standard English.

In "the job interview," one of the student-written skits, Demetrius says, "I need me an application for salesman, please." When Jackson asks what language Demetrius is speaking, a few students answer that it's standard English. Why? Because he said "please," so it sounds formal.

"Demetrius has manners, but he's speaking African-American language," Jackson explains. "Just because he says 'please' doesn't mean he's speaking mainstream English. I'm trying to get you guys out of that mindset."

Similar questions arise when a sentence has a contraction: Many students automatically think the person is speaking in dialect.

LeMoine, along with some linguists, maintains that the language many black students speak is rooted in the African languages of the Niger–Congo region, which share many basic grammatical rules. Since the slave descendants of the region's inhabitants were prohibited from using their native tongues, they adopted English vocabulary. But, since they were never taught "proper English," they continued to lay those English words on top of African structures.

Those patterns have been passed down to today's generation of African-Americans, LeMoine says, because children learn their basic language structures unconsciously from birth to age 4. Therefore, these students must be taught the new rule system of standard English the same way speakers of other languages have been.

LeMoine has argued before the U.S. Congress that African-American students who speak this language should be classified as "limited mainstream English proficient" and should be eligible for instruction with federal bilingual-education dollars. The U.S. Education Department and the National Association for Bilingual Education have opposed that proposal.

"That opens up a whole other set of questions: What about Appalachian white kids who speak a regional dialect?" asks James J. Lyons, NABE's executive director.

The debate over whether the African-American vernacular is a separate language or a dialect of English is "wholly unresolved," says Geneva Smitherman, a Michigan State University linguist who has written extensively on the subject.

In 1978, in what is considered the landmark "black-English case," the parents of 11 African-American students from Martin Luther King Jr. Elementary

School in Ann Arbor, Mich., won a lawsuit against the Michigan state board of education. They charged that students were being improperly placed in classes for the learning disabled because of the way they spoke. A federal judge ruled that the board had to develop a plan to teach the students standard English, saying that it had failed to address, in reading classes, the fact that the students spoke "black English."

The issue, says Molefi Kete Asante, a consultant to numerous school districts and the chairman of the Temple University department of African-American studies, is that "this very powerful, very fluent, very beautiful language has never been adequately recognized."

Linguists generally say that, if two language systems are "mutually intelligible," then they are not separate languages. Thus, since black students can understand standard English (a fact LeMoine does not dispute), the African-American vernacular is not its own language.

But according to the Center for Applied Linguistics, a research and policy group in Washington, there is no set rule to define a language. Many linguists say that it is, in fact, more difficult to learn a second dialect than a language, because the dialect differences can be so subtle.

The argument for labeling what many African-American students speak as separate language is "a political position," says Walt Wolfram, an English professor at North Carolina State University who also has studied African-American dialect. "It emphasizes a unique history and solidarity within a community. It's not justified by any objective linguistic fact," Wolfram says, though he admits that defining a language versus a dialect can be "a can of worms."

Many linguists, including Wolfram, emphasize that many groups other than African-Americans speak nonstandard English dialects and that schools need to do a better job in general about teaching dialect difference and the history behind it so that students learn not to discriminate based on the way someone speaks. In fact, many Hispanic students in the Los Angeles program's schools speak with patterns similar to those of their African-American peers.

Wolfram has developed a dialect-awareness program for North Carolina's smallest school, located on a 15-mile-long island inaccessible except by ferry. Students there speak Ocracoke—a mixture of Appalachian and Elizabethan English, Irish brogue, and other dialects.

Schools also need to convey that, while grammatical norms of English are taught and generally accepted in writing, the idea that there is just one "correct," standard spoken English is a fallacy, many linguists say.

The National Alliance of Black School Educators says it has no official stance on the debate, but its executive director, Santee Ruffin Jr., says black English should be "respected, not romanticized."

"Many African-American educators feel that perhaps the whole idea of black English has been given more status than it deserves," Ruffin adds.

He fears that legitimizing it as a language can "pressure a student to go further outside of the educational mainstream."

The National Council of Teachers of English declines to take a position, but Miles A. Myers, the executive director, says that "in general, we've approached this as a dialect question."

Regardless, many educators say, if a program such as LeMoine's can help insure academic success for more students by validating the language, schools need to sit up and take notice.

When to Correct

A few months ago, one of Jackson's students at the 99th Street Accelerated School was arguing with another boy during an art lesson and blurted out: "I ain't got no glue stick."

Jackson recalls, "I just couldn't leave it alone, I had to get at it." So, he spent 15 minutes explaining that speakers of African-American language often use a form of multiple negation that doesn't surface in standard English, mapping out on the blackboard the different grammatical structures.

But during a recent lesson on adding mixed numbers and improper fractions, students often shouted out answers using nonstandard English: "But how you do dat?" "Naw, Mr. Jackson, I be trying to tell you how I figurin' it."

And they did the same in speaking to one another. "Don't dis here look fresh?" one girl said to another as she made a design with her colored plastic shapes.

Many educators say that the issue is not whether to correct students who use the vernacular, but how and when—and who decides when it is appropriate to use one language over the other.

"None of this is easily reduced to a rule or policy," says Myers of the English teachers' council.

"The key is that kids should not lose their dignity in the process," adds Ruffin of the black educators' alliance.

Johnathan Williams, an African-American who teaches sixth grade at the 99th Street School, says that before he started the language-development program, he "felt like most middle-class white guys: that the students weren't speaking correctly." So, he would tell them, "You don't say it like that." Today, he asks students to come up with "another way" of saying it.

While some educators argue that standard English is the language of school, period, linguists Wolfram and Carolyn Adger, a sociolinguist in the University of Maryland's college of education, say such an approach flies in the face of reality.

"I don't think schools need to draw the line where kids use standard English and where they use dialect, because kids already know what it is," Adger says.

Their work in five predominantly black elementary schools in Baltimore illustrates that most students use standard English in "literacy events," such as formal discussions and presentations. That practice is consistent with when most educators say they would correct their students' language use.

"In math class, if they tell me an answer in dialect, but they have the right answer, I accept their response totally," Williams says.

But "when kids are taught to write essays, it must be edited for standard English. Period," says Deborah M. McGriff, who was the superintendent of the Detroit public schools from 1991 to 1993.

The job-interview skit written by Jackson's students makes a similar point by having the candidate who speaks in dialect brushed aside by a second who speaks standard English and gets an immediate interview.

"My child needs to know that he won't get a job talking like 'Yo man, whazzup,'" says Walter Waddles, the father of two sons in Los Angeles schools.

But, says Brenda Powell-Bolder, who has four sons in the district, "I have enough faith in our kids to decide what's appropriate, once we arm them with the knowledge."

A few teachers using the strategies of the language-development program say that their students have become so sensitized to the differences that they have started to correct each other.

But LeMoine points out that many teachers in her program come to her "dismayed" by the fact that their students still are speaking in dialect on the playground, with their friends, and in class.

"I think the bottom line is that teachers don't want to deal with these sticky problems," says Chris Moggia, a fourth-grade teacher at the 99th Street School. "Most probably wish it would just go away."

"White-People Talk"

Equan Hughey, a 5th grader in Jackson's class, would not speak or write standard English in class one year ago because "most people told me it was white-people talk."

He adds, "But that's why all the white people got the jobs."

Moggia, his 4th-grade teacher, explained to him that as a young white man growing up in Santa Barbara, Calif., he used to talk "surfer-dude" language.

"I never really thought about the differences until I saw Mr. Moggia writing stuff on the board," Equan says. "I used to want to just stay in African-American language. I thought I could use it all through my life, but now I know I can't."

He still speaks mostly in dialect with his friends because he says that if he spoke standard English with them "they be thinking you like a nerd."

Now, Equan says he wants to learn standard English and be able to "switch up" to it as his dad does, so he can be sure to get a football scholarship to a college "far away from here."

There is no research showing conclusively that black youths simply refuse to use standard English, as opposed to not having been taught to speak it properly. Yet, many observers do see such resistance, and say that it only grows more powerful as students get older.

And, some say, that resistance is a reaction at least in part to the subtle or not-so-subtle messages the education system sends to these students about their own self-worth, which is inextricably linked with the way they express themselves.

"If teachers don't connect to you as a human being, then there are a lot of things students won't do for you," McGriff says. "A lot of things surrounding the school environment need to change in order to move this issue" of teacher attitudes toward the language.

"How can you say he talks wrong when that's the way he's talking with his auntie?" asks Yolanda Manigault, who has a son and daughter in Los Angeles schools. "What are you saying about my family?"

Adger notes, "The way these kids talk can bring forth such venom from people."

Or if not venom, then at least a perception of ignorance and ineptitude, says John Baugh, a linguist who has researched issues in black English at Stanford University's school of education.

"Teachers tend to judge as far superior those students of color who orally have mastered the standard English," Baugh says. "And when you add race to linguistic stereotypes, the problem gets more complex."

Previous research has suggested that many African-American students associate academic success with being white. So, if standard English is associated with academic success, it can be tough to sell its advantage. But by validating the home language, LeMoine says, her program is helping to defuse the situation that students are rebelling against.

Like Equan, many students in Jackson's class say they don't speak standard English at home or with their friends for fear of being called white, although they know that standard English can be part of their ticket to upward economic mobility.

"They're really looking for a sense of self by the 6th grade; the recoil can definitely be intense," Williams says. "The attitude in the community is, 'Why does anyone need standard English?' It's my job to show them that it is valuable for life outside the 'hood.'"

Says Kelly Walls, a 4th-grade teacher at Crescent Heights Elementary School: "I don't like to be a dictator. You give them options, give them the choice. Some students are at the point where they say, 'I'll talk any way I want.' I say fine, then explain to them the consequence for not learning how to speak both ways."

DIFFERENT LANGUAGE, DIFFERENT RULES

The following are some of the linguistic differences between mainstream American English and African-American language. The patterns in the latter, some linguists argue, are derived from the rules governing many West African languages and persist in the language that many African-American students speak, using English vocabulary.

MAINSTREAM AMERICAN ENGLISH	AFRICAN-AMERICAN LANGUAGE
The "th" sound is regularly used at the beginning of words.	At the beginning of words, "th" is pronounced as "d." The "th" sound does not exist in many West African languages.
So: then, they	So: den, dey
To show possession, speakers use an apostrophe followed by "s."	To show possession, speakers use word order and word stress.
So: John's cousin	So: John cousin
The "irregular" past tense of the verb "to be":	The "regular" past tense of the verb "to be":

SINGULAR	PLURAL	SINGULAR	PLURAL
I was	We were	I was	We was
You were	You were	You was	You was
He was	They were	He was	They was

Two negatives in a sentence make a positive statement.	The more negatives used in a sentence the more negative the statement becomes.
So: "It isn't likely that there won't be any rain" means it will probably rain.	So: "Nobody don't have no excuse" means everyone is without an excuse.

SOURCE: The Language Development Program for African-American Students, Los Angeles United School District.

The End of Integration
James S. Kunen

In room CCII (make that 202) of Martin Luther King Latin Grammar Middle School in Kansas City, Missouri, Ms. Dickerson's rhetoric students are engaged in a public-speaking contest. Sixth-grader Jo Ann Carter, dressed in the school uniform of white blouse and plaid skirt, has chosen a speech by the school's eponym: "If something isn't done, and in a hurry, to bring the colored peoples of the World out of their long years of poverty, their long years of hurt and neglect," she declaims forcefully, "the whole world is doomed."

Jo Ann's mother, Catherine Carter, looks on approvingly. Jo Ann has earned all A's except for a B in phys ed, and her mother's got the report cards in her pocketbook to prove it. "I was lucky to get her into this school," says Carter, a medical secretary. King, a one-story brick building in a ramshackle area well east of Troost Avenue—Kansas City's approximate racial dividing line—offers an enriched program of classical language and related subjects such as rhetoric. "Well, not lucky—I lied. She didn't get in the first time, so I applied again and said she was white."

This is what things have come to in the latter days of school desegregation in Kansas City. For the sake of desegregation, blacks are sometimes barred from the most popular schools on account of their race, lest they tilt the enrollment too far from the goal of 35% white students. Like most urban systems, the Kansas City, Missouri, School District (KCMSD) has lost white students to the suburbs in droves, which has made the task of achieving racial balance nearly impossible. After deciding that inner-city students could not be bused out to the suburbs as part of a mandatory desegregation plan, a federal district court ordered the state and KCMSD to spend $1.7 billion to create a top-notch system, in part to lure suburban whites. Then, last June, the Supreme Court decreed that the district court had no authority to order expenditures aimed at attracting suburban whites.

When the history of court-ordered school desegregation is written, Kansas City may go down as its Waterloo. Said to be the nation's most ambitious and expensive magnet plan, Kansas City's effort is unlikely to be matched anywhere. In fact, the high court's action has accelerated the pace at which cities across the country are moving to undo mandatory desegregation. And the federal judiciary, which long staked its authority on the enforcement of desegregation orders, appears eager to depart the field. Chris Hansen of the American Civil Liberties Union in New York City observes, "The courts are saying, 'We still agree with the goal of school desegregation, but it's too hard, and we're tired of it, and we give up.'"

SOURCE: *Time*, April 29, 1996, pp. 39–45. Copyright © 1996 Time Inc. Reprinted by permission.

After two decades of progress toward integration, the separation of black children in America's schools is on the rise and is in fact approaching the levels of 1970, before the first school bus rolled at the order of a court. Nationally, fully a third of black public school students attend schools where the enrollment is 90% to 100% minority—that is, black, Hispanic, Asian and Native American. In the Northeast, the country's most segregated region, half of all black students attend such schools. "We have already seen the maximum amount of racial mixing in public schools that will exist in our life time," says University of Indiana law professor Kevin Brown, an expert on race and education. The combination of legal revisionism and residential segregation is effectively ending America's bold attempt to integrate the public schools.

This historic reversal has been welcomed by many in the African-American community. In some cities—Denver, for example—the dismantling of mandatory desegregation has been initiated by black leaders, since it is often black children who bear the brunt of such plans—forced to travel long distances to schools where they may not be welcome. In Yonkers, New York, late last year the local leader of the NAACP was suspended by the national organization for declaring that busing had outlived its usefulness. Clinton Adams Jr., a black attorney who is sufficiently abrasive to qualify as a militant in Kansas City—a town so even-tempered that car horns are blown only to warn of impending collisions—takes an even harder line. "The most egregious injustice is the situation where suburban white kids get priority over resident African-American kids, who are the adjudicated victims of segregation," he says. "That's atrocious. Just to try to achieve some kind of mythical benefit that black kids will receive by sitting next to a white kid?"

Homer A. Plessy, described in court papers as "of mixed descent, in the proportion of seven-eighths Caucasian and one-eighth African blood," bought himself a first-class ticket from New Orleans to Covington, Louisiana, and took a seat reserved for whites on the East Louisiana Railway. He was jailed for violating an exquisitely even-handed, race-neutral statute that forbade members of either race to occupy accommodations set aside for the other—with the exception of "nurses attending the children of the other race." Plessy insisted he was white, and when that failed, argued that criminal-court judge John H. Ferguson had violated his constitutional right to the equal protection of the laws.

In its ruling on *Plessy v. Ferguson,* announced May 18, 1896, the Supreme Court declared laws mandating that "equal but separate" treatment of the races "do not necessarily imply the inferiority of either race," and cited the widely accepted propriety of separate schools for white and colored children. In dissent, Justice John Harlan remarked, "The thin disguise of 'equal' accommodations. . . will not mislead any one nor atone for the wrong this day done."

But the thin disguise endured for a half-century, until a series of school-segregation cases culminating in *Brown v. Board of Education of Topeka.* "Separate educational facilities are inherently unequal" and violate the Constitution's equal-protection guarantee, a unanimous Supreme Court ruled on May 17, 1954. A year later, the court ruled that school districts must admit black students on a nondiscriminatory basis "with all deliberate speed" and instructed the federal district courts to retain jurisdiction "during this period of transition."

The nation is still in that period of transition, observes Kenneth Clark, 81, the black sociologist upon whose work the *Brown* decision in part relied. "I didn't realize how deep racism was in America, and I suppose the court didn't realize it either," he says. Ten years after *Brown,* when only 2% of black children in the South attended schools with whites, the court announced, "The time for mere 'deliberate speed' has run out." In 1968 the court declared that discrimination must be "eliminated root and branch." In 1971, noting that about 40% of American school children routinely rode buses to and from school anyway, the court held in *Swann v. Charlotte-Mecklenburg Board of Education* that the federal courts could order busing to desegregate schools.

Busing broke the back of segregation in the South, where 36.4% of black students attended majority-white schools by 1972. But Chief Justice Warren Burger's opinion in *Swann* also opened the door for the federal courts to get out of the integration business. Once legally enforced segregation was eliminated, he wrote, single-race schools would not offend the Constitution unless some agency of the government had deliberately resegregated them.

Since the end of World War II, as blacks have streamed into the cities in search of work, whites have streamed out—in search of greener lawns and whiter neighbors. Anytime blacks were able to breach the wall of restrictive covenants, brokers' steering and mortgage redlining to begin to integrate a neighborhood, white flight and resegregation quickly followed. By 1970, with the white birthrate plunging, Northern urban school districts, which seldom extend beyond city limits, lacked enough white children to desegregate.

A dearth of whites led a federal court to order the city of Detroit to integrate its schools with those of 53 surrounding districts. In 1974 the Supreme Court struck down that order, holding in *Milliken v. Bradley* that suburban districts could not be ordered to help desegregate a city's schools unless those suburbs had been involved in illegally segregating them in the first place. Justice Thurgood Marshall warned in dissent that the court had set a course that would allow "our great metropolitan areas to be divided up each into two cities—one white, the other black. . . ."

That is exactly what happened. School segregation exacerbated residential segregation, as whites chose not to live in neighborhoods served by predominantly minority schools. Detroit's public school system is now 94% minority. By 1990, in the 18 largest Northern metropolitan areas, blacks had become so isolated that 78% of them would have had to move in order to achieve an evenly distributed residential pattern. The *Milliken* ruling, says Indiana University's Brown, "eliminated all hope of meaningful desegregation in most of the country's major urban areas."

This was the state of affairs when, in 1976, the Federal Government threatened to cut off funds to the KCMSD because it had maintained a dual system of segregated schools. Pro-integration kitchen-table activists who had won control of the KCMSD school board responded by suing suburban school districts and the State of Missouri, arguing that they had worked to confine blacks to the inner city.

Until the *Brown* decision, schools were segregated by law in Missouri; after it, the state allowed desegregation at the discretion of local school boards. Many of the suburban districts (parts of which extended into the city) had not allowed blacks to attend high school, forcing black families to move into central Kansas City in search of education. As the city's minority population grew, the KCMSD redrew school-attendance zones hundreds of times and bused some black children far from their neighborhoods in order to keep the races apart.

Federal District Judge Russell G. Clark, a conservative Democrat, ruled that the state and KCMSD had violated the Constitution, but he dropped the outer districts from the case, finding insufficient proof that they had acted illegally— a decision he would have cause to regret. "The very minute I let those suburban school districts out, I created a very severe problem for the court and for myself, really, in trying to come up with a remedial plan to integrate the Kansas City, Missouri, School District," the judge reflected years later. "The more salt you have, the more white you can turn the pepper. And without any salt, or with a limited amount of salt, you're going to end up with a basically black mixture."

KCMSD's only remaining hope for racial balance was a system of magnet schools designed to lure whites back from private schools and the suburban districts. In 1986 Judge Clark ordered such a plan. After the KCMSD's enrollment became majority black in 1970, the district's voters, who remained majority white, had allowed the schools to literally fall apart, rejecting funding initiatives 19 times while pipes burst and ceilings collapsed. In addition to smaller classes and higher teacher salaries, Judge Clark's order required renovation of 55 schools and construction of 17. When the school district failed to come up with its quarter of the cost—Clark had laid three quarters of the bill on the state— the judge took the unusual step of doubling the local property tax. The money bought, among other things, a planetarium, radio and TV studios, and 1,000 computers for Central High School's 1,069 students. Central, which before Clark's order was awash in broken toilets and overrun by rodents, now occupies a $32 million building that resembles a small city's airline terminal and features an Olympic-size swimming pool.

The KCMSD's annual per-pupil expenditure, excluding capital costs, reached $9,412 last year, an amount exceeded by perhaps 40 of the nation's 14,881 school districts. All together, as of this February, $1.7 billion has been spent under court order in Kansas City.

Sugar Creek Elementary is a French-immersion school. An integrated teaching staff of native French speakers recruited from France, Belgium, Canada, Haiti, Egypt and Cameroon keep the children speaking only French, from the Pledge of Allegiance (*"Je déclare fidélité au drapeau des Etats-Unis. . ."*) through recess to the end of the day. The kids even talk out of turn in French. "They're so eager to learn everything, they pick it up like a sponge," says kindergarten teacher Janet Lawrence.

A third of the students are white, and a third of those come from outside the district—transported by parents such as Virgil Adams. (The state stopped paying for transportation into the district this year.) Adams or his wife make a 28-mile round trip twice a day from Blue Springs, a suburb of tidy lawns and two-car garages, so that Sarah can go to second grade and William to third at Sugar Creek. They were drawn by the foreign-language instruction, but Adams, an FBI agent based in Kansas City, sees the social mix itself as an important advantage. "Somewhere on the news one night the word nigger was used," he recalls. "My son asked me what it meant. I thought that was great; if he'd been around my dad three or four days in a row, he'd have known. We didn't want to bring up our kids that way."

For all its moral appeal, however, the Kansas City plan's achievements appear modest when weighed against its enormous expense. The number of out-of-district white children enrolled at the magnet schools peaked at 1,476 last year. Standardized tests have registered slight gains. White flight, while substantially slowed, has not been reversed: in 1985, the year before the magnet plan began, the district was 73.6% minority; this year it is 75.9% minority. If nothing else, horrible school facilities have been replaced with nice new ones, and for some that is justification enough. "I bet a lot of kids in Kansas City are enjoying their childhood more now that they don't have to go to schools that smell," says author Jonathan Kozol, a longtime chronicler of educational injustice. "A good society would consider that money well spent."

His is not the prevailing view in Missouri, where for the past decade candidates for just about any office have been running against what much of the electorate perceives as Judge Clark's liberal-from-hell spending spree. Attorney General Jay Nixon expresses outrage that the state has spent $2.6 billion on court-ordered school desegregation in metropolitan St. Louis and Kansas City. He is seeking "unitary status"—that is, an end to court supervision based on a judicial finding that the system is desegregated—in both cities. "I'm a Democrat, and I want to help kids' educations," he says. "But to see the fencing team in Kansas City sent to Hungary because it showed up good in the focus groups and the whites would think it's cool, is just ridiculous."

The U.S. Supreme Court evidently agrees. In *Missouri v. Jenkins,* the court held last June that Judge Clark had no authority to order the state and district to pay for a plan aimed at attracting suburban students. Chief Justice William Rehnquist pointedly reminded the district court that its ultimate goal was not to achieve racial balance but "to restore state and local authorities to the control" of the school system. Once the lingering effects of legally enforced segregation were eliminated, it would be perfectly legal for the district to run schools that happened to be all black or all white. As Justice Clarence Thomas explained, "The Constitution does not prevent individuals from choosing to live together, to work together, or to send their children to school together, so long as the State does not interfere with their choices on the basis of race."

For the KCMSD, *Missouri v. Jenkins* portends a big reduction in the state's extraordinary desegregation payments. For court-ordered desegregation generally, the decision's implications could be dire. Says associate director of the NAACP Legal Defense Fund Ted Shaw, who argued the Kansas City case before the high court, "If the courts say unitary status means school districts just have to get to the point where a desegregated snapshot can be taken, and then they can go back to the segregating school assignments they had before — if that's all *Brown* has done, it's been a big charade."

If resegregation is indeed the wave of the future, then the future can be glimpsed in Norfolk, Virginia. Norfolk won federal court approval of a return to neighborhood schools back in 1986, for the stated purpose of increasing parental involvement and arresting white flight. Black parents had sued to block the new plan because it would immediately render 10 elementary schools, many of them serving housing projects, 100% black. Sociologist David Armor, retained as an expert witness by the school board, predicted that if Norfolk's cross-town busing continued, the whole school system would soon become 75% black, making racial balance impossible. "Civil rights groups have always discounted the importance of whites," he says today "which has always been a mystery to me. It's as though their goal were some abstract equity thing, as opposed to actual integration." The court accepted Armor's argument.

"It was turning back the clock. It was like being told you have to go to the back of the bus," recalls Lucy Wilson, then an associate dean at Old Dominion University and one of two black school-board members who initially voted against the plan. When the federal court's ruling rendered the return to neighborhood schools inevitable, Wilson and the other dissenter changed their votes in exchange for a commitment that the all-black schools would be targeted for extra resources, though Wilson doubts the promise will be kept forever. (As Harvard School of Education sociologist Gary Orfield has observed, "A less powerful group isn't going to get disproportionate resources for a very long time from a more powerful group. It requires that water flow uphill.") For the 1993–94 school year, the district's average expenditure per pupil in the black "target" elementary schools was $736 higher than at Norfolk's other elementaries, while class size averaged 20 pupils, two or three fewer than at the other schools.

Still, test scores dropped at the 10 target schools after the end of busing. In 1991 black third-graders in the target schools scored 5 percentage points lower than black third-graders in the remaining integrated elementaries on a battery of tests. Last year black third-graders in the target schools tested 10 percentage points lower.

Young Park Elementary occupies a well-kept building set among the barracks-like structures of Norfolk's Young Terrace public housing project. Of its 341 students, 98% are black and 94% are poor enough to qualify for the free-lunch program. This year so far, the parents or guardians of 60 to 70 kids have joined the PTA. "Some of the children arrive at school not knowing their full name; they just know their nickname," says principal Ruby Greer, who has managed to improve test scores and attendance. "They don't know how to hold a pencil or a book. And it seems like you never catch up."

A five-minute drive away from Young Park stands Taylor Elementary. This is the neighborhood school of white children from the large houses on the surrounding tree-lined streets; and of black children from nearby, mostly working-class neighborhoods. Sixty-one percent of Taylor's 433 children are white, and only 30% qualify for the free-lunch program. One hundred percent of the children's parents are in the PTA, which runs 22 committees. In 1994, 88% of Taylor's fourth-graders surpassed national norms on standardized tests. At Young Park, 7% did.

"The whole discussion of desegregation is corrupted by the fact that we mix up race and class," says Harvard sociologist Orfield. "You don't gain anything from sitting next to somebody with a different skin color. But you gain a lot from moving from an isolated poverty setting into a middle-class setting." National statistics provide suggestive evidence that desegregation raises blacks' achievement (without lowering whites'), despite its apparent failure in such high-profile cases as Yonkers—where middle-class flight left low-income students concentrated in high-poverty schools. A massive 1993 Department of Education study of Chapter One, the compensatory-education program for poor children, found that recipients of Chapter One services in schools where at least three-quarters of the children were poor scored substantially lower in math and reading than recipients attending schools where fewer than half were poor.

And, in fact, since the onset of widespread desegregation in 1971, black 17-year-olds have closed roughly a third of the reading-score gap that separated them from whites. A soon-to-be-released study by Debora Sullivan and Robert L. Crain of Teachers College, Columbia University, reports that among 32 states, the gap between black and white fourth-grade reading scores is narrowest in West Virginia and Iowa, where blacks are least isolated from whites, and largest in Michigan and New York, where blacks are the most racially isolated.

Crain and others have found, however, that academic-achievement tests are only one measure of what schools offer—another important one being what researchers call "life chances." "The great barrier to black social and economic mobility is isolation from the opportunities and networks of the middle class," Crain says. School desegregation puts minority students in touch with people who can open doors to colleges and careers.

In 1966 a randomly selected group of kindergarten-through-fifth-grade low-income students in Hartford, Connecticut, nearly all of them black, were offered the opportunity to attend school in a dozen virtually all-white suburbs. Sixteen years later, researchers tracked down more than a thousand of those who had been tapped for the program and a like number of those who had not. Crain found that males in the test group were significantly more likely to have completed two or more years of college and less likely to have dropped out of high school or got in trouble with the police, and females were less likely to have had a child before age 18.

School desegregation also leads to housing desegregation, not only by promoting tolerance but also, to put it bluntly, by making it impossible to avoid an integrated school by choosing where you live. According to a study by Louisville's Fair Housing Council, Jefferson County's school desegregation program reduced residential segregation to such an extent that by 1990, though only 17% of the area's residents were black, a mere one-quarter of 1% of the population lived in a census tract without black neighbors.

But in the case of Louisville, a great desegregation success story, the city and suburbs are in a single school district. In most Northern cities, white flight has undermined even the best efforts at racial balance, and the measurable benefits of desegregation programs have been spottier—while the burdens, particularly on black students, have often been enormous. There has always been some preference in the black community, as in the white, for neighborhood schools (though these may be more an ideal than a reality for the children of the poor, who tend to move, or be moved, a great deal). And there is a realistic pessimism about the prospects for integration. Says the Legal Defense Fund's Shaw: "My sense is a lot of people are saying, 'We're tired of chasing white folks. It's not worth the price we have to pay.'"

Edward Newsome, an African-American lawyer in the real estate business who himself attended a segregated school in Texas, is a leader of the anti-magnet plan coalition that has dominated the Kansas City school board since 1994. He feels the underlying assumptions of desegregation are patronizing to blacks—as does Justice Thomas. "It never ceases to amaze me," wrote Thomas in his *Missouri v. Jenkins* concurrence, "that the courts are so willing to assume that anything that is predominantly black must be inferior."

Says Newsome: "I welcomed the Supreme Court decision. I saw it as an opportunity for the first time in years to focus on removing the vestiges of segregation. For 10 years we've concentrated on bringing in white kids. There's been no Afrocentric-themed magnet school because it doesn't appeal to white folks."

The J. S. Chick Elementary School represents the kind of school Newsome thinks there should be more of. Chick, whose African-centered program was fashioned by its enterprising principal, Audrey Bullard, occupies a bleak, brown brick building in a rundown east-side neighborhood of Kansas City. Ninety-eight percent of Chick's 327 students are black. "With a Eurocentric curriculum, it appears one race is superior over the others," says Bullard. "The African-centered curriculum makes them feel, 'I'm a part of this. I'm not on the outside looking in.'" Something must be working: Chick's students outscore some of the magnet schools' pupils on standardized tests.

On a recent morning in Lola Franklin's third-grade class, the kids are wearing paper crowns signifying their status as African kings and queens, and they are standing one after another to shout out a dizzying variety of facts. "Welcome to Guinea-Bissau! The official language is Portuguese."

"Sheep, cattle and goats are the principal animals!"

"Who can name an African-American comedian?" inquires Franklin.

"Eddie Murphy!" "Bill Cosby!"

"And some American comedians?"

"Whoopi Goldberg!"

"No, an *American* comedian," she corrects them.

"Roseanne!" a boy calls out.

"Good," says Franklin.

Clint Bolick, litigation director for the libertarian Institute for Justice in Washington, predicts court-ordered desegregation schemes will be gone in 10 to 15 years. Their fatal error was in making racial balance a goal, which eventually led to admissions preferences for whites, "turning *Brown* on its head," says Bolick. "What all this shows is that social engineering doesn't work."

But, a great deal of social engineering went into creating school segregation in the first place, points out William Taylor, a Washington lawyer who has worked on civil rights cases for 40 years. Taylor laments what he sees as the courts' "peculiar notion that segregation is the natural condition and desegregation goes against the natural order of things. The court's own finding in *Brown* was that segregation had been imposed by law and practice for many years. Missouri is a good example. You have racially restrictive covenants, racially restrictive ordinances. The notion that somehow segregation came about all because of people's individual preferences is wrong."

Engineered or not, American society is facing "awesome demographic changes," says Harvard's Orfield. "In around 2050 there's going to be about half nonwhites in the total population, in 2020 about half nonwhites in the school population. We have to figure out how to run our institutions in that kind of a society. 'Separate but equal' is the most well-tried experiment in American history. It was policy for 60 years, and we have no evidence that it can work, given the distribution of power and resources in our society."

Four decades after his research helped decide the case that was supposed to change everything, perhaps Kenneth Clark still puts the issue most succinctly: "Talk about 'separate but equal,'" he says. "If they're going to be equal, why are they separate?"

Cambridge Officials Seek
Income-Balanced Schools
Kate Zernike

CAMBRIDGE—School officials say they will approve a proposal that would make this city the first in the nation to desegregate its schools not only by race but by income level.

"As we moved from racial inequity, I believe we can move to more economic equity the same way," said Alice Turkel, a School Committee member. "We've done it on one hard issue. We can do it on another hard issue."

The idea stems from a School Department report last fall showing that despite the city's nationally renowned program that balances schools by race,

---

SOURCE: *The Boston Globe*, May 5, 1996, pp. 33; 39. Reprinted courtesy of *The Boston Globe*.

schools are segregated between rich and poor. The report also showed that schools with higher concentrations of poor students consistently scored lower on tests.

Economic desegregation, school officials say, can improve academic performance, and assure that students learn in classrooms that mirror society.

"I feel very strongly about this," said Superintendent Mary Lou McGrath, who will ask the School Committee to vote on the proposal Tuesday. "If we're going to be about democracy, we have to have more diversity among students, and that includes diversity of class."

Consultants will design a final plan that could start with kindergarten assignments in 1997.

School Committee members rushed to reassure parents, many of whom worried the plan would mean violations of privacy for the sake of social engineering.

The schools are prohibited by law from asking parents for information about income, except in applications for free or federally subsidized lunch programs. So rather than looking at tax forms or questionnaires, School Committee members say they will use qualification for free or subsidized lunches to identify students as low income.

"We're not advocating parents bringing in their W-2 forms," said David Maher, the committee vice chairman. "We're trying to offer kids a better future. I think we'd serve the entire school system better if we could spread students around."

Committee members said they have yet to decide whether students' current school assignments would be preserved under the new plan. For now, school officials say, the plan will start with kindergartners.

The proposal comes amid growing national debate about desegregation programs established as long as four decades ago.

Nine cities across the country—including Kansas City, site of the landmark *Brown v. Board of Education* desegregation case—are proposing, to do away with their racial balance plans.

In Massachusetts, some state Board of Education members have suggested abolishing the 1974 state law requiring racially balanced schools. At a meeting May 15, the board will consider asking the Legislature to repeal the law.

Cambridge School Committee members say they want their move seen as a strong statement against the trend elsewhere.

"Doing this now is very timely," Turkel said. "Cambridge is saying, 'We refuse to go back to segregation.'"

Cambridge is bound to a racial balancing plan under the state law. But racial balance has not resulted in economic balance.

While almost 50 percent of the city's 8,000 students come from incomes low enough to qualify them for free or federally subsidized lunches, the percentage is as high as 83 percent at the Harrington, in East Cambridge, and as low as 18 percent at the Agassiz, near Harvard Square.

The goal, the plan's authors say, is a more even balance of students whose families are well-off and poorer.

"The nation that we are preparing these students for is going to be even more pluralistic than it is today," said Charles Willie, who drew up desegregation plans for Boston and Cambridge and is the consultant on the new Cambridge plan. "We do a disservice if we educate them in homogeneous settings."

Under Cambridge's 15-year-old controlled choice plan, parents request their top three choices of schools.

Assignments are then made to ensure a racial balance at each school, with preference given to the parents' choice as well as to the school in the students' neighborhood.

The new plan would add economic status to the list of considerations. How heavily income would be weighted will be decided in the final plan.

"I think economic balance is more important than neighborhood schools," said Denise Simmons, a School Committee member. "One of the failures of desegregation plans has been not looking at class."

Whatever the plan, School Committee members emphasized that it would be done with advice from parents.

"We need to have a plan that will not drive children away from the system," Turkel said.

Asians, Whites Join Forces in School Integration Debate
Maria Puente

The decades-old battle over school integration continues around the country, but today there's a new twist: a growing number of Asian parents joining angry whites in arguing that focusing on race rather than academic merit denies their children opportunities.

The new challenges—coming on the heels of recent U.S. Supreme Court decisions hostile to race-conscious remedies—are forcing school districts to confront old questions about integration: How far can they go to achieve it? And are race-conscious remedies permissible?

"There are many desegregation plans in the U.S. and they all have race as a criterion (because) you can't talk about integration without talking about race," says Harvard's Gary Orfield, a leading authority and supporter of desegregation plans. "Schools don't spontaneously desegregate themselves."

SOURCE: *USA Today,* September 11, 1995, pp. 8A–8B. Copyright © 1995, *USA Today.* Reprinted with permission.

Twenty years ago, the issue was forced busing. Now, parents are angry and sometimes suing because their children were denied permission to attend popular "magnet" elementary schools or academically selective high schools because of their race.

The school districts say the children were denied admission to avoid upsetting racial and ethnic balances established by court orders, consent decrees or voluntary desegregation plans aimed at heading off lawsuits or court orders.

But the parents and their lawyers say recent rulings indicate the high court may be ready to reject scores of school desegregation plans as unconstitutional.

"The principle the court seems to be moving toward is you cannot use race to benefit or disadvantage anybody unless it's for a narrowly tailored purpose (such as) to remedy past discrimination," says David Armor, a George Mason University law professor who has studied magnet schools and busing in desegregation cases.

- In San Francisco, three Chinese-American families are suing to overturn a 12-year-old, court-approved desegregation plan that forbids any of nine racial and ethnic groups from dominating a school's student population.

  The parents argue the plan means that Chinese students lose seats to white students with lower test scores in the competition to get into Lowell High School. The 139-year-old academically elite school already is dominated by Asians, especially Chinese, who make up 43% of the student body.

  "Freedom from race-based school assignment is a greater good than integration," says lawyer Daniel Girard.

  But the plaintiffs object only to white students getting in with lower scores, not black and Hispanic students, who together total less than 15% of the freshman class.

  "You could let in every African-American that wants to regardless of scores and we wouldn't care (because) no more than 50 would qualify," says Roland Quan, a leader of the Chinese-American Democratic Club.

  But many Chinese in San Francisco oppose the lawsuit. "Even without a consent decree there will always be people who don't get their first choice of schools," says Henry Der, head of Chinese for Affirmative Action. "The issue is, do other racial groups deserve an opportunity to benefit from schools like Lowell?"

  Ling-chi Wang, chairman of Asian-American Studies at the University of California Berkeley, says the real issue is how to expand to other San Francisco schools the quality of education Lowell offers. "Fighting to get another 50 Chinese into Lowell is not the solution," says Wang, who is advising the district on setting up alternative schools.
- In Boston, where residents have been fighting over integration for more than two decades, a white father is suing to overturn a policy reserving 35% of slots at academically elite Boston Latin School—the nation's oldest school, founded in 1635—for black and Hispanic students.

  The policy was adopted after U.S. District Judge Arthur Garrity ordered Boston schools desegregated in 1974.

Michael McLaughlin, a lawyer representing his 12-year-old daughter, Julia, says she outscored 103 black and Hispanic students who were admitted to Latin, but she was assigned to another school.

"This is an exam school which should be based on merit—period," McLaughlin told Garrity at a hearing.

But if race were ignored, only 15% of the entering class would be black and Hispanic—even though they make up the majority of the district's student population.

"If we did not set aside a percentage of seats for blacks and Hispanics we would substantially resegregate Boston Latin School," says Headmaster Michael Contompasis. "The question is what's the window we're allowed to address desegregation if we're not able to use a race-based process?"

- In Montgomery County, outside Washington, D.C., the school district established a desegregation plan that features 15 elementary-level magnet schools with special programs like Spanish or French instruction.

But parents of three Asian-American children challenged the plan after their children were denied admission to magnet schools. The reason: because their transfers would upset racial balances at their neighborhood schools, leaving the few remaining Asian students there more isolated.

Mary Yee, who is now appealing to the state to get her 4-year-old daughter into a French immersion magnet school, charges the district is trying to create a "pretense" of integration by limiting choices for minority families to avoid angering affluent white families.

"There's no reason why I as a non-white person would want a segregated school, the real issue is how you go about (desegregation)," says Yee.

Christine Rossell, a Boston University political scientist who has studied use of magnets as integration tools, says they're designed to entice white students to leave neighborhoods to attend schools that otherwise would be dominated by minority students. As such, she says, districts control who gets into them, including on the basis of race.

The Montgomery County school district says race is only one of many criteria in school assignment. And in a large district—120,000 students—undergoing rapid demographic change, parents aren't always going to get what they want.

"You have to make the system as fair as you can, but the district has to look at this from a larger perspective and balance a lot of factors," says Maree Sneed, a lawyer representing the district.

Thomas Atkins, a former NAACP lawyer who represented some of the original plaintiffs in several major desegregation cases around the country, says the latest challengers of integration conveniently forget how race was used deliberately in the past to segregate school systems.

"Now race is being used to prevent history from repeating itself," Atkins says. "There will be anomalous results. But if we ignore history and rush into repeating it by permitting schools to be segregated by race, then it will almost certainly lead to educational quality problems."

After Forty Years: The Other Half of the Puzzle
John A. Murphy

Brown v. Board of Education of Topeka, Kansas, was a major turning point in American education. It clearly signaled that our nation would no longer tolerate second-rate education for minority students. School systems wrestled with ways of moving students from one school building to another—moving them to achieve the "ideal" ratio—while, at the same time, *assuming* that the performance of minority youngsters would improve. Well—the assumptions were wrong. In many cases, we achieved the correct mix of students by race but *never* saw the hoped-for improvements in achievement.

After a few years of being on this "treadmill" (or perhaps more appropriately, on this "freeway"), most of us have come to realize that integrating only by the numbers does not work. The number and percentage game is fair neither to students nor to our greater society. By now, I think that most of us realize that (1) integrating schools by numbers without raising our expectations for the performance of minority youngsters will not change the nature of educational outcomes for most; (2) teaching higher-level classes to one group, while others are taught in competency-level classes, is unforgivable; and (3) expecting one group of students to achieve less because of problems that they have *outside* of school is an excuse for inaction *inside* of the school.

Given this perspective, there are two points that I would like to make: first, that the achievement of black students can be dramatically improved in a variety of settings if we are willing to change the ways in which we do business, and second, that we need to initiate a new call for our business and community institutions to become actively involved in the issue of school integration.

The First Point: Improving the Educational Outcomes for Black Students

I have had personal experience with this issue in Charlotte-Mecklenburg, the site of the important and ground-breaking *Swann* decision.[1] This decision required full school system integration and, to its credit, the Charlotte-Mecklenburg community took it to heart. Specifically, the school system instituted procedures that resulted in numerical compliance with the court decree; it created a system that showed the rest of the nation that integrated schools could be created without destroying the social or economic fabric of the community; and it created a school system of which the community can be justifiably proud.

SOURCE: *Teachers College Record,* Summer 1995, pp. 743–750. Reprinted with permission from *Teachers College Record* and the author.

But—the question has to be asked—was the integration of school build-ings the "end" in and of itself, or was there some other key purpose to be served? Of course, although integration by itself is a highly valued condition, it must be accompanied by high expectations and effective education for all stu-dents. Its ultimate purpose should be to create situations in which children of different races and ethnicities attend school together and learn to the same extent and at the same rate. Anything less than this as the ultimate goal is totally unacceptable.

When I arrived in Charlotte-Mecklenburg in 1991, the very first thing that I did was to analyze the state of education for all of the system's children. In those earliest days, I was not interested in knowing how much money was spent, or what the conditions of the textbooks were, or what future plans there were for new schools. My sole focus was to figure out "who was learning what" and to determine if there were any disparities in that learning. (I want to remind you that by 1991, *Swann* had been institutionalized and an elaborate system to inte-grate the schools was in place, including paired schools, schools with satellites of students who were bused from far away, a few magnet schools, and schools with ever-changing boundaries to respond to demographic shifts.)

The results of this review were both shocking and eye-opening. The aver-age performance of black students in Charlotte-Mecklenburg was dismal. It was equally dismal for the students in the few schools that were still predominantly black and for those that were, by any standard, integrated. The fact of the mat-ter was that attitudes and practices that were characteristic of black segregated schools in our past remained in most of our schools and classrooms, no matter what the degree of integration. The course of action was clear—in the context of integrated schools, we had to find a way to improve the quality of education for all of our students.

Before I tell you what we did to address this problem, I want you to under-stand the nature of the results that we achieved in only three years—results that prove, once and for all, that given sufficient flexibility, the right attitudes, and effective practices, we can achieve the dual goal of integration and effec-tive education for all. As you consider these gains, consider that they (1) repre-sented a reversal of past trends, (2) were achieved in only two to three years, and (3) still leave us with "a way to go" before complete equity of educational outcomes is achieved.

I am now going to briefly review our data concerning the academic achieve-ment of black students in each of five areas. Please understand that I am doing this in summary form and therefore may have a tendency to underestimate the significance of the changes.

AREA 1: SCHOLASTIC APTITUDE TEST (SAT) SCORES

From 1991 to 1993, SAT scores for black students rose 32 points (from 711 to an all-time high of 743). Note that this was accomplished *without a re-duction* in the number of black test takers. In fact, 22 percent of all of our test takers are black, compared with only 11 percent nationwide.

In 1992, Charlotte-Mecklenburg black students outscored black students nationwide for the first time (742 in CMS and 737 nationally).

The gap between black and white scores decreased from 202 in 1991 to 193 in 1993 even though white scores increased during this time period.

AREA 2: ADVANCED PLACEMENT (AP) COURSES AND PERFORMANCE

Enrollments in AP courses by black students increased from 84 in the 1990–1991 school year to 376 in the 1993–1994 school year, a 348 percent increase (during the same period, white enrollments increased 198 percent).

The number of black students taking AP exams increased from 28 in 1991 to 86 in 1993, a 207 percent increase.

The number of AP exams "passed" by black students (score of 3 or higher) increased from 14 in 1991 to 42 in 1993, a 200 percent increase.

AREA 3: PARTICIPATION IN HIGHER-LEVEL CLASSES

In 1992, 9 percent of courses taken by black high school students were higher-level, compared with 25 percent in 1994, a 168 percent increase (during the same period, white enrollments increased 100 percent).

In 1992, 25 percent of black secondary school students were enrolled in foreign language courses, compared with 37 percent in 1994, a 50 percent increase (during the same period, white enrollments increased 26 percent).

In 1992, 38 percent of black seventh-graders were enrolled in pre-algebra, compared with 56 percent in 1994, a 48 percent increase (during the same period, white enrollments increased 6 percent). In terms of academic performance, these students are performing quite well.

In just one year (from 1992 to 1993) the percentage of black students who stated an intent to go on to higher education increased from 75 percent to 78 percent.

AREA 4: INDICATORS OF DISCIPLINE AND BEHAVIOR

Retentions are down (from 12 percent of black students recommended for grade retention in 1991 to 11 percent in 1993).

Suspensions are down (from 38 percent of black students in 1991 to 24 percent in 1993).

Fewer students are dropping out (from 12 percent of black students in 1991 to 11 percent in 1993).

AREA 5: INDICATORS OF EARLY READINESS

In 1993, 57 percent of all black first-graders were ready for second grade in reading, up from 51 percent in 1992.

In 1993, 51 percent of black second-graders were ready for third grade in reading, up from 42 percent in 1992.

Given these early but significant indicators of improvement, the question now is how this was accomplished.

First, we addressed the needs of all students in every facet of our operations.

> We developed performance standards that define what every student should know and be able to do at every grade and in every subject.

> The same standards apply to all children. There are *no* exceptions except in the case of severe handicaps.

> We established a public accountability system that did not allow us to hide behind our failures. Included in this information are school-by-school report cards that include disaggregated data, by race.

Second, we gave extra attention to students with traditionally lower achievement.

> We created a schoolwide bonus program in which teachers and others receive a financial bonus if the entire school meets a set of academic goals that are established at the beginning of the school year. It is important to note that for each school we establish separate goals for black and white students, and meeting the academic goals for black students requires that they learn "at a faster rate" than other students. This is the only way that the "gap" will ever be closed.

> We eliminated lower-level and "fluff" courses from the curriculum and replaced them with more demanding courses.

> We developed a set of criterion-referenced tests (CRTs) that are administered several times a year and provide teachers with early warning signs that students are having difficulties. Building principals and others have been trained to assist teachers in adjusting their instruction based on the results of these tests.

> We eliminated the use of IQ tests—tests that had been used to identify and assign black students to long-term, low-level ability groups.

> We allowed and encouraged schools to use staff and time flexibly in ways that increase the direct instructional time for students who are farther behind.

Third, we provided specific programmatic support for each of the outcome measures.

For the SAT:

- We administered the Preliminary Scholastic Aptitude Test (PSAT) to all ninth- and tenth-graders at system/state expense and used the results to assist students in selecting appropriate coursework.

- We provided in-service training to teachers, administrators, and counselors on preparing for the PSAT/SAT and analyzing and using the results.
- We involved parents and students in learning from, and acting on, PSAT results.

For the Advanced Placement Tests:

- We provided additional training to over 100 teachers in AP course content and instructional strategies.
- We added AP courses at every high school.
- We provided financial support to students, when needed, for taking AP exams.
- We moved the AP examination sites from one central location to each high school, eliminating transportation problems.
- We collaborated with the College Board on adding Pacesetter Math/ English to course offerings at pilot sites.

For the Higher Level Courses:

- We eliminated lower-level "fluff" courses.
- We added the International Baccalaureate (IB) program to three high schools, three middle schools, and two elementary schools.
- We added foreign language offerings.
- We added staff development on teaching higher-level thinking skills.
- We provided additional pre-algebra summer staff-development programs for teachers with a practical lab site for students for those with the lowest entry-level achievement.

For First- and Second-Grade Readiness:

- We implemented an assessment process that identifies critical skills areas.
- We initiated literacy projects in those schools with the lowest reading performance—including a literacy specialist for each school and intensive in-service work.
- We expanded school media center offerings.
- We increased staff development for all teachers and made it school-based.
- We distributed brochures entitled *CMS Performance Standards* to parents at each grade level as a means of familiarizing them with what their children should be taught and should learn.

Fourth, we involved the entire community in understanding and addressing the needs of our black students.

I meet regularly with black and other clergy in the community to share concerns and ideas for action.

We have involved all facets of our community in the development and monitoring of *The Charlotte Legacy,* our five-year plan of action for achieving excellence in our schools, and will continue to do so.

Our school board has passed a resolution strongly committing us to integration.

Although we have a long way to go to achieve our ultimate goal of absolute equality of outcomes by race and ethnicity, we are convinced that we know how to get there. You will note that the strategies described above are designed to elevate the entire system with a special focus on those who are not yet competitive. Focusing merely on the equality of outcomes will just not work. Truly eliminating the gap between white and black students requires that the quality of education be elevated for all. It requires that school staffs understand that children who enter their classrooms "behind" in their studies require special services—not remedial services, but accelerated services. This, in turn, requires basic changes in the ways in which our schools and classrooms are run and organized. Embedding these and similar strategies in schools that are also integrated will represent the best case for all. Once again, one without the other is not nearly as powerful, or even acceptable, as the two combined.

I would like to address this point a bit further. Recently, a study was released that claimed that experiences with the Milliken II Programs reveal that they were not successful.[2] Without getting into what I believe was more of an editorial position than a solid piece of research, there is positive evidence that extremely significant outcomes have been achieved in Milliken II Schools. Before going to Charlotte, I was superintendent in Prince George's County, Maryland. In Prince George's we had a very aggressive and successful Milliken program. We used a variety of strategies—several similar to the ones noted above—and the results were striking. For example, between 1984 and 1989 standardized test scores increased for nearly every school in the system. Countywide averages increased from the fifty-ninth to the seventy-fifth percentile; the gap between black and white third-graders closed from 26 to 16 points. The Milliken average, once in the mid-forties, rose to within four percentile points of the system-wide average for all students. The Milliken fifth-grade student scores also increased significantly.

The issue is clearly not which particular integration strategy works (schools that are naturally integrated or integrated via assigned busing, magnetization, or some other strategy, or in court-approved nonintegrated settings such as the Milliken model). We know that the best solution will ultimately include several of these approaches. However, no matter what the strategy, it must be characterized by special efforts to elevate the quality of education for *all* students.

The Second Point: Involving Others in the Integration Issue

We must all recognize the fact that what has been seen as school system policies must be redefined as problems that require community-wide solutions. School districts can continue to move students around with buses, but school systems cannot create policies and practices that determine where they live. As noted by Douglas Massey and Nancy Denton at the University of Chicago, "segregated schools, like high rates of unemployment and minority crime, are the result of white, black, and brown neighborhoods." They continue, "Residential segregation is the institutional apparatus that supports other racially discriminatory processes and binds them into a coherent, uniquely effective system of racial subordination."[3]

School systems can only react to these neighborhood patterns. It will take the full force and commitment of all parties in a community to change those patterns. In the meantime, it would be helpful if our university colleagues and other social commentators could spend more of their energies on finding ways to make this happen, rather than on studying the relative impacts of alternative student assignment strategies on achievement, strategies that in and of themselves are isolated from the academic achievement.

Summary

Until now, the burden of integrating schools has been placed on the courts and on local school systems. In truth, all remedies have the characteristics of compensatory mechanisms—compensating for a lack of integrated housing in our communities. And, as demographics continue to shift, schools will be expected to compensate more and more by adjusting school boundaries and attendance rules. It is absolutely appropriate for school systems to play this role in the short run. But in the long run all citizens and institutions must assume much more responsibility for creating the kinds of communities in which compensating for a lack of integration will no longer be necessary.

NOTES

1. *Swann v. Charlotte-Mecklenburg Board of Education,* 4902 U.S. I 1971.
2. *Milliken v. Bradley (II),* 433 U.S. 267 1977.
3. Douglas Massey and Nancy Denton, interview 1994.

PART TWO

Equality

Chapter 5

COMPENSATORY EDUCATION

INTRODUCTION

Victoria's parents are both college graduates. Her father is a school teacher and her mother is a physician. Victoria's parents have worked around their schedules in such a way that Victoria always has had at least one parent home with her "full time." During her first five years, Victoria's parents read to her for hundreds of hours. For additional hundreds of hours she has listened to her parents and their friends discuss and debate a wide range of topics. Frequently, her parents encouraged her to participate in these "adult conversations." As a result, Victoria has had exposure to, and training in, detecting and dealing with complex cognitive-linguistic structures and she has built an impressive vocabulary.

George, also five years old, is the youngest of five children. He has a mother, but no father, living at home. His mother works full-time and her family "gets by" on her income plus some public assistance. George's grandmother lives with the family and cares for the children during the day. There are few books in his home but this does not seem to matter to George. He much prefers watching television to reading. His brothers and sisters, too, spend hours each day watching television—especially cartoons and action shows—and there is little or no adult supervision. They seldom talk about what they watch; they just watch. When George does converse, it is mostly with his brothers and sisters. The talk is usually concrete and immediate—"What's on next?" George's mother arrives home after supper and is tired. Bedtime arrives soon and there is a sense of practical urgency to get the chore of going to bed out of the way quickly. Talk is typically in the form of short, direct commands—"Pick up your things"; "Shut off the TV"; "Brush your teeth"; "Get to bed."

These, of course, are caricatures. Yet, in reality, many children enter kindergarten with backgrounds very much like those of Victoria and George. The Victorias are well prepared for school; the Georges are not. In all likelihood, the Victorias will do very well in school; they have had a very effective head start. The Georges, already behind the Victorias, probably will fall further behind as they progress through the grades. Various educational programs have been developed in an attempt to compensate for the very unequal backgrounds of children as they enter school. A major question is whether these are, or indeed can be, effective in equalizing a very basic inequality in background and literacy development.

Declining Art of Table Talk a Key to Child's Literacy
Kate Zernike

In the age of two-income families and 12-hour workdays, the nightly family dinner has become nearly as dated as a Norman Rockwell painting.

But Harvard researchers, after spending eight years tape recording the dinner conversations of 80 families from Boston to Framingham, say there are powerful reasons to keep the family dinner ritual.

After analyzing hundreds of hours of discussions, the researchers found that good dinner conversation was the single best predictor of how well a child learns to read—even better than reading to children from an early age. And that is true whether the family is the traditional two-parent unit, or a one-parent household.

It was at dinner that children heard most of the "rare," or vocabulary-building words, that researchers say lead to good reading—words like "carbohydrate," "candidate," even "broccoli" and "asparagus." (Despite what some parents might think, "please" is not a rare word.)

In addition, children tended to get more detailed explanations, and more interest from parents in their questions, at the table.

"In modern life—two working parents, long hours, kids who have to be different places at different times—all those things make it hard for families to eat together," said Catherine Snow, one of the main researchers at the Harvard Graduate School of Education. "But in families that do it even sometimes, and see it as an opportunity for interesting conversation, it is very, very successful."

The conversation need not be heavy intellectual food for thought to be beneficial, Snow and her colleagues found. At dinner, families tend to fall spontaneously into discussions that expand the learning of even the youngest children.

Over a recent casual dinner of take-out Greek lamb and rice, for instance, Gaylee Wheaton of Belmont and her 10-year-old son, Tim, who are among the families being studied, discussed a school project he had to do: the movie *Apollo 13*, and a teacher he doesn't like.

SOURCE: *The Boston Globe*, January 14, 1996, pp. 1; 30. Reprinted courtesy of *The Boston Globe*.

THE ART OF CONVERSATION

Here are transcripts of actual dinner conversations researchers applauded as examples of two kinds of talk—"explanatory" and "narrative"—that lead to improved literacy among children.

Four-Year-Old Female Child

MOTHER: You know what your teacher—you know Michelle told me the other day when we were at the Swan Boats?
CHILD: What?
MOTHER: Michelle said you are the best student she has in her class.
CHILD: I'm a student?
MOTHER: Yeah. 'Cause Michelle's your teacher, so you're her student. You're the best student she has in class because she never has to talk to you a whole bunch of times like she does the other kids. And you never get in any trouble. So she was very happy with you. She says she going to miss you when you do go to a new school.

Three-Year-Old Male Child

(Inviting the child's imaginary friend, a dragon, to sit with him)

MOTHER: Why don't you slide over here a little bit.
CHILD: He's gonna slide, like a slide.
MOTHER: Like a slide?
CHILD: Yeah. On a playground.

continued

Their discussion evolved into a bit of "explanatory" conversation, (how a spaceship falls to earth) some storytelling, and even a few rare words ("suitable," "summon")—all things researchers say help make children better readers.

"When I was growing up, dinner was our time to sit down and talk," said Wheaton, 43, a sales representative for Nynex and single mother who is able to be home for dinner every night.

"I try to keep that up with him. Sometimes we're a little more rushed than I'd like to be. But we still get a chance to talk."

What Snow and other researchers wanted to examine was which situations—dinnertime, school time, play time or being read to—produced more "rare" words, and the connection between those words and later literacy. They defined *rare* as words most children in a given age group wouldn't know.

They chose only low-income families for the study, recruiting from federally subsidized day care and Head Start programs in Boston. Middle and higher-

continued from previous page

MOTHER: Well, sometimes when you say "slide over" it just means scooch over. Like move over a little bit.

CHILD: Oh.

MOTHER: But you're right, it is also a slide at the playground. Same word; sometimes it just means different things.

Three-Year-Old Male Child

(Father supplies a lot of information, and attempts to connect to something child knows, like Pinocchio)

FATHER: Now you know what a dolphin is don't you?

CHILD: Yeah!

FATHER: A dolphin doesn't have to stay in the water all of the time.

CHILD: Yeah!

FATHER: A dolphin can come up, a dolphin is a mammal!

CHILD: Yeah!

FATHER: And a mammal, they live in the ocean, but they can breath our air.

CHILD: Yeah!

FATHER: A whale—a big, big whale? See the big whales? Like in Pinocchio the big whale?

CHILD: Yeah!

FATHER: That's a mammal. It's not a fish.

SOURCE: Harvard Graduate School of Education

income families, they felt, might have other advantages that contributed to good reading skills—such as private school or tutoring.

They found that good dinner conversation promoted literacy even when economics and family circumstance worked against it.

Twice a year, they strapped tape recorders onto the children at school, during play with their parents, while their parents read to them, and at the dinner table.

The children who tested highest on the vocabulary and reading tests throughout elementary school were the ones who had dinner conversations. The children whose parents spent relatively high amounts of time reading to them, but little time in dinner conversation, did not score as high.

Statistically, of the more than two thousand "rare" words the researchers recorded in two years, over 1,000 were heard at the dinner table—compared with only 143 from books.

So what does this mean for literacy, when studies show that a quarter of American families don't regularly sit down to eat as a group?

Snow said other situations, like talking in the car, or at bedtime, can offer just as much benefit—as long as they include the same kind of conversation found at the table.

"It's not so much where," she said, "It's what kind of talk is going on."

And for families who can't remember the last time they heard anything more intelligent discussed at their dinner table than whether there was enough meatloaf for second helpings, Snow and her colleagues offer assurance.

"I think because we're all tired at the end of the day we think we're not saying anything valuable. But interesting conversations are going on," she said.

Wheaton discovered this when she found herself snapping at her son at the dinner table recently, telling him he "exhausted" her.

He asked her what that meant, and she told him to go look it up in the dictionary. He did.

"To wear out completely?" he asked, smiling innocently at her.

Preschool Worth the Cost
Charles Lêroux and Cindy Schreuder

In 1962, children 3 years and 4 years old in a small Michigan city did something that would increase their likelihood of graduating from high school, getting married, owning a home. It would lessen their chance of having a criminal record or going on welfare. It would significantly boost their IQ scores. It would change their lives.

What they did was go to preschool.

For that era, and especially for children such as those impoverished black children who lived near Perry Elementary School in Ypsilanti, an early, intense learning experience was unprecedented. Preschool was almost unheard of then. Head Start, the federally funded program primarily for low-income children ages 3 to 5, was three years away, and only 18 states mandated kindergarten. Toddlerhood was a time for play.

Instead, those 58 Ypsilanti children spent 2½ hours every weekday morning stretching their minds and strengthening their social skills. They learned to recognize series and patterns, similarities and differences, how to deal with conflict, draw and paint and play with clay. They visited the post office, fire station, grocery store and walked through their neighborhood while teachers pointed out differences among trees, leaves and other common objects along the route.

SOURCE: *The Chicago Tribune*, November 1, 1994, pp. 1; 12. Copyright © Chicago Tribune Company. All rights reserved. Used with permission.

Once a week, the teachers visited their homes to help parents reinforce and expand on their children's school lessons.

Follow-up research, most recently done when the oldest were 27, showed that Perry Preschool graduates tended to enter the American mainstream with such hallmarks as jobs, marriages, homes. But a control group of children from the same neighborhood who were not enrolled turned up in greater numbers as burdens on the mainstream. As adults, far more of the second group had prison records, spotty employment histories or were on welfare.

When the Perry project was planned, the researchers had a hunch—but no evidence—that a stimulating program for preschoolers and their parents could significantly change the children's futures. Now, the evidence has come in.

More than 50 research projects in various locations, using diverse curricula and beginning at different ages, all come to the same conclusion. That conclusion is supported by a growing amount of scientific literature on child development that adds biological and neurological research to psychological and sociological studies.

The conclusion is: Early intervention works.

The most recent research on the infant brain suggests a slight change in that declaration: Earliest intervention works best.

Scientists have found that very young children are at the height of adaptability, primed to learn, eager for new experiences. Also, because bonding in the first year is crucial, a child unable to form an attachment at home may find, in an intervention program, someone to love him and teach him to love.

To work, intervention programs must be of high quality. They also must be consistent and persistent—one criticism of Head Start and other such programs is that their effects erode within a few years after the children enter grade school.

The best programs reach out to families, as well, involving them in the children's development and teaching parenting skills. Programs must be accessible—some early-intervention programs for infants in Chicago have waiting lists of four to six months, half a lifetime for those babies.

The recipe for changing lives sounds simple. Provide the newborn with someone who is crazy about him; feed him nutritious food; raise him in a stimulating environment free of domestic and community violence. Provide all of that well into the school years.

But the most important ingredient is something no government agency or program can supply: a loving adult.

The rest of the mix can be considered a long-term insurance policy that society takes out on children to protect against later violence and wasted lives. But many political candidates, cognizant of public fears about crime, have used those concerns to promote instead the short-term security of stricter law enforcement and incarceration.

Even so, the cries of disadvantaged infants to become a part of the American mainstream are just beginning to be heard, amplified by a chorus of interest in children's rights and issues.

For the first time, for example, a U.S. attorney general is suggesting that crime fighting may well be in the cradle.

"Start early," Janet Reno said in August to a national conference on youth violence in Washington. "Unless we start when children are conceived, unless we give them the foundation in [ages] 0 to 3 to grow, we are never ultimately going to succeed."

In an October speech before the International Association of Chiefs of Police in Albuquerque, President Clinton spoke of morality and children. In an earlier speech, the president had mentioned Chicagoan Robert Sandifer, a homicide suspect and murder victim at age 11. In Albuquerque, Clinton focused on the 10- and 11-year-olds who allegedly forced Eric Morse, 5, to fall to his death from a CHA [Chicago Housing Authority] high-rise: "What we must be worried about is wave upon wave of these little children, who don't have somebody both good and strong to look up to, who are so vulnerable that their hearts can be turned to stone by the time they're 10 or 11 years old."

Congress and the president underscored the importance to the nation of early intervention when, in May, they approved legislation extending the Head Start preschool program to an as-yet-undetermined number of children from birth to age 3. The Head Start birth-to-3 program likely will blend educational activities with elements of good infant day care. Those ideally would include not just quality programs but surroundings that allow for private and group play areas, safe ways to climb and slide, muted colors for walls and furniture.

"Adults can't function in a group for 11 hours a day," said Louis Torelli, a designer of infant day-care spaces who is based in California, "and yet we expect that of children. They need to take a break from time to time, and if there's no place to go, they'll have tantrums or get in fights."

Intervention can be expensive. Head Start this year is spending $3.3 billion on 745,000 children, about a third of those who are eligible. That averages more than $4,000 a pupil.

"We can spare $20 billion from defense for Head Start and do more for the defense of this country," said Dr. Julius Richmond, a professor of health policy at Harvard Medical School and Head Start's first director.

But he and others are asking taxpayers to make a leap of faith, to believe that money spent on children today will pay dividends years, even decades, in the future.

"It's true you are putting out expenditures now, but the savings are quite rapid," said David Weikart, president of High/Scope Educational Research Foundation in Ypsilanti, sponsors of the Perry study. "It's the same argument that hotel builders make when they want to build a hotel: Invest now, and you get no money until the guests come—a 10- or 15-year horizon. I don't see any reason why hotels should have better planning than programs for kids."

Perry Preschool spent the equivalent of $7,252 in 1992 dollars on each pupil. But when the monies later spent on welfare, incarceration, special education and similar expenditures were tallied, for every public dollar spent on the program children, $7.16 had been spent on the non-program children by age 27.

"The choice is between spending $1 and spending $7," Weikart said. "People say it costs too much, but that's not the right use of the word 'cost.' What costs too much is not doing it."

More on the Importance of Preschool
Gerald W. Bracey

I have often wondered whether, as adults, the children studied by Jean Piaget felt the unshakable sensation that someone was looking over their shoulders. I now wonder whether the 123 people who formed the Perry Preschool Study feel the same way. Observed from the time that they were 3 years old, they have now reached the age of 27.

The findings of the Perry Preschool Study continue to be exciting and may be more important now than they were when the study originated in the mid-Sixties. At the time, hopes were high in many quarters that a Head Start would be sufficient to overcome the impact of poverty and even that poverty itself would be eradicated in the foreseeable future.

As for poverty, it is more with us today than in previous times and is rising. A graph in the November 3 issue of *Education Week* depicts current and projected poverty rates for major U.S. ethnic groups. The current poverty rates for the three major groups are 48% for blacks, 40% for Hispanics, and 17% for whites. The projections are for the poverty rates of all three ethnic groups to increase, but the rate for Hispanics will climb more steeply and in the year 2010 will nearly converge with the rate for blacks at around 50%.

Thus finding and funding an effective preschool program looks as important today as the National Defense Education Act did in 1958. As I reported in the September 1993 Research [of *Phi Delta Kappan*—Ed.] column, a number of preschool programs have shown long-term positive effects. The data from the Perry Project, however, remain the most complete and the most impressive. Lawrence Schweinhart, who joined the project in its early years, and David Weikart, who was there at the beginning, have summarized the data on the 27-year-olds in the November 1993 issue of *Young Children.*

In terms of achievement, 71% of the group that attended preschool had graduated from high school or attained a GED (General Education Develop-

SOURCE: *Phi Delta Kappan,* January 1994, pp. 416–417. Reprinted with permission of *Phi Delta Kappan* and the author. Gerald Bracey is an independent research psychologist, writer, and author of *Final Exam: A Study of the Perpetual Scrutiny of American Education* (Bloomington, IN: Technos Press, 1995).

ment) certificate, while 54% of the group that had no preschool program had done so. (I remind readers that the 58 children who attended the preschool in the Perry Project were chosen at random from the total group of 123.) Females who attended the preschool graduated at a much higher rate than females who did not attend preschool (84% versus 35%). The high school graduation rate for males yields the lone paradoxical finding of the study: the preschool program had a negative impact on the graduation rate of males. Males who attended preschool were slightly *less likely* to graduate from high school than males who did not attend. No results are reported on whether any of the students in either group attended postsecondary education or training for any length of time.

Not only do those in the preschool group get more education overall, but they also seem to put it to better use in terms of economic advancement. Only 6% of males who received no preschooling reported earnings in excess of $2,000 a month, while 42% of the preschool group did so. Earnings are not reported for females, but 80% of females who attended preschool, compared to only 55% of those who did not, held jobs at age 27. Thirty-six percent of the preschool group—but only 13% of those who did not attend preschool—owned their own homes.

For males, the same proportion of both groups was married, but the males who had attended preschool had been married an average of 6.2 years, while those who had not attended preschool had been married only 3.3 years on average. The rate of out-of-wedlock births for women who attended the preschool was 57%, very near the national average for blacks. The corresponding rate for females who did not attend the preschool program was 85%—substantially above the national average.

Neither group seems to consist of model citizens, but there are differences in the subjects' arrest rates. The preschool group had an average of 2.3 arrests by age 27; those without preschool, 4.6. Five times as many in the latter group (35%) as in the preschool group had been arrested five or more times. The two females in the preschool group who were deceased by the age of 27 had both been brutally murdered in drug-related killings: one, burned to death; the other, bludgeoned.

A cost-benefit analysis estimated that the public received $7.16 in benefits for every dollar invested in the preschool program. Schweinhart and Weikart emphasize that these benefits can be obtained only if the programs are done right: the Perry Project provided not only a high-quality, cognitively oriented curriculum, but also outreach to parents and meals and health care for the children. However, the authors believe that the ratio of children to teachers could be increased from the 5 or 6 to 1 in the original program to as many as 8 to 1 without reducing the effectiveness of the program significantly. This would lower costs substantially.

Causal inferences over such a long period of time are difficult to substantiate, but the authors believe that the Perry Preschool Project had the impact it did because of the way it empowered children, their parents, and their teachers. It encouraged children to initiate learning, it involved parents as full partners with teachers, and it provided teachers with systematic inservice training and support.

To Boost IQs, Aid Is Needed in First Three Years
Rochelle Sharpe

New research on brain development suggests that any attempt to maximize intellectual growth must begin during the first three years of life, much earlier than previously believed.

Scientists have discovered that a child's environment influences the number of brain cells the child keeps and the connections between them, according to a report issued today by the Carnegie Corp. of New York. The findings are prompting the nonprofit Carnegie foundation, as well as some child-development experts, to call on Congress to expand family-leave rights, improve the training of day-care workers and extend the Head Start program for high-risk youngsters to children under age three. "By ensuring a good start in life, we have more opportunity to promote learning and prevent damage than we ever imagined," the Carnegie report says.

Scientists have known for decades that environment affects behavior, but only in recent years have they started to understand that the brain is literally shaped by experience. They now believe an infant's brain develops more quickly in the first year than they had expected and that sensory experiences can affect which brain cells and cell connections live or die.

Babies are born with billions of brain cells, many more than they have at age three and nearly twice as many as they have as adults, recent research shows. During the first months of life, connections between these cells, called synapses, multiply rapidly to 1,000 trillion, forming the structures that allow learning to occur.

Nature acts like a sculptor throughout childhood, scientists say, chiseling away the excessive cells and synapses so the brain can function more efficiently in adulthood. In part it decides which synapses are superfluous by determining which ones never get used. That's why people who take piano lessons before

---

WHAT NEW SCIENTIFIC RESEARCH SHOWS

- Brain development before age one is more rapid and extensive than previously realized.
- Brain development is much more vulnerable to environmental influence than suspected.
- The influence of early environment on brain development is long lasting.
- Environment affects the number of brain cells, connections among them and the way connections are wired.
- Early stress has a negative impact on brain function.

SOURCE: Carnegie Corporation of New York

---

age nine find it easier to play piano as adults than those who didn't start studying the instrument until later in life, says Harry Chugani, a neuroscientist at the University of Michigan Children's Hospital.

By enrolling a child in music lessons, "you've changed the fine anatomy of the brain," Dr. Chugani says.

Animal studies show that brains develop differently in more enriched environments. When rats spend their lives before sexual maturity in cages filled with toys, they develop more synapses than rats in empty cages, says William Greenough, a neurobiologist with the Beckman Institute at the University of Illinois. These rats have 80 percent more capillary volume per brain cell, that is, bigger capillaries and more of them, allowing the brain to receive a better supply of nutrients and oxygen. Meanwhile, the neuroglia, which help keep the nervous system stable, show increases in metabolic rates and size in these rats.

Negative experiences can have lasting effects, scientists say, because they can alter the organization of the brain. Children raised in poor environments can display cognitive deficits by 18 months that may be irreversible, studies show. Severe stress in monkeys and rats, meanwhile, has created serious problems too, resulting in hormonal changes that cause the death of brain cells involved in learning and memory.

"I don't think I'd get paranoid about this, but I would not totally dismiss the idea that stress could have an impact," says Bruce McEwen, a neuroscientist at Rockefeller University who has studied the effect of stress on the brain.

Child experts say the new research shouldn't make parents obsessive about stimulating certain portions of their children's brains but simply make them more aware of the importance of the early years of life. Some parents think a newborn is "kind of a blob," says Edward Zigler, director of the Yale University Bush Center in Child Development and Social Policy and a founder of Head Start.

Stimulating a child properly is simple, he says, but it does take time: putting children on your lap, letting them turn pages when you read to them—normal everyday interactions. "Drop the nonsense about quality time," he says. "It's quantity time that children need."

Mr. Zigler thinks it's best for children to stay home with a parent for the first six months of life, given the child's developmental changes and family adjustments to the newborn. That's why he is a strong advocate of expanding family leave to six months, up from the current requirement that businesses with 50 or more employees allow workers to take up to 12 weeks of unpaid leave. The Carnegie Corp.'s task force on children, which Mr. Zigler serves on, also wants businesses to partially pay parents on leave, since few families can afford to lose months of income.

Children won't be damaged by high-quality day care, experts say. Toddlers who receive good day care will fare as well as if they stayed home all the time with a parent, studies show. But the problem is that good day care is hard to find.

"Child care in America is bad," says Mr. Zigler, citing the Families and Work Institute's recent report that rated only 9% of family child care and relative care arrangements as good quality. The institute concluded that quality could be improved by training day-care workers, a recommendation the Carnegie Corp. wants the government to encourage.

The brain research has far-reaching implications for underprivileged children, who could be spared lives of mental retardation with early intervention. When extremely high-risk children entered educational programs by six months of age, their incidence of mental retardation was cut 80%, says Craig Ramey, a developmental psychologist at the University of Alabama at Birmingham. By age three, these children had IQs that were 15 to 20 points higher than children of similar backgrounds who had not attended programs, Mr. Ramey says. At age 12, these children still functioned at a higher level, and at age 15 the effects were even stronger, suggesting that early educational programs can have long-lasting and cumulative effects.

Children who enter preschool at age three also show improvement, he says, but they never appear to fully overcome what they lost in the first three years.

Such evidence has persuaded Democratic Sen. Edward Kennedy of Massachusetts to seek to expand the Head Start program to include children from infancy to age three. (The current starting age is three to five.) The expansion is expected to be included in Head Start legislation scheduled to be written Wednesday in the Senate Education and Labor Committee, which Sen. Kennedy heads. There will be $120 million set aside for these new Head Starts in the next fiscal year and $600 million by fiscal 1998.

"The evidence is now so convincing that high-risk children can benefit from these interventions that we have to justify to ourselves why we wouldn't provide it," Mr. Ramey says.

Diplomas and Diapers: Schooling for Young Street Mothers and Their Babies
JoAnn Ray and Marilee Roloff

Debbie is 17, and like most teenagers, attends school—but her school is unusual. Each morning Debbie takes her baby, Jessica, to a special Head Start program before she goes to her own school. Debbie is one of the fortunate young mothers to be involved with the Crosswalk School and the special Head Start program for children age birth to 3 in Spokane, Washington.

Debbie's life has not been easy. She left her abusive home when she was only 15, wanting to go as far away from her stepfather as possible. At 15 her options were few. The street was scary, but Debbie learned about Crosswalk from other friends. Crosswalk was helpful to Debbie, providing free meals, school, adults she learned to trust, and a place to "hang out." Debbie could stay overnight at Crosswalk when it was cold and she didn't have anywhere else to go. "I don't know what I'd have done without Crosswalk," observes Debbie.

Debbie's best friend is Mike, who is a year older. Mike also has a violent family. Mike sells drugs to make money. He also uses drugs.

Last year when Debbie discovered she was pregnant, she was frightened but also glad. It would be good to have a baby to love, and someone who would love her. She stopped using drugs altogether, which wasn't difficult because she had never been a heavy drug user.

Debbie moved into Alexandria's House, a transitional home for young mothers, operated by Crosswalk. Alexandria's House provides a refuge for six teen-aged mothers and their children. The house-parent and social worker help Debbie take care of her baby, Jessica. "The staff is so helpful with everything," Debbie says. "You can really rely on them."

Debbie pays $250 of her $440 monthly welfare check for rent, and she sets aside an additional $50 per month in the home's savings program. This money will be returned to her when she leaves.

The other young moms are friends at Alexandria's House, but Debbie is still lonely and depressed. Taking care of Jessica requires more energy and time than she expected. "Life as a young teen mom is hard," she reflects.

Debbie's relationship with her own mother has improved since Jessica's birth. The child is the first grandchild and her mother likes to buy things and babysit with Jessica. Debbie notes, "Mom and I used to fight all the time. Now I can better understand what it means to be a parent."

Mike likes to have a baby, but he can't offer much financial assistance and he gets angry when Debbie can't party with him. "We used to party together,

SOURCE: *Children Today, 23,* no. 2, (1994): pp. 28–31. Reprinted with permission of the author.

but now I want him to help with Jessica instead of hanging out with friends," says Debbie.

Debbie completed her freshman year of high school before leaving home. She is now attending Crosswalk's alternative school. Crosswalk shares the building with a special Head Start program. "I probably wouldn't be in school if it weren't for this program," Debbie points out. "I want to have Jessica close by."

Young Street Mothers

Debbie is typical of many of the young mothers served at Crosswalk. Teenaged mothers who have "street life" experience are proud and devoted mothers, but they have many problems and a highly stressful life. They face difficulties related to a lack of money, concerns about their relationships with the baby's father and their own parents, health issues, depression, and uncertainties about their own and their children's futures.

We are using the term "street kid" to denote those children who identify with the street; that is, they spend their time on the street rather than at school or with their families. Some are still marginally attached to their families. Street kids generally have complicated personal histories. Often their own families are violent and abusive and many street children have been in and out of numerous foster homes. Many have been neglected or physically, emotionally, and/or sexually abused. They often turn to drugs and alcohol and are involved in illegal activities. Their school experiences are often disrupted. These children have fallen through the cracks of social service agencies and are the failures of a society that is not supportive of child rearing.

Street girls represent an even more serious profile than boys, according to intake records at Crosswalk. Girls more frequently report sexual, physical and emotional abuse, express higher rates of depression, and experience more suicide attempts than boys. Pregnant or mothering girls indicate even higher rates of abuse, suicide attempts, depression, family conflict and drug use than other girls.

One-half of the girls were pregnant or mothering two years after intake at Crosswalk, according to a follow-up survey. Infants born to adolescents are apt to be fragile at birth and are at risk for neglect and abuse, and young street mothers are at even higher risk because of street life, drug use, inadequate nutrition, sexually transmitted diseases, and lack of medical care. These young mothers often have few child care skills, and no realistic idea of how they will survive.

A study of the Spokane young mothers concluded that these women are proud and devoted mothers, but are feeling the stresses of trying to raise a child at a young age, with limited income and social supports. The needs of these young women are many, including: housing, financial aid, social, educational, child care, mental health, medical, recreational, and emergency services.

These young women often face difficulty in acquiring needed resources because of restrictive rental, employment and agency policies related to age. Accessing resources is further complicated because the young mothers are often socially isolated, alienated and unable to trust.

These young mothers need a comprehensive, coordinated array of services to empower them to best raise their children and improve their own situations. Providing social services to street youth, including young mothers, requires a non-traditional approach. Services must be "voluntary, free, immediately accessible and on site."

Crosswalk Background

Volunteers of America's Crosswalk, is Spokane, Washington's response for "street kids." Crosswalk was formed as a result of community concern when a Mayor's Task Force—comprised of members from child welfare agencies, law enforcement, juvenile court, and community service groups—identified a significant number of street kids and a lack of adequate services. Volunteers of America opened the doors of Crosswalk in 1985, offering food, "on-the-spot" counseling, and a place for the children to "hang out." Church groups provide meals 365 days a year, and clothing and personal items are available. An array of counseling services, including individual counseling, drug therapy groups, employment readiness groups, and family counseling, are available. Other private and public organizations offer on-site services or accept referral for medical care, employment, vocational training, and substance abuse treatment. Recreational activities, ranging from cake decorating, tie-dyeing, and ballet, to swimming, baseball, volleyball, and field trips, are offered by Crosswalk.

The needs of the young clients have dictated the program's expansion. During the second year of the program, the public school district added the alternative school, and Crosswalk began providing shelter for 15 adolescents during the winter months. The plight of the young mothers was the driving force for developing transitional homes and apartments. The transitional home (Alexandria's House) is designed to provide a supportive supervised living situation for mothers under the age of 18 and their children. The less structured apartments (Apartments for Young Families) provide homes for young mothers 18 to 21, their children, and husbands, if these mothers are married.

Crosswalk moved into its present home in 1992. The spacious building offered the opportunity for another agency to be housed in the same building. The special Head Start program was funded in 1993. This situation allows the young mothers to attend school and be involved with their young children too.

School for Moms

The alternative school at Crosswalk provides the street kids an opportunity to pursue and complete their educations. The staff soon learned that the school was an attraction to the kids: It was the school, not lunch, which brought the kids to Crosswalk. Thousands of teens have attended school during the past eight years and hundreds have returned to neighborhood schools or have earned either their GEDs or diplomas through Crosswalk.

The success of the school is largely due to the choice of its certified teacher, an unusual, gentle man who has empathy and understanding for street kids. The school is flexible, allowing the youths to work at their own level and pace. The curriculum is pragmatic and realistic, focusing on problems and issues facing these children. Ken, the teacher, states that, "Kids like school when it has meaning for them."

In a recent survey, two-thirds of the school attendees stated that their courses were providing them with useful skills for the future. More than three-fourths of the street children agreed that the Crosswalk School made them feel better about themselves.

Since it is located in Crosswalk, the school allows the young mothers easy access to other services. Counseling, clothing, financial assistance and referrals are readily available and delivered in non-traditional ways. The staff has earned a reputation of being caring and trustworthy. Marilee, the past director, states that, "Young mothers don't come with only one problem. You have to impact them from all directions."

School for Babies

The program for the children does not look like a typical Head Start program. The children enrolled are infants and toddlers and their mothers have had street life experience or serious substance abuse problems. The school serves 24 children from three months to three years in two daily sessions.

The Head Start teachers and staff volunteered for this assignment and admit it's a very different program from other Head Start classrooms. "You need tons of flexibility to work with these mothers and babies," says Mary, the lead teacher. This means fewer "formal" presentations and more on-the-spot, spontaneous, two-minute trainings.

The roles of the health advocate and social worker are unique to the program. They spend most of their time in the classroom trying to connect with the parents and babies. In other programs, social workers conduct home visits; in this Head Start program, the teacher and health advocate also visit. This allows all staff to see the home environment and the young mothers feel that "they all care for me."

The staff—especially Crosswalk counselors, the Crosswalk teacher and public health nurses—work closely with other professionals to tackle the many needs of the teen mothers. These relationships, plus the physical presence at Crosswalk, help the staff to understand the complicated problems of the teen moms and to find successful interventions and solutions.

Rules are more lenient at the Crosswalk Head Start. Head Start's strict attendance policies are relaxed because the staff understands the chaotic nature of the street girls' lives. Transportation, drugs, intermittent boyfriends, childhood traumas, health problems and the moms' ages are taken into account.

Although the Crosswalk Head Start program has been modified to meet the young mothers' needs, the basic components are the same as other Head Starts, including parent involvement, developmentally appropriate education, health, social services, and nutrition.

The young mothers whose babies attend the Head Start program are enthusiastic about it. "It's a wonderful place," says Debbie. "It's easy to come up and talk with staff. They make you feel comfortable." The mother of a two-year-old comments, "My baby is learning to say words and play with other kids. Another teen mother believes that the program "helps you more on the next stage in life."

Conclusions

Young street mothers have multiple needs. Cooperative, non-traditional schooling for young mothers and their babies provides an opportunity to give them comprehensive services. Offering diversified services is the ideal approach.

The best plan for Spokane's young street mothers and their children enables the mothers to attend the Crosswalk School, the babies to be enrolled in the Crosswalk Head Start program, and the family to live in the transitional housing. Then mothers and children can be surrounded by caring adults who can gently guide, counsel, educate and be aware of danger signs in the course of the family's growth and development. As Debbie points out, "The Crosswalk program has made it easier for me to be a parent."

Reading Recovery—Program Helps Struggling Pupils Excel
Betsy White

As E Ware-Jones reads aloud about a grumpy, hungry giant, her teacher meticulously charts every syllable the 6-year-old utters.

Behind a one-way mirror, 11 other teachers analyze Wanda Mangum's every move. Throughout the 30-minute "Reading Recovery" session each interaction between teacher and student is dissected and critiqued as if it were the most important task in the world.

That's because, for E and many children like her, it is. Children who fail to grasp the keys to reading by the time they leave first grade rarely recover.

SOURCE: *The Atlanta Constitution*, January 1, 1995, pp. E1; E8. Reprinted with permission from *The Atlanta Journal-Constitution*.

"Learning literacy in the early grades is so fundamentally critical to all future learning and success that it *must* happen for our children, it must," said Colin Martin, a reading coordinator who got the costly program started in Gwinnett County schools.

A carefully designed, one-on-one approach to reading instruction, Reading Recovery is being hailed around the world as a way to reach 6-year-olds who otherwise would not learn to read. It targets the lowest 20 percent of readers in any school's first grade and, in less than half a year, brings them up to the average reading level of their class.

Wowed by those results, 13 Georgia school systems, including six in metro Atlanta, have begun using Reading Recovery in the past three years. They are spending about $2,000 a year per child to let their best teachers work one-on-one with the neediest pupils.

Many of the children who need extra help come from families that are poor, don't read them bedtime stories or don't speak English, but they are by no means the only children who need help.

"You can have a child who's been read to and the parents have done all the right things, and the child still doesn't put all the pieces together," Martin said.

E started first grade as the poorest reader in her class at DeKalb County's Murphey Candler Elementary School. Although she's obviously bright, entire lessons were passing her by.

Now, with 12 weeks of daily Reading Recovery lessons, E has advanced almost to the average reading level of her class. Research says that, even with no more special help, she will stay there.

E's confidence has soared along with her reading level.

"Miss Mangum taught me how to read," she says. "Now I'm super-good!"

Record Recognized Worldwide

Brought to the United States from New Zealand nine years ago, Reading Recovery boasts a phenomenal record. At schools across the nation, virtually every participating student learns to read well.

Suddenly, virtually every education conference, every report, every professional journal is hailing Reading Recovery.

Skeptics say any program that allows good teachers to work with pupils one-on-one would work well.

But in district after district in five nations, Reading Recovery has brought 90 percent of the weakest first-grade readers up to the average level of their class in half a school year or less—something no other approach, whether in groups or one-on-one, can match, according to a study in *Reading Research Quarterly,* a leading journal.

Perhaps most appealing to school systems eyeing the hefty price tag, children who go through 12 to 20 weeks of Reading Recovery keep performing at their grade level for years without requiring extra help.

Training Program Advocated

In metro Atlanta schools, requiring a child to repeat a grade costs about $5,000. Traditional remediation classes cost about $1,500 a year, and students typically remain in them year after year. A year of special education costs about $8,000.

That makes Reading Recovery a bargain, advocates say.

And that is why Georgia State University Professor Clifford Johnson, head of Georgia's only Reading Recovery training program and one of relatively few nationwide, is pushing a $4 million plan to train enough Reading Recovery teachers for every public school in Georgia.

A private foundation, state and participating school systems would each foot a third of the bill—about $335,000 a year from each source—to train 36 teacher-trainers and nearly 2,000 teachers. That would allow 20,000 first-graders to get help each year, a vast expansion from the 1,000 pupils touched by Reading Recovery so far.

Ten other states already provide some funding for Reading Recovery, and state Sen. Mary Margaret Oliver (D-Decatur), chairwoman of the Senate Appropriations Committee's education panel, is hopeful Georgia's legislature will sign on this year.

"I'm going to be pushing for it," she said.

Brainchild of New Zealander

Reading Recovery is the brainchild of a grandmotherly New Zealand education professor, Marie Clay.

As a Fulbright scholar in the 1950s, Clay came to the United States to study with an education professor, but his sudden death forced her to study developmental psychology instead. That unwelcome switch proved a boon, she said, because she learned to observe human development in a way few educators do.

Then, in the 1960s, Clay oversaw a massive research program in New Zealand that provided new insight into how some 6-year-olds become good readers and what trips others up.

Finally, in the 1970s, she put all she had learned into a program that would become Reading Recovery. She waived her rights to any royalties from its use in the United States.

The program has no single method, no easy formula. "We do lots of things that are very different from what people ordinarily do when they try to teach [poor readers] to read," Clay said. Among them:

- Reading Recovery maintains a relentless focus on what the child *can* do, not what he can't. Particularly for poor readers, that can be a huge switch.

  Gwinnett County first-grade teacher Patricia Turner used to spend "a good part of my time thinking about what the children *didn't* know, because that's what I wanted to teach them."

Reading Recovery teachers search for what even low-proficiency readers can do, and they base early lessons on the letters a child has mastered, his name, what he knows about books and topics he wants to read about.

By making carefully chosen, incremental advances, the teacher usually brings about dramatic improvement.

"We all learn better when we're comfortable," said Carole Barnhart, a Reading Recovery teacher in Gwinnett.

- It is highly individualized, recognizing there is no single way children learn to read and no simplistic list of blockades they encounter. Teachers learn to make very specific assessments of each child and to keep precise records of each one's progress.

- While controversy rages over whether phonics or the "whole language" approach is best, Reading Recovery draws on the best of both. As in whole language, Reading Recovery teaches children to read using full sentences and books from their first lessons. (Pupils typically read five short, engaging books in each half-hour lesson.) But it also stresses letter-sound relationships—generally known as phonics—as one important way to figure out what the text says.

- It intervenes early, before the cycle of failure sets in. Many schools start remedial reading in second grade, and by then, children already may have decided they'll never succeed.

Before he left kindergarten, Vince Casey had begun to give up, said his mother, Tracy. "He wouldn't try anything. He would just sit there and say, 'No, I can't do it, I can't do it,'" she said.

Now in Reading Recovery at Gwinnett's Benefield Elementary, Vince is a changed boy. "He will get up there in front of the whole class and read out loud and get into all the discussions," his mother said.

- Reading Recovery aims to teach the child to succeed long-term, not merely in that day's assignment. Problem-solving strategies that will help far down the line are embedded in even the earliest lessons.

- The program emphasizes reading with lots of expression. The idea is to help children understand the meaning of what they're reading to themselves. The dramatic tones also help convey how much fun reading a good story can be.

- All adults in the program, from novice teachers just starting their training to program heads, constantly teach first-graders to read. Education professors long have been criticized for preaching theories of classroom management when they haven't had pupils of their own for decades. That never happens in Reading Recovery.

"You can't learn this program without children," Clay said.

Progress Has Teacher "in Awe"

Reading Recovery came to Georgia in 1991 when Fulton County sent 10 teachers and two teacher-trainers to GSU's training program.

Marietta and DeKalb, Cobb, Douglas and Gwinnett counties have since joined.

Only the best teachers who have at least three years of experience teaching first-graders to read are selected for Reading Recovery. They are given a full year of intensive training.

Sessions such as Mangum's "behind the glass"—teaching a child while colleagues look on from behind a one-way mirror—are an integral element.

To have so many critics watching would terrify many adults, but Reading Recovery teachers say they appreciate the help that other teachers can offer.

And they say the payoff comes as they watch once-defeated children blossom into confident, capable readers.

"I am just in awe about what E is doing now," Mangum said. "She will re-read. She monitors herself. When she runs into difficulty, she keeps working on it and working on it until she gets it."

Reading Skills Recovered
Wendy Fox

Reading Recovery is a one-on-one reading program for first graders that has been used in this country for 11 years and in the Boston Public Schools since 1991. Developed in New Zealand, Reading Recovery is widely credited with being one of the most effective ways of bringing poor readers—or even nonreaders—up to grade level in one semester. Of the city's 5,564 first grade students, about 200 are enrolled in Reading Recovery this year. Another 900 are estimated to need this sort of intensive reading help.

Professor Irene Fountas is director of the Center for Reading Recovery at Lesley College and is responsible for training all the Reading Recovery teacher leaders in Massachusetts. Learning editor Wendy Fox talked with Fountas last week about Reading Recovery and how it works.

Q. *This is reputed to be a very expensive program. Is that true? What does it cost?*

A. The Purpose of Reading Recovery is to work with the lowest children, starting with the bottom child. The idea is that the teacher work with a minimum of four children each day for 30-minute lessons, which would equal two hours of teaching time a day per teacher.

SOURCE: *The Boston Globe,* November 5, 1995, pp. A97–A98. Reprinted courtesy of *The Boston Globe.*

Q. *Each child gets 30 minutes a day?*

A. Yes, it's generally no more than half a teacher's job. The teacher does something else for the other half of the day.

So if we were to think about the cost in terms of salary . . . then somewhere between $25,000 and $50,000 is a teacher salary. So if you were to take half a salary, it would be $12,500 to $25,000.

A teacher should be able to move eight children through the program in a year, four at a time. So that's $2,000 to $3,000 per child. One time.

Now the cost of educating a child in Massachusetts is something like $5,500 a year. So if you are reducing retentions, where a child is going to repeat a grade for $5,500, or if a child is going to special education, which probably costs many more thousands and it's not for one year, it's for several years, then $2,000 to $3,000, in my mind, for a child to have a 10- to 20-week intervention is very cost effective.

The costs of failure in first grade are so great and the child's whole literary path in school we know is largely influenced by what happens in first grade. It would seem to me that kind of investment is an investment in the future of the child.

Q. *Does every child, even the lowest-achieving child who goes through this program, come out reading?*

A. Every child makes progress. Marie Clay, the founder of Reading Recovery, says that if we get these kids early, if we identify them early and work with them early, we should expect to get at least two-thirds of them to the average. In Boston, for five years now, they've gotten over 90 percent of the children to the average.

Q. *When you say get to average, what is average?*

A. An average would differ in various communities. An average would be if this were January in first grade, what would you expect first graders to be reading at this time in January in this school in this community?

And it's not only reaching the average of their peer group, but also . . . they need to show certain strengths as a reader so we have a great deal of confidence that they'll be able to continue to grow.

Q. *For example, those could be what kinds of things?*

A. They would know how to take words apart, and that may be phonetically but it may be in larger chunks. They would know how to use context, they would know how to use language. They would have a variety of flexibility strategies.

What often characterizes poor readers is they have one way of solving problems and if it doesn't work, they don't have a lot of other ways to try. What characterizes successful readers is a set of flexible strategies so when something doesn't work, they have other ways of figuring it out.

So one of the things the child really learns in Reading Recovery is a variety of ways to problem solve as readers.

Q. *There's teacher training, also. How does that work?*

A. The teachers take a graduate-level class for one year after school. They attend class one day a week for three hours and they take turns bringing the children that they are teaching to class and they actually teach a lesson behind a one-way mirror while their class of peers observes the lesson.

It's $2,500 for them to have the year-long course. And there's a set of books that are about $1,700 that the school would buy, a set of children's literature that would become the material of the school. It's a one-time cost.

The training also includes the teacher leader going and visiting them in their school and watching them teach their children and kind of coaching them.

Then what's interesting about Reading Recovery training is that in most education programs, you train and you're done. In Reading Recovery, you're not done.

After their training year, the teachers come back together six times a year, which is usually about once every six weeks, and they take turns teaching for each other again. As long as they're a Reading Recovery teacher, they have this long-term professional development. It's a renewal system.

Q.   *Is that something the school department pays for?*

A.   These teachers would have release time six times a year on their professional development afternoons or whatever, and there's no cost attached to that.

But it depends on how you look at expensive. I would be talking more about impact than expense. When we can talk about doing something for children for 10 to 20 weeks that changes their schooling, I'd pay $10,000 a child. I might even pay $100,000 a child, I don't know.

But the other part is the impact on the system. The system starts to realize that the lowest-achieving children can learn.

For many years, we have bought into institutionalized failure, meaning there will be a percentage of children who will fail the standardized tests and we will put them in special education and we will give them help but we expect that that will be.

Reading Recovery was designed to eliminate literacy failure in the system, one child at a time. And when it happens, it causes teachers to change their views of what can happen for these kids. It causes the system to say, "Ahh, if our kids can do this, what can be our expectations for other kids?"

Q.   *Have you seen that in Boston?*

A.   Yes, and this is why I'm going to get back to impact. The training is not just for these teachers to do Reading Recovery. They're taking all this understanding of how readers develop and how writers develop, and they take that knowledge to their work in the other half of their job.

What do they do for the other half of their job? Special education maybe? Classroom teacher? Title 1 teacher? They take this knowledge to their work with children of other ages and a broader range of children.

Q.   *Let's talk about specifics. What exactly does a Reading Recovery teacher do with a kid for 30 minutes, five days a week?*

A.   For one thing, they read lots of books. They read books that are familiar and easy for the child and have been introduced to the child before.

Q. *Who's reading to whom?*

A. The child reads to the teacher. It's always the child who's reading. The child reads several books.

I'll give you a little capsule of a lesson. The child starts by reading several of what we call familiar books.

Q. *This is a child who can already read?*

A. Yes. And the child who doesn't know how begins by reading a text that's simple, like this one: "I can jump." And the teacher says, "And you know what she's saying? She's saying 'I can jump, too.' You put your finger under it and read. 'I can jump, too.'"

You see how all of a sudden the child is reading the very simplest texts? Very supported by pictures. In Reading Recovery, children learn to read by reading books. Now, it doesn't mean that I might not take the word 'can,' because it's a new and important word for this child, and I might take magnetic letters and work at a magnetic easel and really help them look at 'can' and make it several times. And they look at other words that start like 'can' and really focus on it. So that the child really does develop an understanding of letters and words.

Q. *So phonics and technique are involved in this in addition to context.*

A. Absolutely. The lesson goes like this. First, familiar reading. Then the teacher gives the child the book that she introduced to him yesterday. And she does an assessment on how he reads it all by himself. Then the teacher does some of what we call letter or word work. If the child doesn't know any letters—and it's very typical for a Reading Recovery child not to know any letters—the teacher might work with a letter in a lot of different mediums, like sand and water pen and magnetic letters and big kinesthetic movements and small movements, so the child really gets a letter form.

And then the teacher may have the child sort some letters. The teacher may have the child make some words. That happens for about 2 or 3 minutes, that's letter and word work. Not a whole lot of time, but just enough in each lesson to get the child thinking about it.

Then the child writes a story in what's called a writing book. The child contributes all he can and the teacher teaches him at the top on a practice page some ways of thinking about things he doesn't know how to write. So that he can get his whole message down.

Q. *Is this inventive spelling?*

A. Actually it's not. In the Reading Recovery lesson, we help the child write it correctly. There's a reason for that. Approximated spelling is very useful in the classroom. But for Reading Recovery children if they saw the word spelled differently every time they saw it, it would add to their confusion. And these are children who are easily confused.

Q. *The burden seems to be on the teacher and not on the child in this program.*

A. That's it. You've got it. It is the position of Reading Recovery that if children are not learning, the teacher has not found the right way to teach them. So the Reading Recovery teacher is trained to have a whole lot of different ways of working with the child until the child is successful.

. . .There's also a very comprehensive assessment in Reading Recovery. . . . We've followed children through our center, across the state. We've done a longitudinal study each year, and what we have found is these children continue to progress in second grade and third grade.

Now, do we need to check on them? Absolutely. These were the kids who were most at risk of failure in the system. We've invested in an intervention in first grade and we need to check on them and make sure that if something has happened in their lives or they're starting another school year and they're not feeling comfortable about what they're doing that we check up on them.

What I have found is that more often than not, they're just fine. But once in a while there's a child that you need to pull in for a week or two and read with them to get their confidence back up. We call that a booster dose.

Q.   *What do you think of this new Read Boston effort?*

A.   I think it will take all of us putting our very best efforts together to take responsibility for assuring that every child becomes literate through their experience in the Boston schools.

We can't say these kids can't learn. We can't say they're poor. We can't say their mother doesn't speak English. Those may be true. But those are not things that we can do anything about or penalize children for. I think the fact that there is a broad range of stakeholders taking responsibility for literacy is promising.

What I'm really looking for in Read Boston is measures. I really want us to be able to say this is what we're doing and year by year, we're knowing how much better we're getting at it and where we have to go.

I'm interested in the kind of accountability we use in Reading Recovery. No kid falls through the cracks.

Restore Reading Recovery Program
Editorial, The Atlanta Constitution

Gov. Zell Miller deserves praise for delaying some $17 million in state programs and services. If the General Assembly is going to insist on a $300 million tax cut, that money has to come from somewhere.

Source: *The Atlanta Constitution,* July 10, 1995, Sec. A; p. 8. Reprinted with permission from *The Atlanta Journal-Constitution.*

CHILDREN, PRISONS, PRIORITIES

One year of Reading Recovery	$2,000 per child
One year of special education	$10,000 per child
One year of housing in prison	$17,724 per prisoner
Construction of new cell in typical prison	$34,000
Construction of new cell in high-security prison	$43,400

SOURCE: Wilson Lowrey/Staff

But one program Miller has slated for postponement—though small—underscores the imbalance of priorities that drives state spending. While state officials can come up with $70 million for the construction of prisons, they continue to give short shrift to programs that prevent the need for more prisons.

One of those programs is Reading Recovery, an intense, one-on-one tutoring program designed to catch first-graders who can't read and turn them around before they're programmed for failure. The Legislature appropriated a mere $250,000—the cost of building about six prison cells—to begin the training of teachers in the program's highly successful methods. But Miller cut it out, at least for the time being.

The shortsightedness of that is evident through a visit to the Lee Arrendale Correctional Institution in Alto. There, the sound of construction permeates the air as the prison is readied to accept a new class of young inmates. They're boys ages 13 to 17 whose crimes have earned them adult status and adult punishment under a new law pushed by Miller.

A trait they share is poor reading skills. The average reading level at Alto is the fifth grade.

Reading Recovery alone, of course, wouldn't have kept all these boys out of prison. But it might have saved some.

The governor says he targeted the program because it's new. But it's also the ideal kind of program for government to support. It's cheap: $250,000 to $350,000 a year. It builds on itself: The three Atlanta teachers who were scheduled for training this year would have each trained another 11 teachers next year. It offers immediate savings: Children who go through the program are less likely to wind up in special-education classes, which can cost five times as much.

Furthermore, the state's contribution had leveraged $500,000 more from private foundations and local school systems.

"Preventing the waste of human life that we see at the Lee Arrendale facility should be a higher priority than building new prison cells," says state Sen. Mary Margaret Oliver, who lobbied for the reading program. Though she calls Miller's preschool program for 4-year-olds the best crime prevention program in existence, she adds, "If a child can't read coming out of the first grade, he's in desperate trouble."

The Legislature must still approve the governor's proposed deferrals. And no doubt, there will be much lobbying to save other pet projects. But this is one program that should be restored.

Reading Recovery: Is It Effective?
Is It Cost-Effective?
Gerald W. Bracey

One of the more popular programs for remedial reading instruction in the last decade has been the import from New Zealand known as Reading Recovery. In Reading Recovery, children whose reading skills place them among the lowest 10% to 20% of students are pulled out of classrooms for half an hour of one-on-one tutoring.

The tutor first spends 10 sessions trying to determine what knowledge about reading and print a student already has. The tutor then launches the student on an individually tailored program through a series of books that are graded for difficulty. In each session, the child reads several books, beginning with one that is already familiar. The child may also practice with individual letters or words. When the student has had 60 such sessions or has reached an oral reading level equal to the average of his or her grade, the program ends. The goal is to instill in students strategies for approaching reading that will allow them to continue to improve. It looks like a good approach, and, given its rapid increase in popularity in this country, others seem to agree.

Now, however, in a comprehensive review of the literature that deals with Reading Recovery, Elfrieda Hiebert of the University of Michigan has concluded that the impact of the program may have been overestimated and that the analysis of its cost-effectiveness may have been defective. Her analysis appears in the December 1994 issue of *Educational Researcher*.

SOURCE: *Phi Delta Kappan*, February 1995, pp. 493–494. Reprinted with permission of *Phi Delta Kappan* and the author. Gerald Bracey is an independent research psychologist, writer, and author of *Final Exam: A Study of the Perpetual Scrutiny of American Education* (Bloomington, IN: Technos Press, 1995).

The cost-effectiveness of Reading Recovery was determined by assuming an average salary of $33,000 per teacher and 16 students per teacher, per year. This yielded an annual cost figure of $2,063 per student for the program's services. For comparison purposes, Hiebert points out that the provision of Chapter I services for four years costs an additional $3,772, that special education services for four years cost an average of $6,604 more than a year of regular schooling, and that a year's retention costs $5,208. Hiebert also notes that Reading Recovery teachers typically reach only 11 students, not 16. However, this simple analysis still contains some questionable assumptions: namely, that all Reading Recovery students are successful, that they never need additional services, and that students in alternative remedial programs are not successful. Indeed, the data show clearly that some students in Reading Recovery are going to need additional services and that some are going to be retained.

When Hiebert recalculated the costs per successful Reading Recovery student, she arrived at an annual cost of $8,333 per student. Hiebert questions whether we can afford such a program on a large scale. She calculates that if Reading Recovery were made available to the 26% of first-graders in California who now receive some federal- or state-funded compensatory program, Reading Recovery would occupy 10,593 people full time. Providing Reading Recovery for 15% of California students would require the full-time equivalent of 6,150 people. That's an annual cost of $282,900,000 (since the average elementary teacher in California earned just over $46,000 in 1993–94). Currently, the total number of first-grade teachers in California is only 13,492. Other states might not need to have such a high percentage of Reading Recovery teachers, but Hiebert notes that the need for compensatory resources would be greatest precisely where the resources are least available.

And even then, Hiebert contends, we don't know whether or not the program is successful at its conclusion or whether whatever gains are made will hold up over time. (For some reason, no thought has ever been given to providing Reading Recovery "refresher" courses for students in the later grades.) Hiebert questions Reading Recovery's use of word-level accuracy on an oral reading task as its principal criterion for success, rather than some measure of comprehension or of automaticity (which correlates with comprehension).

The single longitudinal study that has compared Reading Recovery with other treatments did not find much difference. It is problematical, though, that this research has focused on examining mean differences among groups. Hiebert writes:

> When mean differences in performance are the primary way of evaluating the effectiveness of a program, the information that policy makers and practitioners need to make informed decisions can be obscured. In particular, information on who benefits most from the tutoring, the number of children who can be served, the portion of the school population that the children represent, or the aspects of literacy that are promoted by the tutoring may be difficult to glean from analyses of effect sizes.

When Hiebert looked at fourth-graders who had been through Reading Recovery or other treatments, she did not find much difference and did not find high performance. "An average grade-equivalent of 3.0 at the end of fourth grade for the [Reading Recovery]-tutored group suggests that the proficient oral reading performance at grade 1 has not resulted in self-extending strategies to other literacy tasks in subsequent grades," she writes.

Hiebert worries that we may have imported a program that was designed to meet one set of needs and are now trying to use it with students who have different problems. Most children in New Zealand attend small community schools, and the nation has a high literacy level. A program such as Reading Recovery may be sufficient under such conditions. But what about our inner cities and our poor rural areas?

A preliminary report from New York City suggests that reading levels and discontinuation rates are lower in schools with low-income students. The report also suggests that Reading Recovery is adversely affected in these schools by high levels of mobility and absenteeism. Moreover, the criterion for success—reaching the average proficiency of the school—is likely to be too low to ensure a student's future success.

Hiebert does observe that Reading Recovery exhibits five attributes known to be characteristics of successful beginning reading instruction: phonemic awareness, deliberate instruction, high expectations, repeated reading of text, and experimenting with letter/sound correspondences through writing. Hiebert suggests that we take these aspects of Reading Recovery and other programs and try to apply them in nontutoring situations. That might "move American reading instruction away from the elusive search for a single best method to the confrontation of a fundamental issue: Why are the instructional elements that have consistently been associated with high levels of literacy attainment not a given in all Chapter I programs?"

In Loco Parentis
James Q. Wilson

Policy elites, whether liberal or conservative, usually explain the problems of the urban underclass in terms of wrong incentives. Liberals rail at the lack of benefits and opportunities afforded the underclass; conservatives, at the excess

Source: *The Brookings Review,* Fall 1993, pp. 12–15. Reprinted with permission from *The Brookings Review.*

of benefits offered without corresponding obligations. Liberals blame crime on poverty and joblessness; conservatives, on insufficiently severe criminal sanctions. Invariably, the argument boils down to incentives—rewards and penalties.

Ordinary citizens see the matter differently. Though acknowledging that the incentives may be poor—education inadequate, jobs scarce, and the criminal justice system ineffective—the public tends to stress the attitudes of the permanently poor and the habitually criminal, attitudes formed in the family (or, increasingly, the nonfamily) and reinforced by the culture. Those attitudes— which, I would emphasize, are not unique to the underclass, but are particularly destructive in their effect there—are characterized this way: a belief in rights but not in responsibilities, an emphasis on "me" and a neglect of "we," a preference for immediate gratification over investments for the future, and an expectation that if one is lucky or clever enough one can get something for nothing.

Some of these attitudes may be the result of scarce legitimate jobs and abundant criminal opportunities. But if those factors were the whole story, the results of carefully evaluated efforts to change behavior by supplying jobs, providing training, or altering penalties would not be as discouraging as they are. And if the objective conditions of inner-city life were all that mattered, then we would not see such great differences in behavior among individuals and groups confronting similar conditions. Without denying the importance of incentives, I want to side with the view of the average citizen who believes that poor self-control and indifference to the rights of others arise in large part from poor family training.

The Family's Socializing Role

The chief means by which every society induces its members to exercise a modicum of self-control and to assign a reasonable value to the preferences of others is the family. Developmental psychologists are in broad agreement that the parental practices most likely to achieve these goals involve a combination of affection and discipline such that the child's attachment to the parents is strong and the rules of everyday behavior are clearly understood and consistently enforced. Fortunately, most babies are biologically eager for attachment and predisposed to socialization, and most parents love their children and invest without compensation in their rearing.

But individuals differ in the extent to which they have (or reveal) prosocial impulses, and so some children are difficult and some parents incompetent. Unfortunately, since temperament is to a significant degree under genetic control, there is an elevated probability that difficult children will be born to incompetent parents. Socialization failures, if uncorrected, can breed—literally— more failures. Crime runs in families, alcoholism runs in families, impulsive and sensation-seeking behavior runs in families.

Matters become worse if families cease to exist or are transformed into pseudo-families. Poverty, as Daniel Patrick Moynihan steadily and rightly reminds us, has now become a children's problem owing chiefly to the fact that an increased proportion of children live for long periods, sometimes their entire childhood, in mother-only families, a large fraction of which are also poor. A 1988 Department of Health and Human Services study found that at every income level save the very highest (over $50,000 a year), children living with never-married mothers were more likely than their counterparts in two-parent families to have been expelled or suspended from school, to display emotional problems, and to engage in antisocial behavior.

If the family is headed by a teenage mother, the risks are even greater. Children of teenage black mothers are less able to control their impulses, have a lower tolerance for frustration, are more likely to be hyperactive, have more difficulty adapting to school, and, if boys, are more likely to be hostile, assertive, and willful than children of older mothers.

Possibilities for Change

Is there any way to come to the aid of a weakened family, specifically to help it instill in its children the habits of mind and character that will enable them to take better advantage of whatever opportunities they have?

In principle, the answer is yes. Certainly, that is the governing assumption of every religious and of many secular efforts to help social outcasts—alcoholics, drug abusers, and school dropouts—and those efforts have produced many successes. The problem arises in trying to imagine a program that by plan and in the hands of ordinary managers will achieve the necessary personal redemption for large numbers of people.

Efforts to do this on a large scale and by bureaucratic processes have not, on the whole, proved very successful. For example, efforts to rehabilitate large numbers of delinquents or criminals have met with more failures than successes. Though there are some success stories, no one should suppose that we know how to convert large numbers of 18-year-old delinquents into law-abiding citizens.

Nor can one take much hope from recent occasions in which the military had an opportunity to test whether its intensive training and strict discipline could improve the prospects of difficult boys. The first experiment began in 1966, when Secretary of Defense Robert McNamara undertook Project 100,000 as a way of contributing to the War on Poverty, and ended in 1971. The second took place by accident during 1976–80, when the military enlistment test was misnormed and low-aptitude individuals were inadvertently recruited.

Investigators studied veterans of both these quasi-experiments, comparing their economic, educational, and family status with that of people of similarly low aptitude who had never served in the military. Although most of the low-aptitude veterans said that their military experience had been good for them, primarily because it taught them discipline and made them more mature, the belief did not correspond to reality. Project 100,000 veterans were *worse* off than nonveterans in employment status, educational achievement, and income; mis-normed veterans were *no better* off than nonveterans. All were more likely to be divorced than the nonveterans. As the authors of the study concluded, "The military doesn't appear to be a panacea for struggling youth."

Clearly, addressing the problems of temperamentally difficult or low-aptitude youth is not easily done if one waits until they have reached their teens or young adulthood years. What if the intervention could begin earlier? Evidence from early childhood programs is more encouraging but still fragmentary and in some cases inconsistent.

Early Intervention

Scarcely any governmental program is more popular today than Head Start, but even its long-term effects are in doubt (no lasting effects on IQ have been found, and only a little evidence exists on Head Start's effects on such matters as pregnancy, welfare, and crime). The strongest evidence of long-term effects of preschool education comes from one (non-Head Start) program, the Perry Preschool in Ypsilanti, Michigan, whose "graduates" were followed for many years. Compared with a control group, the Perry students were found to be less likely to drop out before finishing high school, less likely to go on welfare, more likely to be working after leaving school and less likely to have been arrested.

Why did the Perry program (and possibly a few other model programs) do so well? One reason is that they *were* model programs conducted by capable people who had received intensive training and ample budgets. Another is that the Perry project was not limited to providing children with preschool experiences for twelve-and-a-half hours a week. It also involved an extensive program of home visits.

Something akin to the Perry results, albeit (thus far) only for the short term, has been reported by the Infant Health and Development Program, which provided intensive services to nearly 1,000 premature infants in eight cities. The infants, at risk for retardation, behavioral problems, and learning difficulties, were randomly assigned to treatment and control groups. Infants and parents in the experimental group received weekly (later biweekly) home visits by trained counselors. After their first birthday the babies attended child development centers five days a week. And parents attended biweekly meetings at which they were given information and could share experiences. At age three, children in the experimental group had higher IQs and fewer behavioral problems than those in the control group. Gains were greatest for children who had the most disadvantaged mothers.

Suppose that the long-term results from the premature baby project parallel those of the Perry Project. What lessons can we infer? The most obvious and (to some) perhaps the most troubling is that intervention programs produce more benefits the more deeply they intervene. For at-risk children, the more the programs either assume parental functions or alter the behavior of parents, the greater the benefit to the child.

Another possibility, albeit one that has as yet only fragmentary evidence, is that long-lasting interventions are likely to make more of a difference than short-term ones. Children cannot be inoculated against behavioral problems as they are against smallpox. Yet beginning at age five or six the only intervention program aimed at children and generally under government control is the school.

The central role of the school has led Americans to focus their hopes for character formation on it, hopes that receive some support from studies suggesting that the schools doing the best job of educating children are also those that do the best job of controlling their behavior. But even the best schools rarely occupy a child more than six hours a day, half the days of the year. And even the best school cannot offset the threats of disorderly streets, the neglect of absent parents, or the discord of unhappy homes.

Is Boarding School an Option?

Families with the necessary financial resources have always had an important way of coping with hard-to socialize children or of escaping their responsibility for socializing them—the boarding school. Families of lesser means have heretofore had no such option for their at-risk children. But could not public resources be used to enable families in underclass neighborhoods voluntarily to enroll their children, beginning at an early age, in boarding schools?

I have in mind no single model of what such a boarding school would do, only a set of guidelines. In the elementary years, a boarding school would simply extend the number of hours the child was under school rather than parental supervision. School might become an all-day affair, with the child given breakfast and dinner and supervised after-class play opportunities in addition to regular instruction. In the extreme case of a child with no competent parent at all, sleeping quarters would be provided. As the child got older, say in the junior high years, it would become a full-time boarding school with home visits arranged by mutual agreement. The schools would be operated, I would hope, by private as well as by public agencies. Enrollment, as stated, would be voluntary but encouraged for at-risk children. The primary object would be to provide a safe, consistent, and enjoyable mechanism for the habituation of the child—that is, for the inculcation of the ordinary virtues of politeness, self-control, and social skills. Another goal for these schools would be either to place their students into a college or to qualify them for entry into an occupation by means of an apprenticeship program.

Instead of leaving matters entirely to chance or voluntary participation in a boarding school program, perhaps better homes could be supplied in other ways. Suppose that unmarried mothers seeking welfare were given a choice: as a condition of receiving financial aid, they must either live with their parents or in group homes where they would be instructed in child care, receive a regular education, and conform to rules governing personal conduct and group responsibilities. The key elements in this idea are threefold. Do not allow welfare to be used for subsidizing independent but dysfunctional households; do not require the mothers of small children to work outside the home; and provide the best and most structured start in life for the next generation of children.

No More Fatherless Families

Boarding schools may be especially important for boys growing up in a fatherless family. Much has been said about the economic and psychological costs borne by such children. But something also must be said about the equally important communal costs. Neighborhood standards and values may be set by mothers, but they are enforced by fathers, or at least by adult males. Neighborhoods without fathers are neighborhoods without men able and willing to confront errant youth, chase threatening gangs, and reproach delinquent fathers.

I do not know any way of requiring this generation of errant fathers to take up their responsibilities. The reach of the law has been lengthened, but we should not be optimistic that this will result in more than a modest increase in the size of family support payments received by some mothers, much less any increase at all in the extent to which fathers would help care for the children. Our chief goal ought to be reducing the number of errant fathers produced by the next generation—that is, increasing the number of young urban males who marry and remain married.

Of all the institutions through which people may pass—schools, employers, the military—marriage has the largest effect. For every race and at every age, married men live longer than unmarried ones and have lower rates of homicide, suicide, accidents, and mental illness. Crime rates are lower for married than unmarried men, and incomes are higher. Infant mortality rates are higher for unmarried than for married women, whether black or white, and these differences cannot be explained by differences in income or availability of medical care. An unmarried woman with a college education is more likely to have her infant die than is a married woman *without* a high school education.

Though some of these differences can be explained by female selectivity in choosing mates, I doubt that all can. Marriage not only involves screening people for their capacity for self-control, it also provides inducements—the need to support a mate, care for a child, and maintain a home—that increase that capacity.

Public Funds, Private Programs

In the past, the institutions that have produced effective male socialization have been private. Today we expect government programs to accomplish what families, villages, and churches once did. I think we will be disappointed. Government programs, whether aimed at farmers, professors, or welfare mothers, tend to produce dependence, not self-reliance. Our policy ought to be to identify, evaluate, and encourage those local, private efforts that seem to do the best job at reducing drug abuse, inducing lovers to marry, persuading fathers to take responsibility for their children, and exercising informal social control over neighborhood streets.

The federal government is a powerful but clumsy giant, not very adept at identifying, evaluating, and encouraging. What it is good at is passing laws, transferring funds, and multiplying regulations. These are necessary functions, but out of place in the realm of personal redemption. When the elephant walks among the chickens, the collateral damage can be great. A government program to foster personal redemption will come equipped with standardized budgets, buy-America rules, minority set-asides, quarterly reporting requirements, and environmental impact statements, and, in all likelihood, a thinly disguised bias against any kind of involvement with churches.

There may be a better way. Public funds might be sent to private organizations that in turn do the identifying, evaluating, and encouraging, all on the basis of carefully negotiated charters that free these intermediaries from most governmental constraints. I know of no example, but people who wish to think seriously about changing the culture of poverty had better start inventing one.

Chapter 6

Bilingual Education

Introduction

He's old now. But when he emigrated from Poland to the United States in 1931 he was only 10 years old. Processed at Ellis Island, his long difficult Polish surname was misspelled and somewhat anglicized. When he went to school, he learned English rapidly by the "sink or swim" method—now called immersion.

He and his wife raised three children. They lived in an ethnic neighborhood and, although proud of their Polish heritage, delivered a clear message to their children: "You don't do the polka here. We speak English." He was proud to be an American, proud of his facility with the English language, and proud of his children's educational and professional achievements—two of whom are now teachers and one a physician.

Today, the old man often expresses his concern for the modern way of educating immigrant children—the bilingual way. He fears that this is not good for the country and not good for the children. He worries that a nation that does not have one common language will become factionalized and ultimately disintegrate. He worries that bilingual educational programs will not result in children mastering English and that as a consequence they will never succeed educationally or professionally. He believes that immigrant children should learn English the same way he did so many years ago.

Are bilingual programs effective in teaching English? Are they effective in producing the net result that, by the time they graduate from high school, students have learned more math, science, history, and so on than they would have if their English language instruction had been by the immersion method? What evidence would count toward establishing an answer to this question? Are bilingual programs more divisive than inclusive? Are bilingual education programs worth the expense?

No Comprendo
Barbara Mujica

WASHINGTON—Last spring, my niece phoned me in tears. She was graduating from high school and had to make a decision. An outstanding soccer player, she was offered athletic scholarships by several colleges. So why was she crying?

My niece came to the United States from South America as a child. Although she had received good grades in her schools in Miami, she spoke English with a heavy accent and her comprehension and writing skills were deficient. She was afraid that once she left the Miami environment she would feel uncomfortable and, worse still, have difficulty keeping up with class work.

Programs that keep foreign-born children in Spanish-language classrooms for years are only part of the problem. During a visit to my niece's former school, I observed that all business, not just teaching, was conducted in Spanish. In the office, secretaries spoke to the administrators and the children in Spanish. Announcements over the public-address system were made in an English so fractured that it was almost incomprehensible.

I asked my niece's mother why, after years in public schools, her daughter had poor English skills. "It's the whole environment," she replied. "All kinds of services are available in Spanish or Spanglish. Sports and after-school activities are conducted in Spanglish. That's what the kids hear on the radio and in the street."

Until recently, immigrants made learning English a priority. But even when they didn't learn English themselves, their children grew up speaking it. Thousands of first-generation Americans still strive to learn English, but others face reduced educational and career opportunities because they have not mastered this basic skill they need to get ahead.

According to the 1990 census, 40 percent of the Hispanics born in the U.S. do not graduate from high school, and the Department of Education says that a lack of proficiency in English is an important factor in the drop-out rate.

People and agencies that favor providing services only in foreign languages want to help people who do not speak English, but they may be doing them a disservice by condemning them to a linguistic ghetto from which they cannot easily escape.

And my niece? She turned down all of her scholarship opportunities, deciding instead to attend a small college in Miami, where she will never have to put her English to the test.

SOURCE: *The New York Times*, January 3, 1995, p. A19. Reprinted with permission from *The New York Times*.

Tongue-Tied in the Schools
Susan Headden

Javier Sanchez speaks English like the proud American he is. Born in Brooklyn, N.Y., the wiry 12-year-old speaks English at home, and he speaks it on the playground. He spoke it in the classroom, too—until one day in the third grade, when he was abruptly moved to a program that taught him in Spanish all but 45 minutes a day. "It was a disaster," says his Puerto Rican-born mother, Dominga Sanchez. "He didn't *understand* Spanish." Sanchez begged the teacher to return her son to his regular class. Her request was met with amazement. "Why?" the teacher asked. "Don't you feel proud to be Hispanic?"

Along with crumbling classrooms and violence in the hallways, bilingual education has emerged as one of the dark spots on the grim tableau of American public education. Started 27 years ago to help impoverished Mexican-Americans, the program was born of good intentions, but today it has mushroomed into a $10 billion-a-year bureaucracy that not only cannot promise the students will learn English but may actually do some children more harm than good. Just as troubling, while children like Javier are placed in programs they don't want and may not need, thousands more children are foundering because they get no help with English at all.

Bilingual education was intended to give new immigrants a leg up. During earlier waves of immigration, children who entered American schools without speaking English were left to fend for themselves. Many thrived, but others, feeling lost and confused, did not. Their failures led to Title VII of the Elementary and Secondary Education Act, which ensured supplementary services for all non-English-speaking newcomers to America.

Armenian to Urdu   Significantly, the law did not prescribe a method for delivering those services. But today, of the funds used to help children learn English, 75 percent of federal money—and the bulk of state and local money—goes toward classes taught in students' native tongues; only 25 percent supports programs rooted in English. That makes bilingual education the de facto law of the land.

Historically, Hispanics have been the largest beneficiaries of bilingual education. Today, however, they compete for funding with new immigrant groups whose urge to assimilate, some educators say, may be stronger. Further, not many school districts can offer classes in such languages as Armenian and Urdu. So for practical reasons, too, children of other nationalities are placed in English-based classes more often than children of Hispanics. The problem, as many see

SOURCE: *U.S. News & World Report*, September 25, 1995, pp. 44–46. Copyright © 1995, *U.S. News & World Report*. Reprinted with permission.

it, is that students are staying in native-language programs far too long. In a typical complaint, the mother of one New York ninth grader says her daughter has been in "transitional" bilingual education for nine years. "We support bilingual education," says Ray Domanico of the New York Public Education Association. "But it is becoming an institutionalized ghetto."

Learning Chinese   In theory, bilingual education is hard to fault. Students learn math, science and other "content" subjects in their native tongues, and they take special English classes for a small part of the day. When they are ready, ideally within three or four years, they switch to classes taught exclusively in English. The crucial advantage is that students don't fall behind in their other lessons while gaining competence in English. Further, supporters claim, bilingual education produces students fluent in two languages.

That would be great, if it were true. Too often it is not. What is sometimes mistaken for dual-language instruction is actually native-language instruction, in which students hear English for as little as 30 minutes a day. "Art, physical education and music are supposed to be taught in English," says Lucy Fortney, a third-grade teacher from Sun Valley, Calif. "But that is absolutely not happening at all."

Assignments to bilingual programs are increasingly a source of complaint. Many students, parents say, are placed in bilingual classes not because they can't understand English but because they don't read well. They need remedial, not bilingual, help. Others wind up in bilingual programs simply because there is no room in regular classes. Luz Pena says her third-grade son, born in America, spoke excellent English until he was moved to a bilingual track. Determined to avoid such problems with her daughter, she registered her for English kindergarten—only to be told the sole vacancies were in the Spanish class.

In some cases, the placements seem to defy common sense. In San Francisco, because of a desegregation order, some English-speaking African-Americans end up in classes taught partly in Chinese. Chinese-speakers, meanwhile, have been placed in classes taught partly in Spanish. Presented with evidence that blacks in bilingual programs scored well below other blacks on basic skills tests, school officials recently announced an end to the practice.

Whether a child is placed in a bilingual program can turn on criteria as arbitrary as whether his name is Miller or Martinez. In Utah, federal records show that the same test scores that identified some students as "limited English proficient" (LEP) were used to identify others as learning disabled. The distinction depended on the student's ethnic group: Hispanics were designated LEP, while Native Americans who spoke Navajo or Ute were labeled learning disabled. In New York City, where public schools teach children in 10 different languages, enrollment in bilingual education has jumped by half since 1989, when officials raised the cut-off on a reading test. Critics say that 40 percent of *all* children arc likely to fail the test—whether they speak English or not.

Misplacement, however, is only part of the problem. At least 25 percent of LEP students, according to the U.S. Department of Education, get no special help at all. Other children are victims of a haphazard approach. In Medford, Ore., LEP students received English training anywhere from three hours a day, five days a week to 30 minutes a day, three days a week. The results? Of 12 former LEP students reviewed by education department officials, seven had two or more F's and achievement scores below the 20th percentile. Four more had D's and test scores below the 30th percentile. In Twin Falls, Idaho, three high-school teachers had no idea that their students needed any help with English, despite their obvious LEP background and consistently failing grades.

Poorly trained teachers further complicate the picture. Nationwide, the shortage of teachers trained for bilingual-education programs is estimated at 170,000. The paucity of qualified candidates has forced desperate superintendents to waive some credentialing requirements and recruit instructors from abroad. The result is teachers who themselves struggle with English. "You can hardly understand them," said San Francisco teacher Gwen Carmen. In Duchesne, Utah, two teachers' aides admitted to education department inspectors that they had no college credits, no instructional materials and no idea what was expected of them.

What all these problems add up to is impossible to say precisely, but one statistic is hard to ignore. The high-school dropout rate for Hispanic students is nearly 30 percent. It remains by far the highest of any ethnic group—four times that of whites, three times that of blacks—and it has not budged since bilingual education began.

Although poverty and other problems contribute to the disappointing numbers, studies suggest that confining Hispanic students to Spanish-only classrooms also may be a significant factor. A New York study, published earlier this year, determined that 80 percent of LEP students who enrolled in English-immersion classes graduated to mainstream English within three years, while only half the students in bilingual classes tested out that quickly. A similar study released last fall by the state of California concluded that students stayed in native-language instruction far too long. It followed an independent investigation in 1993 that called native-language instruction "divisive, wasteful and unproductive."

Not everyone agrees. More than half of American voters, according to a new *U.S. News* poll, approve of bilingual education. Jim Lyons, executive director of the Bilingual Education Association, says the recent studies are flawed because they fail to measure mastery of academic content: "They don't even pretend to address the issue of *full* education," he says. Learning English takes time, insists Eugene Garcia of the education department. "And it's well worth the wait."

Practical Approach   The alternative to native-language instruction is to teach children exclusively in English, pulling them out of class periodically for lessons in English as a second language. Lucy Fortney taught exclusively white American-born children when she started her career 30 years ago; now her classroom is almost entirely Vietnamese, Cambodian and Armenian. "I can't translate one single word for them," she says, "but they learn English."

Today, bilingual education is creeping beyond impoverished urban neigh-borhoods to rural and suburban communities likely to expose its failings to harsher light. Until now, no constituency has been vested or powerful enough to force the kind of reforms that may yet come with civil-rights lawsuits. "Every-body's appalled when they find out about the problems," says Linda Chavez, onetime director of the Commission on Civil Rights and a dogged opponent of bilingual education, "but the fact is, it doesn't affect their kids." That may have been true in the past. But as a rainbow-hued contingent of schoolchildren starts filling up the desks in mostly white suburbia, it is not likely to be the case for long.

Translation—A Barrier to Language Acquisition
Peter Chin-Tang Wang

Translation is commonly used in meetings between heads of states. But it is hardly an effective method for language acquisition or development, nor an ef-fective method of teaching or learning a foreign language. However, translation has been conveniently employed in many bilingual programs and some adult English-as-a-Second-Language [ESL] classes because it simplifies instruction and makes LEP [Limited English Proficient] students feel at ease.

The comfort levels of students cannot be allowed to be a barrier for lan-guage acquisition. Therefore, it is imperative that administrators ensure that translation is not used as a teaching method in their districts.

Strong and Weak Bilingual Teaching Practices

Since Congress passed Title VII of the Elementary and Secondary Education Act in 1967, and since California passed its first bilingual education law—AB 2284—in 1972, millions of dollars have been spent for bilingual programs and training bilingual teachers.

But after more than 20 years of experience with bilingual education, many bilingual programs continue to use the primitive translation approach, in spite of the fact that researchers have developed much more sophisticated language

SOURCE: *Thrust for Educational Leadership,* January 1995, pp. 25–26. Reprinted with permis-sion from *Thrust for Educational Leadership,* published by the Association of California School Administrators.

acquisition methodologies. The purpose of this article is to help school administrators understand strong and weak bilingual teaching practices when they review their district bilingual classes.

The following three examples show how little the approach to teaching LEP students has changed in some districts during the past 20 years.

The Trilingual Translation Approach

In the mid-1970s, I visited a trilingual class in southern California. The school had both LEP Chinese and Latino students. The bilingual expert in the district at that time developed the trilingual program, with simultaneous translation by one monolingual English teacher in the middle, one Latino aide on one side and one Chinese aide on the other, all in front of the class.

When the monolingual English teacher spoke one sentence in English, the Latino aide quickly translated into Spanish, and the Chinese aide followed quickly with the Cantonese translation. After five minutes, I tired of turning my head toward three different speakers, even though I understood both the English and Cantonese used in the class. I could not imagine how the LEP students felt in this intense situation since they only understood one language.

I was totally puzzled by this trilingual approach, and could not determine what the students were learning. I had a brief discussion with the director on this confusing teaching method. Later, a bilingual teacher in that district informed me that it was abandoned the following month after my visit.

Sentence by Sentence Translations

In the spring of 1989, one of my assignments was to review a Title VII bilingual program in a central California school district. The director explained to me that it was very difficult to hire bilingual teachers in this isolated agricultural area. Therefore, the district had taken advantage of the new teacher-exchange law and hired a bilingual teacher from Peru.

When I visited the language arts class taught by the bilingual teacher, I discovered that he spoke one sentence in English and then translated it into Spanish. During a short break, I asked him if he knew whether the students were listening to the English. He indicated that he did not know.

Later I told the director that the students could not learn English this way. The students were not paying attention to the unintelligible and foreign sounds, and were waiting for the next Spanish sentence that made sense to them. The LEP students might have had high levels of comfort in that language arts class, but they were not learning English, particularly since more than 95 percent of the children in the K-6 school spoke Spanish.

Four Years Later

In 1993, while participating in a Coordinated Compliance Review conducted by the California Department of Education at a school district, I visited a high school bilingual class on human growth and development. Again, the guest teacher used the simultaneous translation technique. The regular bilingual teacher during the class translated sentence by sentence, many times phrase by phrase, into Spanish. This is not an isolated situation.

Translation a Hindrance

After more than two decades and hundreds of millions of dollars spent on bilingual education, some of the state's bilingual programs are still at the translation stage. No wonder bilingual education has been controversial and has been described as a hindrance for the LEP students learning English. If bilingual education is translation, it is indeed a hindrance rather than a help for the LEP students as they try to learn English.

We all have watched foreign movies with English subtitles at the bottom of the screen. I challenge anyone to learn a foreign language that way. People do not pay attention to unintelligible foreign sounds. They concentrate on the words that make sense to them.

However, many bilingual teachers and aides are still using this ineffective method, despite the fact that bilingual experts have advised against using two languages at the same time or mixing two languages.

A Better Way

In the example of the high school bilingual class on human growth and development, the guest speaker could have introduced the subject in three to five minutes. The bilingual teacher then could have proceeded in one of two different ways: she could have summarized in Spanish what was introduced in English, or she could have used Spanish to ask questions to determine how much content the students were able to grasp through the English.

Through these approaches, the students must concentrate on the English and try to comprehend as much as they can. If they miss anything, they can pick it up through the questions or summaries in Spanish. This way, the LEP students' comprehension of English is stretched in every class.

Administrators Must Create Better Language Learning Environments

School administrators do not have to be bilingual to discover whether the LEP students are learning English. They can easily tell whether the bilingual teacher is translating or not. If he or she is translating, it means that the teacher needs training on language acquisition and ESL teaching methodologies.

After more than two decades, we have the expertise to teach LEP students more effectively. Monolingual administrators can provide the leadership to correct this ineffective translation method in language acquisition and development.

As illustrated in my visits of bilingual classes in the 1970s, '80s and '90s, the teaching methods in some schools have not changed. It is time for school administrators to create better language learning environments, as the LEP student enrollment has been increasing every year. Effective communication in English is crucial to the future of California.

The Bilingual Integrated Curriculum Project
Sarah Taylor, Lorie Hammond,
and Barbara Merino

Third-grade students are discussing the idea of how heat energy can be generated for cooking. The teacher poses the question of whether the sun can be used to cook. Being from farmworker families in a hot agricultural valley, students know that the sun is a strong source of heat, but that one cannot cook simply by placing food in the sun.

Some remember instances when crayons melted in a car left in the sun. What makes the car "like an oven"? Ideas emerge. The car is enclosed. But then how does the heat get in? Would a box get as warm as the car? Would cars of all colors get as hot? Some students remember that people in Mexico often wear white clothes so they don't get as hot. As homework, some students decide to measure the temperature in white and black cars.

The discussion is in Spanish, and draws from students' life experiences. The students are in an alternate-day bilingual program, in which concepts can be developed in their native language—Spanish—before being discussed in English.

In an adjacent multilingual classroom, Hmong students are previewing the solar oven lesson in Hmong with language assistants, who ask them questions about their experiences with sun in the tropical rain forest. Later, they will discuss the same principles in sheltered English.

After generating the concepts of insulation, absorption and reflection that they will need to design a solar oven, students from bilingual, multilingual and English-speaking groups begin to work with aluminum foil, cardboard, clear plastic and newspapers. The work groups are challenged to create an oven that can achieve the highest temperature after half an hour in the sun.

The possibility of cooking nachos adds to the excitement. However, the lesson will not end with the eating of nachos. Final discussions in English and

SOURCE: *Thrust for Educational Leadership*, January 1995, pp. 16–20. Reprinted with permission from *Thrust for Educational Leadership*, published by the Association of California School Administrators.

the students' primary languages will allow students to share and analyze what they have learned, and to reinforce their new scientific vocabulary by writing about their experiences.

BICOMP

The students described above are participating in the Bilingual Integrated Curriculum Project, a science-centered approach to developing language through challenging subject matter. BICOMP was developed between 1983 and 1988 as a collaboration between Barbara Merino and the Division of Education at the University of California, Davis, and bilingual teachers in Washington Unified School District in West Sacramento, coordinated by Consuelo Coughran, bilingual coordinator.

The purpose of the project was twofold: In keeping with the new state framework, to make constructivist science accessible to language-minority students, and to develop students' linguistic skills in English and in their home languages through experiences in science and thematic "spin-offs" in other subject areas.

This article traces the development of BICOMP in serving a specific bilingual population, and its subsequent expansion to all students in Washington Unified School District and beyond. The BICOMP story illustrates one case of how a curriculum adaptation designed for a bilingual population can lead to innovations that enable all students to succeed.

What Is Sheltered Constructivism?

BICOMP is an evolutionary curriculum and staff development project involving collaboration between district teachers and university researchers. As a Title VII Academic Excellence Project, it must remain true to the basic elements that enabled the project to claim effectiveness in achieving student success. Those elements are blended in the program: a "constructivist" approach to science, a "natural approach" to language acquisition and an integrated, thematic approach to curriculum.

In constructivist science, students are given opportunities to develop their own ideas about the world by experimenting with real objects and discussing the results. Students are encouraged to experience a subject area as a professional in that area would experience it, rather than by reading about it in a book. In the case of science, students engage in scientific inquiry.

Concerns About the Constructivist Approach

Educators of minority students have expressed concern because constructivist approaches can be disadvantageous to students who lack adequate communication skills in English to access the complex discussions usually associated with inquiry learning, or who don't have the academic framework necessary for unassisted scientific inquiry.

"Sheltered constructivism" makes challenging constructivist curriculum available to language minority students by enabling students to access difficult concepts through their home language, delivering instruction in sheltered English, and providing a framework upon which independent inquiry can be based.

In addition, "spin-offs" in other subject areas enable students to connect with science concepts in meaningful ways by seeing their relevance to art, literature, math, computers and problems relevant to their life experience. By choosing themes that relate to the experience of students and their families, by using primary languages in the classroom and in parent interactions, and by providing family science nights, the BICOMP approach enables language-minority families to access their children's science program.

The Process of Curriculum Development

The development of the BICOMP curriculum began in 1983. A collaborative team of district bilingual teachers and university researchers assembled with the purpose of combining knowledge gained through research and practice to improve outcomes for Spanish bilingual students in the areas of science and technology.

When researchers observed bilingual classes, they found that teachers were so preoccupied with teaching two languages that they often did not have time to teach science. To make matters worse, English science textbooks were not comprehensible to many bilingual students, and bilingual teachers, like most elementary teachers, often lacked a strong enough background in science to improvise their own materials. A science curriculum was needed that:

- would integrate with other subjects, especially language arts;
- would be activity- rather than textbook-based; and
- would be user-friendly to teachers inexperienced in science.

As indicated in the *California Science Framework,* it became increasingly clear that many mainstream and multilingual California teachers, attempting to adjust to a new constructivist approach to science, shared bilingual teachers' needs for this kind of curriculum.

BICOMP curriculum was developed and tested in third-, fourth- and fifth-grade bilingual classrooms, and later in kindergarten through second-grade classrooms. By combining research knowledge in language acquisition and science education and the self-defined needs of teachers, the project team developed an integrated model that included:

1. the use of contextualized language;
2. active student participation;
3. hierarchical presentation of concepts;

4. thematic integration of the subject; and
5. cooperative integration of students with differing levels of English proficiency.

By separating English and Spanish by day (alternate-day model) or by activity (preview-review model), all students were given access to native-language and second-language learning opportunities. Specially designed academic instructional techniques were needed for all students, since both English- and Spanish-speaking students would receive some instruction in their second language.

Effectiveness

In 1989, BICOMP received exemplary status from the California Department of Education for its effectiveness. The department said that the "BICOMP curriculum as implemented in the context of a bilingual program affects reading achievement in English to a significant degree."

This claim was substantiated through standardized testing of several grade levels of students, when both limited-English speaking and more fluent bilingual students in the BICOMP "treatment" group were compared to a baseline year in which bilingual students received standard science instruction.

During the past 10 years, significant student gains in both English reading and math have continued to be recorded. A longitudinal, descriptive study measured reading and math gains in bilingual students followed over a three-year period (1991–93) at two BICOMP school sites. At school A, the average percentile in reading as measured by the Stanford Achievement Test went from 16.8 to 25 to 36 over the span of three years. At school B, students began at a higher level of achievement, yet gains of 6.1 percentage points in reading and 19.2 points in math were measured.

Problem-Solving Skills and a Thematic Approach

Why did effective science teaching in Spanish and English lead to increased achievement in reading and math? Two explanations seem plausible.

First, the BICOMP curriculum teaches science through inquiry and problem-solving. These skills become particularly important as language-minority students progress through more advanced curriculum in reading and mathematics. BICOMP "shelters" the experience of learning to think like scientists, thus enabling language minority students to become problem-solvers who excel in challenging mainstream curriculum. This experience appears to transfer to other cognitive tasks, such as taking a standardized test.

Second, the BICOMP thematic approach enables students to experience the concepts that they encounter in science through other subject areas with which they may be more culturally comfortable and which may seem more applicable to their lives than an abstract scientific curriculum. By making solar ovens to cook nachos and doing math through creating quilts, students see how science and math can give them skills that relate to the world they know.

Recognition for BICOMP

In April, 1991, BICOMP received an Academic Excellence award from the Office of Bilingual Education and Language Minority Affairs. This award has been received by fewer than 20 bilingual projects nationwide. Its purpose is to enable exemplary bilingual projects to share their knowledge with other school districts with like needs. BICOMP is currently beginning a second three-year grant period (1994–97) as a dissemination project that offers curriculum materials and training to interested school districts throughout the United States.

■ ■ ■

Bilingual Schools Can Work
Peter S. Temes

CAMBRIDGE, Massachusetts—The leaders of New York City's public schools have conceded that bilingual education is not working—a conclusion that many of us with commitments to bilingualism have resisted for years, even as evidence of failure has piled up in the form of more and more young New Yorkers hobbled by their bilingual classes.

The current movement against bilingual education was spurred by a report from the New York City Board of Education released last fall, which confirmed what many in the schools had figured out by watching bilingual education in New York let down student after student. The report found that students in bilingual programs, which cost the city more than $300 million a year, did not perform as well academically as students in English-only classes.

Some speculate that bilingual education in New York doesn't work because it's just a bad idea, supported only by ethnic blocks who benefit from the demand it creates for Spanish-speaking teachers and education workers.

But nothing could be further from the truth. Bilingual education has been a staple in American schools since the 16th century, when multilingual Roman Catholic missionaries sought to evangelize Spanish speakers in what is now the American West.

SOURCE: *The New York Times*, March 18, 1995, p. 23. Reprinted with permission from *The New York Times*.

Decades later, Puritans brought local tax-supported bilingual schools to Native Americans in Massachusetts and Rhode Island, and in the 19th century German and Scandinavian pioneers in Illinois, Minnesota and Wisconsin built their public schools with a mission to keep their native languages alive.

In our own century, study after study has made the overwhelming case that good bilingual education programs help non-native English speakers learn English faster than direct instruction in English alone. The months a non-English-speaking student spends in class struggling to figure out the rudiments of the English language are months when the entire course content of math, science and history are lost.

How could any typical American expect to jump into a Hungarian school and absorb any of the Hungarian-speaking teachers' lessons when our gray matter would be otherwise occupied trying to figure out how to ask in Hungarian for permission to go to the bathroom, or how to ask for help?

Of course, we would never be able to absorb the facts and skills offered to us in Hungarian until our abilities in that language reached a minimal sufficiency. How wise it would be for our Hungarian educators to teach a bit of Hungarian history to us in English for a few months, or maybe a year, while we were drilled in the Hungarian language for hours a day. That is the essence of bilingual education, and in other cities and countries it seems to work quite well. So why not in New York?

There are two reasons. The first is that the New York City school system has not been able to hire enough qualified bilingual teachers. Rather than have too few, the school system wound up with, in many cases, the right numbers but not the right qualifications.

When I was studying bilingual education as a graduate student at Columbia's Teachers College, we all heard the horror stories of Spanish-speaking teachers hired without legitimate college degrees or any real preparation in teaching. Bilingual education is a good idea, but certainly if the standards for hiring bilingual teachers are unreasonably low, these programs can't work.

Second, bilingual education does not work if it segregates students into ethnic blocks. The best programs expose native English speakers to a second language while also being an essentially remedial program for non-native English speakers. If bilingual education becomes a sign of difference, a stigma, it will not work.

New York may throw away bilingual education, because with mediocre resources and half-hearted support it does not work. English-only instruction seems to do a better job in the face of such burdens. But the changes that would make bilingual education work in New York would make our schools far better places for every student.

Only Place for Kriolu Is Here
Cheryl de Jong

In their native Cape Verde, Paula Nunez and her friends did not speak Kriolu in school.

But in Boston, they do. In a twist on the usual bilingual programs, which normally teach children in the language of their native schools, Cape Verdean immigrants here are taught in Kriolu, a commonly spoken language from the islands that is never used in schools there.

Portuguese is the country's official language, left over from the days of colonial rule, and is the official language of education.

Under the 1971 Massachusetts bilingual education law, a school district with more than 20 children speaking a particular foreign language must provide bilingual education for them in that language. So Boston began teaching in Kriolu, the language many Cape Verdeans speak at home, rather than in Portuguese.

"School is easier in Kriolu," acknowledges Paula. "The instructions are easier and I can learn more."

But the decision to teach in Kriolu brings with it certain complications.

For one, there is no written Kriolu, no alphabet, and so there are no Kriolu books. With no written language, sending notes home to parents, for example, becomes problematic.

Additionally, there are many Kriolu dialects, and teachers often must translate from one to the other for certain children in their class.

"You have got to be flexible," says Viriato Goncalves, a science teacher at the Dearborn School in Boston who has taught in the bilingual system for 19 years. Sometimes, for example, a student from Sao Vicente "gets upset because he's not understanding the Fogo dialect, so you have to go back and help him in Kriolu or Portuguese."

Massachusetts is thought to be the only place in the world to have Kriolu classrooms from kindergarten through high school. Estimates put the number of Kriolu-speaking people in the state higher than anywhere else in the world, including Cape Verde with its 380,000 residents.

Based on those facts, the Cape Verdean government is looking to this state to begin developing a formal orthography and dictionary for the Kriolu language.

"They see us here as models," says Manuel Goncalves, Viriato Goncalves' brother who is a guidance counselor at the Jeremiah Burke and Madison Park Technical Vocational high schools and is a native Kriolu speaker. "We have more practice in schools, in business, immigration and law."

Newcomers and American-born Cape Verdeans who have spoken mostly Kriolu at home can enroll in bilingual classrooms in the Boston, Brockton and

SOURCE: *The Boston Globe*, May 7, 1995, pp. A93–A94. Reprinted with permission of the author.

New Bedford public schools. With about 750 students and 40 teachers, Boston's Kriolu program is the state's largest.

According to Maria Oliveira, a Cape Verdean-born bilingual coordinator for the Boston Public Schools, Kriolu bilingual classes are available at the Burke and Madison Park high schools, the Dearborn middle school and the Ralph W. Emerson, Samuel W. Mason, Joseph P. Tynan and James F. Condon elementary schools.

As with bilingual programs in other languages, says Andanilza Miranda, assistant principal at the Condon School, the Kriolu curriculum includes English as a Second Language instruction and is designed to increase English use in classes until students can be taught exclusively in English.

"The process is called mainstreaming, and we hope to have students mainstreamed in three years," Miranda says. Millie Ruiz Allen, director of the Office of Bilingual Education for the Boston Public Schools, says about 73 percent of all bilingual students meet that goal. She did not have a breakdown for Cape Verdean students.

"A handful stay six years," she says, "and others stay a few months."

More Than Just Language

Some students face even greater obstacles than just a language barrier.

"If they come from the countryside," Viriato Goncalves says, "they are at a real disadvantage because many of them have had no school at all. Here, they are put in school according to age, not knowledge. Those who have had school are competitive, but others are far behind."

Manuel Goncalves is a member of the Committee on Cape Verdean Language Issues, an eclectic group of about 10 people that includes Cape Verdean-born educators, a musician, a secretary and two women who have never visited Cape Verde but are tied to the language through their doctoral studies in education and linguistics. The committee supports the orthography effort.

Those who support Kriolu as a national language realize they face a long haul, says Filinto Elisio Silva, a committee member and bilingual math teacher at the Burke.

"We still have a high rate of phobia against Cape Verdean culture left over by the Portuguese," Silva says. "This causes some people to look down on Kriolu, like it's not a real language."

Similar resistance is felt in this country. As mandated by bilingual education regulations, all paperwork sent to parents must be written in the student's native language.

Eileen Fonseca, a third-grade teacher at Condon, says this often frustrates parents who either cannot read or have never seen written Kriolu.

"When we send home report cards and matriculation papers" in Kriolu, she says, referring to the informal and ever-changing transliteration used by the schools, "parents complain. This is new to them. They have to have it read three times, or they just ask for Portuguese or English, often so it can be read to them" by family or friends.

Says Anizia Pires, whose niece attended a public school in Boston and who is fluent in Kriolu, Portuguese and English, "They sent me a letter apparently to tell me something. I never understood what it was trying to say. I called to say that if the intent of the letter is to communicate, it would be better in Portuguese."

The idea of a written Kriolu, Pires says, "is novel. I don't think in this generation it will do any good. It would take about two or three more generations to accept it."

Where Bilingual Education Is
a Two-Way Street
Lisa Leff

It was an instinctive and timeless gesture, executed with the boyish finesse of a latter day Dennis the Menace. But as Alexis Medrano sneaked a peek at his science partner's paper last week, the freckle-faced fourth-grader, neatly demonstrated why teaching Spanish to U.S.-born children has become the latest rage in educating their classmates who have grown up speaking Spanish.

Alexis, 9, is a pupil at the District's Oyster Bilingual School, where a multicultural student body evenly divides its class time between two languages. As it happens, he is studying science this semester entirely in Spanish. That usually makes classmate Otto Sevilla, 9, a son of Salvadoran immigrants who speak Spanish at home, the one to look to for answers when molecules become *moleculas.*

Giving Latino children a chance to shine in their native language is one aim of a new breed of bilingual education programs cropping up in Washington area public schools. Designed to combat the isolation and second-class status often associated with English instruction for foreign-born, two-way immersion, or dual language, programs that place all students in the same bewildering boat are establishing themselves as egalitarian alternatives.

"When you label a child from the first day of school because the child does not speak English, that is a 'less than' situation. Yet if an English-speaking child learns a second language in high school, that is considered an asset," Oyster Principal Paquita B. Holland said. "Why not look at everything the language-minority child brings to school as an asset instead of deficit?"

Although Oyster has followed that philosophy since it opened as a "model school" in 1971, until recently its influence was felt primarily beyond the

SOURCE: *The Washington Post*, March 13, 1994, pp. B1; B5. Copyright © 1994, *The Washington Post.* Reprinted with permission.

Capital Beltway. Educators from across the nation made pilgrimages to the school's Woodley Park campus to hear kindergartners reciting their ABCs in two languages.

Yet other local school systems remained faithful to the old prototype of putting children with limited English skills into separate, intensive English programs for nonnative speakers.

But the rising number of Latino schoolchildren attending U.S. schools has given new weight to bilingual education, which conservatives often have criticized as a barrier to assimilation. Many educators now believe that allowing Spanish-speaking children to achieve simultaneous literacy in their native language and English, instead of immersing them in English alone, may be better for them academically in the long run.

"The self-esteem of the kids, that's the difference," said Mary Ann Barbery, who teaches English to nonnative speakers at nearby Eaton Elementary and often accompanies out-of-town visitors on tours of Oyster. "Each child has a dominant language, and each child knows what it is to learn a second language."

Barbery noted that at other schools, including Eaton, Latino children hesitate to use Spanish once they have a working command of English, while at Oyster, "they are very proud of their heritage."

Next fall, another D.C. elementary school, H. D. Cooke, will try to replicate the Oyster model, becoming the city's second bilingual public school. The Arlington school system, which already operates two-way immersion programs at three elementary schools and one middle school, plans to extend a modified version of the concept to Washington-Lee High School. Fairfax County and Alexandria each operate one bilingual public school. Both the Montgomery County and Prince George's County school systems have applied for federal funding to start bilingual programs.

There is no doubt that knowing Spanish is valued at Oyster. The school, which takes students through sixth grade, offers Spanish for Speakers of Other Languages classes just as other schools offer intensive English for nonnative speakers. Each class has two teachers, one who uses only Spanish and another who uses only English, and each teacher spends the same amount of time with the students.

The way they switch between languages varies from class to class; sometimes, one period will be conducted in English, the next in Spanish. In the upper grades, a week or semester might be devoted to one language before switching to the other.

Participating in this linguistic do-si-do can be confusing at first, but it gets easier once you learn the second language, said Silas Riener, 9, a fourth-grader with two older siblings who attended Oyster. Silas, who arrived at Oyster knowing only English, is one of the strongest Spanish speakers in his class; the other day, one of his science partners, a U.S.-born girl with Salvadoran parents, looked over *his* shoulder for the correct answer.

"You can speak to people who are not from the U.S., and they understand you," Silas said. "It's sort of like knowing pig Latin."

Although research has not proved definitively that two-way immersion is a better way to teach English to nonnative speakers, some results have been encouraging. Last year, Oyster's 320 students—more that one-third of who were eligible for reduced-price lunches and 63 percent of whom arrived speaking a language other than English—had some of the city's highest standardized test scores.

At Arlington's Key Elementary School, which for eight years has had a small bilingual program modeled after the one at Oyster, native Spanish-speakers are generally fully fluent in English by the time they reach third grade, said Donna Christian, a researcher at the Center for Applied Linguistics in Washington who has evaluated the program. Early evidence shows that the program's students "do as well or better than Arlington as a whole," she said.

Christian, the coauthor of a national directory of two-way immersion programs, said their growth in the last 10 years has been phenomenal. In 1987, researchers knew of about 30, mostly in California and Massachusetts. When she counted again last year, Christian found nearly 170 in more than 15 states.

Explaining the trend, Christian said a growing recognition by non-Latino parents of the advantages of knowing a second language have made programs such as Oyster's "more politically palatable," countering people who think that English should be the only accepted language of instruction. "Although they greatly benefit the language minority, once the broader community sees it can benefit as well, the interest is there," she said.

Generally, however, native Spanish-speakers tend to be the most bilingual of the bunch by the time they graduate, because they live in an English-speaking country and their Spanish is often reinforced at home. Oyster fourth-grader Katie Filardo, 9, pointed out that she often asks Latino classmates for help in Spanish. But it doesn't work the other way around. "They don't ask me that much because there aren't any people who don't know English that well," she said.

Bilingualism: Qué Pasa?
John Leo

A strange story made it onto Page One of *The Washington Post* last week. At least it must have seemed strange to readers who don't keep up with the byzantine politics of bilingualism.

SOURCE: *U.S. News & World Report,* November 7, 1994, p. 22. Copyright © 1994, *U.S. News & World Report.* Reprinted with permission.

"Plan to Meld Cultures Divides D.C. School," said the headline. It was about a $1 million federal grant for a new bilingual program at unsuspecting H. D. Cooke Elementary School, which is about half Latino, half black.

The experiment in culture melding amounts to this: Starting in prekindergarten and kindergarten, and advancing one grade a year, both Latinos and non-Latinos will be taught in Spanish as well as English. Up through third grade, 80 percent of all teaching will be in Spanish. In later grades, it will taper off to half Spanish, half English.

First obvious question: Why would non-Hispanic parents want four fifths of their children's lessons to be taught in Spanish?

Other obvious questions: How did the United States reach the point where bilingualism, which was designed to help immigrant children learn English, turned into a plan to teach nonimmigrants in a foreign language? And if a dual-language precedent is established, how do we then go about withholding the same system in schools that are, say, half Hmong speaking or half Vietnamese speaking?

Bilingual school programs, launched in 1968 with a budget of $7.5 million, evolved into a bureaucratic monster that eats up almost $10 billion a year. Though everyone agrees that non-English-speaking newcomers need help, at no point along the way has anyone demonstrated any connection between money spent and goals sought.

New York City has just issued a gloomy report showing that it apparently gets very little for the $300 million it spends each year on bilingual education: Immigrant children enrolled in bilingual programs in city public schools do less well, on average, and at every grade level, than similar students who take most or all of their classes in English.

$10 Billion Establishment   This is an old story. In 1990, researcher Christine Rossell surveyed studies in the field and found that 71 percent showed that transitional bilingual education was no different from doing nothing at all for non-English-speaking children. Yet the $10 billion bilingual establishment keeps chugging along, sometimes getting what it wants by dangling a million dollars in front of a poor school like H. D. Cooke.

According to the *Post,* parents of Latino students "seemed less informed about the proposal, and they have not organized to support it." Unsurprisingly, black parents and teachers seem angry, particularly the teachers, wondering why their school has to be radically altered.

One reason, it seems, is to avoid the segregation that bilingual classes regularly bring—Spanish-speaking children will not be off by themselves. But the main function of the plan is to establish Spanish as a school language on a par with English. Like Canada, Cooke would officially be bilingual.

This development is softened with familiar rhetoric about the supposed advantages of a fully bilingual system. The *Post* report says: "Through sharing language, Latino and non-Latino children are expected to develop more empathy for one another and their cultures." But such bursts of empathy are rare among those forced to struggle with someone else's language while not yet fluent in their own. (Parents could opt out of the program, but saying no to the bilingual juggernaut has often involved long waiting lists and buses to another school.)

Non-Latinos are supposed to benefit by mastering a second language, but in reality, that won't happen. Diana Walsh of the *San Francisco Examiner* looked hard at a roughly similar plan in her city and concluded: "The English-speaking kids don't learn how to speak Spanish. . . . The school district knows that, and if you push them they will concede that." She says 80 percent of black kids in Spanish-language classes were reading below grade level.

No evidence suggests that the black students at Cooke will do any better under similar conditions. It's a dubious experiment at their expense. Whatever the advantages of learning about Spanish language and culture, the sheer weight of this instruction will displace much of what the black children need to learn to get ahead. Putting English and Spanish on a par obscures the obvious truth that learning English is crucial for Latinos, but learning Spanish, or French, or Chinese, is very much marginal for non-Latinos.

Latino children seem to be pawns here too. The initial idea behind the bilingual movement was that classes were to be "transitional"—temporary and aimed at getting children into the English-speaking mainstream as quickly as possible. The New York City report shows that Korean-speaking and Russian-speaking immigrant children manage this with stunning swiftness. But activists have encouraged Latino children to think of themselves as permanently culturally distinct. So many activists aim to extend "transitional" programs as far as possible, creating jobs for Spanish-speaking teachers and using schools to enforce ethnic solidarity.

This is a corruption of sensible bilingualism, and there's no reason for a school such as Cooke to buy it.

Bilingual Educators Regroup
Amy Pyle

Amid growing public scorn for their profession, bilingual educators from across the state gathered in Anaheim for four days last week, set on preserving what for many is not just a profession, but a religion.

Yet a peek at the thick California Assn. for Bilingual Education [CABE] conference agenda or a brief visit to any of the dozens of generally crowded ses-

SOURCE: *Los Angeles Times,* February 6, 1995, p. B3. Copyright © 1995, *Los Angeles Times.* Reprinted by permission.

sions showed that for bilingual teachers, the central battleground is far from the political din.

While many are worried about their futures, they are consumed by more immediate concerns: teaching English to a teen-ager illiterate in his native tongue or helping a learning-disabled sixth-grader make sense of both Spanish and English.

As she took a break between sessions in the Anaheim Hilton lobby, Clara-cille Murphy chatted with a teacher from Westminster about what had brought her to the conference from 32nd Street School, the USC performing arts magnet where Murphy teaches third grade.

Like many teachers at the conference, Murphy is still perfecting her Spanish and wanted to get some tips on communicating math and science concepts to children with little English or prior schooling—and she wanted to meet others facing similar challenges.

In a bilingual class, "you end up being counselor, mother, teacher and friend," she said. "I had no idea it would be this hard. . . . It's about 12 jobs in one."

The conference was a regrouping time for the beleaguered, and their sheer numbers—about 6,500 teachers, teachers' aides, parents and administrators attended the sold-out conference—encouraged them to think positively. The few hints that their elation might be out of alignment with a reality that includes Proposition 187 and a reinvigorated English-only movement came during keynote speeches, in brief asides during presentations and in casual hallway conversations.

A common theme: Bilingual education is more than a right; it is a necessity in a state where public schools enroll about 1.2 million students who speak little or no English, representing 23% of the current student population and a 150% increase over the past 10 years.

"During the sessions, we're so focused, but in conversations we're all thinking of dealing with it when we get back to school," said Sergio Quintor, who trains bilingual aides and teachers in the Antioch Unified School District, where the number of limited-English-speaking students has doubled in the past seven years.

The political controversy brewing around bilingual education "does seem absurd to us, but it also means some people still need to be educated," Quintor said.

The lack of political activism at the conference was frustrating to Los Angeles CABE chapter president Carmen Sanchez Sadek. During the course of the conference, she handed out hundreds of leaflets encouraging participants to lobby CABE officers to take a more active role.

Sanchez Sadek believes the organization's best entree is the federal government's own Goals 2000—an education reform framework signed into law in April that calls for every adult American to have the math and language "skills necessary to compete in a global economy."

"It's crucial to this country's economic survival," she said. "That's my battle cry."

Conference-goers took Sanchez Sadek's handouts, folded them and filed them in their canvas "CABE 1995" bags amid reams of other handouts.

Sometimes the public references to the struggle ahead were oblique: Conference co-chair Chuck Acosta opened the event Wednesday by describing the passage of Proposition 187 and the election of a more conservative state legislature as an "interesting, unusual event." Author and journalist Ruben Martinez was more direct, saying in his speech that California may be going through the most dramatic upheaval since it was ceded by Mexico in 1848. But he also predicted that current efforts to recoup "a mythical purity" will ultimately fail because California is already bilingual and bicultural.

"Your role is to be at the center of this battle," he said. "You must be public advocates for your students and their parents because they bear the brunt of this attack."

Yet the conference itself seemed a world apart from the fight he described — an unreal world or an ideal world, depending on who is asked. Its official welcome was spoken in four languages; materials were available in Spanish as well as English; the message board had a handwritten note reading, "*Estamos Aqui,*" posted next to one saying, "Meet us at 5."

During sessions, presenters slipped fluidly back and forth between the two languages and audience members followed with ease. When Santa Ana literacy teacher Martha Brambila talked about near-illiterate math students describing unfamiliar objects as "you know, the *cositas* [little things]," those listening laughed freely.

Just being there together was a kind of political statement, said Frank Avalos, a junior high teacher in Davis.

The hundreds of letters to legislators stacking up at the conference's legislative advocacy counter indicated that fretting was not far beneath the surface. There, a map of the state marked with names of Assembly and Senate members guided conference participants who wanted to send a form letter to their elected representative.

"Without help to bridge the language barrier, these students cannot possibly succeed," the letter said in part. "If these children fail, our state faces a deeply troubled future."

CABE officials view legislators as a key to bilingual education's survival in post-187 Sacramento, where direct attacks have been launched in several forums, including the state Board of Education and the governor's office.

The state board is debating the wisdom of teaching foreign students in their native languages before introducing them to English — now the most common practice in bilingual education. Gov. Pete Wilson has twice vetoed legislation that would have required every school district to offer bilingual education.

There also was much excitement among CABE officials and members alike about a new study, presented at the conference, that appears to fortify their latest weapon and the newest wave in bilingual education: two-way immersion, in which foreign language and English speakers are schooled together and all emerge bilingual.

The George Mason University study, delivered to a packed hotel meeting room, showed that such students remained at or above their grade level in their native language and became equally competent in the second language within four to seven years.

As the eagerness to hear about the George Mason study indicates, bilingual teachers know that pinpointing what's working is one of their greatest future challenges, because state politicians and bureaucrats alike are increasingly demanding proof before providing support.

And, as Sacramento becomes more conservative, what CABE is trying to prove may be changing as well and may increasingly rely on practical arguments: Native-language instruction allows schools to involve non-English-speaking parents in their children's education; U.S. businesses will need more bilingual workers as the effects of the North American Free Trade Agreement grow.

Chapter 7

MULTICULTURAL EDUCATION

INTRODUCTION

The social studies teacher called it "multiple perspectives." She divided the class into three groups. One was to argue that Christopher Columbus was a major historical figure, deserving of having a special holiday in his honor. They were to attempt to show that Columbus' greatest accomplishment was opening the "New World" to European settlement. The second group was instructed to take an opposing viewpoint. They were to argue that Columbus Day should no longer be celebrated. Their position was to be that Columbus was a racist who contributed to the destruction of the cultures of the indigenous peoples of the Americas. The third group's assignment was to judge who won the debate.

One of the major thrusts of multicultural education is to convince students that no one culture is better than another. According to this position, for Europeans to have imposed their culture on Native Americans was wrong. Multicultural education does not involve simply teaching about different cultures; it stresses celebrating those cultures. Moreover, it encourages students to identify with the culture of their non-American forebearers. Consequently one is not thought of as an American, but rather as a Mexican American, an Italian American, and so on.

But are the fundamental assumptions of multicultural education in fact true? Is it the case that no one culture is superior to another? Does this mean that all cultures are on a par morally, spiritually, economically, scientifically, and intellectually? Importantly, do multicultural programs lead to greater racial, ethnic, and cultural harmony? Or do they promote divisiveness? But, of course, before any of these questions can be answered we need to know exactly what a *culture* is.

All Brown All Around
Rodney D. Smith

Consuella Lopez is a student in my ninth-grade English class. She is a gang-banger. Every day she struts into my class wearing baggy jeans and an oversized flannel shirt in her gang's color, black. While taking roll, I easily spy the three-inch-high wall of hair that rises defiantly from her forehead as she slouches in the back row. Thick black eyeliner surrounds her brown eyes, and dark burgundy lipstick covers her mouth. From her ears, large silver hoop earrings dangle.

After filling out her detention slip—this quarter she's been tardy five times and suspended once for being disrespectful to another teacher—I ask about her weekend. "Hey, Mr. Smith," she says. "Like I was kickin' it with my homeys. Ya know."

I don't. I know virtually nothing about homegirls or gangbangers or the fierce pride that burns within this Latina girl. I'm an Anglo, born in Wisconsin, teaching in a California school where Asians, African Americans, Pacific Islanders, and Latinos together make up the majority of the students. Consuella's life, like those of so many of my students, differs radically from my own.

And yet, until this year, I have taught the exact same books I read when I attended my predominantly white high school: *The Great Gatsby, Huckleberry Finn, Death of a Salesman, To Kill a Mockingbird.*

This year, for the first time, I am teaching Sandra Cisneros's *The House on Mango Street.* The book tells the story of a twelve-year-old Latina girl coming of age in Chicago.

Before adding this book to my school's English curriculum, my colleagues and I had to overcome criticism of multiculturalism from parents, school-board members, and fellow teachers. Were we instituting multicultural texts for the sake of multiculturalism, regardless of literary merit? Wouldn't this affirmative-action program in English class come at the expense of great literature? What multicultural author, whatever his or her race, sexual orientation, or gender, could match the works of F. Scott Fitzgerald, Mark Twain, or William Shakespeare?

The House on Mango Street rises above such arguments. The book's use of voice, theme, and symbolism, as well as the honesty and clarity of the writing, rivals the best novels I have ever taught.

While teaching *The House on Mango Street,* I often rely on some of my Latino students for clarification. I know nothing about Catholic school, but a few of my Latino students, including Consuella, added their experiences to what the main character describes. When I read Spanish terms, including the word that made most of my Latino students giggle, *mamasota,* the students

---

SOURCE: *The Progressive,* July 1995, p. 38. Reprinted with permission of the author.

helped me define and pronounce them correctly. After a character died, some of my Latino and Filipino students explained to the rest of the class what the Day of the Dead meant to them.

Consuella began to attend class regularly after we read and discussed the chapter entitled "Those Who Don't." This chapter includes the lines, "Those who don't know any better come into our neighborhood scared. . . . But we aren't afraid. . . . All brown all around, we are safe. But watch us drive into a neighborhood of another color and our knees go shakety-shake. . . . Yeah. That is how it goes and goes."

Whenever I'd stop reading to begin a lesson, Consuella pleaded, "Don't stop. Let's keep on reading." Normally, I'm the one who pleads with my students to read and finish a book.

In a journal entry she handed in late, Consuella, the girl with the number thirteen tattooed in black numerals between her right thumb and forefinger, had this to say about the book:

> My favorite chapter in *The House on Mango Street* is "Hips." The reason why is because when I was little I used to jump rope with my friends and make up weird songs to jump to. And my favorite part that she wrote was, "All brown all around." I don't know why, but that just got to me. Sometimes I think back when we read this book and picture me being the main character. . . . It is like, here is this Latina girl writing a book that I really like. I never have gotten into a book like I do now. And that is the truth.

Alternative High—Latino Youth Inc. Gives Dropouts a Second Chance
Rosa Maria Santana

Miguel Lopez didn't want to leave class after the school bell rang because he feared the seven rival gang members standing in the hallway waiting for him.

He told his teacher of the situation. The teacher looked at Miguel, who was then a 15-year-old high school freshman, and said: " 'Don't come to me with your problems. Go talk to your counselor.' "

"I thought, 'These teachers don't really care,' " said Miguel, now 18 and attending Latino Youth Alternative High School. "If these teachers don't care about their students, why should I care?"

"I'll never forget that day because I was really scared. That was the last day I went to [public] school. The next day, I never showed up."

Three years later, Miguel eagerly works on a classroom writing assignment at Latino Youth, a private campus in Little Village for dropouts. Miguel said he left Clemente High School nearly three years ago because he "was always being chased by gangsters."

In fact, many of the students at Latino Youth say they felt disillusioned by public schools. Some say teachers and administrators were uncaring and unresponsive; others say gang rivalries made it impossible to concentrate.

Founded 20 years ago by community activists led by Danny Solis, Latino Youth offers these teenagers—the majority are Mexican-Americans—a second chance to get a high school diploma in a unique setting. They study economics, history and English from a Chicano perspective, meaning the school's curriculum focuses on the contributions of minorities, particularly Chicanos.

Students learn about Mexico's ownership and loss of the Southwest during the Mexican-American War, and they talk about such recent news events as the Indian uprising in the southern Mexican state of Chiapas and the Mexican presidential elections.

Names such as George Washington and Abraham Lincoln are replaced with Pancho Villa and Emiliano Zapata, generals from the 1910 Mexican Revolution revered by the masses for championing agrarian reform and opposing rich hacienda landowners.

Making Learning Relevant

The school also offers the same kinds of core academic courses (world history, physics, math) and electives (journalism, drama, music) as are found in public schools.

Rather than offering the standard foreign language courses in German, French and Spanish, Latino Youth offers a class in Nahuatl, the language of the ancient Aztecs who ruled Mexico before the Spanish conquest in 1521.

Nahuatl, by way of Spanish, gave the English language such words as coyote, tomato and chili, and is still spoken by 1 million people in central Mexico.

The school's purpose is to make learning a relevant experience for Latino dropouts by giving them books and lessons heightening their awareness of Chicano history, said Ester Lopez, director of educational services at Latino Youth.

"Here at Latino Youth we recognize ourselves as who we are," said Lopez, who is not related to Miguel Lopez. "We're Mexicanos, we're mestizos"—people of mixed European and Latin American ancestry—"we're Chicanos, and we need to be affirmative about who we are, and then it's very logical that you'll move to a certain kind of curriculum."

"Studying [Nahuatl] has much more application than German or French because it connects us to who we are," she said. "Really, we need to go back to our history in understanding what the Chicano movement was all about. It was very definite about recognizing our indigenous [roots] and our *mestizaje*," the mixture of Spaniard and Aztec blood. "This school comes from that tradition."

Fighting Dropout Problem

Nationally, Latinos have the highest dropout rate of any ethnic group. About 29 percent of Latinos 16 to 24 years old dropped out of high school in 1992, compared with 14 percent of blacks and 8 percent of whites, according to the U.S. Department of Education. While dropout rates for other groups have fallen in the past decade, the Latino rate remains high.

According to federal studies, the main reasons Latinos drop out are dislike of school, the need to work and teenage pregnancy.

In an attempt to fight this trend, educators in the last five years have increasingly turned to alternative schools, said Jay Smirk, executive director of the South Carolina-based National Dropout Prevention Center. "It is important if you could get their attention and get them to learn of their culture and heritage. They need something they could relate to."

Miguel Lopez, wearing baggy purple shorts that end just below his knees and a white T-shirt with purple etchings, anxiously fidgeted in his seat one recent morning at Latino Youth. Before being given that morning's writing assignment, he left the classroom for a few minutes.

When he returned, he carried Luiz Rodriguez's book *Always Running,* which details Rodriguez's involvement in a Mexican-American East Los Angeles gang in the 1960s.

Though he has read the book, Miguel, an active member of a Latino gang in Cicero, wants to read it again.

"It's about everything that's going on out on the streets—killings, drugs, violence, people going to jail," he said, settling into his seat where for the next hour, he quietly worked on his writing assignment.

One of a Kind

Latino Youth, which has a daycare center for teenage mothers at the school, is the only alternative school in Chicago whose curriculum is overtly Chicano, a term that some experts say came from Nahuatl and that activists in the 1960s adopted as a means of proclaiming Mexican-American nationalism.

The campus is not recognized by the Illinois Board of Education but administrators say they hope it will be by the end of the school year. The school has 22 funding sources, including city and state grants, as well as private donations.

About 90 students attend the school, with a selection committee of students and administrators deciding who gets in. This year Latino Youth received more than 80 applications for the approximately 35 student seats that opened in the fall.

"The fact that you are in a gang will not exclude or include you in this school," said Esther Lopez. "The philosophy [with each student] is, something happened, and it probably wasn't your fault. Come back and try again.

"So what if they are in a gang? They still need some kind of way to connect. What's the alternative? We don't need more jails. There is a significant number of Latinos who live in poverty. How can schools meet their needs? They're not radical changes—like providing child care for students."

When Miguel dropped out of Clemente he worked two jobs; he was a day-time plumber and a nighttime assembly-line worker. On weekends he hung out with his gang. He did this for two years before going back to school.

"I didn't want to sit like a couch potato. I wanted to do something with my life," said Miguel, who hopes to go to college to study either computers or archi-tecture. "This is my second chance, and I'm going to take advantage of it. I don't care what people think."

Miguel joined his Cicero gang when he was 12, after an older cousin whom he admired became a member. Since then he has seen that cousin go to jail and his best friend killed in a drive-by shooting.

"It's hard for me to get out," he said. "It's not easy getting out. You get a good whipping. They jump you. I think I'm going to get out and the next thing that comes to my head is the beating . . . and I don't want that. Probably one of these days I will, but not now."

Miguel Sees a Future

Miguel was fearful of harassment from rival gangs once he decided to go back to school. But at Latino Youth he found that gangs weren't tolerated, which made him feel at home.

"I went into the classroom and they were talking about where you came from," he said. "It freaked me out. They never gave us this in regular high school. They always gave us Abraham Lincoln, blah, blah, blah."

"This is the first time I've stayed [awake] in a history class," he said. He had never heard about Indian agrarian reformer Emiliano Zapata, he said. "He was like Robin Hood, stealing from the rich and giving to the poor. I never really knew about this until I came here."

"I never had plans to go to college, but these teachers help you," said Miguel, eldest of six children and the first in his family with plans to go to col-lege. "Now, I tell myself I'm going to go to college."

While at Latino Youth, Miguel hangs out with friends such as Victor Plas-cencia, 17. After school the two boys linger outside, teasing the girls who walk by and shaking hands with the boys. Latino Youth has motivated Victor in more ways than one.

"You learn about Mexican history—what happened in the past and how we've suffered," he said. "To me, before, 'Mexican' was a word for a human being coming from Mexico. Now I know in the future we'll be the fastest-growing" minority group.

Like Miguel, Victor wants to go to college. He hopes to become a social worker.

"I'll have the knowledge of what I've been through," Victor said. "A lot of social workers have never been in [a gang]. They just talk about statistics. I have knowledge of it . . . the good sides and the bad sides."

Diversity—Or Divisiveness?
Milton Ezrati

Not long ago, my daughter came home from school and asked for our national flag. Remembering a small Stars and Stripes that once marked my place at an international dinner, I fetched it and gave it to her.

"No!" she said, "that is the American flag. I need our national flag." She explained that the school's "diversity lunch" required each student to bring in a flag or symbol of his or her national, racial, or ethnic heritage, as well as a traditional food.

I told her that, like many Americans, our background was mixed and I was not even sure of all its elements. I could not choose a single flag. Besides, we did not feel a particular link to any of our background groups.

She went to school with the Stars and Stripes and some homemade baked goods of indeterminate national origin. But she returned home that day in tears. The teacher was disappointed, and the children accused her of claiming to be more American than others.

The incident was confusing and upsetting. We had sent her off believing that all the students had an equal right to that flag. As it was, my daughter had felt slightly disadvantaged, having to relinquish claim to some special group.

Not long ago, schools projected a very different image of the United States. In that picture, people from all over the world could throw off old prejudices and build a new nation, regardless of their complexion, accent, or the spelling of their name. Race, ethnicity, and gender were held to be almost meaningless compared with an individual's worth or ability to excel. This idealistic image was useful, if only as a guide to what we believe we ought to be.

Now it seems that the image has changed. From the criteria used in President Clinton's cabinet choices, to census classifications, to school programs, the emphasis has shifted from the individual to gender and ethnic or racial blood-

SOURCE: *The Christian Science Monitor,* January 31, 1995, p. 18. Reprinted with permission of the author.

lines. To be sure, all these efforts at diversity are well meaning. Who can argue with the stated objective of cultivating respect for other cultures? But I fear that the present approach creates more self-deception and divisiveness than respect for diversity.

The emphasis on ethnicity, race, and gender often fails to achieve the diversity that people seek. Depending heavily on appearances, it misses the great distinctions between individuals. According to official distinctions used today, a woman of Hispanic origin and a man of Scandinavian descent represent "diversity." But if they are both well-educated and come from professional families, they perhaps share more values and perspectives that this Hispanic woman would with the Hispanic daughter of a migrant worker. Yet official standards would not see any difference between the latter two.

The popular emphasis on gender, race, or ethnic affiliation tends to encourage identification with a group at the expense of individual development. It also distances those in different groups. When the schools and government promote diversity, individuals cease to be simply Americans and become modified Americans with a certain designation, such as African-American, Irish-American, Mexican-American, etc. This practice creates a temptation, especially among young people, to retreat into the group and adopt its identity. It also gives the impression that the individual's prospects are tied to his or her group. This invites individuals to segregate themselves with their particular affiliation and view other groups as competitors.

The U.S. and its Constitution have traditionally emphasized the individual and largely ignored groups as simply agglomerations of individuals. This ideal has created a remarkably open, fluid, and diverse society.

It would be better for teachers and authorities to return the focus to the individual and to cease dwelling on distinctions between groups. They should emphasize the country's common heritage: respect for the individual, regardless of race, creed, gender, or ethnic origin.

Specialist Favors Expansion of District's Afrocentric Curriculum
Sari Horwitz

A consultant hired by the D.C. public schools has concluded that the Afrocentric curriculum launched at a District elementary school last year led to more

SOURCE: *The Washington Post*, September 22, 1994, pp. A17–A18. Copyright © 1994, *The Washington Post*. Reprinted with permission.

parental involvement, better student self-esteem and less disruptive behavior in the classroom.

The evaluation, by Aaron B. Stills of the Center for Multicultural Management Systems Inc. in Columbia, said students in the African-oriented classes at Ruth K. Webb Elementary School in Northeast Washington scored higher on standardized tests than did students at another D.C. elementary school he studied for comparison.

Stills recommended that the pilot program be expanded gradually to junior and senior high schools and that, eventually, similar Afrocentric programs be considered for every D.C. public school. He was paid $18,700 for his study.

In his report, Stills said he conducted the classroom observations with Bernida LaMerle Thompson, director of the Roots Activity Learning Center.

Abena Walker, director of the African-centered project at Webb, based her curriculum in part on a curriculum developed by Thompson.

Even before the favorable evaluation was released yesterday, D.C. Schools Superintendent Franklin L. Smith had decided to expand the Webb project to seventh grade, based on his observations and discussions with parents.

Afrocentrism is broadly defined as an attempt to shift the classroom focus away from Europe to Africa, specifically Egypt, as the origin of culture and intellectual thought.

Supporters of Afrocentric education have promoted it as a way to teach African American children more about their history and to bolster their pride and raise their academic interest and performance.

The introduction of Afrocentric education at Webb last fall sparked a debate among parents and school board members that had less to do with the philosophy behind Afrocentrism than with the credentials of the program director, the instruction given to teachers and the curriculum content.

At-large Board of Education member Valencia Mohammed, a proponent of Afrocentric teaching, raised questions about Walker and her program.

Walker trained D.C. teachers in "African-centered methodology" at the Pan African University, an unaccredited and unlicensed school she founded. She has a master's degree from the same university.

The Stills evaluation itself was the source of controversy this summer. On Aug. 26, a group of parents who participated in the program gathered outside school headquarters and accused officials of suppressing the report because it was favorable.

Some school administrators this summer tried to distance themselves from the Webb project and are emphasizing the new African-Centered/Multicultural High School that opened this month at Spingarn High School in Northeast, which was planned with the help of the Smithsonian Institution and Howard University.

In Walker's program, courses in African languages, martial arts, African music and art are infused into the traditional public school curriculum, along with the contributions of Africans and African Americans, according to the evaluation.

For his six-month study, Stills compared classes at Webb with traditional classes at Shadd Elementary School in Southeast.

He said he saw parent volunteers in most classes at Webb and no parent volunteers assisting classes at Shadd.

The students in the Afrocentric classes at Webb scored "significantly higher" than the Shadd students on several parts of the Comprehensive Tests of Basic Skills.

But the report did not compare scores from previous years and said the difference could not be linked definitively to the new curriculum.

"Consistent with an African-centered philosophy, teachers were observed demonstrating love, patience, and positiveness when interacting with children," Stills wrote.

"Children were observed singing, shaking hands and greeting each other in English and Kiswahili," he wrote. "Students concluded this activity by doing deep breathing and meditations which allowed them to become positively focused on the day's activities."

Webb's program has a $573,814 budget this year, including $37,090 for Walker's salary and $373,976 to pay the salaries of eight teachers.

Stills, a Howard University associate professor of counseling psychology, could not be reached for comment yesterday.

D.C. Schools Open Another Chapter on Afrocentrism
Sari Horwitz

Mr. Shabazz strode to the front of his classroom in a District high school last week, held up his pen and asked his ninth-graders to tell him what it was. "*Hatha al qalam,*" they answered in Arabic.

Down one flight of stairs, Mr. Williams passed out maps of Africa in his geography class. "Name as many countries as you can," he told his students.

Around the corner, Mrs. Grayson's students read aloud "The Return," a short story in their African American Literature textbooks about a Kenyan youth returning from a detention camp after the Mau-Mau emergency.

The classes at Joel Elias Spingarn Senior High School are the first such high school program in the Washington area. They represent the District's second

SOURCE: *The Washington Post,* February 21, 1995, pp. B1; B6. Copyright © 1995, *The Washington Post.* Reprinted with permission.

attempt at Afrocentric education after an effort two years ago became mired in controversy over the director's credentials and the program's curriculum.

District educators, trying to avoid a similar debate, have worked closely with Howard University and the Smithsonian Institution to design the new "Multicultural/African Diaspora" program.

"It's a different horse altogether," said Russell L. Adams, head of Howard's African American Studies Department and a critic of the District's first program at Webb Elementary School, which is still in place.

"This is a far more reasonable, more professional, more responsible, more cautious, less presumptions and, above all, open effort," Adams said.

The Spingarn teachers are using the standard District curriculum but adding other courses such as Arabic and "infusing" lessons about African and African American traditions, literature and history. In biology class, for example, students are studying the heart. But their teacher, Fostina Baker, uses the lesson to tell the students that Daniel Hale Williams, a pioneer in heart surgery, was an African American. She also explains that African Americans and other minority groups are more prone to heart disease.

The educators supervising the project agree that the curriculum is evolving. Their goal is to teach the public schools' 90 percent African American student population more about African and other non-European cultures with the hope of turning them on to learning and keeping them enrolled in school.

Afrocentrism, often an attempt to shift the focus away from Europe to Africa as the cradle of culture and learning, has been a lightning rod for controversy almost everywhere it has been tried in public schools. Critics have said some Afrocentric programs are historically inaccurate, as well as racially inflammatory. But supporters promote the programs as a way to teach African American students more about their history, bolster pride and self-esteem and raise academic performance and interest.

In contrast to the Webb project that began with an avalanche of highly publicized debate over director Abena Walker's credentials and curriculum, the new classes started last semester very quietly.

Educators chose Spingarn to launch the classes for 80 of its new ninth-graders last fall for several reasons. Spingarn's math and reading test scores were among the lowest in the city's school system last year, and its attendance rate ranked in the lower third of District high schools. The school, set on a hill near a large public housing complex and across from Langston Golf Course in Northeast Washington, also had room for the new program because it has only 589 students in a building that can hold 1,309, and school officials hope the new curriculum will act as a magnet for additional students.

In the first year, the students are taking physical education, math, the history and government of the District, an introduction to African Diaspora Studies, English, world geography and science. New courses being developed include contemporary issues in Africa and African/American Caribbean Studies.

In geography, where students will study the effect of African civilization on the world's economic, political, social and cultural experiences, Anthony

Williams divided the course into five units: Three on Africa and one each on Europe and Asia. Tracy Grayson's English literature course also is divided into five sections: Africa, South America/Caribbean, African American, Asia/India and Europe.

For almost every critic who thinks the classes have too much of an Afrocentric slant, there is another who argues there isn't enough of one.

"I've heard from the community that it's not really an African-centered program," said at-large school board member Valencia Mohammed, a proponent of Afrocentric education. "This is multiculturalism. I promoted a pure Afrocentric model."

Most of the students also are taking Arabic, which has raised questions even among some of the program's supporters. "That's a waste of time," said Howard University's Adams, who sits on the Spingarn program's advisory board. "Literature in Arabic is mostly religious. The language for Afrocentrism probably ought to be Spanish or Portuguese. Eight to nine million Africans were taken to Central and South America. I don't see many African Americans going to work or live in Saudi Arabia."

Abdulalim Shabazz argues that Arabic is the native language of 22 African countries and is worthwhile in a global economy. Deputy superintendent Maurice Sykes said that the instructors may add Spanish later but that for now half the battle of keeping students in school is to excite them about what they're learning. "The kids like Arabic," he said. "Part of the hook is to get them interested in something intriguing to them."

Last week, Judith Webb, a consultant and performer who goes by the name Imani, visited the students and acted out a Nigerian folk tale about a talking skull to the beat of drums and the swish of a rainmaker. With her was poet Toni Blackman, who wants to get a doctoral degree in Hip-hop history. All eyes were fixed on Blackman, who urged the students to join her in performing raps on a variety of topics. She then told the students to take five minutes and write a short poem. "You can do it," she encouraged them. "Rap is merely a form of poetry."

She put on a CD of saxophonist Maceo Parker, and the students enthusiastically scribbled away. In a few minutes, Joshua Champ was finished.

I'm sitting outside on a cool, calm day
Doing right just to see another day
At night hearing gun shots, some one yelling my baby, my baby
Her son died, a 30-year-old lady.
Young males dying like flies
Death after death. Cry after cry.
How much longer shall we live in fear of our own race?
Being scared to look in another man's face.

Sykes, the deputy superintendent, and the representatives from Howard University and the Smithsonian say the program is off to a promising start. But they agree it is too early to know whether the classes will boost attendance and grades.

"The success will depend on the teachers," Sykes said.

Throwing the Book at Afrocentrism
Joseph P. Kahn

WELLESLEY—It began, as these collisions sometimes do, with a discourse. At first, Mary Lefkowitz was mildly shaken up. Then whiplash set in.

A student in one of Lefkowitz's classes asked the longtime Wellesley College humanities professor why, since everyone knew Cleopatra was black, Lefkowitz had failed to mention it during one of her lectures. Another student posed a similar question about Socrates, and so on.

With Lefkowitz in attendance, a visiting Egyptologist gave a talk on campus honoring Martin Luther King Jr. He told his audience, made up mostly of black students, that Aristotle had stolen many of his ideas from the great library in Alexandria, Egypt.

Lefkowitz's specialty is the history and literature of ancient Greece. When she rose to challenge this assertion (the Alexandria library was, by most historical accounts, built after Aristotle's death), the race card was played, swiftly and decisively. A heated debate followed. Meanwhile, other Wellesley faculty members and college officials sat by and said little while angry students surrounded Lefkowitz, challenging her right to question the speaker so unsparingly.

By the time Lefkowitz was assigned to write a magazine essay on Afrocentrist literature, her sense of scholarly propriety was deeply violated.

She wanted to know why.

"You can say, oh, this is poppycock. And often that's the attitude," says Lefkowitz, sitting in her cozy office overlooking the Wellesley campus, a campus that has seen its share of ethno-academic tensions in recent years.

A slim, slightly built woman with close-cropped hair and large, round eyeglasses, she looks like a Martin Short character on the old *Saturday Night Live* show. Nerdy, a bit owlish, even. But animated and quick-witted and, at times, indignant.

"It seemed to me, though, that instead of saying, 'Yikes, this is awful,'" Lefkowitz continues, "you could say, 'Yes, this is wrong.' But why do intelligent people believe this stuff? Why does someone I respect and admire on my own faculty believe it?"

SOURCE: *The Boston Globe*, March 20, 1996, pp. 69; 72. Reprinted courtesy of *The Boston Globe*.

Of course, she adds, white people have marginalized the contributions of black people for so long, and discriminated against them in so many other ways, that it's understandable blacks would accuse whites of rewriting antiquity (e.g., presenting a racially deracinated Egyptian queen) to serve their own Eurocentric agenda. Paranoia comes with the territory, she suggests.

"But in fact," Lefkowitz goes on, "I don't think that's what they've done in this instance. This time they're innocent."

Attacking Scholarship

To bolster her argument, Lefkowitz has published two books that attack the underpinnings of modern Afrocentric scholarship. *Not Out of Africa: How Afrocentrism Became an Excuse to Teach Myth as History* is Lefkowitz's primary contribution to the cause. In it, she constructs a careful and methodical response to one of Afrocentrism's central tenets: that the ancient Greeks and Romans hijacked much of their philosophy, theology and science from the ancient Egyptians and passed it off as their own invention.

"Arguing that Afrocentrist writers offer a valid interpretation of history," she writes in the preface, with characteristic bluntness, "is like being comfortable with the notion that the earth is flat."

Lefkowitz is also co-editor of a new anthology, *Black Athena Revisited*, in which 20 leading academics further dissect the Afrocentrist canon. Among the issues examined is the role racism and anti-Semitism have played in classical scholarship, a debate into which Lefkowitz, who is Jewish, has been squarely, if not altogether fairly, thrust.

Not Out of Africa expands on a quest Lefkowitz began in the pages of *The New Republic* four years ago. For the most part it is a calmly reasoned, heavily footnoted weighing of the historical record. Could Socrates have been black? After posing the question, Lefkowitz answers that while absolute truth is hard to establish, his Athenian citizenship effectively ruled out Socrates' also having African roots.

In a chapter titled "The Myth of the Stolen Legacy," she deduces that only in the 18th century, through an obscure novel that inspired the Freemasonry movement, did it become fashionable to believe that the Greeks ripped off the Egyptians rather than merely borrowing from them, as the Greeks did from many other civilizations and sources. Later, Lefkowitz theorizes, this conspiracy paradigm was passed along by, and gained currency through, African Americans who joined the Masonic order.

Sheltered Students

Beyond these and other examples of historical sleuthing, Lefkowitz also writes with uncommon passion about why accuracy matters—and why reworking history to make one group "feel good" about itself does a disservice to all.

"Good as the myths they were hearing may have made these students feel," she writes, recalling her experience at the Wellesley lecture, "so long as they never left the Afrocentric environment in which they were being nurtured and sheltered, they were being systematically deprived of the most important features of a university education.

"They were not learning how to question themselves and others, they were not learning to distinguish fact from fiction, nor in fact were they learning how to think for themselves. Their instructors had forgotten, while the rest of us sat by and did nothing about it, that students do not come to universities to be indoctrinated—at least not in a free society."

Not surprisingly, given the anti-PC backlash sweeping the nation these days, Lefkowitz has attracted cheerleaders from all over the political spectrum.

Conservative columnist George F. Will wrote in *Newsweek* recently, "If truth mattered in this controversy, her book would end the debate." Historian Arthur Schlesinger Jr. praises *Not Out of Africa* for its "learned demolition of various 'politically correct' historical fantasies." Harvard University's Henry Louis Gates Jr. has been an admirer and supporter of Lefkowitz's.

Even leading Afrocentrists like Molefi Asante of Temple University have seized the opportunity to debate Lefkowitz in public. All this has meant a surprising measure of celebrity for someone virtually unknown outside her academic field. Until now, anyway.

"People have been reluctant to speak out because they get called names," she points out. "I think that's too bad. You should be willing to stand up and say what's right and then take the flak if you have to."

A Physical Ordeal

At first blush, Lefkowitz, 60, seems an improbable recruit in the multiculturalism wars. The daughter of a Manhattan stockbroker, she fell in love with Latin and Greek during her prep-school years before matriculating at Wellesley, from which she graduated *summa cum laude* in 1957.

While earning her doctorate at Radcliffe, she joined the Wellesley faculty in 1960 and has been there ever since, with occasional academic sojourns to Oxford and Berkeley. In 1979, Lefkowitz was named the Andrew W. Mellon Professor in the Humanities at Wellesley. Her books and articles include *The Lives of the Greek Poets* and *Women's Life in Greece and Rome,* a widely used textbook.

She has two daughters by her first marriage to a prominent Boston attorney. They divorced in 1981. In 1982, Lefkowitz married Hugh Lloyd-Jones, a distinguished Oxford classicist emeritus who was knighted in Britain in 1989.

Ten years into the marriage, Lefkowitz was diagnosed with breast cancer. With the support of her colleagues and family, she struggled through a difficult year of chemotherapy treatments. The ordeal left her physically depleted but not, she says, discouraged about finishing a project that took her to distant libraries for hours and days of painstaking research.

"Realizing I might not live forever, I saw the project's importance more clearly," Lefkowitz says. "It seemed to me the whole underpinning of academic enterprise was involved." Laughing at the irony, she adds, "I couldn't have lived with myself if I had let these remarks go by."

The Race Card

Lefkowitz has since been given a clean bill of health. More discomfiting, she says, is the state of intellectual integrity on college campuses. At Wellesley, the controversy has flared most conspicuously around Anthony Martin of the Africana Studies department, whom many have accused of teaching anti-Semitic propaganda.

"I certainly raised questions early on about him," acknowledges Lefkowitz, politely refusing to say more about Martin personally. Her reticence may be the result of a lawsuit filed by Martin against Lefkowitz, allegedly over published comments of hers. Preliminary judgment reportedly went against Martin, who is said to be appealing the ruling.

"Not about his teaching," she continues. "I'm a great defender of academic freedom; I believe people should teach what they want. But he ought to be called on it if he or any one says the Jews are responsible for the slave trade. What's your evidence?"

College audiences seldom challenge speakers, Lefkowitz adds, "because often it's arcane stuff they're talking about. Perhaps not to a classicist like myself, but to most students."

Nor does Lefkowitz shy away from speaking out for fear that her own Jewishness will be used against her. Tension between African American and Jewish communities has been around a long time, she notes, and universities are not immune to the virus.

"If it gets into history," she says, "we can deal with it better because we have the material. We know who was involved with the slave trade. Moreover it's wrong when an institution says, 'Oh, this is controversial. Let's not touch it.' I don't like controversy, but I've always cared about the truth."

And the race card?

"It has been part of the response, yes," she says. " 'What do you expect from a white person?' Or, 'What do you expect from a Jew?' That's another nice one. Personally, I much prefer [Afrocentrist scholar Martin] Bernal's comment. He said, 'What do you expect from a classicist?' I rather like that."

Facts, Not Feelings

Lefkowitz does see one sunny side to the movement away from the America-first attitude toward history and civilization. Better, she says, is a more anthropological approach that values other cultures for their considerable achievements.

The bad side to cultural relativism, she says, is this: "You believe there is no objective truth, that each of us has our own narrative. Then you have to say, wait a minute. Either Grant surrendered to Lee, or Lee surrendered to Grant. Both did not happen. There are some rock bottom facts here.

"When [Anthony] Martin made a speech about a Jewish conspiracy against Afrocentrism, I told a colleague that I was upset because his history was wrong. And this man said, 'I don't care who stole what from whom.' I thought, I've got to answer that. Too many people believe that, and it's not right. This is the Greeks' heritage, for heaven's sake. How do the *Greeks* feel about that?

"I don't happen to believe that feelings are where things are at. History is where it's at. Writing a book like *The Secret Relationship Between Blacks and Jews* is not wrong because it hurts Jews. It is lousy history. It distorts reality. That the feelings of Jewish students are hurt is unfortunate. But the real problem for an academic institution is something else."

For Lefkowitz, the bottom line is, and will always be, credibility and accountability.

"It isn't that I care what race Socrates was," she says. "I care that somebody says we were lying. I care about the attitude that says, if this person is such an expert, how come she doesn't know her own subject? Why has she been *concealing evidence?* That's my issue.

"That's why I joined this fight."

Afrocentrism: A Valid Frame of Reference
Clyde Ahmad Winters

During the past 20 years, African American researchers have been developing the idea of Afrocentrism. This field of Africalogical research has been outlined excellently by Asante, who observes that the "Afrocentrist seeks to uncover and use codes, paradigms, symbols, motifs, myths and circles of discussion that reinforce the centrality of African ideas and values as a valid frame of reference for acquiring and examining data."

Although Afrocentric scholars have been writing on Africalogical themes for many years due to the success of Asa G. Hilliard of Georgia State University and Molefi Kete Asante of Temple University, the Afrocentric idea in education

SOURCE: *The Journal of Black Studies, 25,* no. 2, (December 1994): pp. 170–190. Copyright © 1994 by Sage Publications, Inc. Reprinted by permission of Sage Publications.

Note: References have been omitted throughout this essay.

has spread from a small group of advanced African American scholars to high school and elementary school teachers. Africalogy, as explained by Asante, "builds upon theoretical principles outlined by previous scholars. . . . The fundamental theoretical bases for Africalogy are derived from the Afrocentric perspective."

Due to the attempts of many educators to advance Afrocentrism as a part of the multicultural perspective in the social science/social studies curriculum, there has been a White backlash. Given the increasing popularity of Afrocentrism and multiculturalism among teachers around the United States, many White "resisters" have begun a campaign to discredit these educational ideas and the Africalogical field of inquiry.

■ ■ ■

To attack Afrocentrism, the resisters are attacking the great research of Cheikh Anta Diop, who laid the foundations for the Afrocentric idea in education. He laid these foundations using both the historical and the anthropological/linguistic methods of research to explain the role of Blacks in world history.

Before the death of Diop, only one scholar—Mauny—publicly questioned Diop's proof of the African origin of Kemetic (Egyptian) civilization. Today many Eurocentric scholars are attacking Diop's genetic model for African civilization that includes ancient Egypt as a part of the Black world.

There are three components in the genetic model: (a) common physical type, (b) common cultural patterns, and (c) genetically related languages. Over the years, Diop has brought to bear all three of these components in his illumination of Kemetic civilization.

The opposition of many Eurocentric scholars to Afrocentrism results from White hostility to Diop's idea of a Black Egypt and to the view that Egyptians spoke an African language rather than an Afro-Asiatic one. Recently, the resisters have written reviews of Diop's recent book. Although these reviewers mention the work of Diop in their articles, they never review his work properly because they lack the ability to understand the many disciplines that Diop mastered.

■ ■ ■

Due to the rise of the Afrocentric educational idea, the resisters have begun to publicly question ancient Africalogical research by Afrocentric scholars. They cite the shortcomings of *Black Athena: The Afroasiatic Roots of Classical Civilization* (vols. 1-2) by Martin Bernal and a teaching aid produced in Portland, Oregon. During the past couple of years, articles attacking Afrocentrism and Diop have appeared in *The Washington Post, The New York Times, Newsweek, Time,* the *New Republic,* and in educational journals such as the *American Scholar, Educational Leadership,* and *Anthro-Notes.*

In these articles, Afrocentrists are described as cranks and ethnocentrists. Their views are referred to as being based on poor and outdated sources and, as a result, their work is unscientific and lacks adequate proof. Outside of the rhetorical response to Afrocentrism, the resisters attempt to make it clear that the Egyptians were a mixed population, like that of the United States, which got darker and "more negroid" the farther down the Nile one went.

This attack on Afrocentrism is aimed directly at members of school boards and teachers of elementary and high schools that want to add Afrocentrism to the curriculum. Usually a teacher must explain to the department head, principal, or school board why he or she feels changes should be made in the school curriculum. During these discussions, the teacher must be able to defend the soundness of the Afrocentric idea before a curriculum committee at his or her individual school, school district, or school board.

■ ■ ■

Blacks in Greece

Because of the errors in volumes 1 and 2 of *Black Athena,* Eurocentrists have attacked the Afrocentrist evidence of an African foundation for Grecian civilization. Lefkowitz has referred to the errors of historical fact as "the illusions of Afrocentrists."

Lefkowitz and Snowmen perpetuate the myth that the only Blacks in ancient Europe were slaves or mercenaries. This myth is false because the ancient Greek historical works make it clear that many ancient settlers of the Aegean came from Africa, especially the Garamantes and Pelasgians. Parker wrote,

> I need not go into details concerning the ethnical relations of the Romans since they, too, are Mediterranean and are closely related to the same African confederation of races as Greece. Aeneas, their mythical founder, was in direct descent from Dardanus, the African founder of Troy. The *Aenead,* like the *Iliad* and *Odyssey* and all other of the world's great epics, is the poetic story dealing with African people.

The Eurocentrists attempt to prove that there was a large amount of cultural and linguistic continuity in the Aegean from the 12th to 8th centuries B.C.E. Yet there is no way it can be proven that Indo-European Greeks have always been in Greece. This view on the continuity between the Linear B Greeks and later Greeks held by Lefkowitz is disputed by Hopper, who notes that "after all, so much which characterizes Minoan Crete seems wholly alien to later Greece, despite the efforts of scholars to detect 'continuity.'"

Given the wealth of Afrocentric literature, it would seem logical that the resisters review these works and point out the weaknesses within these texts to prove that Afrocentrism is a myth. But, instead of doing just this, the resisters simply mention any text written by Afrocentric scholars and then attack *Black Athena* as if Afrocentrism is based solely on this text.

Black Athena is not the Afrocentric Bible on Black Egypt. We doubt that Diop would even agree with most of the thesis of this book. Trigger observes,

> Although he [Bernal] has acquired an enthusiastic following among exponents of negritude and occasionally describes some of the Egyptian Pharaohs as

"black" or "Nubian," he aligns himself not with Cheikh Anta Diop but with more moderate "Negro intellectuals . . . who . . . do see Egypt as essentially African."

Bernal believes that the Greeks resulted from a mixture of European and Semitic-speaking Mediterranean people.

In volume 2 of *Black Athena,* Bernal outlines his thesis that the "Egyptians" founded Greek civilization. But these Egyptians are not Blacks; they are Semitic speakers. Bernal makes it clear that he believes that the civilization of the Aegean was founded by Semitic-speaking Phoenicians and by the Semitic-speaking Hyksos dynasty of Egypt.

Bernal sees the Hyksos invaders as Hurrian, Semitic, Indo-Iranian speakers. As a result, he believes that the Danaos and Kadmeans, or Egyptian founders of Thebes in Greece, were the Hyksos. In general, Bernal believes that when the Hyksos were driven from Egypt, they settled in the Aegean and developed civilization.

Levine describes *Black Athena* as "an extraordinarily interesting and dangerous book . . . dangerous because in reopening the nineteenth-century discourse on race and origins, the work, sadly, inevitably, has become part of the problem of racism rather than the solution that its author envisioned." Pounder objects to Bernal because "Bernal makes a major contribution to confusion and divisiveness by giving credence to Afrocentrist theories that cannot be supported by historical, anthropological, or archaeological criteria."

Bernal's view of the Hyksos as the founders of Grecian civilization has nothing to do with the work of Afrocentric scholars. The problem with Bernal is that he believes that the "pre-Hellenes" or Pelasgian people were Indo-European speakers. This view is not held by Afrocentric scholars who recognize that the founders of Athens and Attica were Blacks. Diop and C. A. Winters make it clear that Blacks came to Greece in prehistoric times. Therefore, the apparent errors in Bernal's *Black Athena* should not be seen as proving that the Afrocentric scholars are wrong. These errors prove only that Bernal has failed to prove that the Hyksos founded civilization in the Aegean.

Even before Diop, Afrocentric scholars used multiple methods and sources to illuminate the African past. These scholars have sought to illuminate the African past throughout the world. For example, Parker used anthropological, archaeological, historical, and classical sources to prove that Blacks once lived in the Aegean.

Parker used the Greek classics to prove that the Pelasgian were of African origin. He also discussed the origin stories about the Pelasgic founders of selected Grecian cities and proved that these men were Blacks and not Indo-Europeans. Parker also observes that the "great Grecian epics are epics of an African people and Helen, the cause of the Trojan war, must henceforth be conceived as a beautiful brown skin girl."

In the works of Homer, we find that many of the terms have been falsely translated to make it appear that the Greek heroes were a fair-skinned race. As Parker remarks,

Let us consider the supposed testimony to the presence of the fair type in Greece and to its superiority over the darker populations. . . . The truth of the matter is that these translators, like historians, have permitted their prejudices to warp their accuracy. . . . Apollo in Homer is *chrysaeros;* that is to say, bearing a golden sword; while *xanthos,* which has been mistranslated to mean fair, means brown. Artemis is *eustephanos,* which has no relation whatever to fair. Neptune is *kyanochaites;* that is to say, bluish, blackish, like the dark deep waves of the ocean. Neither Hera nor Kalypsos are fair from their descriptive adjectives. Achilles is *xanthos,* which as was said before means brown. Agamemnon is also *xanthos,* and remember, if you please, that he is in direct descent from Epaphos, the black ancestor of the Pelasgic house.

Using archaeological evidence and the classical literature, Winters explains how the African/Black founders of Grecian civilization originally come from the ancient Sahara. Winters makes it clear that these Blacks came to the Aegean in two waves: (a) the Garamantes, a Malinke/Mande-speaking people who now live along the Niger River but who formerly lived in the Fezzan region of Libya; and (b) the Egyptians and East Africans, who were recorded in Greece's history as the Pelasgians. The Pelasgian civilization is discussed in detail by Parker.

The Pelasgians founded many cities. The Pelasgian founding of Athens is noted by Plutarch. According to Herodotus, the Pelasgians also founded Thebes. Winters makes it clear that the Garamantes founded the Greek cities of Thrace, Minoan Crete, and Attica. The Garamantes were also called Carians by the Indo-European Greeks.

The Garamantes or Carians originally lived in the Fezzan. These Garamantes were described by the classical writers as Black or dark-skinned—*perusti, furvi,* and/or *nigri.*

Whereas Lefkowitz argues that Socrates could not have been Black because he was an Athenian citizen, she fails to prove Socrates's racial heritage because the Greeks made it clear that the founders of Athens were Pelasgians. Lefkowitz notes that if Socrates and his parents had dark skin and other African racial features, then it is likely that at least some of Socrates's contemporaries would have mentioned it unless all of the Athenians had African origins as well. But then why, Lefkowitz asks, does the art not depict the Athenians as Africans? This question is easily answered. There are numerous Africans depicted in Greek art. But rather than admit that some of these Blacks were descendants of the Pelasgian and Garamante groups, they are all referred to as Ethiopian slaves or mercenaries.

The works of Diop, Parker, and Winters make it clear that the Afrocentric discussion of the African influence in the Aegean is not based solely on the work of Bernal, as the resisters would have us believe. Use of Bernal as a method to dispute the findings of the Afrocentrists is groundless because his work fails to acknowledge the African origin of the Pelasgians.

■ ■ ■

Conclusion

■ ■ ■

The evidence is clear that the Afrocentric method is based on fact, not fiction. This should encourage more teachers to seek revisions in their local curricula to include Afrocentrism without fear of the resisters because Yurco is a continuation of propaganda begun 100 years ago to deny the influence of African people in the rise of civilization. It is a historical fact that Africans were enslaved. Even Europeans were at one time enslaved. The historical reality of enslavement should not be used to place a burden on the history of the greatness of Black civilizations then or the potential for greatness among African peoples today.

The Dangers of Multiculturalism—The American Experience
Peter Duignan

Since the 1960s American schools have been "force-fed" multiculturalism. Required courses in Western civilization are being replaced by courses in non-Western culture even though they have little or no relevance to the great majority of Americans (80–85 percent) who trace their descent to European and Western culture. Colleges such as Mount Holyoke and Dartmouth, and universities such as Wisconsin and the University of California, require a non-Western study course, but not one on Western culture! Learning about other cultures is, of course, valuable; but students should first know about their own. Too often non-Western and ethnic studies are thin disguises for virulent anti-Western views and attacks on DWEMs (Dead White European Males). The claim is made that the West is the great devil, the great oppressor of women, gays and lesbians and all non-white ethnics who are perceived to be "victims." Recall the recent vicious attack on Christopher Columbus as the destroyer of Indian peoples in the New World. And how could it have been otherwise since multiculturalism grew out of the New Left movement of the 1960s—the alliance of radical students, faculty leftists, sympathetic administrators and advocates of group rights for gays, lesbians, ethnics, feminists and opponents of Western society and capitalism. The cultural revolution of the 1960s was leftist, anti-war,

SOURCE: *Vital Speeches of the Day,* June 1, 1995, pp. 492–493. Reprinted with permission of *Vital Speeches of the Day* and the author.

anti-capitalist and was concerned with race, gender and homosexuality. Out of this witch's brew came multiculturalism and political correctness.

The multiculturalists and the politically correct, while bad mouthing white men and Western culture and values, celebrate cultural relativism and pluralism. The problem of cultural relativism and of holding non-Western culture to be as good as (or better) than Western cultures is that most non-Western cultures have few achievements equal to Western culture either in the past or the present. The modern world of science and technology, of economics, of American institutions, values and achievements came from the West, not the non-West. Non-Western cultures still widely have slavery, caste systems, keep women in a lower status and believe in male superiority. Few non-Western states practice democracy, protect individual rights, but do continue to practice "unnatural acts" such as foot-binding, suttee (wife-burning), female infanticide, female genital mutilation, the pledging in marriage of girl-children, and the killing of twins as so-called witches. Sexual diversity is not allowed in most non-Western societies, in fact homosexuality is not regarded as normal but as abnormal and a moral disorder to be punished harshly—imprisonment in Cuba, shock treatment in China, or death by a firing squad if practiced in a Chinese prison. African societies regard homosexuality as deviant behavior and not to be tolerated within the community.

Multicultural curricula are stirring up controversy around the U.S. Cities with large black or brown populations are pushing ethnic studies. (Afro-centric, native-American, Chicano studies are supposed to give self-esteem to black and brown people by showing them that their ancestors had a great heritage and made great contributions to world civilization.) Ethnic cheerleading is thought to build self-esteem in black and brown children, and for peculiar reasons, is thought to be more relevant to ghetto students than traditional courses in English and American and European history. But what the comings and goings of primitive, pre-literate, small-scale, iron age tribesmen are able to do for blacks and browns is hard to see. While it is understandable to seek out a glorious heritage—most societies have done so—it is bad history because it is false history. The book *Black Athena* claims black Africans created the Egyptian and Greek civilizations. This is a spurious claim, easily refuted by history and linguistics. Egyptians were brown not black; no black civilizations ever approached the Egyptian achievement in anything—not architecture, not agriculture, not science or technology, literacy or medicine.

One of the most controversial curriculum reforms was in New York City in 1989 where scholars such as Arthur Schlesinger, Jr., and politicians such as Governor Mario Cuomo, accused the curriculum report of dividing people and encouraging ethnic separation and antagonism. Yet, advocates of multiculturalism and bilingualism have been making headway in recent years—from kindergarten to high school to the university.

Some Blacks and Chicano radicals also claim they are not part of America and demand multiculturalism and bilingualism in schools. Some Chicanos even want to establish an empire, Azatlan, in the former Spanish Southwest. Cape

Verdeans who speak a pidgin Portuguese (Crioulu) have been successful in getting it taught in New England schools where descendants of Cape Verdeans go to school even though they are a small minority and don't speak Crioulu at home!

And the list of such ethnic chauvinisms grows each year. But there is no justification for any language but English to be taught in schools as their primary language of instruction, even though it is essential to teach foreign languages in schools as we live in an interdependent global world.

Immigrants came to America for a better way of life and most did not want to preserve much of the culture they had left. Although some Germans set up Saturday "Language Schools," most ethnic groups did not, and almost all preferred their children to learn English at school and their native language at home. Most immigrants and all immigrants' children thus learned English and did not seek to differentiate themselves from native-born Americans. Few children of immigrants chose to study their parents' language; few were eager to learn about the old country their parents had rejected. Children wanted to be assimilated as quickly as possible so as not to be differentiated from their peers by speaking a foreign language. The harsh fact is that most children of immigrants have not learned the language or culture of their parents, and while this may be lamented it cannot be undone by bilingual education and should not be done if it serves to divide American society.

There were certainly language ghettos, for example, in New York where Yiddish was widely spoken, or Italian, German and Polish districts where native languages were spoken, but essentially English won out after one generation. No immigrant group succeeded in keeping its language identity separate from American culture. The Germans in the Midwest and the French in Maine certainly tried; the Cajuns (Arcadians) in Louisiana partially succeeded. The Chinese were a partial exception and prejudice probably restricted their assimilation. The road to assimilation and economic success led, most immigrants knew, through the schools where English was the rule and Western culture was taught.

President Woodrow Wilson put it best: "America does not consist of groups."

The efforts of bilingual and multicultural advocates are destructive of America's civic culture and hopefully will fail because all immigrant parents know that the way for their children to succeed is to learn English. (The high school dropout rate of Hispanics may be partially caused by their poor skills in English.) Non-English language training is best done through teaching it as a foreign tongue, not sharing school instruction equally between English and a foreign language. We should not, therefore, let multiculturalism disunite America and set up different ethnic studies centers or language groups or hyphenates in our society. Only the Swiss seem to have kept national unity in a multilanguage country. In Belgium the two language groups dislike each other as do English-speakers and French-speakers in Canada.

The U.S. has been the most successful country in history in assimilating and integrating huge numbers of different ethnic and racial groups. We achieved this by turning foreigners into Americans who were educated in English, did business in English, accepted the American creed and its values, and subscribed to the American constitutional system. And thank God it was that way.

When we look at the ethnic and language quarrels in the former Soviet Union or in former Yugoslavia, or even in Spain and Belgium, we should be glad it was so. We do not want multiculturalism dividing us into separate groups. Let the Chicanos and other ethnic nationals study their ancestors' language and culture, but do so as a second language and after they have done American history. We should teach Western culture through its classic writers; other non-Western cultures may also have "classics" but few are relevant to our society. They are difficult to teach because teachers and students have inadequate knowledge of them, and many, such as Hausa, Yoruba, Indian or pre-Columbian, were pre-literate.

So, English only, should be the rule in schools and in local governments. No more multilingual ballots for voting, no more dual language signs in cities and towns. To become a citizen English is required, so why have non-English ballots and signs in our civic culture? And ethnic studies certainly should be abolished and their subject matter taught in regular departments of social science, language and history. Ethnic histories (there are over 50 groups in the U.S.) should be included as part of American history when they are relevant but not set aside as separate institutes taking time and resources from studying the American experience.

Culture Goes With Curriculum
Mary Faber

Students at Martin Luther King, Jr. Elementary School in downtown Milwaukee learn what other elementary students learn—with one critical difference. While they're learning it, they're immersed in African and African-American perspectives and culture.

Four years into the program, students' reading scores are up. Their school is cleaned up. Parent involvement is up. And African-American professionals come to career days and assemblies to motivate kids.

How did this immersion program make school (and life) better for its 560 K–5 students—who are 99 percent Black and 94 percent poor? By simple changes, say two of its teachers, NEA members Vernice Jordan and Joe Hartlaub.

A kindergarten teacher with a master's degree in computer education, Jordan infuses African-American culture in all she teaches.

Source: *NEA Today*, March 1995, p. 6.

"For example," says Jordan, "when we learn the alphabet, the letter *A* stands for Louis Armstrong. We pretend to blow a horn and sing at a nightclub. The letter *B* is for Benjamin Banneker, who helped plan Washington, D.C. When we reach the letter *Z,* for Shaka Zulu, we learn of the greatness of Africa and talk about conflict and peace."

Hartlaub, who teaches grades 2–5, has a master's degree in international education and was a Peace Corps volunteer in Sierra Leone. In teaching about the slave trade, Hartlaub says he and his students "read and write about it. We study trade between West Africa, Brazil, and the Caribbean. And we calculate distances between West Africa and the New World using both geography and language arts."

But teaching is only one part of King Elementary's immersion program. The program also promotes:

- *Outreach to parents.* Staff make home visits, and a full-time parent co-ordinator arranges for parental participation in classroom and in-service programs.
- *Professional development.* Teachers take 18 credits in African-American history, family life, and culture. Paraprofessionals take the courses they need to become certified as teachers. (Five King teachers started as para-professionals.)
- *Deliberate expressions of ethnic pride.* Principal Josephine Mosely wears African dress often, and Jordan does so occasionally. All students wear uniforms. And staff decorate classrooms and hallways with African and African-American art.
- *Multi-year pairings of teachers and students.* For two to three years, students stay with the same teacher.

"Regardless of ethnic or social class concentration, a key ingredient of learning is high self-esteem," says school principal Josephine Mosley.

"We raise our kids' self-esteem by immersing them in academics and culture — something other minority, majority, and integrated schools can do, too."

Chapter 8

DETRACKING

INTRODUCTION

Tracking is the grouping of students according to some measure of ability to learn—or at least according to some measure of achievement. At the high school level, the typical arrangement is the honors group, the college preparatory group, the standard group, and the basic group. At the elementary and middle school levels the groups have various names, such as "Robins" and "Turtles." Yet, in all cases, the rationale is the same—some students learn at a faster rate and at a higher level than others. Consequently, so the thinking goes, each student benefits the most by being tracked with students of comparable abilities.

Tracking is under heavy attack today. Some claim that all students learn better when there is no tracking in the school. Tracking is said to create artificial divisions; in the real world outside of the school students must get along with and learn with people of various levels of ability and achievement. Others maintain that when students are tracked, teacher expectations are lowered to the point that schooling is little more than custodial at the lower level tracks. Tracking, the argument goes, is inherently discriminatory—all students are not provided with the same level of quality education. And importantly, because large percentages of students in the lower level tracks are black and Hispanic, many believe that tracking amounts to *de facto* racism.

Blowing Up the Tracks
Patricia Kean

It's morning in New York, and some seventh graders are more equal than others.

Class 7-16 files slowly into the room, prodded by hard-faced men whose walkie-talkies crackle with static. A pleasant looking woman shouts over the din, "What's rule number one?" No reply. She writes on the board. "Rule One: Sit down."

Rule number two seems to be an unwritten law: Speak slowly. Each of Mrs. H.'s syllables hangs in the air a second longer than necessary. In fact, the entire class seems to be conducted at 16 RPM. Books come out gradually. Kids wander about the room aimlessly. Twelve minutes into class we settle down and begin to play "O. Henry Jeopardy," a game which requires students to supply one-word answers to questions like: "O. Henry moved from North Carolina to what state—Andy? Find the word on the page."

The class takes out a vocabulary sheet. Some of the words they are expected to find difficult include *popular, ranch, suitcase, arrested, recipe, tricky, ordinary, humorous,* and *grand jury.*

Thirty minutes pass. Bells ring, doors slam.

Class 7-1 marches in unescorted, mindful of rule number one. Paperbacks of Poe smack sharply on desks, notebooks rustle, and kids lean forward expectantly, waiting for Mrs. H. to fire the first question. What did we learn about the writer?

Hands shoot into the air. Though Edgar Allan Poe ends up sounding a lot like Jerry Lee Lewis—a booze-hound who married his 13-year-old cousin— these kids speak confidently, in paragraphs. Absolutely no looking at the book allowed.

We also have a vocabulary sheet, drawn from "The Tell-Tale Heart," containing words like *audacity, dissimulation, sagacity, stealthy, anxiety, derision, agony,* and *supposition.*

As I sit in the back of the classroom watching these two very different groups of seventh graders, my previous life as an English teacher allows me to make an educated guess and a chilling prediction. With the best of intentions, Mrs. H. is teaching the first group, otherwise known as the "slow kids," as though they are fourth graders, and the second, the honors group, as though they are high school freshmen. Given the odds of finding a word like "ordinary" on the SAT's, the children of 7-16 have a better chance of standing before a "grand jury" than making it to college.

SOURCE: *The Washington Monthly,* January/February 1993, pp. 31–34. Reprinted with permission from *The Washington Monthly.* Copyright © by The Washington Monthly Company, 1611 Connecticut Ave., N.W., Washington, D.C. 20009 (202) 462-0128.

Tracking, the practice of placing students in "ability groups" based on a host of ill-defined criteria—everything from test scores to behavior to how much of a fuss a mother can be counted on to make—encourages even well-meaning teachers and administrators to turn out generation after generation of self-fulfilling prophecies. "These kids know they're no Einsteins," Mrs. H. said of her low-track class when we sat together in the teacher's lounge. "They know they don't read well. This way I can go really slowly with them."

With his grades, however, young Albert would probably be hanging right here with the rest of lunch table 7-16. That's where I discover that while their school may think they're dumb, these kids are anything but stupid. "That teacher," sniffs a pretty girl wearing lots of purple lipstick. "She talks so slow. She thinks we're babies. She takes a year to do anything." "What about that other one?" a girl named Ingrid asks, referring to their once-a-week student teacher. "He comes in and goes like this: Rail (pauses) road. Rail (pauses) road. Like we don't know what railroad means!" The table breaks up laughing.

Outside the walls of schools across the country it's slowly become an open secret that enforced homogeneity benefits no one. The work of researchers like Jeannie Oakes of UCLA and Robert Slavin of Johns Hopkins has proven that tracking does not merely reflect differences—it causes them. Over time, slow kids get slower, while those in the middle and in the so-called "gifted and talented" top tracks fail to gain from isolation. Along the way, the practice resegregates the nation's schools, dividing the middle from the lower classes, white from black and brown. As the evidence piles up, everyone from the Carnegie Corporation to the National Governors Association has called for change.

Though some fashionably progressive schools have begun to reform, tracking persists. Parent groups, school boards, teachers, and administrators who hold the power within schools cling to the myths and wax apocalyptic about the horrors of heterogeneity. On their side is the most potent force known to man: bureaucratic inertia. Because tracking puts kids in boxes, keeps the lid on, and shifts responsibility for mediocrity and failure away from the schools themselves, there is little incentive to change a nearly century-old tradition. "Research is research," the principal told me that day, "This is practice."

Back Track

Tracking has been around since just after the turn of the century. It was then, as cities teemed with immigrants and industry, that education reformers like John Franklin Bobbitt began to argue that the school and the factory shared a common mission, to "work up the raw material into that finished product for which it was best adapted." By the twenties, the scientific principles that ruled the factory floor had been applied to the classroom. They believed the IQ test—which had just become popular—allowed pure science, not the whims of birth or class, to determine whether a child received the type of education appropriate for a future manager or a future laborer.

It hasn't quite worked out that way. Driven by standardized tests, the descendants of the old IQ tests, tracking has evolved into a kind of educational triage premised on the notion that only the least wounded can be saved. Yet when the classroom operates like a battleground, society's casualties mount and the results begin to seem absurd: Kids who enter school needing more get less, while the already enriched get, well, enricher. Then, too, the low-track graduates of 70 years ago held a distinct advantage over their modern counterparts: If tracking prepared them for mindless jobs, at least those jobs existed.

The sifting and winnowing starts as early as pre-K. Three-year-old Ebony and her classmates have won the highly prized "gifted and talented" label after enduring a battery of IQ and psychological tests. There's nothing wrong with the "regular" class in this Harlem public school. But high expectations for Ebony and her new friends bring tangible rewards like a weekly field trip and music and computer lessons.

Meanwhile, regular kids move on to regular kindergartens where they too will be tested, and where it will be determined that some children need more help, perhaps a "pre-first grade" developmental year. So by the time they're ready for first grade reading groups, certain six-year-olds have already been marked as "sparrows"—the low performers in the class.

In the beginning, it doesn't seem to matter so much, because the other reading groups—the robins and the eagles—are just a few feet away and the class is together for most of the day. Trouble is, as they toil over basic drill sheets, the sparrows are slipping farther behind. The robins are gathering more challenging vocabulary words, and the eagles soaring on to critical thinking skills.

Though policies vary, by fourth grade many of these groups have flown into completely separate classrooms, turning an innocent three-tier reading system into three increasingly rigid academic tracks—honors, regular, and remedial—by middle school.

Unless middle school principals take heroic measures like buying expensive software or crafting daily schedules by hand, it often becomes a lot easier to sort everybody by reading scores. So kids who do well on reading tests can land in the high track for math, science, social studies, even lunch, and move together as a self-contained unit all day. Friendships form, attitudes harden. Kids on top study together, kids in the middle console themselves by making fun of the "nerds" above and the "dummies" below, and kids on the bottom develop behavioral problems and get plenty of negative reinforcement.

By high school, many low-track students are locked out of what Jeannie Oakes calls "gatekeeper courses," the science, math, and foreign language classes that hold the key to life after twelfth grade. Doors to college are slamming shut, though the kids themselves are often the last to know. When researcher Anne Wheelock interviewed students in Boston's public schools, they'd all insist they were going to become architects, teachers, and the like. What courses were they taking? "Oh, Keyboarding I, Earth Science, Consumer Math. This would be junior year and I'd ask, 'Are you taking Algebra?' and they'd say no."

Black Marks

A funny thing can happen to minority students on the way to being tracked. Even when minority children score high, they often find themselves placed in lower tracks where counselors and principals assume they belong.

In Paula Hart's travels for The Achievement Council, a Los Angeles-based educational advocacy group, she comes across district after district where black and Latino kids score in the 75th percentile for math, yet never quite make it into Algebra I, the classic gatekeeper course. A strange phenomenon occurs in inner city areas with large minority populations—high track classes shrink, and low track classes expand to fit humble expectations for the entire school population.

A few years ago, Dr. Norward Roussell's curiosity got the best of him. As Selma, Alabama's first black school superintendent, he couldn't help but notice that "gifted and talented" tracks were nearly lily white in a district that was 70 percent black. When he looked for answers in the files of high school students, he discovered that a surprising number of low track minority kids had actually scored higher than their white top track counterparts.

Parents of gifted and talented students staged a full-scale revolt against Roussell's subsequent efforts to establish logical standards for placement. In four days of public hearings, speaker after speaker said the same thing: We're going to lose a lot of our students to other schools. To Roussell, their meaning was clear: Put black kids in the high tracks and we pull white kids out of the system. More blacks and more low-income whites did make it to the top under the new criteria, but Roussell himself was left behind. The majority-white school board chose not to renew his contract, and he's now superintendent in Macon County, Alabama, a district that is overwhelmingly black.

Race and class divisions usually play themselves out in a more subtle fashion. Talk to teachers about how their high track kids differ from their low track kids and most speak not of intelligence, but of motivation and "family." It seems that being gifted and talented is hereditary after all, largely a matter of having parents who read to you, who take you to museums and concerts, and who know how to work the system. Placement is often a matter of who's connected. Jennifer P., a teacher in a Brooklyn elementary school, saw a pattern in her class. "The principal put all the kids whose parents were in the PTA in the top tracks no matter what their scores were. He figures that if his PTA's happy, he's happy."

Once the offspring of the brightest and the best connected have been skimmed off in honors or regular tracks, low tracks begin to fill up with children whose parents are not likely to complain. These kids get less homework, spend less class time learning, and are often taught by the least experienced teachers, because avoiding them can become a reward for seniority in a profession where perks are few.

With the courts reluctant to get involved, even when tracking leads to racial segregation and at least the appearance of civil rights violations, changing the system becomes an arduous local battle fought school by school. Those who undertake the delicate process of untracking need nerves of steel and should be prepared to find resistance from every quarter, since, as Slavin notes, parents of high-achieving kids will fight this to the death. One-time guidance counselor Hart learned this lesson more than a decade ago when she and two colleagues struggled to introduce a now-thriving college curriculum program at Los Angeles' Banning High. Their efforts to open top-track classes to all students prompted death threats from an unlikely source—their fellow teachers.

Off-Track Betting

Anne Wheelock's new book, *Crossing the Tracks,* tells the stories of schools that have successfully untracked or never tracked at all. Schools that make the transition often achieve dramatic results. True to its name, Pioneer Valley Regional school in Northfield, Massachusetts was one of the first in the nation to untrack. Since 1983, the number of Pioneer Valley seniors going on to higher education jumped from 37 to 80 percent. But, the author says, urban schools continue to lag behind. "We're talking about unequal distribution of reform," Wheelock declares. "Change is taking place in areas like Wellesley, Massachusetts and Jericho, Long Island. It's easier to untrack when kids are closer to one another to begin with."

It's also easier for educators to tinker with programs and make cosmetic adjustments than it is to ask them to do what bureaucrats hate most: give up one method of doing things without having another to put in its place. Tracking is a system; untracking is a leap of faith. When difficult kids can no longer be dumped in low tracks, new ways must be found to deal with disruptive behavior: early intervention, intensive work with families, and lots of tutoring. Untracking may also entail new instructional techniques like cooperative group learning and peer tutoring, but what it really demands is flexibility and improvisation.

It also demands that schools—and the rest of us—admit that some kids will be so disruptive or violent that a solution for dealing with them must be found outside of the regular public school system. New York City seems close to such a conclusion. Schools Chancellor Joseph Fernandez is moving forward with a voluntary "academy" program, planning separate schools designed to meet the needs of chronic troublemakers. One of them, the Wildcat Academy, run by a non-profit group of the same name, plans to enroll 150 students by the end of the year. Wildcat kids will attend classes from nine to five, wear uniforms, hold part-time jobs, and be matched with mentors from professional fields. Districts in Florida and California are conducting similar experiments.

Moving away from tracking is not about taking away from the gifted and talented and giving to the poor. That, as Wheelock notes, is "political suicide." It's not even about placing more black and Latino kids in their midst, a kind of pre-K affirmative action. Rather, it's about raising expectations for everyone. Or, as Slavin puts it: "You can maintain your tracking system. Just put everyone into the top track."

That's not as quixotic as it sounds. In fact it's long been standard practice in the nation's Catholic schools, a system so backward it's actually progressive. When I taught in an untracked parochial high school, one size fit all—with the exception of the few we expelled for poor grades or behavior. My students, who differed widely in ability, interest, and background, nevertheless got Shakespeare, Thoreau, and Langston Hughes at the same pace, at the same time—and lived to tell the tale. Their survival came, in part, because my colleagues and I could decide if the cost of keeping a certain student around was too high and we had the option of sending him or her elsewhere if expulsion was warranted.

The result was that my honor students wrote elegant essays and made it to Ivy League schools, right on schedule. And far from being held back by their "regular" and "irregular" counterparts, straight-A students were more likely to be challenged by questions they would never dream of asking. "Why are we studying this?" a big-haired girl snapping gum in the back of the room wondered aloud one day. Her question led to a discussion that turned into the best class I ever taught.

In four years, I never saw a single standardized test score. But time after time I watched my students climb out of whatever mental category I had put them in. Tracking sees to it that they never get that chance. Flying directly in the face of Yogi Berra's Rule Number One, it tells kids it's over before it's even begun. For ultimately, tracking stunts the opportunity for growth, the one area in which all children are naturally gifted.

Prom Pictures: A Principal Looks at Detracking
Fredric Cohen

Last year I attended our senior prom with the usual sense of sadness and joy. As I scrutinized each arriving couple and watched them pose for their prom pictures, I realized from my perspective as principal that this was the end of a remarkable educational journey for these special seniors.

The Decision to Detrack

The journey began six years ago when teachers and administrators at Kennedy High School in Bellmore, New York, expressed dissatisfaction with what was

SOURCE: *Educational Leadership, 52,* no. 4, (December/January 1995): pp. 85–86. Reprinted with permission of the Association for Supervision and Curriculum Development. Copyright © 1995 by ASCD. All rights reserved.

then known as our non-Regents track. (In New York state, most students sit for fairly rigorous year-end evaluations known as Regents Examinations. But in almost all high schools, the weakest students take less challenging non-Regents courses and must pass far simpler competency tests.)

Our problem with these non-Regents courses was not based on research calling for higher expectations for all students. Our view then was more limited and concrete. With approximately 225 students in each grade, we had only one or two sections of each non-Regents course per grade. Typically, students weak in math were also weak in English, social studies, and science. We inadvertently segregated this population for almost the entire day, and, except for gym, art, and lunch, these youngsters interacted only with one another.

Two distinct types of poor learners were enrolled in the non-Regents classes: the "can't do's" and the "won't do's." Whenever such groups are brought together and segregated from the rest of the school population, the result is predictably a core of angry, self-loathing youngsters who learn little and are viewed by teachers as hostile and uneducable. This proved to be the case, and most of our teachers disliked teaching these students.

After hearing lengthy faculty complaints about the non-Regents classes, I proposed what was then almost heresy: Eliminate the non-Regents section in all subjects other than math, and integrate these students, a few in each section, into the regular classes. (We chose not to eliminate our honors track, which fed our Advanced Placement program.) Although it took over a year to obtain agreement from all 9th grade teachers and then to sell the idea to parents, the superintendent had long been an advocate of detracking. In fact, he was looking for one of the three high schools in the district to break ground.

Success Versus Struggles

Now, four years later, I looked at our seniors in evening gowns and tuxedos, and I tried to judge how life would have been different for some of them had we not eliminated those low-level classes. First, I thought of the most outstanding of these students. His mother, a high school guidance counselor, had originally felt her son needed slow-paced classes to succeed. Now, she is our biggest supporter; her son not only succeeded in regular classes, but he easily passed Regents exams in all his courses! When he received 92 percent in Global Studies on the Regents exam, his teacher was dumbfounded. How, he wondered, could a student who was viewed as well below average actually become his best student? How indeed!

On the other hand, I watched now as another young man, also one of those students who originally sought entry into a non-Regents program, smiled into the camera for his prom picture. He would have to attend summer school in order to earn a diploma because he had failed his senior English class. In fact, a half dozen seniors were in the same bind. In years past, these students were in the non-Regents program and could pass a class that had only minimal standards. This year, however, with no non-Regents section, there was no golden parachute, and these students would be struggling through their summer making up a class.

What were their chances of achieving academic success this time? We found that the so-called "can't do's" had no difficulty passing, because teachers, after four years of experiencing detracking, were aware of the special needs of these youngsters and how to grade them. The "can't do" students may not have prepared sophisticated term papers, but they did follow the guidelines outlined by their teachers and gave a sustained and maximum effort. But the "won't do's" failed—not because they could not complete assigned tasks, but because they did not attempt them. Now, as I looked at Johnny's smiling face, sadly knowing that he would not earn his diploma in June, I realized that if the non-Regents program had allowed him to pass without requiring an effort on his part, this would have been an even greater injustice.

Encouraging Results

Surely, these two prom pictures neither validate nor negate our efforts at detracking. Nor do I suggest that Regents exams are the only means to evaluate success. In fact, I argue that more modern assessments, based on current research, should be substituted. Still, Regents results can be significant.

For instance, in our district, almost 15 percent more of our students now sit for these exams. This is no small accomplishment because with about 800 students in each grade, this means that an additional 120 students are scheduled for a more rigorous program with far higher expectations. And even though the Regents exams may measure only a part of the curriculum, the students who pass them demonstrate some level of proficiency that is indicative of a solid learning base.

Compared to student achievement four years ago, our students have demonstrated enormously improved performance. In English, 80 percent of our students now pass the Regents exam as compared to 61 percent four years ago. In Sequential Math I, the percentage of students passing the Regents increased from 71 to 87 in Sequential Math III, from 47 percent to 59 percent. We have had similar, but somewhat less dramatic, improvement in other subjects.

To suggest that these improved scores are simply the result of changing students' schedules would be deceptive. We have been forced to change many teaching practices and to expend additional funds. For instance, as is typical in Japanese schools, we have asked our teachers to stress student effort more than student ability. This means that teachers rely less on student recall of factual information and more on research papers, lab reports, homework, and classwork. Most teachers have had to revise old lesson plans and develop a new level of expertise with computers and other technology. We hired additional personnel and developed a partnership with a local university to create a new "intern" position. These teaching assistants have been invaluable in working with 9th graders who attended detracked classes for the first time.

At first, many teachers objected to detracking, and a few may wish we still had non-Regents classes, especially if someone else was assigned to teach them.

Also, we still have an occasional course where the proportion of formerly non-Regents students to Regents students is high, and we have not yet reached our goal of motivating all students to produce solid efforts. But we have challenged many more students, and, perhaps more important, we have eliminated a divisive, nonproductive learning environment that creates a core of self-hating, antisocial adolescents who vandalize our schools and intimidate their classmates and teachers. Although such students continue to exist, we as an institution no longer provide a fertile ground for these seeds of discontent to flourish.

And finally, as I viewed these picture-perfect seniors on prom night in their poses of satisfaction and anticipation, I realized that our efforts thus far have been well focused, and we are surely pointed in the right direction.

Learning to Teach an Untracked Class
Joan Kernan Cone

"When it was snack time," wrote Soo-Jin, recalling her group placement in second grade, "the teacher let groups five and four get the Graham crackers and apple juice first. We would be stuck with the broken pieces—which she gave us two of—and juice that tasted like water." This year Soo-Jin is not in "group zero"; she is in my ninth-grade English class, a heterogeneously grouped college prep class for all but certified gifted students. In that class she has written a number of expository essays and narratives, read *The Odyssey, Jane Eyre,* and *China Boy* on her own in addition to the required literature texts, and earned all A's and one B the first semester in a schedule that includes biology, algebra, world history, PE, French, and English. For all (or perhaps because of) her success in the class, Soo-Jin again feels slighted academically. All evidence indicates that she is an honors student and yet she was not programmed into an honors English class. Why? The answer lies in the rigidity of ability tracking. Soo-Jin's placement in ninth-grade English was decided in second grade when she was not tested for "gifted" and again in eighth grade when she was not programmed into algebra and foreign language.

Next year there will be no Soo-Jins in El Cerrito's ninth-grade English classes. Next year all ninth graders will be programmed into carefully balanced, heterogeneously grouped English classes, the last stage in an untracking effort that has taken eight years to accomplish.

Eight years ago students at El Cerrito High were rigidly tracked into four English class groups: low, average, high, gifted. Teachers referred to their classes by labels: "my third-period low class," "his average juniors," "their gifted ninth graders." For a small group of teachers in the department, however, the labels were as much a description of our expectations for students as a description of student ability, a description that nagged at our awareness of the connectedness of expectation and performance and the workings of self-fulfilling prophesy. In the spring of 1986 we enrolled in an inservice class taught by University of California, Berkeley, psychology professor Rhona Weinstein aimed at creating school success for at-risk students.

When the class ended, four English teachers signed on to do a collaborative research project with Ms. Weinstein and her research assistant.[1] That group — Promoting Achievement through Cooperative Teaching (PACT), as we came to call ourselves — spent the next year reading earlier research, arguing over its validity, relevance, and application in urban classrooms, and gradually created a model for teaching "ninth-grade low" students. Over that year we met every Thursday for an hour and a half after school to discuss more research articles, share teaching successes and failures, and encourage each others' commitment to breaking the cycle of failure for our students.

By the end of the next year, we had learned two important truths. First, classes limited to students testing at the stanine two and three level did not work: No amount of remediation, collaborative learning, parental contact, or shift of locus of responsibility was going to inspire students to succeed if they had no positive peer models of achievement and deportment. We took this concern to our principal and vice principal and got permission to broaden PACT classes to include stanines two through five. The second truth was more complicated: merging "average" and "low" classes was not enough: We needed to learn how to teach heterogeneously grouped classes.

For the next year, teaching strategies became the focus of our weekly meetings. What was the secret of teaching required texts and discourse modes to students with different skill levels? How could the high-achieving students be challenged without leaving the low-achieving students behind? How should discipline problems, absenteeism, and homework policies be worked out? As we developed our pedagogy for teaching at-risk ninth graders, we grew increasingly aware of the damages of ability tracking for all students, high achieving as well as low achieving, twelfth graders as well as ninth. That realization led to a bold move. Inspired by the work of Jaime Escalante and the film *Stand and Deliver,* we decided to untrack Advanced Placement English. Instead of admitting only students with top grades and high scores and glowing teacher recommendations, we invited into AP English Literature and AP English Language all students willing to complete a summer of rigorous writing and reading assignments.

That decision set into motion a commitment to untrack the entire department and led, over time, to the creation of a unique untracking model based solely on student choice. For the past three years all tenth-, eleventh-, and twelfth-grade students at El Cerrito High have self-selected their English class — college prep English or accelerated English (in twelfth grade, AP) — on the basis of their willingness "to work hard or harder." The only exception to self-selection is, or was until recently, ninth-grade English. Despite the disapproval of some PACT teachers, ninth-grade honors English was maintained out of fear that parents of certified gifted eighth graders would abandon the public school system if their children were not programmed into an elite ninth-grade English class.

The results of a recent questionnaire alerted us to the effects of the ninth-grade honors class on our self-tracking model. When asked what influenced their choice of English class, a high percentage of sophomores and juniors and a significant number of seniors mentioned their ninth-grade placement. Typical responses: "I signed up for accelerated because I have been taking honors English classes since ninth grade." "I have always been in honors classes." "I was in honors last year so I just moved along." "I was in college prep last year so I just went with what they gave me." "Because I had [college prep English] all these years." It was clear that students' choice of English class was influenced by a perception of themselves as either accelerated or college prep, a perception established or reinforced by their placement in ninth-grade English.

Twelfth graders' responses indicated the most freedom from the control of that placement. A number of seniors were "crossing over." Scott, a student who had been in accelerated for three years, wrote, "I took college prep because I did not want to do all the work for AP." Joe, a certified gifted student, said: "The idea of reading books over the summer did not appeal to me." Megan, a National Merit Scholar, told us: "The main problem I had with being in AP was facing another year with the same 30 people I've had English with since ninth grade." Mica, new to accelerated classes, wrote, "One of the students in last year's AP class advised me to take this class—I really didn't know much about it. I thought it was only for the gifted." Le said: "I wanted to prove to myself I could do AP work."

After studying the data from the questionnaires, the department voted unanimously to do away with ninth-grade honors English in favor of an untracked, one-tiered class—to empower all students to make future English choices free of high school assigned labels.

Three days after our vote, we announced the change to parents and students at a meeting for incoming ninth graders. Unlike the parents of gifted students who a few years before had literally applauded our decision to open AP, many of these parents were not happy with our decision about untracking freshman English. While there was a smattering of applause, there were many questions, most of them tinted with anger. Why, they wanted to know, why now, why not the next year? And, "How will they [students who had not been in high track classes previously] compete with our children?" And, "How can you guarantee that the best students will be challenged?" Slowly and firmly we explained the why and the how: We don't see education as competition; we see it as working together to learn. Also, the what: Our curriculum will not change, we will continue to teach the curriculum that has challenged students for years. And we asked that they support us as senior parents had and to trust us and our past success. During the next few days our vice principal got calls from parents testing our resolve. We held firm on our position and he held firm with us. We all held our breath. The threats to enroll their children in private high schools did not materialize.

Teaching Untracked Classes

Over the years as PACT members have worked out the structure of our un-tracking model and our philosophy of untracking, we have learned how to teach untracked classes. In the beginning we did not know how important that was. I assumed, for instance, that when I opened AP English Language and Composition to all students willing to commit to a summer and year of academi-cally challenging work, that was all I needed to do: students would rise to the level of the tasks I set. Within the first weeks of the class, however, I realized that creating an opportunity for all students to take AP English was not enough: I needed to create opportunity for success in AP English for all students. That realization led me to change dramatically the way I taught the class.[2]

Two years after that first successful year with an untracked AP class, I re-quested an untracked senior English college prep class. I assumed that what I had learned in my AP class about deadlines, attendance, use of effective talk, and small group instruction could be applied in a college prep class. I was right; but only after I had dealt honestly with the significant difference between the two classes.

To be blunt: I found that college prep students were not AP students. Whereas AP students had read and written essays on three books over the sum-mer vacation, college prep students (with only two or three exceptions) had read none, even though they had been given a list of suggested summer read-ings. In addition, whereas in the AP classes there were no students with poor attendance records, no students on the verge of not graduating, no students who did not intend to go to college, there were many such students in college prep classes. While both classes had a broad spectrum of students in terms of grades and SAT scores, the range was considerably broader in the college prep classes. In AP, for example, there were 12 students who had a weighted GPA of over 4.0; in college prep there was one. In AP 13 percent of the students had under a 3.0 GPA; in college prep only 8 percent had over a 3.0—most signifi-cant, in college prep 20 percent of the students had less than a 1.99. Even more problematic, there were a number of students in college prep classes for whom school was a negative experience. To cope, they had invented strategies. Some cut class regularly, attending just often enough to pass. Some "created them-selves as invisible"—attending class, completing assignments, but making no or minimal connection with other students or the teacher. Some sabotaged classes through disruptive behavior.

The range in the college prep class in terms of attitudes about school, his-tory of school success, and self-perception as learners and the effect those atti-tudes had on the class made learning to teach an untracked college prep class far more difficult than learning to teach an untracked AP class. It took only one year in AP to give me a sense of what worked and what didn't. It has taken three times that long in my college prep classes. Little wonder: The makeup of an untracked college prep class is far more complex than the makeup of an un-tracked AP class. More complex, more demanding, and more reflective of the damaging consequences of ability tracking.

Creating a Safe Environment for Learning

The last few years have taught me that the first task in an untracked class is the establishment of a safe environment. All students must be free to ask questions, share what they know and admit what they don't know, read their writing, make mistakes, take stands and change stands, grow as thinkers. All students must be expected to learn and must see that learning is expected of them. All students must know that rudeness and ridicule will not be tolerated.

The last few years have also taught me that the best way to get across appropriate classroom behavior is not a list of rules but a series of activities that require students to talk with each other and listen carefully. I begin the year with a seating chart lesson. On the second day of school, I hand out a blank seating chart to students and ask them to fill in as many of their classmates' names as they know, working silently and alone. After a few minutes, I introduce myself. "I am Joan Cone. J-O-A-N C-O-N-E." I ask students to raise their hands if they have any questions about the spelling or pronunciation of my name. I then point to the student sitting in the front seat of the first row and ask her to introduce herself, following the model, making sure that she speaks clearly and slowly enough for everyone to hear. During the activity I remind students to raise their hands if a name is not clear. After all students have introduced themselves, I say something like "I was born in Des Moines, Iowa, and my favorite movie is *Apocalypse Now*." Then I call on a student by name and ask her place of birth and favorite film. Thus we make our way around the room a second time, students calling on students across the room tennis match style. Throughout this activity I am strict about politeness and attentiveness; if a student is disrespectful, interruptive, or rude, I stop the class to restate the rules of etiquette gently but firmly. For the next few days, we do variations on the seating chart activity—naming our most difficult classes, listing the first three things we would do if we won the lottery, revealing things about ourselves few people know—so that by the end of the first week students feel relatively secure calling on each other and making their voices heard, safe in an orderly and respectful class in which everyone is expected to contribute, and clear about what I expect in terms of classroom etiquette. This activity also prepares students to assume control of class activities. Once students know each others' names, they—not I—call on each other to read literary passages and to share writing.

The Issue of Attendance and Missed Work

Attendance is not an issue in AP classes where it is rare that a student misses class. It *is* an issue in college prep where sometimes as much as one-fifth of the class is absent. One of the biggest problems with absenteeism is make-up work. In years past, I took responsibility for reviewing class work with absentees and making sure they understood missed assignments. I no longer do that. Now students are responsible for make-up work—their own and their classmates'. When absentees return to school, they do not ask me what they have missed; they check the student-written log book instead. If the log is unclear, they contact the log-writer, a student appointed for a week who records all class activities and assignments in an informative and entertaining way. Make-up work is due the day after the student returns from a one- or two-day absence, a week after a long-term absence.

Logs do not answer all problems related to absenteeism. They are particularly insufficient in assisting students with literature. It is not enough to say to returning students: "Read Act I of *Othello*." This is especially true of students for whom reading is not pleasurable. These students need to know more than the pages covered the day they missed; they need to be invited into the literary work in a way that involves them and makes them want to come back the next day. Years ago I did not know this. When students were absent while I was teaching a piece of literature, I sent them to the library or to an isolated area of the room to read on their own until they caught up with us. Few caught up. Now instead of sending students off to read on their own, I enlist the help of their classmates. Students review the storyline and development of the characters so that the returning student understands well enough to participate in the class. The next day, I ask him to retell the plot to clear up any confusions or errors in his understanding. If he has problems, his classmates help him again. Reviewing in this way serves other students as well as absentees since it assists the whole class in recalling the previous day's reading and gets them focused on the next part of the play or novel.

Strict Deadlines: Showing Respect

It took me over a year to see that the strict rules about deadlines I was setting in AP could be applied in college prep. When it became clear to me that the most dedicated students were meeting the deadlines and the least dedicated were ignoring them, I realized that it was my expectations that were at fault. By allowing students to miss due dates for major papers and take important tests late, I was telling students that a deadline wasn't a deadline unless they wanted it to be. More important, I was telling them, "I don't expect you to get things in on time so I won't be too strict with you." Once I realized the disrespect behind my leniency, I tightened up. Now deadlines are deadlines. Missed homework gets a zero. Late major papers receive credit but no grade. Missed discussions cannot be made up. When discussions are on written papers, I attach a note to the essay to acknowledge the writing as well as the missed opportunity to share in class talk. "Good writing. I wish you could have been here to add your ideas to ours. You missed a great discussion." Admittedly, it is not easy to be strict about deadlines, but every time I fudge, I am sorry. I not only pay on the next assignment ("One more day, please, one more day"), I know that I have lowered my expectations with students who do not need kindness that weakens them.

Talk: The Secret to Success in an Untracked Class

To make my untracked AP class work, I restructured the curriculum so that all students would feel comfortable asking questions, sharing interpretations, reading their writing—joining the real as well as the metaphorical conversation of the class. When I tried to incorporate the same level of talk in college prep, I was unsuccessful. Some students refused to participate in class talk out of fear of being branded nerds or of not knowing the "right" answers. Other students dominated class discussions, seeing them as an opportunity to show off, control the class, or get the class off task to avoid continuing class work.

Before I started the second year of untracked college prep senior English, I analyzed what was going wrong. Most students were not used to "making meaning together"; to them a quiet class was an orderly class. They had been in classes where the teacher or the best readers dominated talk about literature, where little or no emphasis was placed on writing for an audience, where talk meant chaos. To teach them to use speech as a method of learning together, I chose a short but sophisticated work as our first piece of literature: *Sula* by Toni Morrison. From the very first day I stressed the need to ask questions and make meaning together. We had barely finished the first 10 pages of the book, when Melanie blurted out, "What's up with Shaddrack—are his fingers really growing or is he freaking out?" She asked what many students wanted to know and in asking set an example for them. From then on as we made our way through the book, students asked and answered questions constantly, clearing up confusions, defending interpretations, rethinking the text with each other, teaching each other how to read and analyze literature. "Did Shaddrack see Sula kill Chicken Little?" "What did he mean by 'Forever'?" "How could Sula have *hmm-hmm*-ed [laughter] her best friend's husband?" "Did Nel forgive Sula at the end?" "Are Sula and Nel really just two sides of one character—is that what the author is saying?"

From *Sula* we moved quickly to *Othello,* amid groans about Shakespeare. Here, instead of having students ask questions whenever they didn't understand, I had them write at the beginning of each day's class what they understood and did not understand about the previous day's reading. On the second day on the play, for example, I asked them to write everything they knew about the play so far. Phillipa was adamant. "I don't know anything," she said, "I hate this play and I hate Shakespeare."

"Okay," I said, "then write about that for five minutes."

And she did. "I know I hate Shakespeare. I know I don't understand this play. I know nothing about this stupid play." She called me over to show me what she had written.

"Push yourself," I suggested, "or just sit quietly until everyone else is finished."

She resumed writing. "Okay, so I know there's this guy named Othello who is a famous soldier and he fell in love with this young girl. Another guy's in love with her, too. I forgot his name. Her name is Desdemona and she eloped with Othello. And there's this other guy who is jealous of Othello and mad at him. He works for Othello setting out to destroy Othello. Who is black but Desdemona's dad, who is white, doesn't like him because he's black."

Once Phillipa settled down to write, she saw that in fact she did know something about the play—something that she could share with the class. They in turn could share what they knew with her and add to her understanding. Inviting Phillipa to read aloud what she had written was purposeful; I wanted to demonstrate to the class that writing helps us discover what we know. Over the course of our study of *Othello*, I made sure that all students participated in writing and reading what they knew about the play so that they all shared in making meaning of the play. Sometimes in these class openers I asked students to summarize the plot, sometimes to assume the personae of various characters ("All the males write as if you are Desdemona, all the females in the voice of Othello—what is happening to you at this point in the play and how do you feel about that?"), sometimes to guess what would happen next in the play. But always it was writing begetting talk and talk begetting writing and both begetting understanding.

Along with our reading and talk of literature, we read our own writing to each other: first personal narratives, then reflective essays, then expository and argumentative essays—in small groups and to the whole class. When students wrote pieces too private for the whole class to hear, I asked them to come at lunch to read them aloud to me so that they could get a sense of performance about their work.

Thus academic talk came into our class—controlled by me in the beginning, controlled by students' growing sense of appropriate behavior as the year progressed.

Creating Students Through Respectful Tasks

When we first began our untracking efforts years ago, we took as our guiding principle, "If it's good for gifted students, it's good for all students." As I gradually learned to teach untracked senior English, that sentence nagged me. I was increasingly pleased with the *how* of my teaching, but increasingly displeased with the *what*. Specifically, I was concerned that AP students' academic fare was superior to that of the college prep students. In literature, for example, AP students read Baldwin, Conrad, Woolf, and Hong Kingston while college prep students read a majority of texts listed as "adolescent lit," with only an occasional piece by a writer like Morrison. In the words of a college prep student, "They read hard books and we read short ones." I decided to take our motto to heart and to insert into the college prep curriculum works I had previously taught only in AP. The first such assignment was Shelby Steele's "Being Black and Feeling Blue," a provocative essay from his book *Content of Our Character: A New Vision of Race in America* that I had used the year before with AP students. To get students into the piece, I began reading it aloud. Before I had gone three paragraphs, August interrupted, "This sounds like me, I want to read." And he took over, reading as if he were giving a speech, looking up occasionally when students voiced agreement with his/Steele's points. When he had finished, students argued over the essay—some angry with Steele, others agreeing, all excited. At the end of the discussion, a young woman asked, "Why did we have to wait until senior year to read this kind of stuff?" While it was clear that she was talking about the subject matter of the essay, I took her question as permission to bring in more sophisticated pieces that pushed students to think deeply and to struggle with truths.

Since then the distinction between AP fare and college prep fare has faded. Now college prep students read Virginia Woolf, too: not all of *A Room of One's Own* unless they choose to, but all of the first chapter and all of the chapter on Shakespeare's sister. Now *Chronicle of a Death Foretold* is for AP and college prep students, as is *Go Tell It on the Mountain, The Autobiography of Malcolm X,* and *One Flew Over the Cuckoo's Nest.* As I began looking for quality works for college prep I grew excited and daring. From Bay Area newspapers I bring in essays by Ellen Goodman, Clarence Page, Stephanie Salter, and Cynthia Tucker. From the University of California, Berkeley, I have invited Troy Duster and Jabari Mahiri to discuss pieces of their research with us. From the local video store I rent films: *Jou Dou, American Me, House of Games, The Dead, The Meeting.* Every place I look I find new things to teach and new ways to teach old things. This year, after reading the Prologue and eight of the *Canterbury Tales,* my first-period college prep class set up our own Chaucerian competition—using newspaper stories that reflect today's culture and ethics as inspiration for poems, raps, or narratives. The winner received not "a supper at the expense of the Host" of the Tabard Inn, but a dollar from the 16 members of the class who signed up to vie for the title of best storyteller.

These sophisticated reading assignments led me to examine the kinds of writing tasks I was assigning college prep students. In AP I was asking students to write in a variety of discourse modes, to play with diction and tone, to employ sophisticated punctuation, to practice writing to AP prompts under a time constraint. In college prep classes I was assigning descriptions, personal narratives, and simple personal arguments. Once I saw how decidedly different my tasks and expectations were for the two classes, I upgraded the writing curriculum in college prep to include lessons on style and mechanics, argumentation, exposition, and reflection as well as practice in writing to prompts such as those used in college composition placement tests. I also began to assign AP literature type prompts for final discussions and essays on books, to give students practice in writing analytical essays that reflected careful reading and serious thought. As writing from both classes appeared on the bulletin board, it became increasingly obvious that students' choice to take college prep English was a choice of less work, not less quality.

The Role of Choice

Last year as I was experimenting with bringing "non-canonical" writers into the college prep curriculum, a friend suggested that students should have some say in who and what they read. His comment made me think. What would happen if students were given an opportunity to choose their literature? That idea has developed into an important part of my college prep curriculum. In brief, on a designated day, students come to class with the title of a book they want to read and convince at least three other students in the class to read it and discuss it with them. A few days later the book groups meet during class time to begin reading their books (checked out from the library, borrowed from a friend, bought) and to decide on the number of pages they will read each day to finish by the deadline—usually two or three weeks away. While students read their books, class work is limited to activities that do not require homework: plays, mini-lessons on mechanics and grammar, writing and discussions of essays. Generally, I set aside at least one or two days a week during this time for groups to meet to discuss their books. The day the book is due, I ask students to write the whole period on a generic prompt such as, "If you could make a film of your book, which five scenes would you be sure to include? Describe each scene carefully and tell why it is significant. Make sure that your essay demonstrates that you have read the book thoroughly and thoughtfully." I read the papers that night and hand them back the next day for students to use in their discussions. The following two or three days, the groups present their books to the class as a whole and answer questions about them.

In the beginning, I set strict guidelines on the books students could choose: the book had to be at least 250 pages long, written in the last five years, with no film of it and no Cliff Notes written on it. Once I saw that students were taking the activity seriously, I dropped the restrictions: my only criterion now is that the book be a piece of literature appropriate for school reading. What do students read when they are given the freedom to choose? The books my students most recently chose were typical of the range of titles. In first period: *Invisible Man, Alive: The Story of the Andes Survivors, Waiting to Exhale, Mama, Disappearing Acts,* and *Beowulf.* In fourth period: *Alive, Bury My Heart at Wounded Knee, Disappearing Acts,* and *A Season on the Brink.* In both classes there were a few students who read no books, five students in first period and four in fourth.

At the end of last year I interviewed students about the role of student choice in high school literature programs. They were adamant about the importance of choice: "Having choice made me feel powerful." [Kandi] "Having choice gave me freedom—I could read the books I wanted to read with people who were interested in the books I was." [Tassie] They were just as adamant, however, that they not choose all their books. "I think it is a good idea [to have choice] but the teacher needs to choose books, too, otherwise we may not choose the books we're *supposed* to read and we'd feel cheated when we got to college." [Angel] Phillipa agreed, "Even if you don't want to read all the books teachers assign, you need to be exposed to them—otherwise you feel left out—like the teacher didn't think you were capable of reading a certain book so she didn't teach it to you."

This year again I see that giving students choice about their reading encourages them to read good books. When we finished the last book presentations recently, students said things like, "I think we should all read *Alive*—that sounds like a book we need to read as a class." [Becky] "I know what book I'm going to read next—*Waiting to Exhale.* I want to read another Terry McMillan." [Richard] "When do we choose our next book?" [Michael] "I heard *Jazz* is hard, but I want to read it next." [Kanika]

Riding a Bike Is Fine, but First You Need to Learn How

As an advocate of untracking, I often hear teachers and administrators say, "Untracking is fine but first we need to learn how to teach an untracked class." I know what is behind that statement. Fear of parent resistance, classroom chaos, personal failure, school failure. But I know, too, that continuing to stay in a state of not-knowing-how does little good. It is my experience that teachers learn how to teach untracked classes by teaching them, not by waiting to learn how to teach them. And we learn by working with other teachers who are learning: planning lessons together during shared conference hours; talking over successes and failures; encouraging each other to experiment and take chances and read research; seeking help from administrators, counselors, and parents; conducting classroom research on untracking efforts.

To teachers who say, "But first we need to learn how to teach untracked classes," I say: Remember when you learned to ride a bike? You learned not from watching your older brother ride his bike, not from your dad's explanation about the brakes and pedals and handlebars, not even from your mother's steadying the bike for a while. You learned from riding—from practicing every day until you could do it on your own. That's how it has been for PACT teachers in our continuing commitment to learn to teach untracked classes: We needed the support we got from research, university classes, school administrators, and each other. But more than anything, we needed to get in our untracked classes and teach. And as in the days when we were learning to ride our bikes, we sometimes still fall, sometimes get bruised (our egos now, not our shins), sometimes take a challenging road too fast. But for all we don't know yet, we are exhilarated by our new skill and our growing sense of confidence.

REFERENCES

1. R. S. Weinstein, C. R. Soule, F. Collins, J. Cone, M. Mehlhorn, K. Simontacchi. "Expectations and High School Change: Teacher–Researcher Collaboration to Prevent School Failure," *American Journal of Community Psychology 19* (1991): 333-402.

2. J. Cone. "Untracking Advanced Placement English: Creating Opportunity Is Not Enough," *Phi Delta Kappan 73* (1992): 712-717.

BIBLIOGRAPHY

Baldwin, J. *Go Tell It on the Mountain.* (New York: Laurel, 1952).

Bronte, C. *Jane Eyre.* (New York: Washington Square Press, 1972).

Brown, D. *Bury My Heart at Wounded Knee.* (New York: Washington Square Press, 1981).

Chaucer, G. [Lumiansky, R. M., Tr.] *The Canterbury Tales.* (New York: Pocket Books, 1948).

Ellison, R. *Invisible Man.* (New York: Random House, 1947).

Feinstein, J. *A Season on the Brink.* (New York: Simon & Schuster, 1986).

Haley, A. and Malcolm X. *The Auobiography of Malcolm X.* (New York: Ballantine, 1987).

Kesey, K. *One Flew Over the Cuckoo's Nest.* (New York: NAL/Dutton, 1963).

Lee, G. *China Boy.* (New York: Signet, 1991).

Marquez, G. G. *Chronicle of a Death Foretold.* (New York: Ballantine, 1984).

McMillan, T. *Disappearing Acts.* (New York: Viking, 1989).

McMillan, T. *Mama.* (New York: Pocket Books, 1989).

McMillan, T. *Waiting to Exhale.* (New York: Viking, 1992).

Morrison, T. *Jazz.* (New York: NAL/Dutton, 1993).

Morrison, T. *Sula.* (New York: NAL/Dutton, 1987).

Rebsamen, F. [Tr.] *Beowulf.* (New York: Harper Collins, 1991).

Reid, P. P. *Alive: The Story of the Andes Survivors.* (New York: Avon, 1979).

Rouse, W. [Tr.] *The Odyssey.* (New York: Mentor, 1937).

Shakespeare, W. *Othello.* (New York: Washington Square Press, 1957).

Steele, S. *Content of Our Character: A New Vision of Race in America.* (New York: Harper Collins, 1990).

Woolf, V. *A Room of One's Own.* (New York: Harcourt Brace Jovanovich, 1929).

A Stupid Way to Treat Gifted Children
Ingrid Eisenstadter

June 23 was my child's last day in fifth grade. It was also his last day in public school. I'm taking him out a year early because the New York City public school for gifted children my son has been attending bears little resemblance today to the school I selected for him so carefully just a few years ago. His accelerated learning program decelerated till it left him asleep at the wheel.

One of the three private schools we applied to accepted my son with a generous scholarship. Another accepted him with a lavish scholarship. So why are two of the best private schools in Manhattan so interested in having what his public school gives up so willingly?

Budget cuts are not playing a major role in the waning of the gifted program in my boy's former school; educators are. Accelerated education for the gifted is long since out of favor with U.S. educators and today federal funds reserve less than 1% for the gifted. My son, however, always scores in the 99th percentile in the standardized math and reading-aptitude tests and that makes his academic needs an increasing problem for his school—Manhattan's P.S. 6, a "magnet" school—where it is now *de rigueur* to find that all children are born with similar abilities to learn. They're not, of course.

A few years after my son started school, the gifted program was dropped in the lower grades. At home he chose to read *The Complete Sherlock Holmes* (third grade), *The Origin of Species* (fourth grade) and *A Brief History of Time* (fifth grade), while in school he was reading, well, books for little kids.

Next, in keeping with a nationwide trend, our school eliminated "tracking" (keeping the brightest children together in one class). This practice, the theory goes, causes children in less academically gifted classes to get the wrong message about their abilities and become discouraged. They may well get the wrong message, but it does not come from classes restricted to children who excel at academic subjects. It comes from educators willing to imply to any child that he can grow up to be a plasma physicist or knot theorist, and that's just not true.

When did it become shameful to be a butcher or carpenter or an electrician? What's wrong with being a tool-and-die maker or a corsetiere like my father and mother, both of whom apprenticed in their trades to become highly skilled workers?

In a meeting with several school staff members last year I expressed my concern that, as the gifted program deteriorated, my son's schoolwork was increasingly below his abilities. "Our gifted program has depth and breadth, not acceleration," I was told. My son was learning "leadership" and "tolerance." But did he have classes in leadership and tolerance? No. What he had was arithmetic long after he heard the siren call of algebra and geometry.

I started teaching him at home. This added to his boredom in class. In time I heard—always from other parents, never by official communication from the school—that in sixth grade gifted and nongifted children were now in the same classes for numerous subjects, among them art history, three times a week. Art history? Three times a week?

Around this time, the head of the PTA withdrew her child in despair to teach him full time from home. Working mothers, of course, do not have that option.

The downgrading of the gifted program is a tragedy particularly because my son is by no means exceptional in his school. His buddy Jason taught himself to read before kindergarten. I was there. I saw it. I heard my son's friend Robert, who stayed at our home when the boys were in first grade, read my son a bedtime story, and it wasn't "See Dick Run"—it was C. S. Lewis's novel, *The Lion, the Witch and the Wardrobe*. And in the back of our car one third-grade day, my son and his friend Zachary talked about the states of matter, wondering if gels held a legitimate place among liquids, gasses and solids—nothing they'd learned in school.

I made an appointment with the district superintendent, Anthony Alvarado, to ask him, "What is the academic benefit to gifted children when you eliminate tracking?" I arrived for the appointment to find he was out of town. I asked the assistant superintendent, "By what yardstick are you measuring the success or failure of the changes in the gifted program?" She answered, "When the children stop being successful, we'll know the program didn't work."

That's not good enough. Exactly how do you gauge the loss—to these bright children, to the public school system, to society—caused by the academic challenges these leaders of the next generation did not have to rise to meet?

The bell tolls for excellence in public schools. Is anyone listening?

Volatile Mix: Parents Flunk Schools That Put Gifted Pupils With Lower Achievers
Sarah Lubman

SEATTLE—At least once a week, Howard Schwartz goes through his daughter's school notebook while she is asleep. He frets that Rachel, a gifted ninth-grader, is getting dumbed-down course work at her public high school, where honors English classes are now open to any student who wants to take them.

"There's a denial that kids are different, and the sense that everyone can be equal," Mr. Schwartz gripes about James A. Garfield High School's experiment of mixing high- and low-achievers in the same English classes. If the year-old experiment becomes standard practice, he warns, parents like himself "would seriously look at private schools."

Mr. Schwartz's anxiety is at the heart of a heated debate over educational privilege that is once again pitting parents against public schools around the country. Just such a debate spawned gifted-program mandates by most states in the 1970s and 1980s and surfaced repeatedly during the outcry over court-ordered busing in the late 1960s. But as broader definitions of intelligence have gained sway in recent years, an influential group of educators has argued that sorting students by test scores and academic ability should be scrapped because it is outmoded, elitist and perpetuates racial gaps.

New Learning Theory

"Kids are not smart and dumb, they're just different in the way that they learn best," says Robert E. Slavin, a research scientist at Johns Hopkins University in Baltimore and a leading opponent of "ability grouping," which, like "tracking," divides students according to their academic ability. Mixing children, the theory

SOURCE: *The Wall Street Journal*, May 23, 1995, pp. A1; A11. Reprinted by permission of *The Wall Street Journal*. Copyright © 1995 Dow Jones & Company, Inc. All rights reserved.

goes, exposes the academic whizzes to other kinds of intelligence, promotes cooperation instead of competition, and boosts the quality of education for those less academically inclined.

Moreover, budget-squeezed public schools are finding it harder to cater to students' special needs, which can involve costly programs. At Garfield High, parents who favor restricted honors classes "want a private school—but they want a public school to do it for them," says Jodee Reed, the head of the school's English department.

While ability grouping remains widespread, opposition to it is rising. Of 570 administrators polled in 1992 by the National Association of Secondary School Principals, 82% said their schools separated students by ability. But 36% of the principals were considering stopping the practice, and another 7% planned to do so, imminently.

Racial Overtones

As schools like Garfield put the theory to the test, parents like Mr. Schwartz are putting up a fight. They are pressuring schools not to adopt mixed-ability classes, seeking legal recourse, and even yanking their children from public school. The parents say they are simply concerned about the caliber of their own children's education. They invoke a 1992 analysis of 120 academic studies by a University of Michigan researcher showing that after one year of mixed classes, gifted students trail their peers who remain in gifted classes by at least half an academic year.

But the fact that activist parents of gifted students are overwhelmingly white and affluent—"Volvo vigilantes," as education-equity guru Jeannie Oakes of the University of California at Los Angeles calls them—has laced the debate with ugly overtones of race and class.

Meanwhile, the threat of driving away such parents dogs the public schools, as administrators worry about everything from losing funding because of declining enrollment to being unable to attract top-notch teachers: Seattle's public-school population has shrunk to 45,600 in 1994, from a 1960s high of 100,000, due to a combination of demographic changes and "white flight" to the suburbs.

Legal Challenges

"You don't come off real well when you tell people your kid is the smartest in the grade. But frankly, my kid couldn't be accommodated," says Peggy Varnado, who three years ago removed her daughter, Christine, then 12, from sixth grade at public Lily Burney Elementary School in Hattiesburg, Miss. She decided to teach the girl at home after Lily Burney converted from an academic magnet school to mixed-ability classes.

In other cases, parents of gifted students are turning to legal channels, much like parents of disabled children. Since gifted education isn't federally mandated, though, cases are hashed out in administrative hearings and rarely reach court. Jennifer Rotigel of Greensburg. Pa., has been embroiled in a hearing for 10 months to demand separate instruction for her bright 12-year-old son, Daniel. "Gifted kids are underdogs, too," she argues.

In school districts where race isn't a factor, the mixed-ability movement is sometimes short-lived. Last spring, at mostly white Rancho San Joaquin Middle School in Irvine, Calif., parents derailed a year-old experiment by demanding meetings with incoming principal Mark Reider and persuading him to revert to gifted-only classes. One of the parents was Marc Klau, a physician who complains that his gifted 13-year-old daughter, Elena, "had a lot of extra time" in the mixed-level class she took last year—although he concedes that Elena herself wasn't complaining.

"It was fun to not have to do any homework and get an A," Elena says. But she adds that she was bored, and that the transition to eighth grade has been tough as a result.

And some of Rancho's teachers applaud the change back. Michelle Rosenblum, who teaches gifted seventh-grade humanities classes, says the only way to manage her mixed 36-student class last year was to teach to the middle. She dropped *Jane Eyre,* a favorite book for gifted students, and substituted *The River,* a simpler book by contemporary "youth novelist" Gary Paulsen.

Quick reversals are less likely in places like Amherst, Mass., where race looms large. Amherst is moving toward mixed classes in a settlement with the local chapter of the National Association for the Advancement of Colored People. The NAACP sued the school district in federal court in 1992, charging that it was violating minority children's rights by steering them into lower-level classes. Similar cases are brewing elsewhere as gifted classes nationwide remain largely white and Asian.

But more often than the courts, it is members of school communities who are forcing the issue.

School Within a School

Such is the case at Garfield High, a massive maroon-brick edifice in a gritty black neighborhood in central Seattle, where bused-in white and Asian teenagers troop upstairs to honors classes, literally leaving their black peers behind on the ground floor. One of Seattle's best public high schools, Garfield consistently produces more National Merit finalists on the Pre-Scholastic Aptitude Test than any other public or private school in the state.

But in the wake of the 1992 Los Angeles riots, Garfield held race-relations forums that revealed strong antihonors sentiments. "Many students felt that dividing students on the basis of 'honors' vs. 'regular' is elitist and has a tendency to separate black and white students," 12 students wrote in a report summarizing views from the forums. "Garfield's academic program structure leads to 'a school within a school.'"

Numbers bear them out. Despite Garfield's diverse 1,540-member student body—52% white, 33% black, 10% Asian, and 5% Hispanic and other—honors and advanced-placement classes in English and history have been disproportionately white and Asian. In spring 1994, for example, 63% of freshmen in honors English classes were white, 13% Asian and 19% black.

In response, Ms. Reed, the English department head, suggested eliminating lower-level and honors-only sections, and teaching all students with honors materials. Several dozen parents of top-performing students in Seattle's Accelerated Progress Program objected immediately. In a contentious meeting with Ms. Reed, they were particularly galled by the argument that mixed-level classes would aid their children. The APP group—short for "Anxious Protective Parents," some joke—proposed keeping separate honors classes while Ms. Reed tested mixing students in a few classes.

Taking the Heat

As a compromise, Ms. Reed agreed to let honors survive but to make all students eligible for it. Starting last fall, any freshman was permitted to take honors English—or, alternatively, opt to do extra work for honors credit in a "regular" section. Fully 61% of the freshman class enrolled in honors, up from 54% in 1992 before any changes were made. The "honors option" system was extended to juniors this spring, but APP parents are still demanding separate honors sections.

So, Garfield's black principal, Ammon McWashington, now is taking the heat. In a recent meeting with 40 wary parents of gifted eighth-graders headed for Garfield in the fall, he assured them that open access to honors wouldn't "drag anyone down."

But many parents don't buy his argument. The day after the meeting, Mimi Winslow, a lawyer and parent of two gifted teenagers at Garfield, pokes her head in Mr. McWashington's doorway. Ms. Winslow, editor of Garfield's parent newsletter, has challenged Mr. McWashington frequently. This time she wants another meeting between parents of gifted students and Garfield's English teachers.

"For my kids, having an accelerated curriculum for a number of years and then slowing down in high school is going the wrong direction," says Ms. Winslow, who is white, at her kitchen table in Seattle's affluent Laurelhurst neighborhood. A day spent at Garfield attending both honors and nonhonors English classes convinced her she was right.

Impact Uncertain

Joan Irvin, whose daughter, Lois, is in the 10th grade at Garfield and tests into the gifted range, agrees. "If you're on a crutch, you're not going to make the track team. Sorry, but it's the reality of life."

It is too soon to tell whether Garfield's attempt to level the academic playing field will help or hurt the team as a whole. Although more students are taking honors English classes, standardized test scores fell slightly this year, a possible indication that some students are indeed being dragged down.

But others are being pulled up. Kathryn Sperling, a senior, transferred to Garfield as a sophomore because she had heard honors classes were more accessible. She took honors English and got her first A ever in the subject; her grade point average has risen to 3.2 from 2.9. "I realized what I'd been missing," she says.

And many gifted students, like Rachel Schwartz, don't object. "I'm not suffering or anything," she says. Nor does she mind her father's outspokenness—or even his notebook prowling—but thinks he sometimes overreacts. Rachel, who is 14, adds that she likes Garfield's renowned science and music programs and wants to stay there—although she may take English classes at a community college, an option for qualified students who can afford the book costs.

One Unconcerned Parent

And not every parent of a gifted student is anxious. "I'm willing to let class be watered down if it would raise standards for other African-American children," says Mary Bogan, who is black and the mother of a 17-year-old honors student at Garfield.

In any case, mixed classes have done little to ease the acute awareness among students of where each fits in. In Ann Schuh's 31-student freshman English class, the six nonhonors students sit in a clump in the middle of the room. While the honors students must write at least three pages on today's assigned book, the nonhonors students only have to write three paragraphs.

Students must also choose several books from a reading list. William Jones, a nonhonors student, raises his hand. "Can't I read a short one, with the big fat print for the illiterate kids?" he asks wryly.

Georgia Superintendent Battles a Subtle Racism
The New York Times

EDISON, Georgia—During his 20 years teaching English at Calhoun County High School here, Corkin Cherubini gradually concluded that black students, regardless of ability, were being steered into lower-level classes. But he said nothing for fear of losing his job.

SOURCE: *The New York Times,* February 14, 1995, p. A10. Reprinted with permission from *The New York Times.*

In 1992, he won election as superintendent of schools in this rural southwest Georgia county, and Dr. Cherubini broke his silence. He called in the Federal Education Department last year to investigate whether the 1,200-student Calhoun County system, which is 70 percent black, was grouping students by race rather than class performance, a practice known as *racial tracking.*

"I realized I needed help," Dr. Cherubini said. "I saw the futility of one person trying to correct a long-standing tradition."

For stirring the waters, Dr. Cherubini, a soft-spoken white man of 50 and a self-proclaimed outsider in this county of peanut and cotton farms and only 5,700 people, has become the target of bomb threats, hate letters and oral taunts from white parents and students.

Some white families have been angry enough to leave the district.

"Since school started, we've lost 85 students, predominantly white," said Frank Miller, a white member of the school board and a critic of Dr. Cherubini. "When you lose white kids, when you lose their families' support, it's going to hurt the school system."

But Dr. Cherubini is resolute. "Racial tracking is not much more than segregation," he said.

Under the district's system, students were placed in classes ranked A, B, C and D. The A classes were unofficially considered the college preparatory classes and tended to get the more experienced teacher and more money, Dr. Cherubini said. The D classes were considered the vocational track. The problem, he said, was that the elite classes were largely white and the lower-level classes entirely black.

Students could petition to move to a higher level, but by the seventh or eighth grade, their track was pretty well determined. "One of the biggest things is that the kids know where they are," he said.

Dr. Cherubini also asked Federal officials to investigate the cheerleading squads, which for years were made up of white girls for football, black girls for basketball.

Last November, the Education Department's Office of Civil Rights and Miami Equity Associates, a federally financed civil rights organization, concluded that blacks were indeed being placed by race instead of test scores, grades or teacher evaluations, a violation of the Civil Rights Act of 1964.

Working with the Federal officials, the district decided to abandon the four-tier classification. To make the schools more equitable, the Education Department will provide money to send teachers to conferences about how to end racial tracking and to bring in teachers and principals from other school districts for counsel. The investigators also ordered the integration of the cheerleading squads.

Although many white parents are angry, Nancy Peck of Miami Equity Associates asserted that by asking for help before the Government came in uninvited, which she said was inevitable, Dr. Cherubini made it much easier for his schools.

"I think it was an extremely courageous thing for Cherubini to do," she said.

Racial tracking, Dr. Peck said, is all too common, particularly in Southern districts where the administrators are white and at least half of the student body is black. She said the elite, majority white classes are sometimes consciously created to prevent white flight. More often, she said, the imbalance results from white parents' clamoring to get their children in the best classes and the mistaken feeling that black students are not as smart.

Black parents had known of the tracking for many years, said Willie Taylor, vice chairman of the Calhoun County School Board and the first black person elected to the board. "But every time a black parent would go over to the school and ask to have their child moved up to a higher level, they would always tell them that there was no room in the class," Mr. Taylor said.

Until a few years ago, many black parents worked on the farms and in the houses of white residents, said James Gibson, a former member of the school board who is black. If those blacks had complained about the inequitable class breakdown, he said, they would have lost their jobs.

Dr. Cherubini, too, said that as a new teacher at Calhoun County High School in the early 1970s he felt pressure not to upset the status quo. "Being elected superintendent, to actually be able to do something, allowed me to say something," he said.

Dr. Cherubini said he also believed that his status as an outsider enabled him to speak out. Reared in New Jersey and Massachusetts, he is not a member of the local Lions Club, attends a Unitarian Church in Tallahassee, Fla., and has a name that looks as out of place as a skyscraper would in downtown Edison.

"I've never fit in real well here with the cliques and the church groups," he said.

Some critics said Dr. Cherubini's motives were political, that he wanted the school board, which has a black majority, to give him another term in 1996 when Georgia law eliminates elected superintendents.

Dr. Cherubini said people are just angry about the changes. "There will be plenty of resistance," he said. "But we are definitely going to come into compliance, whatever it takes."

Mamie Williams, a teacher and the cheerleaders' sponsor, said it was for the best that the racial tracking was brought to light. "If Cherubini hadn't acted," she said, "it would have never happened."

Chapter 9

INCLUSION

INTRODUCTION

Inclusion has its roots, in part, in the Civil Rights movement of the 1960s. At its foundation is the principle of respect and equality for all people. In education today, "inclusion" is the term generally used to describe the practice of including as many physically, intellectually, emotionally, or otherwise handicapped or challenged students as possible into the mainstream of the school. There are, in fact, federal and state laws that require inclusion into regular classrooms under certain conditions.

On the one side, there are the emotional concerns of the parent who wants the very best for a challenged child. On the other side, there are parents who do not want their children "slowed down" because of the extra demands for attention that a challenged student might put on the teacher.

The major issues surrounding inclusion are those of effectiveness, cost, and morality. While there are various anecdotes and moving personal testimony on both sides of the question, educators must strive to base their decisions on hard data regarding the *real* impact of inclusion, both in terms of its educational and social benefits—or lack thereof—for *all* students and on its cost effectiveness to school systems, many of which already are financially strapped. Finally, there is the moral issue of the rights of challenged students to the same opportunities and quality of education as the nonchallenged.

"Inclusion" Shuffle: Some Students Getting Lost as Schools Try to Cope
Jeffrey Bils

On the first day of school the girl with cerebral palsy was there with her walker, ready to join her classmates for her first tentative trip into a regular classroom.

The only problem: No one had told her teacher.

Dale Steele was ready to teach a classroom full of 1st graders at Frost School in Mt. Prospect last year—but she was not prepared for the little girl with the walker.

And she was not alone.

As more and more Illinois school districts join the movement to place children with severe disabilities in ordinary classrooms, teachers often are not given advance warning or the assistance they need, teacher advocates say.

As a result, the practice known as *inclusion* has become a top concern among the state's teachers, many of whom complain that the laudable effort to integrate such pupils robs teachers of precious classroom time they need to teach the rest of the class.

"Over the last three years, I've gotten the most calls, the most heart-rending stories over inclusion," said Susan Shea, instruction and professional development director for the Illinois Education Association, the state's largest teachers union.

Countless teachers have reported incidents of "dumping," Shea said, in which teachers are "told on Friday the kid will be there on Monday." Others have reported varying degrees of miscommunication that show a widespread pattern of children with and without disabilities losing out on their chances to learn, Shea said.

All that has dampened enthusiasm for a movement that many educators hail as an inspired approach to teaching children with disabilities, an approach that promises to tear down the social barriers that hold back those who traditionally have been stigmatized as "handicapped."

Even teachers who have had troubling experiences often are fervent supporters of inclusion in principle. For example, Steele said that after the initial surprise of learning that she would be responsible for a girl with cerebral palsy, the experience improved.

"I never had a class that had such a sense of family and support as that class last year," said Steele. This year, Steele said, the district has hired an aide to help with the girl's needs. Steele praised the district for its efforts.

But even as some districts respond to teachers' concerns, others do not try to make their inclusion programs work effectively. This has left many teachers apprehensive and skeptical about how inclusion is practiced in their schools.

Recently, for example, a middle school teacher in Wheaton was told on Monday that four students with disabilities would be included in his regular classrooms on Tuesday.

"If I had known ahead of time, like at the beginning of the year, I would have been better prepared," said the teacher, who asked that his name not be used.

The teacher said nobody told him the nature of the children's disabilities. Though an aide has been assigned to help him, the teacher still had not had a chance to be in on planning sessions in which the children's needs and educational goals are established.

"Somebody needs to be realistic as to what the goals are for these kids. What is the expected outcome?" the teacher said. "A normal classroom is a bit overwhelming, even for a veteran teacher, because of the range of abilities in there."

Another teacher, who would be identified only as a language arts teacher in a western DuPage County middle school, said, "I walk in the door, and there sits an inclusion student in my classroom, with no prior notification, no training, and no aide. It's happened to me for three years."

Though she doesn't have a disabled student this year, the problem continues in other classrooms, she said.

"The situation at the school is that we are promised personnel, and then when school year starts, things are the same way. It's just chaos," she said. "Students, both inclusion as well as regular education students, are not receiving what they need."

Most teachers are reluctant to discuss their concerns over inclusion, even anonymously, because they fear retaliation or they believe it is more effective to work through internal school district channels, observers said.

But many teachers have deep concerns. Mary White, a 4th-grade teacher at Pattern School in Naperville, used to be one of them.

White's reaction was not unusual when she found out that Greg Morris, a child in a wheelchair with multiple disabilities that rendered him unable to speak, would be in her class last year.

Said White, "I was scared."

But White said she became a convert to inclusion as a result of the excellent support services provided by Indian Prairie Community Unit School District 204, services that helped Greg achieve a level of socialization that might otherwise have been impossible.

Greg, now 11 and in the 5th grade, has been in regular classrooms in the school district since he was in the 1st grade, despite his spina bifida and other disabilities. A nurse is with him throughout the school day, helping him take part as much as possible in classroom lessons and with other pupils.

"The people who are his classmates now are going to be the employers of the future," said Greg's mother, Louise Morris. "Those kids are going to remember it when they grow up."

And Greg's classmates have become accustomed to being around him.

"It's like a new experience for me. It's a good thing," said Darryl Webb, 10, who has been Greg's classmate since the 4th grade. "It's good for us to learn about people with disabilities."

The success of the Indian Prairie's inclusion program has attracted national attention, said Michael Byrne, the district's director of student services. The key to success, Byrne said, is the ample communication and assistance for the teachers.

Throughout the state, Shea said, there are examples of school districts such as Indian Prairie that devote enough resources to inclusion programs. But there are many other districts, she said, that do not.

Cindy Terry, a supervisor in the State Board of Education Special Education Department, characterized the concerns as "growing pains." Her office has been providing inclusion training for teachers for two years.

Since 1975, federal law has required that all students be educated in the "least restrictive environment," Terry said. "That law has never changed. It's just that perhaps it hasn't been as fully implemented.

"Within the last few years, there have been a lot of parents and administrators who have been saying, 'Wait a minute. We're not fully implementing the least restrictive environment.'"

Teachers in the state's largest school district, Chicago Public Schools, have experienced the same types of problems, said Gail Purkey of the Illinois Federation of Teachers, which includes the Chicago Teachers Union.

"You have students placed in regular education classrooms without support services that are needed," Purkey said. "There are going to be places in the Chicago Public Schools where inclusion is doing well, places where it's doing mediocre and places where it's hurting the students that it's supposed to help."

Purkey echoed concerns raised by teachers throughout the state: "There's a whole teamwork approach that needs to be in place before you include a special-education student in a regular classroom."

That teamwork approach generally includes specialized aides—and the assistance can be expensive.

"Some districts look at inclusion as a way to save money," said Katherine Avard, a member of the IEA [Illinois Education Association] Regular Education Initiative Committee.

"Educating these kids in a regular classroom, when done right, usually costs more," Shea said. "Unfortunately, the dollar dictates many times what's going to happen."

Stepping Into the World
Russell Martin

WOODLAND PARK, Colorado—In the fall of 1989, Ian Drummond began first grade. After a year in special-education kindergarten, this nonspeaking autistic boy was deemed ready to take another step into the world.

But before Ian started at Gateway Elementary in Woodland Park, Colo., his mother came to school to describe her son to his future classmates. She showed them a videotape—images of a blond boy, who looked normal, swinging and sliding on their playground. His mother explained that Ian had a sister named Sarah and a dog, that he liked stories about animals and that he loved to watch movies.

Yet, she explained, the kinds of sounds Ian would make wouldn't quite be words. She warned that sometimes he would push them out of his way but only when he really needed to go where he's going. Sometimes he would get upset and cry and scream for no apparent reason. He would spend lots of time alone, she said, even when they wanted him to join them, but it would not be because he didn't like them.

When Ian came to the room, his classmates were excited—some afraid, others eager to meet him but within an hour or so his presence was taken for granted.

Ian took this step in his own kind of stride. He ate his lunch at a table with other kids in the cafeteria. With the help of a teaching assistant, he was attentive during math and reading time. He still spent half of each day in a room with special-education students, yet his clockwork coming and going between the two classes seemed to suit his innate need for organization.

He initially sat at the edge of the cluster of kids who crowded around the teacher, Barbara Myers, as she read. But after a few weeks he began moving into their midst. Entranced by books, Ian made a point of investigating the new titles Mrs. Myers would display on the chalk tray.

One day in November, on the heels of Halloween festivities that hadn't seemed to interest Ian at all, he sat at his desk looking at an illustrated story called "The Farm Concert." By chance, everyone was quiet at the moment he nonchalantly said "cow" in a throaty whisper. Then he said "cow" again—audibly, distinctly and the room erupted, his classmates shouting "He said 'cow!' Ian said 'cow!'" Most of them rushed to his desk. Mrs. Myers was beside him as well, tears streaming down her face. "Say it again!" the students encouraged him. And he calmly said "cow" another time.

SOURCE: *The New York Times,* February 22, 1994, p. A21. Reprinted with permission from *The New York Times.*

By the beginning of the next school year, Ian was speaking about two dozen words, and flashcard exercises showed that his reading vocabulary was growing. He remained a first-grader, held back because he had been the youngest in his previous class. Now that he was one of the oldest, his parents and teachers hoped that his skills would more closely match that of his classmates and that he might begin to form friendships.

Ian had shared toys successfully in the special-education class, and he soon made friendships with kids in the larger class. It clearly didn't matter much to them that Ian could say so little, or that the words he could pronounce sounded strange. And with his friend Eddie—a rugged boy who assumed the role of Ian's companion and confidant—a one-way flow of words seemed more than adequate. Eddie developed an uncanny ability to sense what Ian could tolerate and what he could not. Eddie knew when a crisis was looming, and even how to push Ian to try some new things.

It seemed clear to the staff at Gateway that if Ian could prove so capable of inclusion, then virtually any other student could as well. And it didn't seem to benefit only Ian; sometimes inclusion's greatest value seemed to be what it offered the regular kids who had contact with him.

One day the next spring, Ian stood calmly at the front of his classroom, a giant-sized edition of "The Farm Concert" on an easel in front of him and his classmates sitting on the carpet at his feet. In the loudest voice he could muster, his words spoken clumsily but intelligibly, Ian announced the title and began to read, his cadence and inflection surprisingly appropriate:

"Moo, moo," went the cow.
"Wuff, wuff," went the dog.
"Quack, quack," went the duck.
"Oink, oink," went the pig.
"Baa, baa," went the sheep.
"Quiet!" yelled the farmer. "I can't sleep!"

Then, mimicking the way in which Mrs. Myers and his parents had read the story to him a hundred times, his voice just a whisper, he continued:

"Moo, moo," went the cow.
"Wuff, wuff," went the dog.
"Quack, quack," went the duck.
"Oink, oink," went the pig.
"Baa, baa," went the sheep.
"Good," said the farmer. "I *can* sleep."

Ian's classmates erupted in applause, and a boy near him quickly extended his palm and shouted, "give me five!" Then a dozen hands were extended; the kids up on their knees, pressing toward him and hollering, "give me five!"

Ian stood calmly, his face expressionless, his eyes turning to survey each of them yet appearing uncertain how to react to this ceremonial stuff of giving five. Then Eddie jumped up to help, guiding Ian's hand into the 20 open palms with a quick and hearty slap, Eddie saying, "yeah, Ian, cool, *now* you're giving five!"

An Interpreter Isn't Enough
Leah Hager Cohen

It's a few minutes before the class will start. Everyone's fishing notebooks from knapsacks and sharpening pencils, and it's all "What did you put for the last answer on the algebra?" and "Tomorrow's the last day for yearbook money, right?" and "If we want to stay for the game, Toni says she can give us a ride." All of the eleventh-graders are speaking or listening, directly or indirectly. Except for one student, sitting down front. She is neither speaking nor listening; she is not involved; she is deaf.

I am her sign-language interpreter. I stand at the front of the class, poised to begin signing whenever she looks at me, but she doesn't; she is resting her eyes on the sky outside the window. When at last she does turn her face, it is not to see what her classmates are saying but to chat with me about her weekend, about the book I am reading, about her dog, my sweater, anything. She is hungry for communication and chooses me—an adult satellite paid to follow her through the school day—rather than her peers, who do not speak her language.

Class begins. She pays attention for a while. Sometimes when the teacher asks a question, she signs a response, which I interpret into spoken English—always a little late, just a few seconds after the other students. Sometimes the students all talk at once; their voices overlap and I have to choose one thread to follow, or compress them all in a quick synopsis inserting who said which thing to whom and in what tone of voice.

Sometimes I make a mistake and have to correct myself and then we both fall behind and I scramble, signing extra-fast to catch up. Sometimes, when I am speaking for her, I don't understand something she has signed. I have to ask her to repeat it, and I can see her flush, both of us sensing the polite and condescending impatience of the teacher and the class.

Sometimes the teacher uses a roll-down map or an overhead projector, and all the students train their eyes on the visual information while listening to the teacher. I move closer to the map or screen, trying to make my hands make

SOURCE: *The New York Times*, February 22, 1994, p. A21. Reprinted with permission from *The New York Times*.

sense of all the information. The girl looks at me, then at the visual display. The teacher talks on. By the time the student looks at me again, she has lost three sentences. She looks at her notes and loses more sentences. Frustration flickers across her face, her eyes go blank and she gives up, returning her gaze to the sky.

I do not eat lunch with her, but I have seen her in the cafeteria at a long white table with other students. She is able, sort of, to participate in conversation, if someone makes a point of turning and speaking directly to her. Because she has trouble lip reading and they have trouble understanding her speech, she often resorts to pen and paper. The students are patient. But conversation usually ricochets across the table too rapidly for her even to pretend comprehension, so she takes a bite of her sandwich. She chews carefully, almost surreptitiously; she has been told that deaf people make funny noises when they eat.

More often, she doesn't go to the cafeteria at all. She spends her lunch period at the library, in woodshop, on the basketball court shooting hoops. She's a good athlete. She runs with the cross-country team, but she doesn't participate in school government or school plays or the literary magazine or cheerleading. She prefers activities in which she can excel alone.

Her parents are proud that she attends a regular public school. They do not use sign language. On Mondays she comes to school ravenous for conversation with me. She signs gregariously before class and even during class, and I smile in a small way and sign back: wait, wait, we'll talk about it later, the teacher's speaking now.

Her teachers ask me how I think she's doing. I tell them that I cannot say; as the interpreter, I'm not permitted to give an opinion. I say, "Maybe you would like to ask her? I'd be glad to interpret if you'd like to ask her yourself." They do not take me up on it.

This girl could go to a federally financed school for the deaf, where all the students can converse with each other, all the information is presented visually, teachers sign and deaf adults serve as role models, deaf kids lead the student government and star in the school play.

These schools prepare students for jobs and college. They also give the students access to the deaf community, which has its own language, folklore, traditions, social clubs, periodicals, athletic teams and political events. The schools have always served as the cultural center of the deaf community. Yet proponents of inclusion would like to close them, claiming that it would liberate deaf people from the "discrimination" of separate schooling and give them equality. All it would require are some sign-language interpreters to smooth out the differences, they say.

To many deaf people, this is at best maddeningly naive; at worst it is chauvinistic. The history of deaf people is one of mandated assimilation: we can make you more like hearing people, we can make you more normal.

Proponents of inclusion should ask themselves why it looks so appealing. Is it the policy that will best serve deaf people? Or is it simply a way to further that great American myth, the one we seem to need like oxygen, that says we're all created equal?

Addressing Learning Differences Right From the Start
Elizabeth Heron and Cheryl M. Jorgensen

James is a gregarious 9th grader who is labeled learning disabled in both language and reading. He has problems with decoding and serious weaknesses in vocabulary and content-area knowledge. His writing is poor, and he has trouble understanding textbooks and articles even when they are read to him.

During elementary and middle school, James's reading and language arts instruction was in pull-out programs; now he is fully included in a high school where he takes a full load of coursework and participates in extracurricular activities. A special education teacher is present in some of his classes and works with him to complete assignments during class time. James also goes to a writing center that provides help to students.

Last semester, James participated in an interdisciplinary unit on the Civil War. Students read *The Killer Angels,* a novel by Michael Shaara about Gettysburg; watched Ken Burns's Civil War documentary; and read from their history textbook. The students raised the money for a class trip to Gettysburg, and their final assignment was a research paper.

James floundered despite the activity-based focus of the classroom. The novel was too long and had difficult vocabulary. The textbook had some pictures, but the reading level was well above his ability. His special education teacher got him the movie *Gettysburg,* based on the book *The Killer Angels.* After watching the movie alone during a free period, James said that it was good, but he couldn't retrieve many details. He knew the North won, that Martin Sheen led the South's troops, and that the regiment from Maine was brave.

The trip to Gettysburg was a high point. James was deeply stirred by the number of casualties and chose to research the battle of Gettysburg. He began gathering sources; the encyclopedia was useful, but most of the other books in the high school library were at a high reading level. The learning disabilities specialist helped James cull information from a few sources for his note cards. He completed a traditional outline and went to the writing lab for help with his paper. The writing specialist realized that James knew something about Gettysburg but had not mastered the information in his notes and had difficulty expressing his ideas verbally. James only had time to complete one draft. The paper was two pages long, with stodgy sentences, and three references. James turned it in and the team accepted it with reservations.

What's Wrong With This Picture?

James's experience is typical of many students with disabilities who are in inclusive programs. Without careful attention to James's strengths and weaknesses, learning style, language processing abilities, and reading level, he and students like him miss the opportunity to master both the content of the Civil War—essential knowledge for a successful student—and to develop basic skills in research, reading, and writing. While physically included, James feels intellectually excluded, and acutely inferior to his peers. No one is to blame; everyone did their jobs to the best of their abilities. Yet, how might the Civil War unit be planned to address the learning needs of students with disabilities and still retain the rich content-area resources about the Civil War? The following are suggestions for addressing students' needs within the restructured inclusive classroom.

Providing Support and Promoting Excellence

When first planning the Civil War unit, teachers need to collaborate with special educators and reading specialists. Special educators could provide teachers with information about the students' abilities and help to design classroom activities and projects that give students with disabilities a chance to engage in content-area study. As part of this effort, the curriculum could offer a range of reading materials on the Civil War at different grade levels. Students might be required to choose several readings, one of which provides a historical overview of the war, others that provide greater insight into a specific aspect of the war.

In-class readings for group discussion can be high-interest articles from the popular media or primary sources. Texts might be read out loud in small groups and then analyzed and summarized in the students' own language. For example, a teacher who wishes the students to read and discuss the Gettysburg Address during the class period might first ask students to write or tape their own eulogies to the battle, drawing on their knowledge gained from readings, film, and the field trip. James would be an ideal candidate to tape his eulogy as he would become frustrated at being unable to write a coherent passage in the available time. Students can share their eulogies in small groups by reading them or playing their tapes.

For the actual reading of the Gettysburg Address, several students might volunteer to give a dramatic rendition of the speech. Students in small groups could then translate the Address into contemporary English. Repetitive reading and translation activities serve two functions. They help all students decipher archaic vocabulary, and they help them work with difficult grammar. Students must work through the speech line by line, reading it aloud to the whole group and then writing a contemporary translation. James can listen or participate, but as the dialogue unfolds and the modern translation emerges, he has a good chance of understanding the Gettysburg Address.

In the process, the whole class moves into the heart of the speech, probes the beauty of its language, and examines the nature of its message. For James, this class provides opportunities to learn the Gettysburg Address without asking him to initially use his least preferred and least successful learning styles—reading and writing. To evaluate the students' understanding of the meaning, the teacher might ask them to do a short free-write or taped response to the question "Did Lincoln justify the war in the Gettysburg Address?"

Assigned reading outside of class provides a different kind of opportunity for James. Prior to the Civil War unit, the teaching team, which includes either or both the special education or reading teacher, might identify the critical information and goals that all students must meet. The texts and readings are chosen to reflect students' reading abilities and goals. The learning disabilities specialist provides information on students' reading abilities and helps search for a range of materials in both print and other media. Optimally, these sources are both at and just above students' comfort zones as independent readers. James's outside-of-class reading would be challenging, and while he might be required to do less total reading than other students, he might get much of the same information as his peers.

Another important aspect of the restructured curriculum is diversity of classroom activities. Students might work in small groups, or gather for a large group discussion, or work independently. Decentralized classroom activities allow more students time to work one-on-one with a teacher or a peer. In this way, James receives direct instruction in reading, and strategy instruction to practice sight words, word attack skills, and content-specific comprehension skills appropriate to his instructional level.

Using Media for More Than Entertainment

Although the original unit used video and film to present information about the war, certain strategies can ensure that students are active rather than passive movie watchers. The students might view the film in 20-minute segments and have a discussion after each segment. Small groups of students could outline the salient features. The use of semantic or graphic organizers is well suited to this type of in-class outline because they provide a way to organize information conceptually and spatially. For example, if the section viewed was the battle of Gettysburg, then the graphic organizer might be a large sheet of paper representing the battlefield, with essential characters and battle strategies shown in different colors, symbols, and words.

For more abstract topics in the documentary, such as causes of the war, the class could use a semantic organizer to provide a spatial array of interrelated information and concepts. The entire class could construct a mural-sized semantic/graphic organizer and concept map that would become a reference for further discussion and analysis. Every student, including James, could participate in and benefit from viewing a movie this way.

Frontloading Adaptive Teaching Methods

This model of curriculum development accommodates students' learning differences right from the start. Support in the form of adaptive teaching methods, repetition and analysis, and multi-modal, multi-level sources of information are frontloaded during curriculum planning, rather than provided in a remedial or catch-up method as the unit progresses. Successful implementation of this model requires active participation and collaboration by all members of the teaching team. The general education teachers identify key concepts and skills relating to the Civil War. Reading specialists and special educators shed light on individual students' needs for accommodation in materials, expectations, support, and assessment. All members of the team can contribute to the task of finding materials for the unit.

Training Teachers for Diverse Classrooms

The characteristics of students in today's diverse classrooms demand that all teachers diversify. Special educators and reading educators must be trained in content-based education and general education practices. Simultaneously, regular education teachers must be trained to understand and to address the diversity and special needs of students with reading and learning disabilities.

The current system of teacher education does not provide the common learning experiences and skills that all teachers need, regardless of whether they are training to be regular, special, or reading teachers. Courses in curriculum development and assessment must teach the development of multi-level goals for different learners within a common curriculum. Courses in methods and materials development must target different learning styles, and teach strategies for adapting existing materials when variety is not possible.

Finally, all of this attention to accommodation must not ignore students' right to strive for literacy. Mainstream classrooms can support and develop literacy skills if modifications like those described here are implemented. In many cases, however, these supports will not be sufficient. Students like James will continue to need direct instruction, even one-to-one instruction, from reading and learning disabilities specialists. The point is not to replace effective instructional practices for students with disabilities, but to reconfigure those efforts with effective, inclusive classroom practices. James is already a physical presence in his courses. The time has come to welcome him to the intellectual community of his peers. We are only beginning to understand how that welcome might look.

Essential Questions—Inclusive Answers
Cheryl M. Jorgensen

When Cathy Fisher, a 10th grade social studies teacher, taught a unit on slavery and the Civil War, she posed this question: "Can you be free if you aren't treated equally?" Some students answered by referring to what they had read about the Civil War and by analyzing the progress of civil rights in the United States. Amro, a student whose native language is Egyptian, and who communicates by pointing to letters on an alphabet board, found it easier to use his own experience to relate to Civil War issues. He knows that he is treated differently than others. In this unit, he gained an understanding of what the lives of slaves were like. He compared their loss of freedom to the lack of freedom he experienced when he was in a segregated special education class.

Support for All

At Souhegan High School, all students—including those with mild to severe physical and emotional disabilities—are fully included in non-tracked, heterogeneously grouped classes. There are two math tracks throughout the grades, but in the 9th and 10th grades, all students take the same English, social studies, and science class—there is no honors English or college-prep science.

Souhegan accommodates high-achieving students by offering an honors challenge within each major unit's final exhibition or class presentation. Any student can accept the challenge for one unit or for every unit that semester and possibly receive designations of "distinction" or "honors" along with his or her grades.

The school takes pride in nurturing each student's passions and interests and providing each with academic and social support. Small student advisory groups meet with faculty daily. The school is governed by a democratic council of faculty, students, and community leaders. And an innovative wellness program replaces the traditional sports-oriented physical education curriculum.

Outcomes First

Full inclusion is possible at Souhegan High School primarily because of three program components:

    1. *Collaborative planning time.* Despite a school's philosophical commitment to inclusion and heterogeneous grouping, long-term success is

SOURCE: *Educational Leadership, 52,* no. 4, (December/January 1995): pp. 52–55. Reprinted with permission of the Association for Supervision and Curriculum Development. Copyright © 1995 by ASCD. All rights reserved.

possible only when its structure and schedule support curriculum planning by both special and general education teachers.

2. *Curriculum design characterized by planning backwards* from expected outcomes and a final student exhibition to the details of lesson design.

3. *"Essential questions"*—overarching questions (or statements) used to guide performance-based curriculum development.

Consider first a lesson *without* these components:

The teacher informs the students they will be reading *The Autobiography of Malcolm X* for Black History Month. A few students who are interested in African-American issues sit up straighter. Others have watched the movie several times and feel they can ace this unit without opening the book. Three girls object to yet another book about a male hero. And the special education teacher in the back of the room appears panic-stricken: this is the first he's heard about this assignment. He must call the Talking Books people to see if they have a copy in stock and if they can send it in time for the students who need it. He worries, too, about Sam. What will this student do during reading time?

At Souhegan High School, in contrast, when a teacher considers a topic for a particular unit, he or she decides on the content by asking the following questions:

- How accommodating will it be for students with different learning styles, interests, talents, and challenges?
- Will it challenge the most well-read student in the class?
- Will it motivate and engage students who are not terribly interested in school?
- Can I find high-interest, low-level reading materials on the topic for students who don't read or who read with great difficulty?
- What about students with extraordinary learning challenges who may not understand the topic regardless of how I present it? How can I fully include them in every class period?
- What do I expect students to remember about this unit? What should they be able to do a year from now when they have forgotten all the details?
- Can all my students achieve some of these outcomes?

Throughout the learning process, teachers must build in the following components:

- an opportunity for students to follow their own areas of interest within a broad, common topic;
- a variety of learning materials and sources;
- a requirement that students interact with one another;
- coaching from teachers and support staff;
- options for different performance based exhibitions;
- personalization of some learning outcomes; and
- personalization of standards by which students are evaluated.

The Right Questions

Essential questions is a term used by Souhegan and other members of the Coalition of Essential Schools, which was formed by Theodore Sizer at Brown University (Sizer 1992). The questions (or statements) are designed to create a unified curriculum in which all students can learn.

Consider the question a 10th grade science teacher wrote on the board: "If we can, should we?"

> The teacher asked the students to get into groups of four and gave each group a large sheet of newsprint paper and some markers. She then asked them to divide the paper into two columns, listing in the first column all the dilemmas or issues to which this quotation might refer, and in the second, their answer to her question for that issue. One group thought the question might refer to the atomic bomb—"If we have the atomic bomb, should we use it to stop another country from invading an innocent neighbor?" They wrote "No. Atomic energy is too dangerous. You should use diplomacy or conventional weapons instead."

Finally, the teacher told the students they would in fact be studying human genetics for the next several weeks. Every student would have to answer an essential question through a performance-based exhibition: "If we can influence the incidence of birth defects through genetic selection and prenatal diagnosis, should we?"

Note that these questions and the ones in the Civil War unit share certain characteristics:

- They have no one right answer.
- All students can answer them.
- They enable all students to learn.
- They involve thinking, not just answering.
- They make students investigators.
- They are provocative—they hook students into wanting to learn.
- They offer a sense of adventure, are fun to explore and try to answer.
- They require students to connect learning from several disciplines.
- They challenge students to demonstrate that they understand the relationship between what they are learning and larger world issues.
- They enable students to begin the unit from their own past experience or understanding.
- They build in personalized options for all students.

Interdisciplinary Team Teaching

The 11th and 12th grades at Souhegan are organized like a traditional high school. However, in grades 9 and 10, teachers and students are grouped in two teams for each grade, with about 85 students on each team. English, science, social studies, and special education teachers share two blocks of time each day—two and one-half hours in the morning and an hour in the afternoon. They may organize instruction any way they wish. Students often spend about one hour in each class, but teachers may schedule longer blocks for a subject area when the time is needed for interdisciplinary teaching or for a comprehensive project.

This past year, Team 10D implemented several interdisciplinary units. The team's science teacher, Jennifer Mueller, and English teacher, Scott Laliberte, jointly taught a unit called "Lives of a Cell." The essential questions that guided the unit were:

- What is life?
- What are the characteristics that define life?
- Why do we need to know if some thing is living?

Mueller and Laliberte hoped all students would achieve the following outcomes, in part through their final class exhibitions:

- acquire and integrate critical information in academic and non academic domains,
- interpret and synthesize information,
- express ideas clearly,
- effectively communicate through a variety of media,
- create quality products,
- work toward group goals, and
- assess and monitor their own behavior within a group.

For the final exhibitions, groups of four to six students were expected to perform a play or produce a video depicting one of the major life processes of a cell—for example, reproduction, energy use, or differentiation. As an interim step, each group designed a 10-minute lesson on the life process. The class had to use many modes of presentation—lectures, demonstrations, visual aids, overhead transparencies, and hands-on group activities—so that every student could be involved.

During some lessons, the teachers taught classes separately. In English class, students read Lewis Thomas's *Lives of a Cell*. In science, they learned about mitosis, meiosis, DNA, energy production, and differentiation.

Toward the end of the unit, English and science sections were combined and both teachers coached students in developing their final group exhibition. Mueller's contribution was in the area of cell structure and function; she provided multi-level reading materials, charts, videos, and filmstrips as information resources for each group. Laliberte coached students in organizational and presentation skills, and helped them view life's biological processes from the unique perspective of a writer.

Tailor-Made Challenges

A school is not truly inclusive unless every student, including those with significant learning, behavioral, and physical disabilities, can participate in learning and strive toward challenging outcomes. The following questions form the basis for curriculum adaptation for students with special needs (Tashie et al. 1993).

1. *Can the student participate in this lesson in the same way as all other students?* When a student with significant disabilities first enters a regular class, teachers often think they will have to modify most every aspect of the lessons. After they get to know the student, however, they usually find that he or she can take part in many activities with no changes.

2. *What supports and/or modifications are necessary for the student's full participation if he or she is unable to participate fully without accommodation?* Students may need support from a classmate or an adult; modified, adapted, or substitute materials; or assistive technology. Or, the teacher may have to modify expectations, perhaps by assigning less work, by changing the priority learning objectives of a particular lesson, or by changing how the student demonstrates what he or she knows.

For example, Brandon has visual impairments. For multiple-choice tests, a teaching assistant reads him the question and the answer choices, and he then points to the letters *a, b, c,* or *d* written in four quadrants of a portable white board.

Amro, the student described earlier, benefits from sitting next to a student who rephrases questions for him during discussions. In his integrated math class, Amro uses a calculator to solve addition and subtraction problems while the other students are working on two-step equations. He was, however, able to participate in his chef's class with very few modifications, and earned an *A.*

Jessica's lines in theater class are tape-recorded by a classmate. At the appropriate time in the performance, Jessica leans her head against a pressure switch connected to the tape recorder, which then plays her lines.

Arthur and several other students built picnic tables to be used at the school. Arthur demonstrated his knowledge of mathematics by following a blueprint, using measuring and cutting tools accurately, and assembling the table in the correct pattern.

The Bottom Line

After only two years of operation, the strides made at Souhegan are nothing short of remarkable. Most students with disabilities are doing well socially and academically. Most of their parents are thrilled at the perceptible changes in their children's self-esteem and learning as a result of the confidence expressed in their ability to succeed. And many teachers have expressed a new respect for these students' abilities.

New and veteran teachers are successfully developing teaching strategies for heterogeneous classes. They are also developing respect for one another's experience and perspectives, and are looking forward to working even more effectively on interdisciplinary teams next year.

Teachers and administrators are clear, nonetheless, about challenges that lie ahead:

- Not all students with disabilities who live in the Amherst area are attending Souhegan.
- Many difficult issues surround heterogeneous grouping. For example, can one set of educational outcomes apply to all students? How can differences in talents and interests be accommodated without sacrificing academic rigor?
- The support model and the roles of special education and regular education teachers are still confusing to many teachers.
- Only a few of the teachers have experience working collaboratively with their regular education colleagues, much less those in special education. They all need to improve their group-process and problem-solving skills.

Despite these ongoing challenges, Souhegan is well on its way to becoming a school where all students belong, are valued, can do quality work, and can learn with others who are different from themselves. The result is a richer experience for everyone involved.

REFERENCES

Sizer, T. (1992). *Horace's School: Redesigning the American High School.* Boston: Houghton-Mifflin.

Tashie, C., S. Shapiro-Barnard, M. Schuh, C. Jorgensen, A. Dillon, B. Dixon, and J. Nisbett. (1993). *From Special to Regular: From Ordinary to Extraordinary.* Durham, N.H.: Institute on Disability/UAP, University of New Hampshire.

As Loudoun Goes, So May Other Schools
Debbi Wilgoren and Peter Pae

Nine-year-old Mark Hartmann is autistic. He can't speak or write. If he is upset or confused, he flaps his hand and screeches—a strangled, grating sound.

But in happier moments, Mark blends in with the other children in his Loudoun County neighborhood. His skin is tanned and his thick hair bleached from a summer of playing and swimming. In the airy living room of his family's yellow Victorian house, he takes pride in knowing how to work the VCR.

This month, Mark's life took a new turn: The tall, sturdy youngster became a symbol in a national debate over whether, and how often, disabled youngsters should be educated alongside their non-disabled peers.

Advocates on both sides are watching intently to see whether Loudoun school officials succeed in their unusual effort to have Mark transferred, over his parents' objection, from a regular classroom to a program for autistic children in a public school 10 miles away.

Proponents of "full inclusion" for severely disabled students fear that if a state hearing officer rules in Loudoun's favor, that could persuade other school systems to take similar steps, thus damaging those children's chances of functioning in the mainstream world.

But such a ruling would be vindication for others, who said they believe that full inclusion is not possible for every child and that the concept has jeopardized worthy specialized programs for disabled students.

"What's at stake here is a message that will go out to other [schools] that are struggling with the issue," said Jamie Ruppman, of Vienna, an advocate of full inclusion whose adult son is autistic. "Families are worried that their kid will be next."

Mark, a second-grader last year at Ashburn Elementary School, is one of six severely disabled youngsters enrolled in regular classes in Loudoun. Other school districts in the Washington area also have a few children with severe mental, physical or emotional disabilities assigned full time to regular classrooms.

That setup was unimaginable a generation ago, when teachers with training in special education worked with small groups of disabled students, often in buildings far away from regular schools. They focused on life skills and vocational activities rather than academics.

Even as those programs were developed in the mid-1970s, however, many professionals in the field were forming the theories that now fuel the inclusion movement. They said it was unfair and unwise to separate disabled children from their peers because youngsters learn best from imitating those around them. Moreover, they argued, inclusion would provide non-disabled children a lesson in tolerance.

The movement got a boost from the 1990 Americans With Disabilities Act, as well as from recent court rulings saying public schools must find the resources to educate disabled children in regular classrooms.

"Instead of proving that you have the right to be in, you *start* with the right to be in. It's a different premise," said Kathleen B. Boundy, an attorney with the Cambridge, Mass.-based Center for Law and Education.

Last year, the Department of Education said a record one-third of children with special education needs were spending their school days in regular classrooms. Most of them had learning disabilities or speech impediments rather than conditions as severe as autism or mental retardation.

In some cases, there have been dramatic successes. Joseph Pauley of Potomac said his daughter Cecelia, who has Down's syndrome, has improved her IQ score by 25 points after two years of full inclusion at Winston Churchill High School in Montgomery County.

But the trend also has generated substantial opposition. Teachers' unions say instructors often do not get the resources and training needed to teach disabled and non-disabled at the same time, and they have questioned whether regular teachers should be given such a burden. And some specialists and parents of disabled children object to the notion that a regular classroom is the best environment for every child.

"When you talk about full inclusion, you're talking about getting rid of everything else," said Bernard Rimland, the director of the Autism Research Institute in San Diego, whose 38-year-old son is autistic.

"Inclusion wouldn't have helped my son," Rimland said. "His best progress was in small classes with dedicated teachers."

In Montgomery, parents formed separate advocacy groups with dueling acronyms: CASE (Citizens for Alternatives in Special Education) and PISCES (People for Inclusive School and Community Education Services). They have clashed over the number of teaching positions devoted to inclusion rather than special education classrooms.

School administrators in the Washington area said they are feeling conflicting pressures.

"We don't have all the answers," said Rosy McGuinness, a special education coordinator in Fairfax County. "We don't want to deny children their right to be included, but we also must recognize that inclusion may not be appropriate for some children."

Federal law requires school administrators to meet with parents of disabled youngsters each year to review their course of instruction. Either side may propose full inclusion.

Inclusion can mean assigning a full-time aide to work with the disabled child. In many cases, it also means modifying the classroom curriculum for that child—using a reading assignment to improve the youngster's attention span, for example, even as other children in the room are studying the same pages for theme and character development.

School officials said the overall cost of inclusion is about the same as that of separate, specialized classrooms.

Where inclusion has succeeded, educators said, it has been the result of extensive preparation.

The school system in Boyertown, Pa., spent three years phasing in students from a special education center into their neighborhood schools. Among them was a quadriplegic who is blind and deaf.

In the District, special education director Garnett Pickney is working closely with the staff at LaSalle Elementary School to include a youngster with Down's syndrome in the fourth grade.

Last year, the child was in a third-grade classroom but received no special support. Pickney said the result was "chaotic." This year, teachers, administrators and a psychologist have spent hours figuring out how to include the child in academic activities without frustrating him or boring others.

Inclusion "is just better for the kids overall—provided that everyone's prepared," Pickney said. "If everybody's not prepared, then it turns into a battle: 'Am I going to help the special ed kid or the regular ed kid?' It should never have to be a choice."

But it was for Diane Johnson, Mark's second-grade teacher at Ashburn. During the Aug. 15 hearing on whether Mark should be taken out of Ashburn, Johnson testified that she often had to speak over his screeches to teach the other children. She also said she rarely gave individual instruction to her other students, choosing instead to spend time working with Mark.

"I think I neglected the students in my class," Johnson said. "I can think of two children in particular who struggled through the year who could have done better if I had more time with them."

Loudoun school officials said Mark is frustrated at not being able to keep up with his classmates and would show more progress in a special ed class.

But Mark's parents, Joseph and Roxanna Hartmann, said they blame the county for not sufficiently training Johnson or Mark's aide in how to teach autistic youngsters and for failing to send in experts to work out difficulties as they arose.

They said the suburban Chicago elementary school where Mark attended kindergarten and first grade took those steps and had more success.

Since the family moved to Loudoun a year ago, Roxanna Hartmann said in an interview, Mark has regressed. Sometimes he hits himself or impulsively pulls off his clothing, signs of frustration she said she hasn't seen since he was 5.

The hearing on Mark's final placement will resume in late September.

Among those in the audience will be Eleanor Voldish, of Loudoun. Voldish sat through all eight hours of testimony on Aug. 15, listening to people talk about Mark while she thought of her 6-year-old son, Gregory.

Gregory, who has Down's syndrome, has been in regular classes since preschool. Although he lags behind his peers in speech and writing skills, he begins first grade Monday at Sterling Elementary School.

Kathleen Mehfoud, the Loudoun school system's lawyer, said school officials remain committed to including disabled children whenever possible. The Hartmann's case, she said, involves only what's best for Mark.

But Voldish said she wonders what would happen if the Hartmanns lose and her son, who thrived last year in kindergarten, begins to have problems.

"They could easily come back and say Gregory shouldn't be included," she said. "It could set back years of work."

Loudoun Can Take Autistic Boy Out of Regular Class

Peter Pae

A Virginia hearing officer granted Loudoun County's request yesterday to re-move an autistic boy from a regular classroom over his parents' objection, handing at least a temporary victory to educators who have argued that such placements are disruptive to teachers and other students.

After reviewing five days of testimony, Hearing Officer Nancy McBride con-cluded that 9-year-old Mark Hartmann's educational needs were not served last year in his second-grade classroom at Ashburn Elementary School.

McBride gave Loudoun school officials permission to place Mark in a spe-cial program for children with autism, in a school 10 miles away, although he would continue to attend art, music and physical education classes with non-disabled students.

Her 26-page decision, released yesterday, was a bitter disappointment to Mark's parents, who had said that their son's future depended on his going to school with non-disabled children.

"They are quite disappointed," said Gerard S. Rugel, the Hartmanns' attor-ney. "They put their heart and soul into this. They want the best for their child." He said the parents would have no immediate comment on the ruling.

Rugel said the Hartmanns will appeal the decision to the state Board of Edu-cation, allowing Mark to remain in a regular third-grade classroom while the ap-peal is pending. The state board's ruling can be appealed in court. But Rugel said the Hartmanns, who have spent $20,000 in legal fees, also want to explore the possibility of a compromise with school officials.

The case has been closely watched as a test of how far school systems must go to include disabled youngsters in regular school activities. Although about a third of the children with special education needs now spend their school days in regular classrooms, very few of them have conditions as severe as autism, a developmental disorder that disrupts the brain's processing of information and retards academic and social skills.

Mark cannot speak or write. His second-grade teacher at Ashburn testified that he repeatedly had tantrums in class, cutting into the time she could spend with other students, and that he seemed to get no benefit from being with non-disabled children.

"Oh, gosh, thank you," said Linda Burgin, whose daughter sat next to Mark last year, when she was informed of McBride's decision. "It was so obvious that

Mark was in the wrong place. Not only did it not benefit Mark, but it was detrimental to other children."

The Hartmanns agreed that Mark's experience at Ashburn Elementary had been a disaster, but they blamed the school system for not providing enough training to Mark's teacher and full-time instructional aide. They pointed to Mark's progress at the Illinois school where he attended regular kindergarten and first grade before the family moved to Loudoun, and they argued that it was crucial to Mark's social development that he go to school with his non-disabled friends.

But McBride, an Alexandria lawyer appointed by the Virginia Supreme Court to hear school disputes, said the Loudoun school system had made a "substantial effort" to help Mark succeed in a regular classroom. She noted, for example, that school officials reduced his second-grade class from 26 to 21 children and assigned students who were the least likely to need extra attention.

Loudoun School Superintendent Edgar B. Hatrick said yesterday that the Hartmann case should not be seen as a setback for disabled children.

"Since the beginning, this has been a case about one student's education, not about inclusion in general," Hatrick said. "We remain committed to providing appropriate educational opportunities to our disabled students in accordance with their needs and will continue to make professional judgments on a case-by-case basis."

In Autism Case, Hearing Is Over, but Battle Isn't
Debbi Wilgoren

No one knows how much Mark Hartmann comprehends about the legal battle that is swirling around him. He can't tell his parents, or his attorney, what he thinks of a hearing officer's order that he be moved into a class with other autistic children.

But Mark's mother believes that although the 9-year-old can't speak or write, he knows his place in Mrs. Fatz's third-grade class at Ashburn Elementary School is in jeopardy. She cites the tears that flowed unexpectedly at dinner recently when Mark's sister asked if he would be going back to school.

SOURCE: *The Washington Post*, December 27, 1994, pp. D1; D6. Copyright © 1994, *The Washington Post.* Reprinted with permission.

"It was different than Mark's normal crying when he's angry," Roxanna Hartmann said, stifling her own sob to tell the story. "It was sadness. It was grief."

On Dec. 15, a Board of Education hearing officer ruled in favor of Loudoun County school officials who want to place Mark in a special education program. But her decision didn't end the anguish of parents on both sides of the dispute.

For Roxanna and Joseph Hartmann, the agonizing question is what their next move should be.

Should they appeal the ruling and continue to carry the torch for a national movement that seeks full inclusion of disabled youngsters in school activities? Should they leave their brand-new home in Ashburn and Joseph Hartmann's senior-level job at the State Department, to search for a school system in the United States or abroad that might be more accommodating? Or should they seek a compromise with Loudoun officials that would provide Mark with a mix of special education and time in a regular classroom?

The Hartmanns must decide by the end of January, the deadline for filing an appeal.

In other homes in this suburban enclave 30 miles northwest of Washington, the parents of some of Mark's classmates also are torn. They are loath to criticize neighbors, and they support, in theory, the grouping of disabled and nondisabled children together as a means of teaching tolerance.

But they also trust the teachers and principal who educate their youngsters and who argue that Mark's presence in a regular class is hurting him as well as their children. And they are frustrated that Mark would stay where he is during any appeal process.

"My son has basically lost a year," said Debbie Mattens, mother of 8-year-old Anthony. She blames her son's recent slip from A to B work on his difficulty in concentrating during Mark's frequent outbursts.

"I feel for the Hartmanns. I feel for Mark. [But] if no one is going to speak out for my son, I have to do it. That's what I'm here for."

Loudoun school officials have turned down reporters' requests to observe Mark in class. They say they don't want to add to the overwhelming media interest in the case, which already has been chronicled in *People* magazine, on network television's morning news programs and in Spanish-language newspapers here and in Roxana Hartmann's native Costa Rica.

According to parent volunteers and school staff, Mark rarely stays seated, often cries, and almost never interacts with his peers other than to push them away when they get too close. His academic progress comes from one-on-one tutoring, and he gets no apparent benefit from class exercises.

School officials want to send Mark to Leesburg Elementary School, about 10 miles away. He would be in a class with four or five other autistic youngsters and would join nondisabled children for art, music, gym, library and recess. They say the setup would maximize Mark's academic learning while preserving his chance for social development.

To the Hartmanns, however, it is a recipe for disaster. They argue that un-expected change is extremely upsetting for autistic youngsters and that Mark's encounters with nondisabled peers would be of little value if they were only occasional.

The Hartmanns do not measure the benefits of Mark's inclusion in a regular classroom in terms of his academic performance. Rather, they look at how Mark recently has started to imitate his classmates by closing the door behind him when he goes to the bathroom. In an autistic class, Roxana Hartmann said, such social norms would not exist.

"It's growing up. You have to grow up with your peers," Joseph Hartmann said. He said Mark is learning "the fact that you don't touch the other person [at random], the fact that you have to wait, the fact that you have to stand in line. And the fact that you don't talk when someone else is speaking."

The Hartmanns are driven by memories of Mark's year in a first-grade class in Illinois, before the move to Loudoun. At the Illinois school, according to its prin-cipal, Mark participated in activities and eventually stopped having tantrums.

Roxanna Hartmann dreams of her son someday holding a job, perhaps us-ing his organizational and computer skills to file returned tapes at a video store and enter the titles into the database.

It's easy to imagine, watching him ride in the car with her to McDonald's, unbuckling his seat belt as the car approaches the entrance. Inside the restau-rant, he shakes his head "yes" or waves his hands "no" to answer questions and follows her instructions to sit up straight, take off his jacket or fix his glasses.

Back at home, he dashes upstairs unassisted, changes from school clothes to shorts and pops in an *Alice in Wonderland* videotape. He fast-forwards and rewinds to find his favorite parts, tilting his head to the side in anticipation of Alice's tumble into the rabbit hole.

But in Denise Fatz's classroom, youngsters and parent volunteers describe a totally different youngster, one who screeches, hits classmates and wanders around.

Among those distracted by his behavior, said Polly Mizelle, is her 8-year-old son, Danny. Danny is a slow reader, his mother said, and he often stops his work to watch Mark or to offer his help.

Mizelle, [a] trained pediatric nurse who volunteers in the class about once a week, said she has not seen any progress in Mark and doubts he can succeed in a regular class.

"How much do they just want to believe?" Mizelle said of the Hartmanns. "I've seen it happen in the past with parents. They want something to happen so bad, they believe it, even if it isn't there."

"Until I walk in [their] shoes, I don't know. But if the experts are saying, 'This is what's best for your child plus these other 20 children,' then why aren't they listening?"

The Hartmanns have seen similar sentiments expressed in letters parents have sent to local newspapers. They say they understand, perhaps more than anyone, parents' concerns about their children's education. But the criticism still hurts.

"I finish reading it and I say [to the letter writer], 'Hey . . . aren't you blessed?'" Roxanna Hartmann said. "'Aren't you blessed that you don't have this problem?'"

Full Inclusion Is Neither Free nor Appropriate
Albert Shanker

What happens when a 4th grade teacher with a class of 30 or 35 finds that several new students have severe behavioral disabilities? The teacher has no previous training in working with disabled children, and the principal says that getting any extra classroom help is out the question—the school district simply can't afford it. The teacher's main resource, the special education aide, who must serve 60 children in four schools, is stretched pretty thin. As the year goes on, the teacher finds that math class is disrupted every single day by the demands of one or another of the special needs students. How can the teacher meet these extraordinary demands without robbing some students? Many teachers are facing problems as difficult as this—and far more difficult—as the result of a movement known as *full inclusion*.

Rush to Include

Since the passage of the landmark Education for All Handicapped Children Act (P.L. 94-142) in 1975, youngsters with disabilities have had a right to a "free and appropriate public education in the least restrictive environment." Until recently, this usually meant some kind of special placement. Now, state departments of education and school districts, as well as some advocacy groups for the disabled, are pushing to have all handicapped children educated in regular classrooms, regardless of the nature and severity of their handicap. And inclusion advocates are taking advantage of court decisions that favor their position to move ahead quickly.

Advocates for full inclusion raise the issue of equity. They say that disabled youngsters are burdened with an additional handicap when they are segregated

SOURCE: *Educational Leadership*, 52, no. 4, (December/January 1995): pp. 18–21. Reprinted with permission of the Association for Supervision and Curriculum Development. Copyright © 1995 by ASCD. All rights reserved.

from their nondisabled peers because they are denied the chance to develop the social and academic skills necessary to function in the mainstream of society. Many local school boards, state departments of education, and legislators also back full inclusion, but for a different reason. They see it as an opportunity to cut back on expensive special education services. These services have become a crushing financial burden, especially because Congress has never appropriated funding at the level promised by P.L. 94–142, leaving states and local school boards to shoulder most of those costs.

Not all advocacy groups are enthusiastic about full inclusion. Many—including those for blind, deaf, attention-deficit-disordered and learning-disabled children—believe a one-size-fits-all approach will be disastrous for the disabled children themselves. Nevertheless, we are seeing a rush to inclusion regardless of the disability.

Who Pays?

Of course, disabled children placed in regular classrooms are supposed to get special services so they can participate academically and socially and so the other students' learning is not disrupted. That's the behind-the-scenes reality in the documentary film *Educating Peter,* which won an Academy Award in 1993. Filmgoers see a moving story about a child with Down syndrome who learns to work and play with his new classmates. What filmgoers *don't* see is that the class was relatively small—19 students—and Peter's teacher was intensively prepared for his arrival, as were the parents of his classmates. Moreover, a full-time special education aide was with Peter every minute of the day, and an "inclusion specialist" worked with him daily and was available to help his teacher and classmates.

This kind of comprehensive help is expensive. Because states and school districts are putting disabled children into regular classrooms as a cost-cutting measure, such expenditures are the exception rather than the rule. Instead, the responsibility for disabled youngsters, who may need specialized medical attention (like having catheters changed or mucus suctioned out of their lungs), falls on teachers and paraprofessionals. Unlike Peter's teacher, most have no more than a few hours of training. And they are largely on their own when it comes to figuring out how to help the child fit in, and how to tailor lessons to his or her requirements, while keeping other students up to speed in arithmetic and reading and science.

Full inclusionists say this ad hoc approach to inclusion must change and all the supports for disabled children in special education settings must follow them into regular classrooms. This is the ideal, but given the reason most states and school districts are adopting full inclusion—to save money—it is no more likely to happen for disabled children than it did for mentally ill people who were de-institutionalized years ago. Their supports were also supposed to follow them, but now, as we know, large numbers of these people are out on the streets. That's one reason that many parents of disabled children oppose full inclusion.

They fear their children will lose the range of services now available and end up, like those who were deinstitutionalized, with nothing.

Who Benefits?

Who are we helping if we put disabled students into regular classrooms without the supports they need? If they get these supports, a regular class would be the best possible placement for many of these youngsters. But will a child with multiple physical disabilities or behavioral disorders learn to socialize with other children simply because he or she has been put into a class with them? Will the other kids receive that child as a friend in the absence of special encouragement and support, or will they ignore or tease that child and make his or her life a misery? What happens to attempts to raise the reading or math achievement levels of other children when their teacher must devote extraordinary time and energy to disabled classmates? (In the documentary, Peter's classmates learned to live with him and accept him—and Peter himself improved—but the film does not address his impact on their education.)

Staying Put

Finally, what happens when a child whose disability has led to disruptive and even dangerous behavior must, as the law requires, remain in class because a judge refuses to have the child removed? Those who created P.L. 94–142 and its subsequent amendments wanted to prevent these kids from being jerked around from one placement to another. But one of their tools, the "stay-put" provision, has turned out to be a nightmare for other students and for teachers. According to "stay-put," once a child has been placed in a class, he or she can't be excluded because of behavior related to a disability for more than 10 days a year without consent of the parents or a formal hearing process that could take months. This means that a student with a behavioral disorder who constantly disrupts the class—or even assaults a teacher or schoolmates—cannot be excluded.

Recently, I received a letter from Edward Martin, who was the first director of the U.S. Bureau of Education for the Handicapped and now heads an advocacy group for the disabled. He, too, opposes full inclusion, and he is especially troubled by the idea of making sweeping changes without any data or research to support them. Where are our figures on how well disabled students in regular classrooms do in comparison with those in special education settings? How many drop out? How many go on to college or vocational programs? Without this information, we have no way of knowing what is working for these youngsters and what is not. "Special education programs," Martin says, "must be judged on their successes, not on our wishes for a more inclusive society."

Separate but Equal

Full inclusion is often justified by an analogy with the racial segregation practiced during a large portion of our history. "Separate but equal" always meant "inferior," and inclusionists feel the same is true of any separate classes for any disabled children. But the analogy is faulty. African-American children have the same range of abilities and needs as white children. They were excluded only because of the color of their skin, which was irrelevant to their ability to function and benefit in a regular classroom. This is quite different from putting a blind youngster into a special class so he or she can learn Braille, or from excluding a youngster who is emotionally disturbed because he or she will disrupt the education of others while deriving little benefit.

When I was growing up, the great majority of children with disabilities were not allowed to come to school at all. And the ones who were—mostly children who were considered mentally retarded—were warehoused in "opportunity" classes where their capabilities and needs were ignored. It's a good thing those days are gone. However, this bad policy is being replaced by another bad policy. In calling for all disabled children to be placed in regular classrooms regardless of the severity and nature of their difficulty, full inclusion is replacing one injustice with another.

We need to discard the ideology that inclusion in a regular classroom is the only appropriate placement for a disabled child and get back to the idea of a "continuum of placements," based on the nature and severity of the handicap. Make the ability to function in a regular classroom, given the necessary support services, a condition for placement there.

A Better IDEA

If we are to reject full inclusion, however, how do we ensure that all students do get an education that challenges them to meet high standards of achievement? One way is to further revise P.L. 94-142. Congress has been considering reauthorization of the 1975 special education legislation, which in 1991 was amended and renamed the Individuals with Disabilities Education Act (IDEA). As members of Congress rethink its provisions, we would do well to remind them of the following.

- *Congress must pay its fair share for educating children with disabilities* as promised in P.L. 94-142. In 1975, Congress agreed to provide 40 percent of the cost of educating handicapped children, but in nearly two decades, it has funded no more than 12 percent of the costs (7 percent this year)—even though it has continued to add new requirements. With resources scarce, providing the rest of the money is a hardship for all but the wealthiest school districts. Many, in fact, have had to cut back their regular programs to pay for these unfunded mandates. (In New York City, 60 percent of all new money for the schools goes to special education, even though children with disabilities represent less than 20 percent of the school population.)

    Many other districts are trying to control costs by simply dumping students with disabilities into regular classrooms, without the necessary help for either the youngsters or their teachers. This undermines the education of *all* students. Ironically, because regular programs have been cut back to pay for legally mandated services, many children with learning problems, who normally could get the help they need in a regular classroom are pushed into special programs.

- *The law needs to be amended to require school districts to provide adequate training for all teachers who work with disabled students.* The success of any placement depends to a large extent on the classroom teacher. Yet many teachers and paraprofessionals, particularly those in regular classrooms, are ill-prepared or unprepared to work with students who have disabilities.

- *A rewritten law should give equal weight to requests from parents and referrals by teachers for special education services.*

- *The law should specify that a child's teacher—not some proxy appointed by the school district—must be part of the team writing a child's individual education plan.* Except for parents, teachers know better than anybody what a child needs.

- *The revised law should allow teachers to report failure to provide services and offer protection to those who might hesitate to blow the whistle for fear of reprisal.* The teacher is in the best position to know whether or not the services called for are actually being provided.

- *The "stay-put" provision should be rewritten to allow responsible alternative arrangements for disabled students who are violent or disruptive until the issue of their placement is resolved.* These youngsters' rights can be protected without sacrificing the education of other students—some or all of whom may also have disabilities—or endangering their safety and that of their teachers.

One final issue: There is often a larger number of minority children in special education—especially classes for the learning disabled—than their numbers in the school population would seem to warrant. This, some minority advocates believe, indicates that special education classes are being used to re-segregate schools. As a result, many members of minority groups are vocal supporters of inclusion. This is an important but separate problem. It can't be forgotten or pushed to one side as we try to make our system for educating disabled children flexible enough so that the welfare of one group is not sacrificed for the welfare of another.

PART THREE

Quality

Chapter 10

ACHIEVEMENT

INTRODUCTION

We had the "space race" and the "weapons race" and now many claim we are engaged in the "education race." This time the contest is between the United States and Asia, especially Japan. Many worry that we are involved in a "life or death" struggle for manufacturing and trade supremacy in the new global marketplace. And a key to our victory—or defeat—is our educational system, they maintain.

Many view the American and Japanese school systems as standing in stark contrast, one with the other. They believe that the academic achievement of American students has declined over the years to a point at which today it simply does not measure up to that of the Japanese—or for that matter to many other countries.

It is easy to imagine a television special designed to emphasize the poor showing of American education in comparison with Japanese education. The camera focuses on an American school, its state-of-the-art gymnasium packed with students cheering a sports team. A montage of scenes rapidly follows, supposedly capturing life in the typical American high school—students wearing earphones connected to tape recorders, no books in their hands; in math class, a student, head on his desk, sleeping; students during a free period gathered in the parking lot, listening to car radios.

Next we see students at a Japanese high school. Altogether different images are conveyed. Forty or so students, dressed in dark blue uniforms, fixated on their calculus teacher—no heads on their desks; no daydreaming in this class. Then some Japanese students are interviewed and they respond in reasonably good English. Everything they talk about deals with *academics*. When asked what they do in their spare time they report that they go to tutoring school where they "catch up" on anything they may have missed in their very intensive regular classroom.

These, however, are images that, although they correspond with many people's *beliefs,* may or may not correspond with *reality.* One critical question here, of course, is: Have the academic achievements of American students actually declined significantly over the last 25 or so years? Where exactly do we stand in relation to other countries? And what about the tests that are used to measure achievement? Are they solid instruments that provide valid data?

Commission on Education Warns "Tide of Mediocrity" Imperils United States
Edward B. Fiske

WASHINGTON—A bipartisan Federal commission called today for a significant upgrading of American education at all levels.

In an "Open Letter to the American People," the 18-member National Commission on Excellence in Education said that America's economic, cultural and spiritual role in the world was being threatened by lax standards and misguided priorities in the schools.

"The educational foundations of our society are presently being eroded by a rising tide of mediocrity that threatens our very future as a nation and as a people," it declared. "If an unfriendly foreign power had attempted to impose on America the mediocre educational performance that exists today, we might well have viewed it as an act of war. As it stands, we have allowed this to happen to ourselves."

The commission was appointed in August 1981 by T. H. Bell, the Secretary of Education, to address what he termed "the widespread public perception that something is seriously remiss in our educational system." The project, which cost $785,000, was financed by the Department of Education.

Mr. Bell said the department would now "hold meetings all across the country" to promote a "commitment to excellence" in education.

These were some of the changes the commission urged:

- High schools should tighten requirements in the "new basics"—English, mathematics, science, social studies and computer science—and colleges and universities should raise their admissions requirements in these areas as well as in foreign languages.
- Students should spend more time in school. School boards should consider extending the school day from six to a total of seven hours and increasing the school year from 180 to as many as 220 days.
- High school students should be given "far more homework."

Source: *The New York Times*, April 27, 1983, pp. A1; B6. Reprinted with permission from *The New York Times*.

- Salaries for teachers should be increased, and their contracts should be extended from 9 to 11 months to allow time for curriculum planning and helping students with special needs.
- Financial incentives should be used to attract "outstanding students" into the teaching profession, and "master teachers" should be used to train them.

The commission did not offer recommendations in several areas that have been priorities of the Reagan Administration, including tuition tax credits, prayer in the schools and abolition of the Department of Education.

In his remarks late this afternoon at a White House ceremony in which he was given a copy of the report, however, President Reagan said, "We'll continue to work in the months ahead for passage of tuition tax credits, vouchers, educational savings accounts, voluntary school prayer and abolishing the Department of Education."

The commission urged American citizens to provide "the fiscal support and stability" necessary to bring about these reforms. "Excellence costs," it declared. "But in the long run mediocrity costs far more."

Beyond this appeal, the report did not address the question of how to pay for changes such as higher teachers' salaries. "We were not asked to offer any advice on how to finance education," said David P. Gardner, president of the University of Utah and chairman of the commission, at a news briefing.

Comments About Financing

Much of the initial reaction to the 36-page report focused on how the proposed reforms might be financed.

The National Education Association, the country's largest teachers organization, called the document "exciting" and said the panel's recommendations would require "additional billions of dollars—and a big boost from the Federal Government—to achieve their sweeping objectives."

Representative Carl D. Perkins, the Democrat from Kentucky who is chairman of the House Education and Labor Committee, said he was glad to see recommendations such as increasing teachers' salaries but added that the report came "after three years of Administration efforts to cut back on education programs."

"I believe the President ought to take a signal from this report and put an end to his questioning of whether the Federal Government should be involved in education," he said.

Responsibilities Discussed

The report said state and local officials have the "primary responsibility for financing and governing the schools" but added that the Federal Government shares responsibility for meeting the needs of gifted, handicapped, disadvantaged and bilingual students. The Federal Government also has "the primary responsibility to identify the national interest in education," it said.

At the ceremony this afternoon, Mr. Reagan interpreted the commission's position as a "call for an end to Federal intrusion," adding that that "is consistent with our task of redefining the Federal role in education."

The commission staff, which was headed by Milton Goldberg, surveyed existing educational research and commissioned its own studies on topics such as curriculum trends and how American students fare in relation to those of other countries. It also held hearings at which students, teachers, school officials and other citizens were invited to testify.

In its report, entitled "A Nation at Risk: The Imperative for Educational Reform," the commission presented a wide range of evidence that the quality of American education has been deteriorating over the last two decades.

Declining Test Scores

The document noted, for example, that achievement test scores of both high school and college graduates have been declining consistently and that there has been a "steady decline in science achievement scores of American 17-year-olds as measured by national assessments of science in 1969, 1973 and 1977."

Excerpts From the Report on Excellence in Education

Following are excerpts from "A Nation at Risk," a report by the National Commission on Excellence in Education that was released today at the White House.

Our nation is at risk. Our once-unchallenged pre-eminence in commerce, industry, science and technological innovation is being overtaken by competitors throughout the world. This report is concerned with one of the many causes and dimensions of the problem, but it is the one that undergirds American prosperity, security and civility. We report to the American people that while we can take great pride in what our schools and colleges have historically accomplished and contributed to the United States and the well-being of its people, the educational foundations of our society are presently being eroded by a rising tide of mediocrity that threatens our very future as a nation and a people. What was unimaginable a generation ago has begun to occur—others are matching and surpassing our educational attainments.

The Risk

History is not kind to idlers. The time is long past when America's destiny was assured simply by an abundance of natural resources and inexhaustible human enthusiasm, and by our relative isolation from the malignant problems of older civilizations. The world is indeed one global village. We live among determined, well-educated, and strongly motivated competitors. We compete with them for international standing and markets, not only with products but also with the ideas of our laboratories and neighborhood workshops. America's position in the world may once have been reasonably secure with only a few exceptionally well-trained men and women. It is no longer.

The risk is not only that the Japanese make automobiles more efficiently than Americans and have government subsidies for development and export. It is not just that the South Koreans recently built the world's most efficient steel mill, or that American machine tools, once the pride of the world, are being displaced by German products.

It is also that these developments signify a redistribution of trained capability throughout the globe. Knowledge, learning, information and skilled intelligence are the new raw materials of international commerce and are today spreading throughout the world as vigorously as miracle drugs, synthetic fertilizers and blue jeans did earlier. Learning is the indispensable investment required for success in the "information age" we are entering.

Our concern, however, goes well beyond matters such as industry and commerce. It also includes the intellectual, moral and spiritual strength of our people, which knits together the very fabric of our society. A high level of shared education is essential to a free, democratic society and to the fostering of a common culture, especially in a country that prides itself on pluralism and industrial freedom.

Indicators of the Risk

The educational dimensions of the risk before us have been amply documented in testimony received by the commission. For example:

- International comparisons of student achievement, completed a decade ago, reveal that on 19 academic tests American students were never first or second and, in comparison with other industrialized nations, were last seven times.
- Average achievement of high school students on most standardized tests is now lower than 26 years ago when Sputnik was launched.
- Over half the population of gifted students do not match their tested ability with comparable achievement in school.

These deficiencies come at a time when the demand for highly skilled workers in new fields is accelerating rapidly. For example:

- Computers and computer-controlled equipment are penetrating every aspect of our lives—homes, factories and offices.
- One estimate indicates that by the turn of the century millions of jobs will involve laser technology and robotics.
- Technology is radically transforming a host of other occupations, including health care; medical science; energy production; food processing; construction; and the building, repair, and maintenance of military equipment.

The Learning Society

In a world of ever-accelerating competition and change in the conditions of the workplace, of ever-greater danger, and of ever larger opportunities for those prepared to meet them, educational reform should focus on the goal of creating a learning society. At the heart of such a society is the commitment to a set of values and to a system of education that affords each member the opportunity to stretch one's mind to its full capacity, from early childhood through adulthood, learning more as the world itself changes. Such a society has as a basic foundation the idea that education is important not only because of what it contributes to one's career goals but also because of the value it adds to the general quality of one's life.

A Word to Parents and Students

The task of assuring the success of our recommendations does not fall to the schools and colleges alone. Obviously, faculty members and administrators, along with policy makers and the mass media, will play a crucial role in the reform of the educational system. But even more important is the role of parents and students, and to them we speak directly.

To Parents   You know that you cannot confidently launch your children into today's world unless they are of strong character, and well educated in the use of language, science and mathematics. They must possess a deep respect for intelligence, achievement and learning, and the skills needed to handle them; for setting goals; and for disciplined work. That respect must be accompanied by an intolerance for the shoddy and second rate masquerading as "good enough."

You have the right to demand for your children the best our schools and colleges can provide. Your vigilance and your refusal to be satisfied with less than the best are the imperative next step. But your right to a proper education for your children carries a double responsibility. You must be a living example of what you expect your children to honor and to emulate.

Moreover, you bear a responsibility to participate actively in your child's education: Encourage more diligent study and discourage satisfaction with mediocrity and the attitude that says "let it slide"; monitor your child's study; encourage good study habits; encourage your child to take more demanding rather than less demanding courses; nurture your child's curiosity, creativity and confidence; and be an active participant in the work of the schools. Above all, exhibit a commitment to continued learning in your own life.

Finally, help your children understand that excellence in education cannot be achieved without intellectual and moral integrity coupled with hard work and commitment. Children will look to their parents and teachers as models of such virtue.

To Students   You forfeit your chance for life at its fullest when you withhold your best effort in learning. When you give only the minimum to learning you receive only the minimum in return. Even with your parents' best example and your teachers'· best efforts, in the end it is your work that determines how much and how well you learn.

When you work to your full capacity, you can hope to attain the knowledge and skills that will enable you to create your future and control your destiny. If you do not, you will have your future thrust upon you by others. Take hold of your life, apply your gifts and talents, work with dedication and self-discipline. Have high expectations for yourself. Convert every challenge into an opportunity.

A Final Word

Our final word, perhaps better characterized as a plea, is that all segments of our population give attention to the implementation of our recommendations. Our present plight did not appear overnight; and the responsibility for our current situation is widespread. Reform of our educational system will take time and unrelenting commitment. It will require equally widespread, energetic and dedicated action. Help should come from students themselves; from parents, teachers and school boards; from colleges and universities; from local, state and Federal officials; from teachers' and administrators' organizations; from scholarly, scientific and learned societies; from industrial and labor councils; and from other groups with interest in and responsibilities for educational reform.

It is their America, and the America of all of us, that is at risk; it is to each of us that this imperative is addressed. It is by our willingness to take up the challenge, and our resolve to see it through, that America's place in the world will be either secured or forfeited. Americans have succeeded before and so we shall again.

Mythology and the American System of Education
David C. Berliner

What is wrong with the American public school system is that it runs on myths. As we all know, myths are functional. Thus the myths about the American public school system must be serving the purposes of some, though not necessarily

SOURCE: *Phi Delta Kappan,* April 1993, pp. 632–640. Reprinted with permission of *Phi Delta Kappan* and the author. Many of these arguments are extended in Berliner, D. C. and Biddle, B. J. (1995). *The Manufactured Crisis.* Reading, MA: Addison-Wesley.

all, citizens. But the myths about the American public schools may also be misleading the majority of the citizenry and undermining the American people's confidence in one of their most cherished institutions.

What is right about the American education system is that the myths are so far off the mark. Contrary to the prevailing opinion, the American public schools are remarkably good whenever and wherever they are provided with the human and economic resources to succeed.

Let us examine a baker's dozen of these myths about U.S. education and see if they hold up. As we challenge the myths about what is wrong with our schools, we may learn what is right about them.

Myth 1. Today's youth do not seem as smart as they used to be.

Fact   Since 1932 the mean I.Q. of white Americans aged 2 to 75 has risen about .3 points per year. Today's students actually average about 14 I.Q. points higher than their grandparents did and about seven points higher than their parents did on the well-established Wechsler or Stanford–Binet Intelligence Tests.[1] That is, as a group, today's school-age youths are, on average, scoring more than 30 percentile ranks higher than the group from which have emerged the recent leaders of government and industry. The data reveal, for example, that the number of students expected to have I.Q.s of 130 or more—a typical cutoff point for giftedness—is now about seven times greater than it was for the generation now retiring from its leadership positions throughout the nation and complaining about the poor performance of today's youth. In fact, the number of students with I.Q.s above 145 is now about 18 times greater than it was two generations ago. If the intelligence tests given throughout the U.S. are measuring any of the factors the general public includes in its definition of "smart," we are now smarter than we have ever been before.

Myth 2. Today's youths cannot think as well as they used to.

Fact   The increased scores on intelligence tests throughout the industrialized world have *not* been associated with those parts of the tests that call for general knowledge or for verbal or quantitative ability. We could assume performance in those areas to be positively affected by the increase in schooling that has occurred throughout the industrial world during the last two generations. Rather, it turns out that the major gains in performance on intelligence tests have been primarily in the areas of general problem-solving skills and the ability to handle abstract information of a decontextualized nature.[2] That is, the gains have been in the areas we generally label "thinking skills."

If we look at statistics on the Advanced Placement (AP) tests given to talented high school students every year, we find other evidence to bolster the claim that today's American youths are smarter than ever. In 1978, 90,000 high school students took the AP tests for college credit, while in 1990 that number had increased 255% to 324,000 students, who took a total of 481,000 different AP tests. Although the population taking these tests changed markedly over this time period, the mean score dropped only 11/100 of a point. Meanwhile, the percentage of Asians taking the AP tests tripled, the percentage of African-Americans taking the examinations doubled, and the percentage of Hispanics quadrupled.[3] Something that the public schools are doing is producing increasingly larger numbers of very smart students, for those tests are very difficult to pass.

Myth 3. University graduates are not as smart as they used to be and cannot think as well as they did in previous generations.

Fact When we look at objective data, such as the scores on the Graduate Record Examination (GRE), we discover that the talented students who take this exam are smarter and think better than students have for some time.[4] It is a myth to believe that today's college graduates are less talented than those from some previous time.

In the verbal area these students perform at about the same level as graduates did 20 years ago. But in the area of mathematical skills they far exceed the graduates of two decades ago. And in analytic skills—a measure of what we usually mean by "ability to think"—their performance has gone up during the decade that such skills have been measured.

Reliable data exist that appear to challenge the myth of poor performance by high school and college graduates. A very good data-based case can be made that the K–12 public schools and the colleges and universities are conferring many more degrees than in previous generations, and the products of all those schools are smarter than ever before.

Myth 4. The Scholastic Aptitude Test (SAT) has shown a marked decrease in mean score over the last 25 years, indicating the failure of our schools and our teachers to do their jobs.

Fact To be sure, since 1965 the average SAT score has fallen. The *scaled* scores showed 70- or 90-point declines, a drop that frightened many government officials and the press. The scaled scores, however, are distorted records of performance. Not noted, for example, was the fact that, if we multiplied those scores by 10, the declines would have been 700 or 900 points—and we could have scared more people—while if we divided those scaled scores by 10, the decline would have been only 7 or 9 points over a 30-year period. If we use the *raw* score to judge performance over time, as we should, the decline has actually been only 3.3% of the raw score total—about five fewer items answered correctly over a period of 30 or so years.

Far from being ashamed of this loss, educators should celebrate it. Why? Because it is explainable by the fact that much greater numbers of students in the bottom 60% of their graduating classes have been taking the SAT since the 1960s.[5] As educational opportunities and higher education became available to rural Americans and to members of traditionally underrepresented minorities, more of these students started taking the SAT. Since they were frequently from impoverished communities and from schools that offered a less rigorous academic curriculum and fewer advanced courses than wealthier schools, it is not surprising that they tended to score lower than advantaged, suburban, middle-class white students. This is why the mean number of items correct is less than it was. Most of the drop actually occurred between 1965 and 1975, not since. And the drop was primarily in the verbal, not the mathematics, measure.

Anyone rearing a child during the 1950s probably noticed an increase in television viewing. Associated with that change in the nature of childhood was a decrease in book reading and other verbal skills among the students who graduated from high school during the 1960s. Between the changes in the population taking the test and a changed pattern of child rearing because of TV, the decline we witnessed in SAT performance seems perfectly reasonable and not easily attributable to inadequate teachers or a failing school system. In fact, one might properly ask why we do not test our children on decoding information from complex audiovisual displays, or on remembering information presented in auditory or visual forms, or on comprehending extremely fast-changing video arrays of information, and so forth. The media through which our children learn about the world changed dramatically in the 1950s, and so did our children's cognitive skills. Our assessment instruments, however, have not changed at all, and therefore some decrease in measured verbal ability is to be expected.

Actually, as an educator, I am filled with pride that we have played a major role in the achievement of two of America's most prized goals of the 1960s—a higher high school graduation rate, particularly for minority children, and increased access to higher education. We accomplished both goals with a loss of only a few correct answers on the SAT.

This is a remarkable achievement, I think, particularly when we look at other data. For example, from 1975 to 1990 the mean SAT scores of white, African-American, Asian-American, Native-American, Mexican-American, and Puerto Rican high school students went up.[6] Every one of the subgroups for which there are data has increased its average score on the SAT over the period during which the mean score dropped. The most likely cause of this nationwide increase in measured student achievement is an improvement in education. The decline of the average SAT score, used to bolster the myth that the schools are failing, seems meaningless in light of this increase in the scores of *every* subgroup that attends our public schools. These data can more easily be used to make the point that our public schools must actually be improving.

Myth 5. The bottom students now score better on achievement tests, but the performance of the better students has declined. Our top students are not as good as they were.

Fact   There has been some concern that, while the performance of under-achieving students in the U.S. (primarily the poor, primarily those black and brown in color) has gotten better, it has been at the cost of underserving the better students (primarily the richer and whiter students). But that myth also appears not to be true. The SAT performance of all test-takers between 1975 and 1990 was unusually stable. Whatever drops there were in performance oc-curred prior to 1975; since then, scores have remained steady. But if we look at the performance of only those students who match the profile of those who *used to* take the SAT (students who were primarily white, suburban, middle and upper-middle class, higher in high school class rank, and so on), we see an increase between 1975 and 1990 of more than 30 SAT points—more than 10 percentile ranks.[7] Among these advantaged, primarily white youths, who were supposedly achieving less because they suffered from harmful desegregation policies (including forced busing), low standards of performance, poor teachers, no homework, too much television, low morals, and a host of other plagues, we find considerable improvement in performance on the SAT. What boosts my pride as an educator even more is that the Educational Testing Service, the de-veloper of the test items for the SAT, has admitted that the test today is more difficult than it was in 1975.[8]

What have we learned about our students when we look at the facts about SAT scores? Three things stand out. First, the supposedly great loss in America's intellectual capital, as measured by the average score on the SAT, is trivial, par-ticularly since the average scores of every minority group went up for 15 years. Even the traditional college-bound students (those white middle-class students more likely to have taken the examination in 1975) are doing dramatically bet-ter today than they did in the Seventies. Second, more American students are graduating from high school and thinking about college. That is why the mean SAT score did fall somewhat. Many of the students who took the SAT actually did go on to college, with the U.S. achieving one of the highest rates of college attendance in the world.[9] Third, the data we have from this well-accepted indi-cator of educational achievement will not support the accusation that, overall, we have a failing school system and inadequate teachers. The public and many educators bought this spurious charge in the past, and they should not do so any longer.

Myth 6. The performance of American students on standardized achievement tests reveals gross inadequacies.

Fact   This myth can be examined first by looking at the data collected by the National Assessment of Educational Progress (NAEP). The NAEP tests are given to national samples of 9-, 13-, and 17-year-olds in the subjects of mathematics, science, reading, writing, geography, and computer skills. Since the 1970s modest gains, at best, have been the rule. But what is more important is that one group of scientists reviewing the data believes unequivocally that the "national data on student performance do not indicate a decline in *any* area" (emphasis in the original). They have concluded that "students today appear to be as well educated as previously educated students."[10]

Summaries of the NAEP test results, purporting to be the nation's report card, inform us only that our students are performing the same over time. But there are other data in which we can take greater pride. When you investigate the norming procedures used with the most commonly purchased standardized tests, you find that it takes a higher score now to reach the 50th percentile rank than it did in previous decades. For example, on average, students in the 1980s scored higher on the California Achievement Tests than they did in the 1970s. Similarly, on the venerable Iowa Tests of Basic Skills, at the time of the last norming of the test, the test developer said that achievement was at an all-time high in nearly all test areas. The same trend was found in the renorming of the Stanford Achievement Test, the Metropolitan Achievement Tests, and the Comprehensive Tests of Basic Skills.[11]

In both reading and mathematics we find meaningful annual gains in percentile ranks from one representative norming sample to the next. If a school district does not gain more than one percentile rank a year in reading or mathematics, it loses out in the subsequent norming of the test because every other district is doing better than it did previously. If a district at the 60th percentile in reading and mathematics on the last set of norms kept the same program and teachers and had the same kinds of students, that district would be at about the 50th percentile on the new set of norms, without any change in performance having occurred. Each renorming sets the mean higher—clear evidence of the increased productivity of the American schools.

Major standardized tests are renormed, on the average, approximately every seven years. A reasonable estimate is that, over one generation, norms have been redone around three times. Thus we can estimate that about 85% of today's public school students score higher on standardized tests of achievement than the average parent did.[12] But, as in the high jump, the bar keeps getting higher, and it takes better performance today than it did around 1965 to hit the 50th percentile.

While on the subject of standardized test performance, we should also examine the social studies survey developed by Diane Ravitch and Chester Finn and discussed in their gloomy 1987 book, *What Do Our 17-Year-Olds Know?* Their answer was that 17-year-olds know embarrassingly and shockingly little! Their conclusions were part of a barrage of similar arguments showered on the American people by E. D. Hirsch in his book *Cultural Literacy* (1987), by Allan Bloom in his book *The Closing of the American Mind* (1987), and by William Bennett in his report *To Reclaim a Legacy* (1984).[13] The popular press, of course, promoted the claim that today's children know less than they ever did and, therefore, that we are surely a nation at risk. The authors and the editorial writers throughout the land seemed to see nothing but doom for America if we didn't return to our old ways as a nation and as a people, to those mythical halcyon days.

Dale Whittington decided to check the claim that the 17-year-olds of the 1980s knew less than their parents, grandparents, or great-grandparents.[14] She examined social studies and history tests administered from 1915 onward and found 43 items on the Ravitch and Finn test that corresponded to items from other tests given at other times. Today's students were less knowledgeable than previous generations on about one-third of the items. They scored about the same on about one-third of those items. And they scored better on about one-third of the items. When compared to historical records, the data in Ravitch and Finn's study do not support the charge that today's 17-year-olds know less than any previous generation. In fact, given the less elitist composition of today's high schools, the case can be made that more 17-year-olds today know as much about social studies and historical facts as previous generations.

There may never have been any halcyon days to which to return. Every generation of adults has a tendency to find the next generation wanting. This social phenomenon has been recorded for about 2,500 years, since Socrates condemned the youths of Athens for their impertinence and ignorance. Ravitch and Finn, continuing this grand tradition, are merely disappointed that the next generation does not know what they themselves do.

What may we reasonably conclude from these studies of standardized tests? First, there is no convincing evidence of a decline in standardized test performance. This is true of intelligence tests, the SAT, the NAEP tests, and the standardized achievement tests used by local school districts. If any case for a change in these scores can be made, it is that the scores on standardized aptitude and achievement tests are going up, not down. Educators—working under almost intolerable conditions in some settings—have not failed society. It is incredibly difficult to keep academic achievement constant or to improve it with increasing numbers of poor children, unhealthy children, children from dysfunctional families, and children from dysfunctional neighborhoods.[15] Yet the public school system of the U.S. has actually done remarkably well as it receives, instructs, and nurtures children who are poor, who have no health care, and who come from families and neighborhoods that barely function. Moreover, they have done this with quite reasonable budgets.

Myth 7. Money is unrelated to the outcomes of schooling.

Fact   Current income can be predicted from the characteristics of the state school systems in which men received their education during the first half of the century. After the usual statistical controls are applied, it is found that teachers' salaries, class size, and length of the school year are significant predictors of future earnings. States that had spent the most on their schools had produced the citizens with the highest incomes.[16]

It has also been found that higher salaries attract teaching candidates with higher academic ability and keep teachers in the profession longer.[17] Clearly, both of those benefits pay off for students.

An unusual set of data from Texas looks at the effects of teacher ability, teacher experience, class size, and professional certification on student performance in reading and mathematics. Data on millions of students in 900 districts were examined longitudinally from 1986 to 1990. Two rather simple findings emerged. First, teachers' academic proficiency explains 20% to 25% of the variation across districts in students' average scores on academic achievement tests. The smarter the teachers, the smarter their pupils appeared to be, as demonstrated by results on standardized achievement tests administered to both groups. Second, teachers with more years of experience have students with higher test scores, lower dropout rates, and higher rates of taking the SAT. Experience counts for about 10% of the variation in student test scores across districts. The effects are such that an increase of 10% in the number of teachers within a district who have nine or more years' experience is predicted to reduce dropout rates by about 4% and to increase the percentage of students taking the SAT by 3%. Dollars appear to be more likely to purchase bright and experienced professionals, who, in turn, are more likely to provide us with higher-achieving and better-motivated students.[18]

The Texas data also show that, in grades 1 through 7, once class size exceeds 18 students, each student over that number is associated with a drop in district academic achievement. This drop is estimated to be very large—perhaps 35 percentile ranks on standardized tests—between a class size of, say, 25 and a class size of 18.

Furthermore, the percentage of teachers with master's degrees accounted for 5% of the variation in student scores across districts in grades 1 through 7. So we learn from the Texas study *and other data that support its conclusions* that academically more proficient teachers, who are more experienced, who are better educated, and who work with smaller classes, are associated with students who demonstrate significantly higher achievement.

It costs money to attract academically talented teachers, to keep them on the job, to update their professional skills, and to provide them with working conditions that enable them to perform well. Those districts that are willing and able to pay the costs attract the more talented teachers from neighboring districts, and they eventually get the best in a region. Those districts can improve their academic performance relative to other districts that are unable to pay the price, resulting in an education system that is inherently inequitable.

For those who point out that education costs have been rising faster than inflation, it is important to note that special education populations have been rising as well. It costs 2.3 times as much money to educate a child in special education as it does to educate a student in the regular education program.[19] Most of the real increases in educational expenditures over the last 20 years have been the result of increased costs for transportation, health care, and special education. They have not been connected with regular instruction or teachers' salaries.

Myth 8. The American public school system is a bloated bureaucracy, top-heavy in administrators and administrative costs.

Fact   The average number of employees that each administrator supervises in education is among the highest of any industry or business in America. With 14.5 employees for every one administrator, education is leaner than, for example, the transportation industry (9.3 to one), the food products industry (8.4 to one), the utilities industry (6.6 to one), the construction industry (6.3 to one), and the communications industry (4.7 to one). Central office professionals plus principals, assistant principals, and supervisors in the public schools make up a mere 4.5% of the total employee population of the schools. If all these supervisory personnel were fired and their salaries given to teachers, the salaries of teachers would rise no more than 5%. And if those supervisors' salaries were redistributed to reduce class size, the size of classes nationwide would be reduced by an average of one student![20] The administration of education is not a major cost factor. That is a myth.

Myth 9. American schools are too expensive. We spend more on education than any other country in the world, and we have little to show for it.

Fact   Former Secretaries of Education William Bennett, Lauro Cavazos, and Lamar Alexander said we spend more on education than do our rivals Germany and Japan. Former Assistant Secretary of Education Chester Finn wrote in *The New York Times* that we "spend more per pupil than any other nation." And, just before the education summit of 1989, John Sununu, once President Bush's chief of staff and close advisor, declared that "we spend twice as much [on education] as the Japanese and almost 40 percent more than all the other major industrialized countries of the world."[21] But it appears that the people who made these claims, like David Stockman before them, made up the numbers as they went along.

The U.S., according to UNESCO data, is tied with Canada and the Netherlands, and all three fall behind Sweden in the amount spent per pupil for K–12 education and higher education.[22] We look good in this comparison because we spend much more than most nations on higher education and have two to three times more people per 100,000 enrolled in higher education than most other countries. When only the expenditures for preprimary, primary, and secondary education are calculated, however, we actually spend much less than the average industrialized nation.

In 1988 dollars we rank ninth among 16 industrialized nations in per-pupil expenditures for grades K–12, spending 14% less than Germany, 30% less than Japan, and 51% less than Switzerland. We can also compare ourselves to other countries in terms of the percentage of per-capita income spent on education. When we do that comparison, we find that, out of 16 industrialized nations, 13 of them spend a greater percentage of per-capita income on K–12 education than we do. If we were to come up just to the *average* percentage of per-capita income spent on education by the 15 other industrialized nations, we would have to invest an additional $20 billion per year in K–12 education![23] The most recent report by the Organisation for Economic Cooperation and Development on education in the European Community and some other industrialized nations also finds the U.S. low in its commitment to education. That report places the U.S. behind 12 other industrialized nations in the percentage of Gross Domestic Product devoted to public and private education.[24]

Perhaps we do not teach as much in the K–12 schools as some would like. But we do not have to. A relatively large percentage of our students go on to postsecondary studies, where they can acquire the learning the nation needs them to have. Our nation has simply chosen to invest its money in higher education. Consequently, our education system ultimately provides about 25% of each year's group of high school graduates with college degrees, and it is the envy of the world. We run a costly and terrific K–16 school system, but we must acknowledge that we run an impoverished and relatively less good K–12 school system.

Moreover, in many of the countries that spend more per capita than we do, the funding is relatively even across regions and cities. But in our nation, we have, to use Jonathan Kozol's scathing formulation, "savage inequalities" in our funding for schools.[25] Even though the national *average* for per-pupil expenditures in the primary and secondary schools is relatively low, included in the calculation of that figure are the much, much lower annual per-pupil expenditures of those school districts at the bottom of the income distribution. To our shame, conditions in many of those districts resemble conditions in the nonindustrialized nations of the world.

Former President George Bush perpetuated the myth we address here when he declared at the education summit of 1989 that the U.S. "lavishes unsurpassed resources on [our children's] schooling."[26] What he should have said was that we are among the most cost-efficient nations in the world, with an

amazingly high level of productivity for the comparatively low level of investment that our society makes in K–12 education.

Myth 10. Our high schools, colleges, and universities are not supplying us with enough mathematicians and scientists to maintain our competitiveness in world markets.

Fact   There are solid data to suggest that the supply of mathematicians and
scientists is exceeding the demand for them! First of all, we now exceed or are
at parity with our economic competitors in terms of the technical competence
of our work force—for example, in the number of engineers and physical scientists we have per hundred workers.[27] So, if we have lost our economic edge
in the world marketplace, it may well be because of poor business management
and faulty government economic policies, but it is certainly not because of the
lack of a technically skilled work force. But that is the present situation. Projections of the future supply in these fields do look gloomy, but that is true only as
long as the economy's demand for such individuals is not examined. When demand and supply are examined together, it turns out that the economy is not
now able to absorb all the scientists and engineers that we produce. With no increase in the rate of supply of scientists and engineers, we will accumulate a
surplus of about one million such individuals by the year 2010. Given the probable reduction in military spending during the next few years, the glut of trained
scientists is likely to be even more serious than was forecast a year or two ago.
Moreover, the National Science Foundation recently apologized to Congress for
supplying it with phony data a few years back. That agency now admits that its
predictions of shortages in supply were grossly inflated.

In my most cynical moments, I think that the business community and the
politicians are demanding that the schools produce even more engineers and
scientists because the labor of these individuals is currently so expensive. An
oversupply will certainly drive down the salaries of such workers.

The myth of the coming shortage of technically able workers has been de-
bunked by many economists.[28] In fact, it has been estimated that, if the entering
workers had an average of only one-fourth of a grade level more education than
those now retiring from the labor force, all the needs of the future economy
would be served.

How can this be? The answer is in the mix of jobs available in the future.
The five most highly skilled occupational groups will make up only about 6% of
the job pool by the year 2000. On the other hand, service jobs, requiring the
least technical skill, will actually grow the fastest overall in the next few years,
and they will constitute about 17% of the job pool by the year 2000. Apparently
this nation is not in any danger of failing to meet its technological needs.

Furthermore, research has found that, during the first eight years on the
job, young adults without a college education receive no rewards from the labor

market for their abilities in science, mathematical reasoning, or language arts.[29] The fact that so many American high school students avoid rigorous mathematics and science courses may actually be a rational response to the lack of rewards for these skills in the labor market.

Myth 11. In our science laboratories and our graduate schools we train foreign students who leave us to return to their native lands.

Fact   Many of our graduate degrees in mathematics and the natural sciences do go to foreign-born students. But we are blessed with the good luck that more than half of these enormously talented individuals choose to stay in the U.S.[30] We are draining the world of its talent, which is a moral problem, but our good fortune serves the national interest just fine. These individuals—Pakistanis, East Indians, Asians, Latin Americans—become law-abiding, relatively high-salaried American citizens, who increase our international competitiveness. Opposition to such students is probably based more on xenophobia and racism than on any economic argument that could be made.

Myth 12. The U.S. is an enormous failure in international comparisons of educational achievement.

Fact   I would ask some questions about international comparisons before I would worry about our students' relative performance. First, I would like to know if we Americans want our children to experience a childhood like those of Japanese, Korean, Israeli, or East Indian children. I do not think so. Other countries rear children in their ways, and we rear them in our way. As you might expect, we have a vision of what constitutes a "normal" childhood that is uniquely American.

My middle-class neighbors seem to agree that their children should be able to watch a good deal of TV; participate in organized sports such as Little League, basketball, and soccer; engage in after-school activities such as piano lessons and dance; spend weekends predominantly in leisure activities; work after school when they become teenagers; have their own cars and begin to date while in high school; and so forth. To accomplish all of this, of course, children cannot be burdened by excessive amounts of homework. This kind of American consensus about childhood produces uniquely American youths. According to many visitors to the U.S., we have some of the most creative and spontaneous children the world has ever seen. And these students do go on to more challenging schooling at the college level, in numbers that are the envy of the world.

It is clear that our system is not designed to produce masses of high-achieving students before the college years. You cannot have both high levels of history, language, mathematics, and science achievement for great numbers of students and the conception of childhood that I have just sketched. But our nation is certainly not at risk because of that conception. Enough able workers are being trained to meet our national needs.

Second, I would like to know whether the students tested in international comparisons have all spent the same amount of time practicing the skills that are to be assessed. It is not clear that this is so. Given the additional school days in the Japanese school year, multiplied by 10 years of schooling, we find by the simplest arithmetic that the typical Japanese student has the equivalent of more than two years' more schooling than the typical American student when they are both 16 years old. Moreover, with the additional time they spend in private "after-school" schools and in Saturday schools (the *juku* schools, attended by a large percentage of the Japanese school-age population), Japanese children accumulate still greater amounts of education, such that by age 16 they have more than three years' more schooling than their American counterparts. Furthermore, the immense (at least by American standards) amount of homework assigned to and completed by Japanese students means that they accumulate huge quantities of extra time practicing school subjects at home and on weekends. Suppose you now compare these groups in terms of their mathematics and science achievement in the 10th grade. It would be truly newsworthy if the results were any different from what they are now. The results we get are exactly what we should expect.

Third, before taking the international comparisons at face value, I would want to make sure that the samples of students who take the test are somehow equivalent. It is easy for the U.S. to produce a representative sample of 13- or 16-year-olds for an international comparison. Is that also true of some of our international competitors? Some of the nations in these studies have neither an accurate census nor a school system that attempts to keep everyone in school. We have a larger percentage of our school-age population in school than most other nations. Thus our representative sample is culturally and economically more heterogeneous.

In the first international assessment conducted by the International Association for the Evaluation of Educational Achievement, from which we learned how awful the U.S. was doing, the average performance of 75% of the age group in the U.S. was compared with the average scores of the top 9% of the students in West Germany, the top 13% in the Netherlands, and the top 45% in Sweden.[31] Could the results have been predicted? In the most recent international comparisons of science and mathematics achievement, the U.S. did not do as well as Korea and Taiwan. But in our sample we had more children at lower grade levels for their age than they did. All other things being equal, when around 10% of our sample has attained one or two fewer grade levels of schooling than the sample of the same age from Korea and Taiwan, we have a sampling problem.[32] What could be newsworthy about differences in achievement when the samples are not equivalent?

Fourth, I would like to be sure that the different groups in the international comparisons all had the opportunity to learn the same things. We should note that school systems that do not hold as many children as we do until high school graduation and that have fewer students continuing on to higher education need to teach many things at an earlier point in the curriculum—calculus and probability, for example. Because we are a nation that is rich enough and democratic enough to attempt to retain our youngsters longer in school and because we send a comparatively large number of them on to college, we often look weak in the international comparisons. Many of our students learn what they need to learn later than students in other countries.

We need to remember that students will not do well on any content to which they have not been exposed. Opportunity to learn a subject is probably the single best predictor of achievement that we have. If you cannot control for it, you have no basis for comparing achievement. The findings of the Second International Mathematics Study are a case in point.[33] Do we see, in the performance of the Japanese and others, evidence of efficiency and effectiveness in education—or merely evidence that national curricula differ?

If we look at the 273 eighth-grade math classes that made up the U.S. sample, we find that they were actually labeled as remedial, typical, pre-algebra, and algebra classes. To no one's great surprise, only the pre-algebra and algebra classes—about 25% of the U.S. sample—had had nearly the same amount of exposure as the Japanese classes in the sample to the algebra items that made up the test. Three-quarters of the classes in the U.S. sample were simply not exposed to the same curriculum as were the Japanese! Can you guess what the result might be in such a comparison? If we look only at the eighth-grade algebra classes among our sample, we find that American performance in algebra meets or exceeds the performance of the Japanese eighth-graders.

The differences in achievement between nations are most parsimoniously explained as differences in national curricula, rather than as differences in the efficiency or effectiveness of a particular national system of education. International comparisons such as these make us realize that American students, including the most ordinary ones, are capable of learning more mathematics at earlier ages—if that is what we want them to learn.

But while we should wrestle with these legitimate curriculum issues, we need not blame our students and castigate their teachers for gross failure. Our nation, particularly at state and local levels, has made curricular decisions that are in accord with prevailing views of childhood and of education. We can change those decisions if we want. But the system has actually been serving the nation well for decades, and, as noted, it is producing all the mathematicians and scientists this economy can use for the foreseeable future.

Finally, in considering the results of international comparisons, I would like to be assured that the motivation of the students who took the tests was similar across different nations. It is not clear that this is the case. The Koreans, for example, take the tests for the honor of the nation.[34] The American students often use the test to rest for two hours, knowing that neither their teachers nor their parents will see the results.

I cannot find much to worry about in the international comparisons. Every nation has its visions of childhood, development, schooling, equality, and success. While our nation heatedly debates and gradually modifies these visions, as a dynamic society must, let us just note that the system we created has been remarkably successful for a large number of the children and parents it serves.

Myth 13. American productivity has fallen, and a major factor in that decline is the education of the work force.

Fact   According to the 1992 report of McKinsey and Company, one of our nation's most prestigious management consulting firms, there has been no decline in American productivity.[35] It is true that productivity in other countries has grown at a faster rate than ours, but since their productivity was historically much lower, that is not surprising. Their rates of increase are not nearly as steep as they approach our rate of productivity. McKinsey and Company estimates that overall economic productivity is lower in Germany by 14% and in Japan by 28%. In the service areas, where the U.S. is beginning to lead the world, our productivity rates are even higher when compared with those of other nations.

When we examine the various factors that can influence the productivity of a nation—market conditions, labor unions, government regulations, behavior of management, available capital, skill of the labor force, and so on—only one variable predicts productivity in the service sector across nations. That factor is the behavior of management. The educational level of the labor force is unrelated to productivity. As we now realize, it was the management of General Motors, the management of Sears, and the management of Pan American Airlines (remember them?) that caused the economic hardships those companies have undergone. The educational level of the labor force was not an issue, though that makes a nice target when arrogant and intransigent managers are looking for scapegoats for their billion-dollar blunders.

Let me be clear. We have failing schools in this nation. But where they fail we see poverty, inadequate health care, dysfunctional families, and dysfunctional neighborhoods. Where our public schools succeed—in Princeton, New Jersey; in Grosse Pointe, Michigan; in Manhasset, New York—we see well-paying jobs, good health care, functional families, and functional neighborhoods. Families that can live in dignity send the schools children who have hope. Those children we can educate quite well. Families that have lost their dignity function poorly. They send us children with no hope for the future. Those children we cannot easily educate.

The agenda America should tackle if we want to improve schooling has nothing to do with national tests, higher standards, increased accountability, or better math and science achievement. Instead, we should focus our attention and our energies on jobs, health care, reduction of violence in families and in neighborhoods, and increased funding for day care, bilingual education, summer programs for young people, and so forth. It is estimated that 100,000 handguns enter the schools each day. It seems to me that this is a greater problem than the nation's performance in international mathematics competitions.

NOTES

1. J. R. Flynn, "Massive IQ Gains in 14 Nations: What IQ Tests Really Measure," *Psychological Bulletin,* vol. 101, 1987, pp. 171–91.
2. Ibid.
3. Paul E. Barton and Richard J. Coley, *Performance at the Top: From Elementary Through Graduate School* (Princeton, N.J.: Educational Testing Service, 1991).
4. Ibid.
5. C. C. Carson, R. M. Huelskamp, and T. D. Woodall, "Perspectives on Education in America," Third Draft, Sandia National Laboratories, Albuquerque, N.M., May 1991.
6. Ibid.
7. Ibid.
8. Ibid.
9. Organisation for Economic Cooperation and Development, *Education at a Glance* (Paris: Centre for Educational Research and Innovation, 1992).
10. Carson, Huelskamp, and Woodall, op. cit.
11. Robert L. Linn, M. Elizabeth Graue, and Nancy M. Sanders, "Comparing State and District Test Results to National Norms: The Validity of Claims That 'Everyone Is Above Average,'" *Education Measurement: Issues and Practice,* Fall 1990, pp. 5–14.
12. Robert L. Linn, personal communication, February 1991.
13. Diane Ravitch and Chester E. Finn, Jr., *What Do Our 17-Year-Olds Know?* (New York: Harper & Row, 1987); E. D. Hirsch, Jr., *Cultural Literacy: What Every American Needs to Know* (Boston: Houghton Mifflin, 1987); Allan Bloom, *The Closing of the American Mind: How Higher Education Has Failed Democracy and Impoverished the Souls of Today's Students* (New York: Simon & Schuster, 1987); and William J. Bennett, *To Reclaim a Legacy: A Report on the Humanities in Higher Education* (Washington, D.C.: National Endowment for the Humanities, 1984).
14. Dale Whittington, "What Have 17-Year-Olds Known in the Past?," *American Educational Research Journal,* vol. 28, 1991, pp. 759–83.
15. National Commission on Children, *Beyond Rhetoric: A New American Agenda for Children and Families* (Washington, D.C.: U.S. Government Printing Office, 1991).
16. David Card and Alan B. Krueger, "Does School Quality Matter? Returns to Education and the Characteristics of Public Schools in the United States," Working Paper No. 3358, Bureau of Economic Research, Washington, D.C., 1990.
17. Charles F. Manski, "Academic Ability, Earnings, and the Decision to Become a Teacher: Evidence from the National Longitudinal Study of the High School Class of 1972," in David A. Wise, ed., *Public Sector Payrolls* (Chicago: University of Chicago Press, 1987); and Richard J. Murnane and R. J. Olsen, "The Effects of Salaries and Opportunity Costs on Duration in Teaching: Evidence from Michigan," *Review of Economics and Statistics,* vol. 71, 1989, pp. 347–52.
18. Ronald F. Ferguson, "Paying for Public Education: New Evidence on How and Why Money Matters," *Harvard Journal on Legislation,* vol. 28, 1991, pp. 465–98.

19. Glen Robinson and David Brandon, *Perceptions About American Education: Are They Based on Facts?* (Arlington, Va.: Educational Research Service, 1992).
20. Ibid.
21. Both Finn and Sununu are quoted in M. Edith Rasell and Lawrence Mishel, *Short-changing Education: How U.S. Spending on Grades K-12 Lags Behind Other Industrialized Nations* (Washington, D.C.: Economic Policy Institute, 1990).
22. Ibid.
23. Ibid.
24. Organisation for Economic Cooperation and Development, op. cit.
25. Jonathan Kozol, *Savage Inequalities* (New York: Crown, 1991).
26. George H. Bush, speech delivered at education summit, University of Virginia, Charlottesville, 28 September 1989.
27. Carson, Huelskamp, and Woodall, op. cit.
28. Lawrence Mishel and Ruy A. Texeira, *The Myth of the Coming Labor Shortage: Jobs, Skills, and Incomes of America's Workforce 2000* (Washington, D.C.: Economic Policy Institute, 1991).
29. John H. Bishop, "The Productivity Consequences of What Is Learned in High School," *Journal of Curriculum Studies,* vol. 22, 1990, pp. 101-26.
30. Carson, Huelskamp, and Woodall, op. cit.
31. Iris C. Rotberg, "I Never Promised You First Place," *Phi Delta Kappan,* December 1990, pp. 296-303.
32. Archie E. Lapointe, Janice M. Askew, and Nancy A. Mead, *Learning Science* (Princeton, N.J.: Educational Testing Service, 1992); and Archie E. Lapointe, Nancy A. Mead, and Janice M. Askew, *Learning Mathematics* (Princeton, N.J.: Educational Testing Service, 1992).
33. Ian Westbury, "Comparing American and Japanese Achievement: Is the United States Really a Low Achiever?," *Educational Researcher,* June/July 1991, pp. 18-24.
34. Lapointe, Askew, and Mead, op. cit; and Gerald W. Bracey, "Why Can't They Be Like We Were?," *Phi Delta Kappan,* October 1991, pp. 104-17.
35. McKinsey Global Institute, *Service Sector Productivity* (Washington, D.C.: McKinsey and Company, 1992).

American Education: The Good, the Bad, and the Task
Harold Hodgkinson

My aims in this brief article are to describe the unique diversity of the American student body and the magnitude of the demographic changes that are to come, to consider our accomplishments with this student body by looking at test data,

Source: *Phi Delta Kappan,* April 1993, pp. 619-623. Reprinted with permission of *Phi Delta Kappan* and the author.

to point out the failures of the system in working effectively with certain students, and to indicate what needs to be done to make the system work more effectively for *all* young Americans.

Diversity

While the national population grew 9.8% during the 1980s, certain groups grew very rapidly, and others posted only small increases. The number of non-Hispanic whites grew by 6%; of African-Americans, by 13.2%; of Native Americans, by 37.9%; of Asian-Pacific Islanders, by 107.8%; of Hispanics of all races, by 53%.

While about 22% of the total population can be described as minority, 30% of school-age children are minority, a number that will reach 36% shortly after the year 2000. A look at immigration rates can give us a clue as to why this is so. Between 1820 and 1945, the nations that sent us the largest numbers of immigrants were (in rank order): Germany, Italy, Ireland, the United Kingdom, the Soviet Union, Canada, and Sweden. The nations that send us the most immigrants now and that are projected to do so through the year 2000 are (in rank order): Mexico, the Philippines, Korea, China/Taiwan, India, Cuba, the Dominican Republic, Jamaica, Canada, Vietnam, the United Kingdom, and Iran.

It is clear from the former list that we have not really been a "nation of nations," as both Carl Sandburg and Walt Whitman proclaimed; rather we have been a nation of Europeans. There was a common European culture that the schools could use in socializing millions of immigrant children. The latter list indicates that we face a brand-new challenge: the population of American schools today truly represents the world. Children come to school today with different diets, different religions (there were more Moslems than Episcopalians in the U.S. in 1991), different individual and group loyalties, different music, different languages. The most diverse segment of our society is our children. While these children bring new energy and talents to our nation, they also represent new challenges for instruction.

In the 1990 Census, for the first time in history, only three states accounted for more than half of the nation's growth in a decade. These states were California, Florida, and Texas. They also picked up a total of 14 seats in the U.S. House of Representatives, while New York, Pennsylvania, Ohio, Indiana, and Illinois lost an equivalent number of seats. California will have to prepare for a 41% increase in high school graduates by 1995, with 52% of them being "minority," a term that loses its meaning in such a situation. By the year 2010, the number of minority young people in the U.S. will increase by 4.4 million, while the number of non-Hispanic white young people will decline by 3.8 million.

The states that are growing fastest have high percentages of "minority" youth. If the large minority population of New York is added to the large and fast-growing minority populations of California, Texas, and Florida, these four states will have more than one-third of the nation's young people in 2010, and the youth population of each state will be over 52% "minority." In 2010 about

12 states will have "majority minority" youth populations, while Maine's youth population will be 3% minority. It makes little sense to focus solely on the national changes when the states are becoming much more diverse in terms of ethnicity, age of population, job production, population density, family types, and youth poverty.[1]

Children at Risk and Schools

In 1993 more than 23% of America's children were living below the poverty line and thus were at risk of failing to fulfill their physical and mental promise. This is one of the highest youth poverty rates in the "developed" world and has shown little inclination to decline. Most of these children live in our nation's inner cities and rural areas, in about equal numbers. (The issue of youth poverty in rural America has not been addressed seriously by the nation's leaders.) Because these children bring the risks with them on the first day of kindergarten, it becomes a vital job of the schools to overcome these risks. Schools should be assessed on how well they and other agencies responsible for youth development meet the challenges posed by these children.

Since the publication of *A Nation at Risk* in 1983, there has been a general impression that American students have slumped from a previous position of world leadership to near the bottom in terms of academic achievement. (Of course, we have had similar waves of criticism of public school standards in previous decades; Arthur Bestor's *Educational Wastelands,* James Bryant Conant's reform movement, and the many responses to Sputnik I—suggesting that American students were hopelessly behind those of the Soviet Union—spring immediately to mind, along with a long list of books suggesting that American education is "falling behind.")

Behind what? That question is seldom voiced, though its implied answer is clear to readers of the literature of decline: schools are falling behind some previous Golden Age during which American public school students were the world's best in every aspect of the curriculum. In reality, if you look at the data from 30 years of international achievement testing, you will find *no* period during which American students led the world in school achievement.

Anyone who questions the methodology of the international comparisons on which much of the literature of decline is based will usually be accused of advocating "complacency." Those who ask such questions are thus shown to be enemies of excellence. However, a variety of data suggest that the picture is not as universally bleak as it is sometimes painted.

A report from the Sandia National Laboratories, carefully assessing a wide variety of data sources, concluded that American education has done well in most areas of performance. That report has never formally seen the light of day. The largest-ever international study of reading, directed by a distinguished U.S. researcher, tested thousands of students in more than 30 countries. It found that U.S. students were among the best in the world in reading, surpassed only by Finland. Only *USA Today* covered the story, and the U.S. Department of

Education immediately discredited the results by saying that higher levels of difficulty were not assessed, and therefore the U.S. was not interested in the findings. Actually, the data were politically unacceptable rather than cripplingly flawed.

The fact is that all the international studies of educational achievement have a number of built-in flaws. First, translation is an art, not a science, and an item in one language can seldom be translated into another language with the identical set of culturally derived meanings. All items have a cultural "spin" based on the values behind the words. If a student can correctly identify a harpsichord as a musical instrument, we learn little about that student's intelligence but a lot about his or her family and social class. Moreover, there is no way to control for the differing motivation of the students who take the tests.

In addition, international comparisons are not diagnostic: they don't help students (or nations) understand their mistakes in order to improve performance. They don't help policy makers figure out what is wrong with an education system in order to improve it. Outside of a major preoccupation with finding out who's "number one" in some vague terms, it is hard to see how any education system in any nation has been helped by these tests. It's hard to tell from these test scores what specifically needs to be fixed in American education. One can wonder what the return has been on this considerable investment.

Test Data in the United States

Let's look at test data from our own country and see what we can make out of them, starting with the performance of younger children and ending with that of graduate students. For this purpose I'll rely on an excellent compendium titled *Performance at the Top*, recently issued by the Educational Testing Service (ETS).[2]

With regard to reading, the data show that one 9-year-old in six can search for specific information, relate ideas, and make generalizations—the same fraction as in 1971. But we also learn that whites do much better and that Hispanics actually do a little better than blacks, despite the complications associated with English as a second language for many Hispanic children. Most important, there are spectacular differences in reading that are associated with parents' level of education: 22% of children whose parents have had some college can read at this higher level of comprehension, but only 6% of the children of high school dropouts can. Indeed, parents' level of education is one of the very best predictors of students' educational achievement.

The implications of the importance of parents' education for our education reform efforts are huge, and they have been largely neglected by the reform initiatives that issued from the Bush White House under the banner of the America 2000 strategy. Poverty would seem to be the root cause of educational deficiency (college graduates being unusually low on poverty measures), yet the reforms suggested as part of America 2000 seldom mention poverty or disadvantage.

If a child who was poor and a member of a minority group is allowed to enter the middle class—as happens if the parents become college graduates and move to the suburbs—then that child will tend to perform in school like other children whose parents are college graduates living in suburbs. This means that we should not let go of the American Dream just yet; if given the chance, it still works.

In math, slightly more 9-year-olds (20%) can perform at intermediate levels. Again, there has been no change over the years, although the first data are from 1978. But whites still do far better, and the scores of blacks are slightly lower than those of Hispanics. Geographically speaking, the Southeast and the West don't do as well as the Northeast and the Central U.S. But again, differences in parents' level of education reveal much: 29% of the children of college graduates perform at the intermediate level, while only 6% of the children of high school dropouts do so.

In science, about one-fourth of 9-year-olds can apply basic scientific information, a figure unchanged since 1977. Here, racial and ethnic differences are somewhat smaller, and blacks do a little better than Hispanics. Regional differences are also smaller. But once again, the differences between the children of college graduates and the children of high school dropouts are the greatest: 36% of the former do well in science versus only 9% of the latter. (Oddly enough, children whose parents had some additional education past high school do better than the children of college graduates, but only by 3%.)

The data on the performance of 13-year-olds in reading reveal patterns similar to those of 9-year-olds. Again, whites do better than minorities, but the differences have narrowed among the 13-year-olds, and the scores of blacks are slighter higher than those of Hispanics. Regional differences are also smaller. However, differences associated with parents' level of education remain quite large: 15% of 13-year-old children of college graduates read at the "figuring out" level, but only 6% of the children of high school dropouts can. (Other subjects use different comparisons and are therefore not included. Among 17-year-olds, the data for comparing regions and parents' education are not comparable, although there is no evidence of systematic declines in subject areas.)

As we look past high school, some fascinating numbers are present. The Advanced Placement (AP) testing program has grown rapidly since its inception—jumping by more than 500% in the last two decades. The numbers of minority test-takers have also shown large increases, reaching about one-fifth of all test-takers in 1990, though Asian-Americans make up about half of all the minority students tested. The program has become very popular in a variety of schools, ranging from the inner cities to the wealthy suburbs; the number of test-takers grew from about 100,000 in 1978 to 320,000 in 1990.

In most testing situations, expanding the pool of test-takers lowers the average scores. The AP program proves to be the exception, as the scores have remained virtually stable for the past two decades. One interpretation in the ETS report suggests that the limits of the pool have not been reached and that many more students could successfully complete college work in high school through

AP-type programs. (This is particularly exciting for low-income and minority youths, as I have contended that inner-city students will often rise to a challenge, no matter how depressed their background may be.) The data certainly suggest that the consistency of AP scores cannot be explained by the conventional wisdom that all schools are terrible and getting worse.

When we finally get to scores on the Scholastic Aptitude Test (SAT), we find that the declines of the 1970s were largely recouped during the 1980s in terms of the percentage of students scoring 600 or above on either the verbal or the math sections. (The percentage of students achieving high scores in math has been about twice as large as the percentage achieving high verbal scores, which could have some useful implications for high schools.) Even more interesting with regard to the "high end" scores are those for the College Board's Achievement Tests, which are designed to test what is actually taught in high school courses. About 8% of high school seniors take these tests. Their average SAT verbal and math scores have steadily increased since 1977, and their average scores on the Achievement Tests have increased since 1979. It seems clear that the performance of our top students is, in some senses, improving over time.

If we look at issues of equity with regard to college attendance and graduation, we find that about 23% of all white high school graduates in the classes of 1972 and 1980 received a bachelor's degree, while the corresponding figure for black high school graduates actually declined from 17.5% for the class of 1972 to 13.9% for the class of 1980. The rate at which Hispanics earned college degrees actually improved a little, from 10.7% in 1972 to 11.2% for the 1980 class, even though Hispanics' percentages of college completion were consistently below those of blacks. The 1992 *Almanac of the Chronicle of Higher Education,* however, shows an increase in college enrollment for all minorities during the 1980s, although degree data are not given.

It seems that during the 1980s, when minority scores were improving on many K–12 measures, *access* to higher education was slipping for many minority groups. Whether this was a result of shifts in financial aid policies (converting grant programs to loans) or of other factors is not clear. However, half of our graduating seniors enter college, and about one-fourth of them receive bachelor's degrees. Two percent then enter graduate school, and 3% enter professional schools. While minorities were steadily increasing their numbers through high school graduation, their participation in the higher education pipeline showed some disturbing trends. In 1992 minorities represented about 30% of public school students, 20% of college students, and 14% of recipients of bachelor's degrees. (Note that an increase in the number of high school diplomas earned by minorities will take five or more years to show up as an increase in bachelor's degrees.)

Even more striking is a look at the ETS data on high-ability students. While half did earn a bachelor's degree, 10% of high-ability seniors did not attend *any* higher education program after high school, and 40% of those who did so attended a community college, from which some transferred later to four-year programs. Given our stereotype that community colleges have virtually none of the high-ability students, it appears that they actually enroll about two-fifths of them, which may explain why students who transfer to four-year programs do quite well.

When we come to the question of entrance to graduate school and consider scores on the Graduate Record Examination, we find even more interesting issues. From 1981 to 1990, the number of test-takers increased 16%, from 135,000 to 157,000, while the mean verbal score rose 16 points, the mean quantitative score rose 36 points, and the mean analytical score rose 30 points. The average score on the Graduate Management Admissions Test has gone from 481 in 1982 to 503 in 1990, while the number of test-takers surged from 114,000 in 1984 to 160,000 in 1990. Scores on the Medical School Admissions Test and on the Law School Admissions Test have also shown great stability (and some score increases), even with a more diverse group of test-takers. From these data it appears that both the diversity and the quality of our future scientists, researchers, and professional workers have increased simultaneously.

An Explanation

We now need to try to find some way of explaining all the data we have examined. Below, I offer a brief summary, and then I propose one explanation that fits all the data.

First, the top 20% of our high school graduates are world class—and getting better. However, talented minority youths do not get as far in the educational pipeline as they should. (The production of black Ph.D.s declined by more than one-third during the 1980s, a factor that cannot be explained in terms of declining test scores for blacks or declining numbers of blacks in the pool.)

As Iris Rotberg and others have pointed out, 40% of all research articles in the world are published by U.S. scholars; no other nation produces more than 7%.[3] There seems to be little doubt that the American intellectual elite, particularly in math and the sciences, is retaining its dominant position. The problem is that, if all public schools are doing such a miserable job, how do colleges make up for that loss and produce the world's best graduate students? (Note that the vast majority of U.S. graduate students are U.S. citizens, not Asian citizens; only at the doctoral level in the areas of engineering and computer science are U.S. students not holding their own.) The data on the AP tests and graduate school admissions tests certainly suggest that our best are already world class, have been improving, and probably will continue to improve, despite more diversity in the examinees.

Second, the 40% right behind the top 20% are mostly capable of completing a college education, although some will need remediation in writing and science. A large number of minorities are probably now in this group, the first generation in their families to get a crack at a college education. Many students from low-income backgrounds are also in this group. We have colleges that serve a wide range of student abilities in the U.S., which explains the large

American middle class. Having a wide range of undergraduate institutions that specialize in different kinds of students from different backgrounds is vital to success in a highly diverse nation.

Third, the lowest 40% of students are in very bad educational shape, a situation caused mostly by problems they brought with them to the kindergarten door, particularly poverty, physical and emotional handicaps, lack of health care, difficult family conditions, and violent neighborhoods. (Using indicators of these conditions, it is very easy to predict in the early grades which children will be at risk of school failure.) Because many of these children stay in our schools until age 18, while in most other countries they would be on the streets, our test scores reflect our commitment to try to keep them in school. These are the children who are tracked into the "general" curriculum in high school, which prepares them neither for college nor for a job. We know exactly where most of these very difficult students reside—in our inner cities and in our rural areas.

If we can locate the young people who need help the most, why do we not target our resources and focus our concern on improving the entire system by working on the students who are at the highest risk of school failure? Most of our top students are going to do well with very little effort from the school system. But the students in the bottom 40% have few resources they can bring to the school: their parents are often high school dropouts, and they know very few people who have benefited from education. Without assistance and concern from the school, they are destined for failure. If half of the students in the bottom third of U.S. schools were stimulated to do well, developed some intellectual and job skills, and moved into the middle class, everyone in the nation would benefit.

The best way to deal with this problem is to provide a "seamless web" of services, combining education, health care, housing, transportation, and social welfare. Such efforts represent an attempt to reduce the vulnerability to school failure of the lower 40% of students. Head Start and follow-up programs can give very young children a sense of their own accomplishment and potential and can help in building a supportive and enthusiastic home environment. Chapter 1 can continue the battle in the early grades, while TRIO, Upward Bound, and Project Talent can keep the achievement level up through the high school years and on into college, where other programs are available to improve graduation rates.

On the health-care front, one of the best ways to improve education would be to make sure that every pregnant woman in America received at least one physical exam during the first trimester of her pregnancy (which would reduce births of handicapped infants by around 10%); a second way would be to make sure that every child is immunized against polio, diphtheria, and measles before entering school. All the components of the "seamless web" of services are in place, but it's not clear that we know how to coordinate these services in the best interests of young people. That would make a fine agenda for the next decade.

It is also clear that American students have regained any ground lost during the 1970s and that students are doing approximately as well as when the National Assessment of Educational Progress began more than two decades ago. Some might say that that level of achievement is not high enough for today's world, and that's a reasonable position. But then one must specify what level is needed and why. The idea of making America "number one in math and science" is meaningless unless we understand what skills and habits of mind we wish to develop and *why*. Certainly becoming numero uno on the existing international tests would not necessarily increase the number of graduate students in science and math, would not increase the scholarly output of our universities, and would not increase the number of patents or inventions (indeed we might see a reduction in creativity, since these tests do not reward innovative or divergent thinking). Broadening the educational pipeline to include more disadvantaged students with an interest in science might work, but no one has proposed that.

So where should the U.S. bend its energies and talents in education? It seems very clear to me: we should focus on the students who are at greatest risk of school failure, numbering close to one-third of the children born in 1992. These children will become the college freshmen of 2010. We know where these children are; we know that they are smart and energetic, even when doing illegal things; we know what they need in order to become successful students; and, generally, we have the resources they need (although local, state, and federal programs are largely uncoordinated). What we lack is the will to make this a national direction. Yet if we were told that an unfriendly foreign power had disabled one-third of our youth, rendering them incapable of reasonable performance in school, we would view it as an act of war. We don't need to imagine a foreign enemy; by systematically neglecting the needs and potential of disadvantaged children, we have done the damage to ourselves.

Notes

1. For a complete discussion of diversity, see Harold Hodgkinson, *A Demographic Look at Tomorrow* (Washington, D.C.: Center for Demographic Policy, Institute for Educational Leadership, 1992); and Harold Hodgkinson, Janice Hamilton Duttz, and Anita Obarakpor, *The Nation and the States* (Washington, D.C.: Center for Demographic Policy, Institute for Educational Leadership, 1992).
2. Paul E. Barton and Richard J. Coley, *Performance at the Top: From Elementary Through Graduate School* (Princeton, N.J.: Educational Testing Service, 1991).
3. Iris Rotberg, "Measuring Up to the Competition: A Few Hard Questions," *Technos,* Winter 1992, pp. 12–15.

The New Mythology About the Status of U.S. Schools
Lawrence C. Stedman

This is a warning against complacency. A flurry of recent reports have portrayed education quite positively (Bracey 1991, 1992b, 1993; Carson et al. 1993; Huelskamp 1993; Rotberg 1990). Thanks to them, we can now say confidently that U.S. schools are *not* in a general decline, but this good news is only part of the story.

No Better; No Worse

Student achievement in most subjects is at about the same level it was 10, 20, and even 30 years ago (Stedman 1993). During the 1980s, most test scores remained steady and some even improved. There was no "rising tide of mediocrity," as the Reagan administration's *A Nation at Risk* report maintained. Moreover, high school completion rates are higher than they have been in decades. The research has also successfully challenged the popular notion that in international comparisons, the United States consistently ranks near the bottom. In the most recent assessments, for example, American 9-year-olds ranked second in the world in reading and third in science, while our 14-year-olds had reading scores in the top third of the tested countries (Stedman 1994a).

Given the enormous changes in school populations and in the society at large, this generally stable educational achievement is impressive. Educators and school officials, who have felt unfairly disparaged for a decade, understandably have welcomed these findings.

The bad news is that these findings have prompted a one-sided, rosy portrait that threatens to foster complacency. This outlook—a new mythology about U.S. education—could stand in the way of much-needed educational reform.

Separating Fact From Fiction

This new mythology rests on several major claims—widely circulated as truisms in newspapers and educational journals—that are not supported by the evidence (Basler 1993, Bracey 1993, Geiger 1994, Raspberry 1993, Tanner 1993, Wilson 1994). I will assess four of these unsubstantiated claims:

- There really wasn't an SAT decline.
- Test scores are at all-time highs.

Source: *Educational Leadership*, *52*, no. 5, (February 1995): pp. 80–85. Reprinted with permission of the author.

- The top half of American students are internationally competitive.
- The crisis in education is not general; it concerns inner-city schools and poverty.

Although U.S. schools are not in a general decline, student performance remains low. Students have done well internationally in reading, but their performance has been dismal in mathematics, uneven in geography, and often poor in science—particularly at older ages. Fundamental school reforms are warranted—including far-reaching overhauls of funding, governance, organization, pedagogy, and evaluation.

Myth 1. There really wasn't an SAT decline.

The new mythology attributes the SAT decline *entirely* to demographic changes. Analysts at the Sandia National Laboratories claimed that the reason "is not decreasing student performance," but more students from the bottom half of their high school classes (Carson et al. 1993). Bracey points to the dramatic growth in minority test takers—from less than 3 percent to over 25 percent—and concluded that "no decline exists or ever existed" (1991).

In fact, changes in class rank were minor, and there was a major decline in white students' scores (Stedman 1994b, Murray and Herrnstein 1992). Factors that did depress the scores included changes in students' social class, region, type of high school, age, and birth order. In addition, more nonselective universities began requiring the SAT. According to the most careful analyses, compositional changes explain about 50–75 percent of the SAT decline (College Board Advisory Panel 1977, Morgan 1991, Stedman and Kaestle 1991). Even Harold Howe (1985), the former U.S. Commissioner of Education, who mischievously called for another SAT decline because it would mark another expansion in educational opportunity, believes that only half the decline was caused by demographic changes (1985).

The best evidence suggests that there was a real decline in SAT scores in the 1970s, particularly in verbal performance. If one believes the test measures verbal skills that are critical to academic literacy and thinking, then the decline could represent a worrisome deterioration in educational quality.

The SAT test, however, is largely one of endurance—students must answer more than 200 questions in three hours, or more than one a minute. It does not measure achievement in most high school subjects. The test's origins help explain its limitations. Carl Brigham, who created the SAT for the College Board, had helped run the Army's World War I testing program (Gould 1981). Although he later recanted, he became convinced there were racial and ethnic differences in intelligence. In developing the SAT, he copied the Army Alpha test's worst features: ranking test takers by mental aptitude rather than by academic achievement; stressing verbal and numerical gymnastics, and speed; and using analogies, antonyms, and math puzzlers. In addition, both tests suffered from a cultural bias that perniciously sorted out army draftees and college prospects.

FIGURE 1

NAEP Science Performance of 17-Year-Olds, 1969–1990

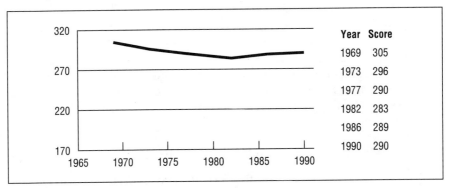

Year	Score
1969	305
1973	296
1977	290
1982	283
1986	289
1990	290

SOURCE: Data from National Center for Education Statistics, 1992.

The recent SAT revisions are largely cosmetic. Replacing the word "aptitude" with "assessment" should help the Educational Testing Service market the test in an era of authentic assessment. But the open-ended math problems will still be few, the new writing sample will be optional, and the deleted antonyms section will not be replaced by subject matter questions.

Other SAT-related evidence counters the notion of an educational decline. Scores on the College Board achievement tests—which do measure academic achievement—rose over the past decade even as more students took them. And the scores of nationally representative samples of high school students who took the PSAT, a short version of the SAT, were generally stable from the 1950s through the 1980s.

Myth 2. Test scores are at all-time highs.

Some say most test scores have been improving (Tanner 1993), but there are even stronger claims that "achievement is at an all-time high in nearly all test areas" (Wilson 1994; see also Raspberry 1993 and Bracey 1991) and that our public schools are now "better than they ever have been" (Wilson 1994; see also Bracey 1992b). Both claims are only partly supported by the evidence.

Many elementary school tests have shown improvements in reading and mathematics. Scores on some of these, such as the Iowa Tests of Basic Skills (ITBS), are indeed at all-time highs. But these gains likely were as much a result of teaching to the test as genuine improvement (Linn et al. 1990, Stedman and Kaestle 1991). The Lake Wobegone effect (Garrison Keillor's fictional town where all the children are above average) is too well established to be ignored, even in test publishers' renorming studies.

Linn and his colleagues concluded that the renorming gains were partly caused by students' "familiarity with a particular form of a test." The back-

FIGURE 2

Mathematics Performance for 13-Year-Olds, 1991 (Average Percent Correct)

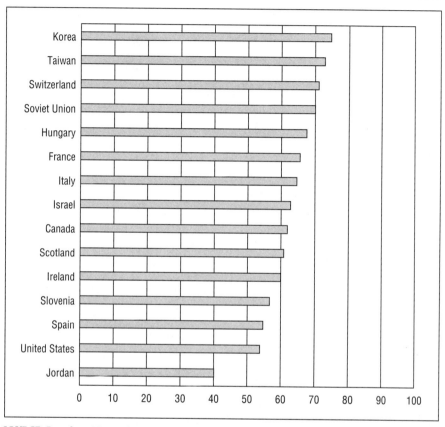

SOURCE: Data from National Center for Education Statistics, 1992.

to-basics movements of the 1980s also may have helped improve scores at the expense of learning by focusing on frequent testing and a narrow skill-based curriculum.

The secondary school test score evidence is mixed. On many indicators, these students are *not* performing as well as they once did. Reading scores on the MAT and SRA declined in recent renormings (Linn et al. 1990), and high school gains on the Stanford achievement tests evaporated in the late 1980s (Rothman 1991). Scores on the National Assessment of Educational Progress (NAEP)—our best barometer of national achievement—are also not at all-time highs. While 17-year-olds' reading and mathematics scores have been basically level, their science scores fell greatly during the 1970s and rebounded only part way during the 1980s (see Fig. 1). Their civics scores have been declining slowly since the 1970s.

NAEP reading scores of 9- and 13-year-olds have generally held steady for the last two decades.

Myth 3. Our top half is internationally competitive.

According to the new mythology, the top half of our students do well in international comparisons (Basler 1993; Bracey 1992b, 1993; Raspberry 1993; Wilson 1994). This claim originated with Westbury's research comparing American and Japanese achievement (1992, 1993). His studies, however, involved only one subject—mathematics—and used data that were more than a decade old! Back then, the top half of our 8th graders did well in arithmetic, but lagged greatly in algebra, geometry, and measurement. Popularizers have ignored Westbury's analysis of American calculus classes, which was telling because it tested our best math programs given to our best students. These classes fared poorly, substantially trailing the *average* Japanese class in every area tested (Stedman 1994a).

In recent assessments, American students have consistently performed near last in mathematics (see Fig. 2). In 1991, for example, the United States finished 14th out of the 15 countries whose populations were comprehensively sampled. The top half of our students also have not kept pace. In 1988, only 40 percent of U.S. 13-year-olds reached middle proficiency in math—the worst national performance (Lapointe et al. 1989). By contrast, 70–80 percent of the students in British Columbia, French-speaking Quebec, and Korea achieved this level.

The gaps in science were almost as large, with only 42 percent of U.S. students reaching middle proficiency. Clearer evidence supports Tanner's (1993) narrower claim that our best students—the top 10 percent—are competitive. This is true even in math and science, where our 95th percentiles match those of most other countries (National Center for Education Statistics 1992). (The 95th percentile roughly reflects the average performance of the top 10 percent.) To the extent that there is a connection between academic achievement and economic competitiveness, we need more than the top slice of our students to be world-class.

Our nation's poor position has been attributed to the misleading nature of rankings, but in math, the rankings have reflected large differences in performance (see Fig. 2). Geiger (1994), president of the National Education Association, tried to explain away the results by claiming that "most international comparisons rate *all* American students against the top 20 percent of students from other countries," but this is simply untrue.

In reading and elementary school science, American students have been among the world leaders (National Center for Education Statistics 1993). This is important and overlooked news, but even so, we have a serious problem: Our students seldom read on their own, have little outside interest in science activities, and spend far more time watching television than reading or doing school work (Stedman 1993).

FIGURE 3

Percent of High School Seniors Answering NAEP History Questions Correctly

---

68% President Abraham Lincoln wrote

the Bill of Rights

the Emancipation Proclamation

the Missouri Compromise

Uncle Tom's Cabin

43% The Missouri Compromise was the act that

granted statehood to Missouri but denied the admission of any other new states

settled the boundary dispute between Missouri and Kansas

admitted Maine into the Union as a free state and Missouri as a slave state

funded the Lewis and Clark expedition on the upper Missouri River

41% Who is associated with the founding of settlement houses to help the urban poor?

Jane Addams

Cary Nation

Susan B. Anthony

Mary McLeod Bethune

31% What is Magna Carta?

The Great Seal of the monarchs of England

The foundation of the British parliamentary system

The French Declaration of the Rights of Man

The charter signed by the Pilgrims on the Mayflower

SOURCE: Ravitch and Finn 1987.

Myth 4. The crisis in education is not general; it concerns inner-city schools and poverty.

Although the recent reports have acknowledged that education could be better—schools can always use some improvement—they explicitly reject the view that the "typical school is failing" (Bracey 1992b). Instead, these researchers have argued that reform should focus on urban minority students because the system "works well for others" (Bracey 1992a, 1993; see also Carson et al. 1993, Hodgkinson 1991, Houston and Schneider 1994).

No one familiar with Jonathan Kozol's *Savage Inequalities* could deny the pressing need to focus resources on inner-city schools, to reduce segregation, and to overhaul the educational financing system.

What is troubling, however, is that the new mythology ignores the vast body of evidence that shows that general educational performance is low and has been for decades (Stedman 1993). To cite some specifics:

- *Mathematics.* NAEP analysts recently concluded that less than half of high school seniors "appeared to have a firm grasp of 7th-grade content," and only 5 percent "attained a level of performance characterized by algebra and geometry—when most have had some course work in these subjects" (Mullis et al. 1991).

- *Reading.* In the 1992 NAEP reading assessment, only 37 percent of our seniors demonstrated proficiency, while a quarter were unable to reach the basic level.

- *Writing.* Most high school students are competent in punctuation and grammar, but have weak expository, narrative, and compositional skills. Few have performed well on the NAEP writing tests. Only about a third wrote adequate papers, and only a small percentage were able to write "elaborated" papers.

- *Literacy.* Outright illiteracy in this country is rare. Contrary to an old canard, our high schools are not graduating scores of illiterates (Stedman and Kaestle 1987). Nevertheless, our functional illiteracy rate continues to hover around 20–30 percent—meaning that millions of Americans have trouble with common day-to-day reading tasks. The latest national study of adult literacy suggests that the problems may be even more extensive (Kirsch 1993).

- *History.* Many students' basic historical knowledge is poor (see Fig. 3). In the late 1980s, national assessments showed that about two-thirds of our 17-year-olds could not date the Civil War, did not recognize Upton Sinclair and Ida Tarbell as muckrakers, and did not know that the Scopes trial dealt with evolution. A *New York Times* survey of college freshmen in the 1940s revealed similar weaknesses.

- *Geography.* In 1988, the Gallup Organization repeated a survey given to adults in 1947 and concluded that "Americans' geographic literacy has gotten worse in the last 40 years." They found that "from outline maps, the average American can identify only 1 of 12 European countries, less than 3 of 8 South American countries, and less than 6 of 10 U.S. states" (Gallup Organization 1989). Geographic knowledge was also low in the 1940s, however. Even though World War II had just ended, U.S. adults could identify only half of the major countries in Europe!

- *Civic literacy.* Civics knowledge has remained at modest levels since World War II. In spite of increased educational attainment and media coverage, the public still knows little about the structure of government, basic political and economic concepts, and major political events and issues.

- *General knowledge.* Problems with general knowledge also have a long vintage. In the late 1950s, for example, high school graduates, ages 25–36, averaged only 34–65 percent correct on items dealing with public figures, current events, history, humanities, geography, and science.

What Can Educators Do?

Where does all this leave you, as an educator? The national data may not apply to your local school district, so you should investigate the following:

- How well are *your* students learning *your* curriculum?
- Can your students demonstrate high levels of general knowledge as well as *sustained* problem-solving?

To judge this and encourage high intellectual standards, your district should consider adopting performance assessment, standardized tests of subject matter knowledge, and exhibitions of mastery for graduation. The assessments should go beyond achievement:

- Are students well-read?
- Do they have a work ethic?
- Do they have a sense of ethics, civic activism, and social responsibility?

We are, after all, preparing students to participate in a democratic society, so reform should not become a mere quest for higher test scores.

The quality of school life is also important. The environment should be safe and supportive, the students treated with respect and challenged intellectually.

I would recommend setting up teams of students, teachers, parents, community leaders, and school officials—one for each school and one for the K–12 system—to create ethnographic portraits of school life. This new form of assessment is invaluable; Elliot Eisner's work (1991) can guide the effort. The teams could use these portraits to prepare comprehensive reform plans that the public would debate.

The teams should consider proposals from across the educational spectrum—E. D. Hirsch's *Cultural Literacy,* Mortimer Adler's *Paedeia Proposal,* Ted Sizer's *Horace's Compromise,* and Ann Bastian and colleagues' *Choosing Equality* (1985). The process is as important as the product. A deliberative, democratic, and community-driven inquiry is essential; it must not be school district-directed and -dominated. In sum, while education at the national level is not deteriorating, it is certainly not succeeding. At the local level, concerned educators and community members should determine how extensively schools need to be reformed and in which directions to take them.

REFERENCES

Basler, G. (November 28, 1993). "New Schools of Thought." *Press and Sun-Bulletin:* E1.

Bastian, A., N. Fruchter, M. Gittell, C. Greer, and K. Haskins. (1985). *Choosing Equality: The Case for Democratic Schooling.* Philadelphia: Temple University Press.

Bracey, G. (October 1991). "Why Can't They Be Like We Were?" *Phi Delta Kappan:* 105-117.

Bracey, G. (March 1992a). "How Bad Are Our Schools?" *Principal:* 14-18.

Bracey, G. (October 1992b). "The Second Bracey Report on the Condition of Public Education." *Phi Delta Kappan:* 104-117.

Bracey, G. (October 1993). "The Third Bracey Report on the Condition of Public Education." *Phi Delta Kappan* 75: 104-117.

Carson, C. C., R. M. Huelskamp, and R. D. Woodall. (May/June 1993). "Perspectives on Education in America." *The Journal of Educational Research* 86: 259-310.

College Board Advisory Panel. (1977). *On Further Examination.* New York: College Board.

Eisner, E. (1991). *The Enlightened Eye.* New York: Macmillan.

Gallup Organization. (1989). *The Gallup Poll Public Opinion 1988.* Wilmington, Del.: Scholarly Resources.

Geiger, K. (March 20, 1994). "Myth, Reality, and the Public Schools." *The Washington Post:* C4.

Gould, S. J. (1981). *The Mismeasure of Man.* New York: W. W. Norton and Company.

Hodgkinson, H. (November 26, 1991). "We Know Where the Bad Schools Are?" *The Washington Post:* A20.

Houston, P., and J. Schneider. (June 1994). "Drive-by Critics and Silver Bullets." *Phi Delta Kappan* 75: 779-782.

Howe, H., II. (May 1985). "Let's Have Another SAT Decline." *Phi Delta Kappan:* 599-610.

Huelskamp, R. (May 1993). "Perspectives on Education in America." *Phi Delta Kappan:* 718-720.

Kirsch, I. S. (1993). *Adult Literacy in America.* Washington, D.C.: National Center for Education Statistics.

Lapointe, A., N. Mead, and G. Phillips. (1989). *A World of Differences.* Princeton, N.J.: Educational Testing Service.

Linn, R. L., M. E. Graue, and N. M. Sanders. (Fall 1990). "Comparing State and District Results to National Norms: The Validity of Claims That 'Everyone Is Above Average.'" *Educational Measurement: Issues and Practice:* 5-14.

Morgan, R. (1991). *Cohort Differences Associated with Trends in SAT Score Averages.* New York: College Board. (Ed 336 409)

Mullis, I. V. S., J. A. Dossey, E. H. Owen, and G. W. Phillips. (1991). *The State of Mathematics Achievement.* Washington, D.C.: U.S. Department of Education.

Murray, C., and R. J. Herrnstein. (Winter 1992). "What's Really Behind the SAT Score Decline?" *The Public Interest:* 32-56.

National Center for Education Statistics. (1992). *Condition of Education 1992.* Washington, D.C.: U.S. Department of Education.

National Center for Education Statistics. (1993). *The Digest of Educational Statistics 1993.* Washington, D.C.: U.S. Department of Education.

Raspberry, W. (October 8, 1993). "The Brighter Side of American Schools." *The Washington Post:* A27.

Ravitch, D., and C. Finn. (1987). *What Do Our 17-Year-Olds Know?* New York: Harper and Row.

Rotberg, I. (December 1990). "I Never Promised You First Place." *Phi Delta Kappan:* 29-303.

Rothman, R. (November 13, 1991). "Revisionists Take Aim at Gloomy View of Schools." *Education Week:* p. 1.

Stedman, L. C. (1993). "The Condition of Education: Why School Reformers Are on the Right Track." *Phi Delta Kappan* 75, 3: 215-225.

Stedman, L. C. (1994a). "Incomplete Explanations: The Case of U.S. Performance in the International Assessments." *Educational Researcher* 23, 7: 24-32.

Stedman, L. C. (January-February 1994b). "The Sandia Report and U.S. Achievement: An Assessment." *Journal of Educational Research:* 133-146.

Stedman, L. C., and C. F. Kaestle. (Winter 1987). "Literacy and Reading Performance in the United States, From 1880 to the Present." *Reading Research Quarterly:* 846.

Stedman, L. C., and C. F. Kaestle. (1991). "The Great Test Score Decline: A Closer Look." In *Literacy in the United States,* edited by C. F. Kaestle, H. Damon-Moore, L. C. Stedman, K. Tinsley, and W. V. Trollinger (Chapter 4). New Haven: Yale University Press.

Tanner, D. (December 1993). "A Nation 'Truly' at Risk." *Phi Delta Kappan* 75: 288-297.

Westbury, I. (1992). "Comparing American and Japanese Achievement: Is the United States Really a Low Achiever?" *Educational Researcher* 21, 5: 18-24.

Westbury, I. (1993). "American and Japanese Achievement. . . Again." *Educational Researcher* 22, 3: 21-25.

Wilson, J. C. (January 1994). "Urban Education: A Board Member's Perspective." *Phi Delta Kappan* 75: 382-386.

Chapter 11

OUTCOME-BASED EDUCATION AND PORTFOLIOS

INTRODUCTION

For the past decade, liberal-minded educators—from kindergarten through college—have attempted to, and in many instances have succeeded in, implementing plans for reforming education, the most notable of which are outcome-based education and portfolio assessment.

Associated with both of these approaches is the notion of cooperative learning. Seen by many as the educational equivalent to medicine's newest "wonder drug," cooperative learning is billed as a broad-spectrum, all-purpose teaching-learning strategy that will upgrade achievement and solve problems of motivation, even in the most difficult of our nation's classrooms. Moreover, its proponents claim, cooperative learning will not only close the "learning gap" between students from different socio-economic levels but if practiced routinely in math and science classes will obliterate the "gender gap," leading millions of school girls to high-paying careers in various scientific and technological fields.

Cooperative learning, along with the strategies of outcome-based education and portfolio assessment, has captivated the minds of many educators. Indeed, if one were to do a content analysis of proposed solutions to America's educational problems—as found in scholarly journals and academic symposia conducted in colleges of education—cooperative learning would rank first among all of the other topics discussed.

In one respect, attempts at large-scale educational reform are not new. There have been many during the past 40 years. Two notable examples are what was known as "the new math" (or "modern math") and the "open classroom." Each of these reforms was abandoned after only a few years. Whether outcome-based education, portfolio assessment, and cooperative learning will suffer the same fate as both the modern math and open classroom movements remains to be seen.

Debate Still Raging Over How Kids Should Learn
Diane Loupe

Duluth first-grader James McGehee proudly reads the paragraph he's typed out on a computer terminal:

"Wut we do in ferst grad we doo math out sid time lunch sints and riting to read."

Like millions of other students nationwide, James writes sentences like that every day with the help of IBM's "Writing to Read" program. It encourages students to express themselves without stifling them with concepts that can be taught later.

"If you correct every word, they're not going to write," said Florence Magee, a teacher at James' school, B.B. Harris Elementary. "They're going to hate it."

But in Gwinnett County, many parents regard the whole-language program as just one symbol of a misguided and dangerous movement in education.

Bobbi Davis believes Writing to Read did more harm than good for her 9-year-old son, Rob.

"I don't believe Rob learned to spell well. Learning has been more difficult, trying to unlearn bad habits," she said.

Bronwynn McGehee, James' mother, gushes with praise for Harris and its whole-language program:

"They're not getting yelled at because they're not spelling everything correctly. They're proud of themselves because they're writing their own stories."

Exactly the point, language arts experts say after years of testing the program at schools across the country, where students of all skill levels are demonstrating improved reading and writing abilities.

But here and across the nation, political and religious conservatives complain that the Gwinnett program and dozens of others like it "dumbs down" schools and puts their children at a competitive disadvantage.

Those conflicting viewpoints symbolize a confrontation that has shaken Gwinnett for the past year. The debate has divided parents' groups, dominated newspapers' editorial pages and spurred voters to oust two school board members last summer.

The controversial Gwinnett programs came to be defined loosely, and often inaccurately, as outcomes-based education (OBE), a business-driven reform movement intended to shift educators' focus from what students are taught to what they have learned.

SOURCE: *The Atlanta Journal/The Atlanta Constitution*, October 16, 1994, pp. D1; D10. Reprinted with permission from *The Atlanta Journal/Constitution*.

At its core, the OBE movement intends to ensure that students fully understand the material and have not simply memorized it. But detractors say it abrogates parental authority, violates children's privacy and scuttles academics with its concern for values and behavior.

Parents in Clayton, Henry and Hall counties also have warned their school boards against adopting OBE techniques.

But the Gwinnett programs included some that might be found in any American classroom: mainstreaming of special education students, cooperative learning, peer tutoring, conflict mediation, mastery learning.

Despite few changes in classroom procedures, the Gwinnett furor has subsided a year after it started. But there are signs it may not be over:

- Superintendent George Thompson, a frequent target of OBE critics, said Monday he will resign to take a job at an educational think tank by Dec. 31, the day before a new, divided school board is sworn in.
- Two new board members take office in January after waging anti-OBE campaigns. One new member, Dan Seckinger, decried the "edu-crats" who favor "reforms at all costs" and wants to scale back the whole-language program that employs the Writing to Read software.

And member-elect Bob McClure urges caution about further reforms. "We have to be careful to adopt an 80,000-student experiment," he said. "If you set a hurdle everybody can jump over, it has to be a pretty low hurdle."

- One Christian school opened this fall in Gwinnett with 123 students, crediting its enrollment in part to dissatisfied Gwinnett parents. Families in the county are home-schooling 1,175 students this year, 143 more than last year.
- At Harris, a focal point for the OBE debate, a number of parents have placed their children in private school or home schooling. Enrollment is down from a projected 1,200 to 1,100, although there are no verified explanations for the disparity.

Thompson said he's not being driven out, but OBE critics applaud his departure. Others fear the controversy may make it harder to recruit a new superintendent.

Much of the criticism dealt with techniques that were said to focus too much attention on "at-risk" children or that emphasized group learning over individual performance.

"They're trying to do away with individuality, with groups and group grades, and doing away with competition," said parent Doug Ford. "I don't believe you can hope to do the best for each kid if you throw into one big pool all levels of academic achievement."

Martha Brady, Gwinnett's director of elementary schools, calls it the "scarcity mentality," a feeling that "some children because of their needs will demand more, and therefore my child, who does not need as much, will not get enough."

For now, Gwinnett's critics appear largely to have been silenced by the school system's response. Officials convened focus groups, hired consultants to survey parents' attitudes, discontinued some programs and slowed the pace of others, and replaced a thick, jargon-filled master plan of educational goals in favor of a much thinner and less specific document.

Nevertheless, at least a dozen parents pulled their children from B. B. Harris, saying they couldn't risk their future on an educational strategy that may not work.

"I wasn't willing to gamble these precious years by putting her in a situation where I wasn't confident she was going to excel," said Anne Schultz, who withdrew her 7-year-old daughter, Emily, for home schooling.

"My friends had bright fourth- and fifth-graders who didn't know basic math facts and wrote run-on sentences," she said.

Gwinnett's anti-OBE movement was fueled in part by the rhetoric of Christian conservatives. Church leaders were among the critics, and detractors studied anti-OBE literature distributed by national religious right groups. As the unrest developed, Phyllis Schlafly's Eagle Forum held a daylong conference in Atlanta with a seminar on OBE.

School officials say critics misrepresented the classroom changes and other proposed programs. They say parents erroneously claimed the school system was committed to year-round schooling and to eliminating grades and the gifted program—ideas that were only points for discussion.

Thompson said such tactics are chilling reform efforts and that some school systems avoid certain new programs for fear of attacks by OBE opponents.

"You'll have a hard time convincing me it's not a political issue," Thompson said. "It's very much like McCarthyism."

The anti-OBE parents at Harris and other schools emphatically deny they are pawns of the religious right. They contend the labels make it easy for school officials to dismiss them.

Many said they felt a professional arrogance from educators. Linda Bubb said she moved her second-grader to private school when she couldn't get a satisfactory explanation for the academic reasons for the new programs.

"When we asked questions, we became a problem," Bubb said. "They nodded, smiled and didn't hear a word we said."

Third-grade teacher Jinny Hayden said Harris' emphasis has shifted from rote skills to more complex problem-solving, which better prepares students for secondary school, college and life after graduation.

"We teach children what to do with the facts," said Hayden.

Thompson said he has come to believe that some parents won't be satisfied with *anything* the school system does.

"On no issue do we make all people happy," he said. "It's impossible to do that."

Outcome-Based Education: Kentucky's Approach
Linda Olasov

Educational instruction in Kentucky has undergone massive changes as a result of the Kentucky Education Reform Act of 1990 (KERA); it is now outcomes-based. Six learning goals, desirable and achievable by all of the commonwealth's students, were developed in response to the needs and concerns of its citizens. Learning outcomes, developed by state-wide task forces of teachers, administrators and university faculty, further define what students should know and be able to do.

For education, times are changing, and nowhere is this more true than in the Commonwealth of Kentucky. The Kentucky Supreme Court declared Kentucky's schools unconstitutional in 1989, a response to a class-action suit brought by several school districts serving very poor communities. The court found that the common school finance system in Kentucky was unconstitutional. It also cited major inequities in student achievement and governance issues. The Kentucky Education Reform Act (KERA) was a legislative response to this Kentucky Supreme Court mandate requiring the educational system to undergo massive changes so that every child in the commonwealth would be provided with an equal opportunity to have an adequate education.

One of the major components of that change, indeed one of the most significant, was curricular reform; there were concerns that Kentucky students would not be prepared to live in a competitive world. Kentucky business and industry also expressed concern about the education level of a potential work force. To address these concerns about what Kentucky students should know and be able to do, as well as how to assess the results, the governor appointed a twelve-member Council on School Performance Standards (CSPS). By talking directly to employers, parents, community leaders, and 800 Kentuckians surveyed by phone, the council translated the expectations and concerns into six learning goals.

Six Broad Learning Goals

Six broad school goals were incorporated into KERA, and the CSPS was charged with further defining these goals so that they could be measured. The goals are for students:

- to possess basic communication and math skills for purposes and situations similar to those encountered in life;

SOURCE: *The Delta Kappa Gamma Bulletin, 60,* no. 3, (Spring 1994): pp. 26–30. Reprinted by permission of The Delta Kappa Gamma Society International.

- to apply core concepts and principles from mathematics, sciences, humanities, social studies, and practical living skills (health education, home economics, physical education) to situations or problems similar to those encountered in life;
- to be self-sufficient;
- to demonstrate productive group membership in a family, work group or community;
- to think and problem solve in both school situations and a variety of other situations similar to those encountered in life; and
- to connect and integrate experiences and new knowledge from all subject matter fields into her/his own existing knowledge base.

Since teachers would be teaching toward the goals, the goals must contain what is essential and most important to learn. They should describe what is expected for all students. Learner outcomes are not defined as minimum competencies, but as standards of performance for educated citizens.[1]

Learner outcomes, then, are a further definition of Kentucky's six broad learning goals. They were determined by eleven task forces chosen by the CSPS and composed of teachers, school administrators, college professors and representatives from Kentucky's Department of Education. The 125 members of the task forces represented a broad geographic area. Working during 1990–1991, they identified and described seventy-five learner outcomes related to the six learning goals named in the reform law.

Learner outcomes require students to demonstrate that they can use skills and knowledge in situations they might experience in life; for example, writing a business letter, producing a report, making an oral or video presentation, solving a problem, creating a new product, choosing and supporting the best course of action, and working independently or in groups. These performances are called *learner* outcomes because they are learner centered, and they actively involve the learner in every phase of the assessment and instructional process. They are outcomes-based; learning is assessed through authentic tasks or products that are useful or significant to life experiences.[2]

Learner outcomes are not detailed descriptions of all the knowledge and individual skills students will have to acquire in order to achieve each outcome, but are broad statements of what is essential for a Kentucky graduate to know and to be able to do. *Transformations: Kentucky's Curriculum Framework* was developed by the Kentucky Department of Education in 1992 and was disseminated to local school districts. It suggests related content for each of the seventy-five learner outcomes as well as learning strategies and resources for the classroom teacher in order to implement Outcomes-Based Education (OBE) in public schools.

Assessment

Learner outcomes must be measurable. KERA mandated that all Kentucky students would be assessed in grades four, eight and twelve. Assessment takes three forms: traditional paper and pencil tests, like those given by the National Assessment for Education Progress; event tasks which can be completed the same day or in a class period by a student and which require the application of knowledge and skills in situations similar to those they might encounter in real life; and lastly, longer assignment tasks that may take students several days to complete and may require the work of an individual student or the collaborative efforts of a group of students. This performance task might measure the outcome of an entire unit, module or grading period. Examples of student assessment efforts and work are maintained in a portfolio available for parents and students to see.

The following are examples of event tasks and performance tasks in health education at grades four, eight and twelve.

Learner Outcome   Students demonstrate effective individual and family life skills. Related concepts are relationships with family, peers, dating, marriage; rights and responsibilities in relationships; parenting; human life cycle, relationship skills, sexuality, personal safety/prevention of family violence; family crisis related to divorce, suicide, blended families, teen pregnancy, death and dying, and substance abuse.

GRADE 4—EVENT TASK

You and your sister or brother argue constantly about the use of the television. Your parents have stated that they will take television privileges away from both of you unless you can come to an agreement and share the television. Through a role-playing situation you are to come up with three possible solutions to the problem. The role play between you and another student who plays your sister or brother should be conducted in a positive manner with no yelling or name calling. Decide what the two of you did right in the problem-solving process. Determine what things you could have done better.

GRADE 4—PORTFOLIO TASK

Students keep a journal for two weeks, reacting to a scenario such as a parent being hospitalized, a sibling being confined to a wheelchair, a new baby in the family, or a grandparent moving in with the family. The journal should cite resulting problems for the family and individual family members, inner personal feelings of the student, and possible adaptations.

GRADE 8—EVENT TASK

The class is divided into four groups to generate possible solutions, role play, and be videotaped while presenting to the class the following case studies:

(1) gossip; (2) peer pressure concerning sexual relationships; (3) copying homework; and (4) friends using others for an alibi with parents.

GRADE 8—PORTFOLIO TASK

Student teams react to the following situation and write an article for the school newspaper regarding a blended family. The eighth grader's mother has recently remarried; the family now includes a man and his children (ages 5, 13 and 17). The student will now share a room with the thirteen-year-old. Students brainstorm for ways to make the transition easier, including ways to assume responsibility of family chores, share rooms, and communicate effectively.

GRADE 12—EVENT TASK

Students research and write an article for the student newspaper highlighting the problems relating to premarital sex (e.g., teen pregnancy, sexually transmitted diseases, HIV/AIDS, dropout rate, and emotional/social problems).

GRADE 12—PORTFOLIO TASK

Students research activities that address the social-emotional needs of a four-year-old. Students plan and carry through with a nursery school program for a three-hour block of time for one week. Activities might include a learning activity, musical activity, group game, refreshments and a rest period.

The examples described define outcomes-based education; that is, they clearly articulate what students should know and be able to do. In defining these outcomes, it is critical that educators focus on learning that really matters: content related to meaningful understanding and expressions of concepts, higher-order thinking skills, and capacities required in our modern information-based society. Contexts for learning must be authentic, that is, related to students' present life experiences and similar to what they will encounter in their future. And, finally, educators must provide demonstrations that engage students in role performances related to situations which are engaging, open-ended, and realistic.

The Kentucky Department of Education has developed and published *Transformations: Kentucky's Curriculum Framework,* a two-volume work designed to provide direction to teachers as they design student-centered curriculum, instruction and assessment. Volume II contains material that addresses outcomes-based education, making connections across disciplines, alternative ways of learning, curriculum and assessment connections, technology and multicultural education. It presents ways in which the learning environment can be transformed to foster sustained learning for all students. In addition, it outlines a process ensuring that instruction is organized around meaningful and real-life issues, problems, or questions, that the major focus of a unit is aligned with the learning goals and outcomes, that content is used as a vehicle for teaching the learning goals and outcomes, and that curriculum is aligned with assessment.

This new outcomes-based education will require change in what we teach and how we teach in every discipline. Some teachers have always provided students with authentic, experiential opportunities for learning and evaluation because of a philosophical belief in the efficacy of this pedagogical approach; for them there will be few changes. They believe that transfer of learning and behavior change are most likely to occur with this approach.

Expectations

With the shift to outcomes-based education, students and educators are expected to move: [3]

- from focusing on knowledge and skills to focusing on the completion of tasks with a quality performance,
- from searching for the one right answer to selecting and supporting the most appropriate solution for alternatives generated,
- from progressing through a scope and sequence curriculum to revisiting key skills and concepts on a developmental path from novice to expert,
- from measuring aptitude to assessing performance that is a product of ability and effort,
- from relying on textbooks for content to using a variety of experiences and materials as content for learning,
- from confining learning to classroom experiences to using resources for learning wherever they may be found,
- from restricting enrichment experiences to the gifted and talented to providing interesting and exciting learning experiences for all students,
- from reproducing knowledge to producing knowledge through thinking, problem solving and reflection,
- from assessment as a distinct event to assessment as a "dip stick" in the process of learning,
- from learning in separate disciplines to integrating learning across disciplines.

As expected, this kind of educational revolution in Kentucky requires inservice programs, as well as revamping teacher preparation programs in state colleges and universities in order to prepare current and future teachers for the new instructional perspective. Thomas C. Boysen, Kentucky Commissioner of Education, asserts that "the achievement of the school reform goals will be an even greater step for the nation's education than landing on the moon was for the space program." [4]

In December 1991, the governing body for Kentucky education, the State Board for Elementary and Secondary Education, adopted outcomes-based education. By law all changes will be in place in all Kentucky public schools by 1996. The foundation for improved education is in place, the future will tell when the vision "to guarantee every child an internationally superior education and a love for learning"[5] will become a reality.

REFERENCES

1. Council on School Performance Standards. "Kentucky's Learning Goals and Valued Outcomes." Technical Report. Draft, September 1991: 4.
2. Ibid.: 5.
3. Ibid.: 90.
4. Pankratz, Roger S. "Frankfort Hotline: Kentucky's Shared Vision of Schooling." *KAHPERD Journal,* 27(1). Spring 1991: 6-12.
5. Council on School Performance Standards: 10.

Traditionalist Christians and OBE: What's the Problem?
Arnold Burron

Any attempt to speak for Christians on any point of controversy may just lend credence to the adage "Fools rush in where angels fear to tread." Christians—even so-called Fundamentalist Christians—no more speak with one voice than do Hispanics, African Americans, or any other identifiable group. Nevertheless, as a Traditionalist Christian and a university professor who has presented public school informational seminars to Traditionalist Christians throughout the United States, I would like to offer some insights about the "Religious Right" that may be of help to public school educators.

What Educators Should Know

Public educators appear to be woefully ignorant of Traditionalist Christians' belief in *supersessionism,* the belief in the exclusivity of Christianity that states that

SOURCE: *Educational Leadership, 51,* no. 6, (March 1994): pp. 73-75. Reprinted with permission of the Association for Supervision and Curriculum Development. Copyright © 1994 by ASCD. All rights reserved.

only through faith in Jesus Christ's atonement can eternal salvation be attained. This belief has a profound influence on how this group of Christians responds to OBE.

If Christianity is the only true religion, assert Traditionalist Christians, then any element of the curriculum that propounds that all religions are equally valid and acceptable—as opposed to teaching that all people have an equally valid and acceptable *right to practice* whatever religion they choose—threatens the eternal well-being of their children. Further, because they believe that their eternal well-being is more important than any temporal tranquillity, they will relentlessly oppose any attempts to deprecate their concerns about what they see as the public schools' insidious inculcation of universalism.

Public educators may disagree with this exclusivity; nonetheless, supersessionism is the sine qua non of the Traditionalist Christian viewpoint and the source of almost all Traditionalist criticisms of the curriculum. Any aspect of public schooling that detracts from this belief or from the moral values associated with it will evoke opposition. Knowing this fact could help public educators respond to challenges sensitively and judiciously.

A second important point to consider is that Traditionalist Christians link topics as diverse as the debate over whole language versus synthetic phonics, multicultural education, social services on campus, and site-based management to OBE. For example, the lack of structure in the whole language philosophy appears to be consistent with what they see as deliberate attempts by restructuring proponents to achieve ambiguously stated objectives in OBE. Traditionalist Christians respond emotionally to these issues, and because they fail to prioritize their relative importance, they treat whole language phonics with the same gravity as, say, globalism: all are "subversive." Public educators should be aware that apparently minor issues may be seen as significant because of their perceived ties to OBE.

Closely related to the failure to discriminate among issues is the fact that some Traditionalist Christians are not well-informed about specific details of issues. Neither their public school administrators nor their Christian leaders have presented them with a balanced analysis of the issues. Public school educators may find themselves attempting to explain something that their audience may not have the background to understand. Again using whole language versus phonics as an example, many of these Christians will either not know about the different kinds of phonics approaches, or they will have been programmed to reject any attempt to teach reading using an analytic approach. Approaches that do not have a clearly defined scope and sequence, they believe, lead to nebulous goals and subjective outcomes.

Most Traditionalist Christians, however, are eager to learn, and they have been receptive to presentations that challenged their most cherished notions, provided that they see the presentations as objective. If they believe that public educators will listen, they also welcome suggestions on how to diplomatically present their concerns. Unfortunately, experience has led them to anticipate that they will be stonewalled and their concerns will be disparaged. Educators seem neither to desire nor respect their input. As a result, they often resort to aggressively presenting their concerns.

Although Traditionalist Christians agree that OBE contradicts their values, there is no consensus on the specific elements of OBE to which they object. Participants at my presentations have raised a number of points that could be summarized in two major concerns: they object to affective emphases in content courses, and they oppose the covert indoctrination of social, political, and economic values.

Concerns About Affective Goals

An objective from *Maine's Common Core of Learning* illustrates how a seemingly benign objective, if couched in ambiguous terminology, can evoke controversy:

> Students with a common core of knowledge work cooperatively and actively in group decision making, whether in small groups or in the larger society; are able to listen, share opinions, negotiate, compromise, and help the group reach consensus.

Traditionalist Christians challenge this objective because it seems to promote relativism as a desirable goal. They object to fostering the abilities to "compromise" and "reach consensus" when such practices could lead in certain situations to capitulation to group pressure or to approval of behaviors that a Traditionalist interpretation of Christian Scriptures prohibits, such as homosexuality. They fear that their children's advocacy of moral absolutes, which preclude their having an attitude of "tolerance" or other secularly sanctioned "virtues," will detrimentally affect their children's grades and academic placement. They believe that their children will have to demonstrate politically correct behaviors, and that the goals, processes (such as group problem solving and cooperative learning), and evaluations used in OBE deliberately attempt to undermine their children's values, individuality, and commitment to personal responsibility.

Both public educators and Traditionalist Christians need to understand one another's perspectives on the question of ambiguous, affective outcomes. Most Traditionalist Christians, when presented with hypothetical situations that illustrate how their children are affected by classmates who do not know how to achieve peaceful compromise, begin to understand why such OBE objectives have been formulated. Yet I have found no evidence of an equal level of understanding on the part of public educators regarding the concerns many of these Christians have about formalizing affective goals. How many educators understand that many Traditionalist Christians view a goal such as Maine's "Have a basic understanding of the changing roles and rights of women and men" as being diametrically opposed to their belief that the husband is the head of the house and the wife is the helpmeet who is to submit to the husband's authority? How many educators would attempt to accommodate this concern?

Concerns About Indoctrination

In addition to concerns about affective objectives, Traditionalist Christians believe schools using OBE are indoctrinating children with social, political, and economic values in subjects such as science, health, social studies, and the visual and performing arts. Environmentalism, globalism, and multiculturalism are supplanting ideas such as the prudent utilization of resources, "my-country-right-or-wrong" patriotism, and America the melting pot. Many of the views presented on political issues such as gun control, abortion, homosexual activism, and the welfare state violate deeply held Traditionalist Christian beliefs.

Traditionalist Christians have, for some time, asserted that indoctrination has been occurring within traditional education, but OBE exacerbates their concern. OBE, they say, makes covert indoctrination overt. Ambiguously worded objectives legitimize the politicization of the classroom and the curriculum, and they sanction educators to "come out of the closet" with political perspectives antithetical to those embraced by most of these Christians—perspectives students will be held accountable to when demonstrating various outcomes.

Concerns About Process

In addition to these two major concerns, the process by which OBE and other restructuring initiatives have been adopted disturbs Traditionalist Christians. Many of them feel manipulated or disenfranchised by their public servants, some of whom they perceive as duplicitous or dishonest.

For example, one state legislator approached me at a restructuring seminar and showed me an invitation he had received to an institute at Harvard University on reform in public education. A session-by-session analysis of the agenda could be the subject of a whole article on why the process of achieving reform angers Traditionalist Christians, particularly as it relates to OBE. The description of the last formal presentation of the conference says:

> The most difficult part of systemic reform is not in finding consensus with each other. . . the hardest task may be in "selling" the package to the public. . . . This session examines how legislators can package education reform and offers suggestions for dealing with vocal opposition groups.

The conference sponsors appear to assume that legislators, presumably invited to discuss the need for and the nature of reform, will buy into all the reforms presented, that consensus will be achieved, that the specifics of the reforms will need to be "packaged" and "sold" to the public, and that opposition will be stifled. Traditionalist Christians have too frequently noted a similar arrogance on the part of their public school administrators when they implement OBE.

■ ■ ■

Using Students' Portfolios to Assess Mathematical Understanding
Harold Asturias

■ ■ ■

Portfolios have long been used successfully to evaluate a student's work in the arts and writing. In recent years, mathematics teachers have used portfolios in their classrooms to make instructional decisions. The mathematics education community is currently trying to define what it means to use mathematics portfolios as a way to assess what students are learning.

Why Use Portfolios in the Mathematics Classroom?

The use of portfolios to assess students' progress toward important goals offers many advantages.

As students begin to work on portfolios, they take an active role and assume some responsibility in their own assessment. When they judge the quality of their work while selecting the pieces to be included, they begin to reflect on their own learning and on ways to improve it. Portfolios contrast with on-demand assessment in that they allow students to include work at different stages of completion as drafts, revisions, and final versions. In so doing, students can include pieces of longer, sustained work completed in and outside the classroom.

As a work in progress, portfolios show students and their teachers concrete evidence of the progress made toward preestablished goals and yield more information about what and how students learn than do other, more traditional forms of assessment. Continually examining the contents of the portfolios in

SOURCE: *The Mathematics Teacher, 87,* no. 6, (December 1994): pp. 698–700. Copyright © December 1994 by the National Council of Teachers of Mathematics. All rights reserved. Reprinted with permission.

progress presents opportunities for midcourse adjustments that students and teachers can make in their instructional interaction.

■ ■ ■

Create a Portfolio Culture in the Classroom

Making portfolios an integral part of their instructional day remains a challenge for many mathematics teachers. The following suggestions can help teachers create a portfolio culture and make portfolio use a worthwhile classroom routine for themselves and their students.

- Make students responsible for keeping their portfolios up to date and organized and containing the work they consider most representative of themselves as learners of mathematics.
- Use portfolios on an ongoing basis rather than only at the end of a period of time or on specific days.
- View portfolios as part of the learning process rather than merely as record-keeping tools, as a way to stimulate and enhance students' learning of mathematics. Portfolios allow students to include work on topics in which they have a particular interest or extended pieces of work they have been creating over time.
- Create a shared, clear purpose for using portfolios. Students should clearly understand whether they are creating their portfolios for self-reflection about their learning, for a parent–teacher spring conference, or as a special exhibit for an external assessor.
- Share the criteria that will be used to assess the work in the portfolios as well as ways in which the results are to be used. Students should be familiar with the rubrics used to assess their work, how each piece counts, and how the scores they get in their portfolios affect their overall evaluation.
- Give students access to their portfolios. Students will then take responsibility for their portfolios, and teachers can implement their use daily. The main responsibility for managing the portfolios should rest with the students.
- Create multiple opportunities for feedback on the use of the portfolios from student to student, teacher to student, and so on. During these periodic conferences, students can discuss with each other the value of different pieces of work they want to place in their portfolios. Another example includes conferences in which teachers can discuss the use of portfolios with their students.

How to Assess the Portfolios

On the basis of individual needs, decide ahead of time how students' work included in their portfolios will be assessed and communicate that decision to them. One portfolio-assessment effort under development involves a joint venture by New Standards and Balanced Assessment. (The New Standards is an effort to set national standards for assessment: Balanced Assessment is a National Science Foundation-funded project to create "balanced" assessment packages to be used by teachers, schools, districts, states, and so on.) The following, though a work in progress, illustrates one way to evaluate the portfolios to promote balance—a representative variety rather than coverage—in the work included in the portfolio. Using *A Framework for Balance* (Daro 1993), which defines this balance, Figure 1 suggests dimensions to be assessed in the portfolios.

What to Include in the Portfolio

The items that students include in their portfolios are tied to the general purpose for which it is created. The New Standards portfolio asks students to give evidence of the various topics they are studying by using (1) investigations and (2) gap fillers. Five investigations are defined: statistical survey studies, mathematical model[s] of experimental data, designs for physical structures, resource planning and managing, and pure mathematical investigations.

In Figure 2, students are asked to include three different investigations out of the five described.

Even though the investigations clearly address more than one particular standard, other standards or topics are not sampled. When students collaborate with their teachers to identify gaps in the content of their portfolios, they will be asked to include medium and small-sized pieces of work to fill those gaps.

Conclusion

Portfolio use is a powerful tool that helps students become responsible for their own learning. It stimulates students' thinking by connecting other areas of study with their lives outside the classroom. The self-assessment aspect makes students aware of areas that need improvement. Students gain a deeper understanding of the concepts they are learning and are able to communicate better mathematically. Portfolios are instrumental in working with students to meet high expectations and perform to the NCTM's Standards. In short, portfolio use is one of the best venues through which educators can ensure mathematical power for all students.

FIGURE 1

New Standards/Balanced Assessment Portfolio Assessment: Dimensions for Balance

Communication

Students will be expected to demonstrate their ability to communicate their mathematical ideas effectively by using a range of tools to do so. Some of these tools might include, but not be limited to, a picture, diagram, sketch, table, chart, spreadsheet, coordinate graph, equation, formula, prose, oral discussion, model, map, manipulatives, network, tree, matrix.

Problem Solving

Four main aspects of problem solving to be assessed in the portfolios are *understanding, approach, decisions,* and *generalizations.*

Content

The content standards for grades 9–12 are outlined in the *Curriculum and Evaluation Standards* (NCTM 1989). The goal is not to include a piece of work in each and every standard but rather to present a collection of pieces of work that show the various topics that students have studied in their mathematics classes. Some pieces of student work will exemplify more than one of those standards.

Circumstances of Performance

Another dimension that should be balanced across the portfolio is the various circumstances under which students do mathematical work. Three main aspects of the actual work follow:

- Time—two to three class periods, one to two weeks, three weeks or longer
- People—individual, group, interacting with teacher, peer feedback
- Resources—information and tools

Reflection

Reflection is an essential part of the portfolio. It renders insight into students' thinking as they do their work and justifies the choices of work that students include in their portfolios. Reflecting is also a tool for self assessment, which allows students to judge the quality of their own work as well as to demonstrate how they have grown as learners of mathematics.

Adapted from Daro 1993.

FIGURE 2

Investigations: Kinds of Work to Include in the Portfolio

Students must choose three investigations from the five described here.

Statistical Survey Studies

Students identify, investigate, and draw conclusions about a social question or situation of interest to them or their community. This activity entails making decisions about how to collect and display data as well as drawing conclusions and making recommendations after interpreting those data.

At the high school level, students could investigate the attendance patterns of students at their own school and neighboring schools and compare them. In carrying out the investigation they would summarize, analyze, and transform the data to test hypotheses and draw inferences. In their report they would include the raw data; a representation of the data in charts, tables, or graphs; a description of the adjustments they made as they collected the data; the conclusions they reached; and how tests help validate their inferences. This investigation would last three to six weeks during which students revise their projects. Those revisions are included as part of their report and taken into consideration when drawing conclusions from the data collected.

Mathematical Model of Experimental Data

Students choose a physical phenomenon to investigate. They identify and collect the relevant data and develop a mathematical model for that phenomenon using the data they have collected. Finally they draw conclusions about the applicability and limitations of their model.

At the high school level, students might investigate the geometry of shadows and create a mathematical model to represent their findings.

Designs for Physical Structures

Students design and produce an item from the areas of architecture, engineering, art, or city planning. Students' work on the design should focus on two perspectives:

1. Product—setting or meeting the criteria for a design and demonstrating an understanding of how the finished work meets these criteria.
2. Process—communicating the design and the process of carrying it out clearly enough so that another person could understand the design and reproduce it or use it.

At the high school level, students might design, make, and advertise a proposed fund-raising game based on probability. Their product would

(continued)

(continued from previous page)

include the game itself or a picture of it, a full description of how it works, and clear communication about how to build it and use it. Students could devise, test, and vary the game according to cost per play, number of players, probability of winning, size of prize, or payoff. They could predict the amount of funds the game would raise under certain conditions then enact those conditions.

Resource Planning and Managing

Students work on projects that allow them to show what they can do in the areas of risk analysis, planning and scheduling, design of games, software design, and optimization.

At the high school level, students could investigate the system design of manufacturing factories and evaluate the effectiveness of the system by testing different alternatives. They would define constraints, goals, alternative plans of production, recommendations, and justifications for their choices.

Pure Mathematical Investigation

Students formulate the mathematical questions about which they are curious. They pose a question, note a phenomenon, identify a pattern. or make an observation. Their exploration of the mathematical idea may or may not lead to a single, definitive solution; the investigation may proceed along several fronts or in an idiosyncratic sequence; real-life applications may not be apparent to the student. Students do, though, record the discoveries and connections they have made as well as their analysis of the question, phenomenon or pattern with which they began. Many explorations will take students up blind alleys, just as with mathematicians. Exploring blind alleys are valid investigations.

At the high school level, students could explore the limits of the magic-square problem ("Using the numbers 1–9 once each, arrange them in a 3 × 3 grid so that the sum of each row, each column, and each diagonal is the same"). Students could produce a series of mathematical questions that vary the conditions of the magic square, present solutions or explain why a solution is impossible, and relate the mathematical significance of their findings. Questions students might pose and test include the following: Does more than one way exist to solve it, or only one? Can one construct a magic square with the sequence 1, 3, 5, 7, . . . ? Can one do it with 2, 4, 6, 8, . . . ? Will every sequence work? With the original problem, the sum of every row, column, and diagonal is 15. Could a set of workable numbers sum to 21? Could they sum to 22? Can one construct magic squares of 4 × 4? Magic squares of 5 × 5? If so, what are their properties?

BIBLIOGRAPHY

Daro, P. *A Framework for Balance.* Oakland, Calif.: The New Standards Project, 1993.

Kuhs, Therese M. "Implementing the *Curriculum and Evaluation Standards:* Portfolio Assessment: Making It Work for the First Time." *Mathematics Teacher* 87 (May 1994):332–35.

Mumme, Judith. *Portfolio Assessment in Mathematics.* Santa Barbara, Calif.: University of California, 1990.

National Council of Teachers of Mathematics. *Curriculum and Evaluation Standards for School Mathematics.* Reston, Va.: The Council, 1989.

———. *Professional Standards for Teaching Mathematics.* Reston, Va.: The Council, 1991.

———. *Assessment Standards for School Mathematics.* Working draft. Reston, Va.: The Council, 1994.

Petit, Marge. *Getting Started: Vermont Mathematics Portfolio—Learning How to Show Your Best!* Cabot, Vt.: Cabot School, 1992.

Stenmark, Jean Kerr, ed. *Assessment Alternatives in Mathematics: An Overview of Assessment Techniques That Promote Learning.* Berkeley, Calif.: University of California, 1989.

———. *Mathematics Assessment: Myths, Models, Good Questions, and Practical Suggestions.* Reston, Va.: National Council of Teachers of Mathematics, 1991.

Portfolios Fine-Tuned in Vermont
Sally Johnson

MONTPELIER, Vermont—With five years' experience behind them, Vermont educators are fine tuning the state's pioneering portfolio assessment program with an eye toward making a good system better.

As "outcomes-based assessment" becomes increasingly popular across the country, specialists at the Vermont Department of Education are using results compiled since the project began in 1990 to fix the glitches and find out what teachers think of the system.

Nationally, the project has received so much favorable attention that late last month IBM awarded the state $2 million to help computerize and expedite portfolio assessments. It was the third of 10 awards IBM is making nationally as part of its $5 million "Reinventing Education" campaign. In a ceremony at the IBM plant in South Burlington, IBM chairman Louis Gerstner Jr. said Vermont "passed the first and only test: a commitment to fundamental reform."

SOURCE: *The Boston Globe,* May 21, 1995, pp. 101; 103. Reprinted with permission of the author.

In general, educators of every stripe, from state education officials to principals and teachers, give high marks to the portfolio system, which is designed to assess how well students can read, write and reason based on a compilation of their schoolwork. Supporters say portfolios offer a broader view of a student's ability to reason and communicate than do standardized tests.

"We're learning lots of wonderful things through this system," said Sue Rigney, coordinator of the Vermont Assessment Project at the State Department of Education. "Teachers are telling me that the quality of student work has improved dramatically."

Detractors, even some of those who admire the program conceptually, lament the amount of time needed to assess the portfolios and the time and money necessary to train teachers. Some educators also are concerned that the growing pressure to hold schools accountable for student performance may cause the public and the state to draw unfair comparisons between richer and poorer districts.

"The comparing of schools and the public reporting of results is what I worry about," said Laura Johnson, principal of the East Montpelier Elementary School, noting that a few samples of work collected from a tiny rural school may not give a true picture of student achievement there. "The threat exists that a poorly achieving school may suffer a loss of state funding."

The concept behind portfolios, which are gaining popularity around the country, is that a student's written work is a better indicator of educational achievement than a fill-in-the-boxes test, which can determine only whether an answer is right or wrong, not how well it was reasoned out.

In the arena of language arts, educators are interested in whether a student's writing conveys organization and a sense of purpose in clear, articulate prose. In math, they want to see whether a student can analyze a problem and then come up with a logical solution.

This year, to understand better what classroom teachers think of portfolios, Majorie Lipson and Jim Mosenthal, reading specialists from the University of Vermont, are surveying fifth-grade teachers around the state to see how they are implementing the writing portfolios.

"This issue hasn't been studied from a teacher's point of view," said Lipson, who won a grant from the Spencer Foundation to carry out the survey. "As a general proposition, we've been impressed by what teachers are willing to take on."

Still, says Johnson of East Montpelier Elementary, "My teachers would agree that it's a good system, but they don't like the amount of time and effort involved. One of my teachers counted a total of 20 days out of the classroom for training."

Portfolio assessments were instituted in 1990 as a pilot program in 138 Vermont schools. By the second year, the program was extended to all of the state's 322 primary and secondary public schools. In the 1994–95 school year, all but six public schools chose to participate.

Portfolios are but one piece of a national education reform effort to revise teaching practices, both in terms of curriculum and testing. So far, variations of portfolio assessments, some mandatory and some, as in Vermont, voluntary, are in use in Arizona, California, Kentucky, Maine and New Mexico.

The Vermont Assessment Project begins as an interaction between students and classroom teachers. Before school ends in June, fourth, fifth and eighth graders will pull together their best efforts at writing and math.

Each portfolio must include selections in certain basic categories. An eighth-grade writing portfolio, for example, must include a piece of writing; a letter about the piece; a short story, play or narrative; a personal response to a book or play; and three prose pieces from an area outside language arts.

First, the students score their own work, based on a scoring chart. For example, a student could solve a math problem but not explain the reasoning behind the solution and get a score of 2, whereas a student who could explain the solution and apply the reasoning to another type of problem would score a 5.

The portfolios then are scored by the student's classroom teacher. Finally, the State Department of Education collects a random sampling of 8,000 math and writing portfolios from the roughly 25,000 students statewide in all three grades. The samples are scored by a team of evaluators as a kind of reliability check on the classroom scoring.

Jan Scipione, an eighth-grade math teacher at Middlebury Union Junior High School, was on the committee that decided what type of math work should be included in the upper-grade math portfolio. She is passionate about the benefit of the portfolio system.

"We were looking at what could be assessed through a uniform test and what couldn't be assessed that way," she said in a recent interview. "We decided that one of our most versatile tools would be a portfolio. We wanted to be able to see that students took risks in their learning. We wanted to see them project an idea, test it and then revise it if need be, to see them developing a healthy curiosity about math."

Her enthusiasm seems to have rubbed off on her students. Ari Margolis, now in ninth grade, believes the portfolio she put together for Scipione last spring represented some of the best work she has ever done.

"I think of portfolios as a way of keeping track of yourself," said Ari. "I really look forward to the feedback from my teachers. I value those comments more than a grade."

One of her favorite pieces was a career budget, in which she laid out her life's plan to become an athletic trainer. She estimated the job would pay her an annual starting salary of $12,000. She then had to figure out how to pay for food, housing and transportation. She also had to repay her education loans.

"It was sort of shocking," said Ari of her immersion into the real world of personal finance. "I barely made it."

Marnie Wood, a teacher, has seen a growth both in her own teaching skills and in her fourth graders at the Bridgeport Central School. Now in her 12th year as a teacher, she said the portfolio system "is undergirding my curriculum in positive ways."

At the same time, she acknowledges that the emphasis on problem-solving in math has been a stretch for her, as it has for a number of primary-grade teachers, many of whom are not specialists in math.

"I'll admit the amount of actual problem-solving I did with the kids prior to portfolios was much more limited," she said; "I'm always looking for new math tasks. I grab them wherever I can find them."

Riding the wave of 1994 Winter Olympic fever, she asked her 8- and 9-year-old students to solve math word problems based on the number of gold medals won by the competing countries. In another problem, they had to explain whether it would be cheaper to take one friend to the movies twice or two friends to the movies once.

"The emphasis on problem-solving rather than straight computation helps with life skills in general," said Wood.

To be sure, problems with portfolio assessment remain. One particularly thorny issue has been how to ensure that portfolios are scored uniformly throughout the state, since many of the judgments that go into scoring are subjective.

Even so, Scipione believes that making the effort is worthwhile.

"We knew this would be a 10 year process when we began," she said. "People think of the Vermont portfolio as a done deal, and it's not. This was never meant to be limited to a few grades. It was meant to be expanded to all grades, which has happened in some schools, not in others.

"The idea is that we want students to be able to communicate their ideas through a variety of forms. But for me, the biggest change has been learning about assessment. No students have ever had clear, consistent, public criteria for evaluating their work. Now, for the first time, they know what the standards and the expectations are. The keeping of a portfolio is an incredibly important thing for a child to do."

Regents Exams Are Being Redesigned, for "Portfolio" Answers
Sarah Kershaw

The New York Regents exams, the primary measure of high-school achievement for more than a century, are being overhauled for the first time since multiple-choice questions were introduced in 1923.

The changes, which officials expect to complete by the end of the decade, seek to make the tests a more reliable reflection of what students know. Instead of multiple-choice questions, some exams being tested in pilot programs require long-term projects like poems, essays and memoirs collected over a year or scientific experiments performed over a week.

SOURCE: *The New York Times,* September 11, 1995, pp. B1; B8. Reprinted with permission from *The New York Times.*

The tests, which cover subjects like mathematics, science, English, foreign language and history, have molded high-school education since 1865. They are not required for graduation, but colleges use them to evaluate applicants, and passing grades are needed to earn a coveted Regents diploma, the New York equivalent of graduating with distinction.

But for all their history and power, the exams have been criticized as rigid and anachronistic, particularly by teachers who complain about having to take time from regular classes to prepare students in crash courses for the exams.

In 1990, New York high-school students did not learn, at least in their Regents courses, that the Soviet Union had collapsed, because it was not on the global studies test that year.

"It's just never been a good test," said Marcia Lubell, an English teacher at Yorktown High School in Westchester County who has prepared students for the Regents for 20 years. "It doesn't resemble anything we do in the classroom."

While committing themselves to updating the exams, officials said they wanted to avoid the problems of other states like California, Connecticut and Virginia, which abandoned new-style tests amid complaints that they were too subtle, too amorphous and, in some cases, too personal.

For that reason, New York officials are not planning a drastic overhaul of the tests, which drive the high-school curriculum by covering specific material in courses like algebra, physics, American literature and Spanish.

The pilot programs, in 10 districts in the last school year and 50 this year, are experimenting with "performance-based" testing, emphasizing critical thinking and analysis over rote learning. Instead of taking a multiple choice test for reading comprehension, students would hear a lecture and write a summary. In math, scratch work would count for credit.

"Over time, the Regents exams have been equated with high standards, with a real dedication to excellence," said Carl T. Hayden, Chancellor of the Board of Regents, which sets state-wide educational policy. "But the process offers merely a snapshot of our students. It does not present an occasion for a useful exchange between student and teacher."

Each year 450,000, or 60 percent, of the high-school students take the exams, which are given three times a year, in biology, chemistry, earth science, physics, global studies, United States history and government, English, mathematics and six languages. Last year, 37 percent of the graduating seniors received Regents diplomas, meaning that they passed the required courses and the exams.

The changes would be similar to those that Vermont began under Richard P. Mills, a national expert on testing innovations who was recently confirmed as Education Commissioner in New York. When he was Education Commissioner in Vermont, that state became the first to use student portfolios extensively. The portfolios are collections of work gathered over the school year, in evaluating student progress.

"When I visit a school," Mr. Mills said, "the first thing I ask is, 'Can I see the portfolios?' The portfolios reveal the standards."

The portfolios would be important in testing subjects like English, science and math. Portfolios on computer disks are being tested in a middle school in Croton-on-Huson and University Heights Alternative High School in the Bronx.

The Regents will receive results about the tests this fall and, over the next year, hold hearings on changes. State officials have begun similar changes in standardized tests for grade-school pupils.

The reinvention of the Regents exams has proceeded quietly, with few parents and students, other than those in the districts trying the new tests, aware of the changes. But with haunting reminders of similar programs that failed in other states, officials are preparing for skepticism.

"When you tamper or when you look at something that's been taught for thousands of years in the same way, people think that if you change it you are watering it down," said Joyce R. Coppin, Superintendent of the Brooklyn High School District, which has developed and used an alternative to the Regents biology exam.

A particular concern about the new tests is the reliability of scoring.

"We're not satisfied that what we have is real good reliability," said Edward T. Lahler, the assistant state commissioner for curriculum, instruction, assessment and innovation. "The same work scored in a different location by a different scorer at a different time could produce a different result."

Referring to the current system, he added: "The American public is used to seeing things like 85 and 76. They know what that means, what B work is, that the 60's are a danger zone. We'rc going to have to work with the public on this."

For parents, the move can spur confusion. For teachers, administering and scoring the new tests almost always require much more work.

Yorktown received a waiver from the State Education Department to use portfolios as a substitute for 35 percent of the 11th-grade Regents. Mrs. Lubell said scoring required many more hours than scoring the traditional Regents exams.

The waiver required that two teachers score each portfolio, Mrs. Lubell said, noting that some teachers had 120 portfolios to score, taking 35 to 40 minutes each to grade.

"Teachers who are going to work the contract are not going to do this," she added. "I can't even begin to tell you how many hours it took to do this. But there are some of us who are crazy enough to want to do it. I've never seen so much learning take place in an English classroom as I did this year."

New York plans to spend $500,000 a year for five years to develop and administer the redesigned exams, Mr. Lahler said. The full cost has not been determined.

Nationally, the cost of administering and scoring a multiple-choice test is $2 to $3 a student. Performance-based tests cost at least $10 a student, according to the State Education Assessment Center.

One of Mrs. Lubell's students, Sonia Werner, assembled a portfolio of essays, book reports and poems as part of her 11th-grade English Regents exam last year.

PAST, PRESENT, FUTURE: EXCERPTS FROM REGENTS EXAMS

1895 Version: Essay

A sample question from an Elementary English exam:

> *Tell from what stem each of the following is formed and give the meaning of each stem: abbreviate, compassion, loquacious, vocation, capture.*

The Test of Today: Multiple Choice

A sample question from an English exam given in June:

> *In the space provided on the separate answer sheet, write the number of the word or phase that most nearly expresses the meaning [of] the word printed in heavy black type.*
>
> *The little girl's sleep was* **fitful.**

1. refreshing 2. irregular 3. brief 4. quiet

A New Kind of Exam: Portfolio

The state is now experimenting with portfolios, collections of student work gathered over the school year. At Yorktown High School in Westchester, Marcia Lubell's class was asked to submit essays, poems, short stories, a memoir and the following assignments:

Analyze Thomas Wolfe's "Far and the Near" and Rita Dove's poem "This Life," comparing the role of dreams in the two pieces. Then put the assignment away until the end of the year.

Using a list of vocabulary words that appear in the literature, write a dialogue or monologue in which one of the protagonists of the stories goes into a bar and explains his experience.

Analyze the "Kingfisher" and Theodore Roethke's "My Papa's Waltz," comparing the father–son relationships in each.

Compare the first and last assignments and explain what you learned.

"Dear Sir or Madam," Miss Werner wrote in the introduction to her 200-page collection. "Shall I say welcome to my portfolio or shall I say welcome to me? What you are holding is not merely a medley of papers bound by a plastic spine and branded with the name Mastery Portfolio. Inside these pages you will find my blunders, my successes, my hopes and my dreams. In many cases, myself and these pages are interchangeable."

In his reflection on creating a portfolio, another of Mrs. Lubell's students, Anthony Cacciola, wrote:

"When I heard Mrs. Lubell tell us that we were going to improve greatly in our reading, writing and thinking skills by the end of this year, I thought she was nuts. How was I, Mr. Slacker, Mr. Screwup, going to improve in anything by the end of the year? Now I see that she was absolutely correct. I don't know how or when it happened, but I have become a decent writer."

Chapter 12

STANDARDS AND SCHOOL CHOICE

INTRODUCTION

As liberal educators implement their agenda of outcome-based education, portfolio assessment, and cooperative learning, their more conservative-minded counterparts view their efforts with skepticism—and in some instances outright disdain. One example of the practices to which the conservatives object is a "literacy task" for English courses developed recently, such as the following.

Students are instructed to work in groups of four and to pretend that four characters from books they have read have come together in a particular place. The students are instructed to write a little play in which they will interact in the roles of these characters. At the same time, the play can have nothing to do with the plots of the books in which the characters originally appeared. In developing the play, the group is instructed to pay particular attention to such things as costumes, scenery, and props. The students are to perform the play before their classmates, and afterwards they are to write a reflective essay on their personal experiences as they participated in the project.

This is the sort of thing to which conservative educators object, for they see it as an emphasis of form over matter, as the celebration of process over content, indeed, as the near total abandonment of academic standards.

On the conservative side of the educational spectrum there has been a growing, consistent call for a return to what they perceive as the high academic standards of the past. The charge is that liberal-minded educators are seriously injuring a whole generation of children with the result that very many—far too many—high school graduates simply do not know what they should know and lack even rudimentary skills. They argue for a clear set of academic standards to which the whole educational establishment—students, teachers, school administrators, and colleges of education—can be held accountable.

An enduring problem for many conservatives, however, has been that the majority of the groups put in charge of developing standards have been dominated by liberals. Consequently, the standards that these groups produce are generally not acceptable to conservatives, who maintain that they improperly stress process over content. One of the major controversies today is not so much whether we should have standards, but rather just what those standards should be. At the same time, conservatives do not want to separate the question of standards from the question of content. Given that certain outcomes should be achieved, for example, that certain standards should be met, the conservatives have some very definite opinions concerning precisely *what* we should teach so that this will happen. Moveover, according to many conservatives, we need to spend more time teaching the core curriculum. Consequently, many want to lengthen both the school day and the school year.

Another group of conservatives believes that all attempts to reform education from *within* the current system are doomed to fail because the liberal establishment is so firmly entrenched in the public schools. Their solution is to give parents vouchers, worth several thousands of dollars, which they can use to send their children to the public—or *private*—schools of their choice. These conservatives believe that most parents share their dissatisfaction with the quality of education their children receive today in the public school. And, they reason, if given the choice, most parents would opt for schools that incorporate high standards with strong academic content. They maintain that giving parents the freedom to choose schools for their children would force public schools to reform in order to survive.

New Math Plan: A Plus for Pupils
Richard Lee Colvin

If you're a parent of a student in a California public elementary or middle school, prepare to feel out of touch come next fall when your child sits down to do math homework.

The assignment will probably contain more words than numbers—or no numbers at all—with an essay replacing calculations. Students might be asked to measure potatoes or survey family members on their favorite flavor of ice cream.

When adding, subtracting, multiplying or dividing is required, it might not matter if a student uses a calculator. And if your child says there is no right answer, he or she is probably telling the truth.

Sound disorienting? Discouraging? Don't feel too bad, because in all likelihood your son or daughter's teacher will be confounded as well.

That statement is not meant to be snide. Rather, that is the assessment of some of the most progressive math education experts around the state. They

Source: *Los Angeles Times*, March 12, 1995, pp. 1; 16. Copyright © 1995, Los Angeles Times. Reprinted by permission.

estimate that between 50% and 90% of the state's teachers are ill-prepared for what is described as the most dramatic change in the teaching of mathematics this century.

Beginning next fall, California's decade-long effort to reform math instruction will kick into high gear, as public schools introduce new teaching materials that emphasize student discovery over calculation, deep understanding over repetitive practice.

Teacher training experts say the state would have to spend more than half a billion dollars annually—or $75,000 per school—for the next several years to get all its teachers ready. And those pushing the new teaching methods do not want to wait.

"If we wait for everybody to be ready, it's just not going to happen and we are going to lose that whole new generation of kids. . . just at the time when, for the economic viability of the country, we need people who are mathematically, scientifically and technologically literate," said Eunice Krinky, who heads a state-funded math teacher training project at Cal State Dominguez Hills.

Up and down the state, schools are in the midst of selecting from a list of approved textbooks, calculators, videotapes and guidebooks that conform to the new way of teaching, which emphasizes concepts over calculation and formulas, relies as much on group problem-solving as individual effort, and begins introducing sophisticated subjects such as geometry and algebra in the earliest grades.

Those reforms began seeping into California classrooms 15 years ago, as part of an effort to increase enrollment in advanced math courses, better prepare students for college and improve the capacity of workers to think mathematically on the job.

Now, the advent of new textbooks and materials will pressure all teachers to subscribe to the reforms.

The result, many teachers believe, will be confusion and resistance. Not only are many unprepared to teach in a new way, but some experts believe that no amount of training will make it possible for teachers with little math background to make the switch. Others worry that the methods remain untested, particularly with low-achieving students and those still learning to speak English.

Even Walter Denham, the state Department of Education's top math expert, agreed that next year will be an experiment. "We don't have empirical evidence that it will work in tens of thousands of classrooms," he said.

California school districts will spend about $250 million this year and next on the new texts. Those most in line with the new "thinking" curriculum will require teachers to perform what will be, for some, the challenging role of coach and guide.

Rather than just checking pupils' answers, teachers in every grade will be expected to question them about how they arrived at their solutions and to deduce from the responses their level of understanding. Even in the primary grades, teachers will need to be familiar with such areas of math as probability and statistics, geometry and algebra.

"You will find teachers who. . . find that these materials are a shock, but they will be teachers who haven't kept up with their profession," said Paul

Giganti, a math education expert at the Lawrence Hall of Science in Berkeley and president of the California Math Council. "I think many teachers are ready and anxious to implement the new materials."

But he acknowledged that parents—many of whom equate math homework with the endless calculations that past generations performed—are in for a surprise.

"There are a lot of parents who do not understand the changes. . . and it is our fault," Giganti said. "We have good reasons for all of the things we have done, but. . . we have kept them largely to ourselves."

His organization is working to address that. So are textbook publishers and school principals, who are hosting meetings to reassure parents that their children will still learn to calculate, and that high-achieving students will not be held back by the emphasis on group problem-solving.

Reed Middle School in North Hollywood began trying out one of the new textbook series last fall and found that students who previously had been adept at working math problems were struggling.

"The kids. . . were more used to having a math book give them an example and then 20 problems like it," said Larry Tash, Reed's principal. Now, however, the students are doing better and most parents have become supporters of the new curriculum, he said.

But in some school districts, parents have prevailed upon administrators to go slow in choosing textbooks or reject the new methods altogether.

In Palo Alto, parents objected to a state-sponsored program to promote the "thinking" curriculum in middle schools. Parents' fears that children were being steered away from math fundamentals led to angry confrontations with teachers, and some parents threatened to pull their children out of the highly regarded school district.

"Parents would call the teacher and ask for help and some of the teachers. . . were not able to satisfy the concerns that were being raised," said Jack Gibbany, the district's director of curriculum and instruction. Partly as a result, the district has delayed buying new math textbooks until next year.

The Chino United School district in San Bernadino County has also put off selecting from among the new materials, in response to parents' concerns. Supt. Stephen Goldstone said the district may decide to stick with the almost decade-old books it uses now. He appointed parents to a committee to help advise the district on which way to go.

"There are some very good and very interesting aspects of some of these new textbooks, but some of them are so far-fetched that, it's like, what are kids really going to learn about math when they are done with this class?" asked Anne Gluch, the parent of a Chino fifth-grader, who is serving on that committee.

Sales representatives of the publishers said that between a quarter and a third of the state's 1,000 school districts are delaying making a choice, although some are doing so for financial, not philosophical, reasons.

One of the most vocal critics of the new textbooks has been Maureen DiMarco, Gov. Pete Wilson's top education adviser. She and others warn of a repeat of the 1960s debacle known as "new math," a highly abstract teaching method that was introduced into schools nationwide without adequate preparation for teachers and parents.

Those opposed to the latest changes in math have begun referring to them as the "new new math."

"I'm truly alarmed that some radicals have taken a hold of the curriculum, and are convinced that basic skills are not important, when everybody knows that solid basic skills are the foundation on which you work to get to the higher order skills," DiMarco said.

Furthermore, she said, there is no research that shows that children will understand math better if taught the new way. Even some mathematicians believe that the approach is misguided, no matter how well it is taught.

Cal State L.A. math professor Wayne Bishop has been campaigning for years against the state's math framework, and the national guidelines on which it is based.

He argues that the approach is a retreat from standards and from true math—a rejection of substance in favor of form. "Learning your math by solving interesting problems is going to die—it's just a matter of how long it will take," he said.

But the publishers of the new-style books, and backers of the state math guidelines on which they are modeled, are convinced that the changes are essential.

In the past, they say, students were taught a standardized way of doing long division, but not necessarily whether the answer they produced made any sense. Now, they will be asked to think mathematically about real-world problems.

Although math textbooks always have included "story problems," those in the new books are more open-ended and more ambiguous and are known as "investigations."

One such problem, drawn from a fifth-grade textbook, is the following: A student crouching by a field of tall corn sees 72 legs of cows and chickens. How many different combinations of cows and chickens might there be?

The answer is 17. Some students might work out the solution using algebraic equations. More likely, they would write down a series of numbers showing the possible combinations and count them. They also might represent the combinations using toothpicks.

Usually, students would be expected to work cooperatively. Afterward, they would explain how they arrived at their answers, either orally or in essays.

In another typical problem, for younger students, the teacher would ask how many pencils would have to be purchased to furnish two for each of 30 students per week for a year. The answer is 3,120.

The Los Angeles Unified School District last month received a five-year, $15-million National Science Foundation grant that will help pay for teacher training. But Los Angeles, like other districts statewide, also will have to divert funds to training from other purposes because it is highly unlikely that the state will foot the rest of the bill.

Recognizing that many teachers might not be ready, or willing, to drastically change their approach to teaching, some of the publishers of the new math textbooks preserved more of the traditional lessons.

Teachers "can't possibly be up-dated as much as we would like them to be" to take on the challenges of the new textbooks, said Carole Greenes, associate dean of the Boston University school of education and one of the authors of a series published by Silver Burdett Ginn. "We developed a series. . . that is within the power of all teachers to get a handle on."

But other publishers downplay that issue and offer step by step guidelines to help teachers cope with the new style. Charlotte Gemmel, president of Creative Publications of Mountain View, Calif., said teachers will have no trouble using her firm's material even though they are far different from traditional texts.

"The book takes the teacher by the hand, with questions [and] responses of kids, and the book itself becomes a tool to learn and feel comfortable with this new approach," she said.

But teachers are clearly ambivalent and that is showing up in sales meetings as the publishers visit schools to pitch their materials.

Donna Batson, a consultant for Addison-Wesley, recently presented that company's materials to about a dozen teachers at Menlo Avenue School, just south of the Los Angeles Coliseum. Much of her talk was spent trying to reassure teachers that the series had not dispensed with traditional drills.

"I know it's coming hard and fast. . . but if you take it slowly and try it out, I think you will have good results and enjoy what you are doing," Batson told the group.

Afterward, teachers were divided in their assessment. Michael Rosner, who had tried the materials out with his third-, fourth- and fifth-grade students, was a believer. "I think it's the best thing I've ever seen," he said.

But third-grade teacher Nicholas Kelly was skeptical. "I've had parents come to me and ask me for more computations," he said. "I will still do that. I don't believe in throwing out the basics."

And Charles Ferreira, the teacher who headed the school's selection committee, said he is trying to moderate between the two views. "Personally, I don't have a lot of faith in it," he said. "But if we adopt it, we will go with it."

A TEACHER'S GUIDE

This fall, many California schools will begin using radically different textbooks and other teaching materials that incorporate a new approach to mathematics. Here is a sample from the *Mathland* teacher guide, demonstrating a classroom exercise for fourth-graders.

The Problem

The teacher writes the problem 12×5 on the chalkboard. She asks the class for their answers and discussion ensues.

A Sample Discussion

TEACHER: "One answer we have down for 12 times 5 so far is 60. Does anyone get a different answer?"

STUDENT: "It might be 50."

TEACHER: "Let's add 50 to our list. I wonder which of these answers is right. What do you think?"

STUDENT: "I got 50. . . because I learned last year you're supposed to start with the 'ones' and do 5 times 2, then you write 0 for the 'ones,' and then I multiplied 5 times 1 and that's 5 for the 'tens.' So it's 5 and 0. That's 50."

TEACHER: "Convince me. Use what you know about the numbers to prove your answer is right."

STUDENT: "Well, I know that five tens is 50. Oh, but it must be more because there are 5 twos, too, and that's 10. So 50 and 10 makes 60."

The Intent

According to Micaelia Randolph Brummett, an author of the series: "The point is that the student who makes the error thinks it through and corrects him or herself. Instead of doing computation. . . kids do discussions of a few problems in class, but they do them very, very thoroughly. [The teacher] takes off the mantle of the authority. . . and gives that power to the student. They get excited about trying to defend their particular choice. . . and when they come to that final answer they believe in it."

The NCTM Math Standards
Are a Very Bad Joke
John H. Saxon

I recently read with dismay a newspaper article in which Jack Price, the president of the National Council of Teachers of Mathematics (NCTM), announced that he has appointed a commission on the "Future of the *Standards*" to be chaired by past President Mary Lindquist. The *Standards* are the highly touted *Standards for School Mathematics* whose recommendations have produced no measurable gains in any school system in America since they were published in 1989. Many schools are trying to follow these unworkable recommendations and refuse to consider that they are unworkable. As a result, the disaster in math education will continue unabated.

If we look at this document carefully, we can see that the so-called *Standards* are not standards at all, but constitute a very bad joke. I cannot understand how an organization with a track record of abject failure can believe it is in the best interest of America for them to continue to make wild guesses in an attempt to rectify the disaster their predecessors' guesses have caused. I would like to review the past history of the NCTM and ask the reader if it is most probable that the leaders of this organization have had no idea of what they have been doing for over thirty years and have no idea of what they are doing now. It is time to think the unthinkable—that the leaders of this organization are totally inept and that we should demand concrete proof of the efficacy of future recommendations before we even consider implementing them.

The NCTM has been producing "fads for the decade" for a full generation and none of these fads has worked. First came the new math of the sixties and seventies, which asked schools to switch emphasis from fundamentals to the study of the properties of real numbers and to other off-the-wall concepts such as the over-emphasis on the study of number systems whose base is not ten. Instead of telling the students that numbers could be added in any order and could be multiplied in any order, students were told of the *commutative properties of real numbers under the operations of addition and multiplication.* To make things abundantly clear, they were told that $A + B = B + A$, and that $AB = BA$ for any real numbers A and B. Of course, the use of big words with small meanings led to great confusion about a topic that was very simple.

Students were taught to write the numbers twenty-one and fifty-five in base-two numerals as 10101 and 110111. The leaders of the NCTM seemed to believe that if students could demonstrate their understanding of base-two

SOURCE: *Education Week, 15,* no. 20, (February 7, 1996): pp. 28–29. Reprinted with permission of the author and *Education Week.*

numbers, it would enhance their understanding of base-ten numerals. The Russians had just launched Sputnik and there was a mad dash to "catch up with the Russians." The cold war was at its peak. So, the decision to implement the new math without testing it beforehand was somehow reasonable because we could not take a chance of being left behind in technology. The NCTM used its regional and state organizations to force the "new math" into schools all over the nation. The teachers objected to being forced to switch their emphasis away from fundamentals, but teachers wanted to do what was right, so they went along. Anyone who objected was considered unpatriotic. Parents were bewildered and some students cried a lot. But, the teachers still sneaked in the topics and concepts they knew were important, so the scores of students did not decline precipitously at the outset.

By 1978 or so, the leaders of the NCTM realized that things were not going well, so they threw together another set of recommendations that were totally untested and titled them *The Agenda for the Eighties*. The cold war was still going strong and we could again stomach the failure to test before implementation. By the end of the eighties, many of the older teachers had retired and the new teachers were the product of the new math era. The decline in the mathematics abilities of American students became more apparent. The NCTM responded by calling together a new set of experts and in 1989 published the *Standards for School Mathematics*. These people who had been unsuccessful in teaching American students the math necessary for the twentieth century believed they knew exactly what mathematics would be necessary for the twenty-first century. Their "vision" was clear. They agreed that paper-and-pencil algorithms were inherently bad and therefore unnecessary, and that practice was really drill in disguise. They hated the word *drill* with a passion. They saw "clearly" that much more emphasis should be put on the use of calculators. They believed that we should avail ourselves of everything that technology has to offer. They believed that we should introduce calculators in elementary schools and let the individual students decide whether a computation required just an estimate, or could be completed with paper and pencil, or whether a calculator should be used. They have pushed the use of calculators in elementary schools with reckless abandon. As a result, our middle and high schools have an overabundance of students who do not know basic math facts and who cannot estimate well enough to know whether a calculator's answer is even in the ballpark.

This result is most apparent in schools with heavy minority enrollment. The leaders of the NCTM refuse to face up to what they have done. Instead, they believe that minorities can be brought up to speed if we water down the tests we use. I quote from the *Assessment Standards* of the NCTM:

> Too often, tests designed for other purposes have been used unintentionally as filters that deny underrepresented groups access to the further study of mathematics. Today the mathematical development of each child in a diverse multicultural society must be valued. Assessment procedures must no longer be used to deny students the opportunities to learn important mathematics.

I am intrigued by the euphemism "underrepresented groups." I assume that this appellation means African-Americans, Native-Americans, and Hispanics. The idea that we cannot teach these students the same mathematics that Asian and Caucasian students learn is outrageous. The job of the NCTM is to find a way to do it. We do not need to change the tests. All Americans must compete in the same job market and applicants are selected for jobs based on their ability to produce, not on their racial background. If students score poorly on norm-based math tests, this tells the teachers that more time should be devoted to their math education. The idea that testing denies students the opportunity to learn important mathematics is repulsive.

The introduction of the *Standards* says that we need (1) mathematically literate workers, (2) lifelong learning, (3) opportunity for all, and (4) an informed electorate. The explanation of (3), opportunity for all, is interesting.

> 3. *Opportunity for all.* The social injustices of past schooling practices can no longer be tolerated. Current statistics indicate that those who study advanced mathematics are most often white males. Women and most minorities study less mathematics and are seriously underrepresented in careers using science and technology. Creating a just society in which women and various ethnic groups enjoy equal opportunities and equitable treatment is no longer an issue. Mathematics has become a critical filter for employment and full participation in our society. We cannot afford to have the majority of our population mathematically illiterate: Equity has become an economic necessity.

What a wonderful job of breast-beating. You can't say that on the surface the authors of this document do not seem to care. The *Standards* have produced no gains in the number of women who take higher level math courses or in the number of minorities who do so. Such gains will never accrue because the fundamental philosophy of the *Standards* is not valid. If gains were possible, the NCTM would have been able to find a teensy-weensy gain somewhere and would have shouted the results to the world. Instead, what they recommend will cause the gap between the knowledge of the gifted and the less gifted to become greater and will cause our society to become more polarized.

The people who wrote the *Standards* are good people and have worked hard on this document. They really, really care and want to help. They are almost all professors of education who have been long removed from the public school classroom. They say right up front that there is no data to buttress their claims. They say that they want to create a **vision** of what is possible. In fact, they use the word **vision** twenty-four times in the first volume of the *Standards*. Their description of their **vision** is the total content of the *Standards*, and is nebulous at best.

The authors say that the *Standards* are necessary to "protect schools from shoddy products." Publishers want to sell books and if following the recommendations of the *Standards* is the way to sell books, they will try to follow these recommendations. The administrators in our schools are afraid to think for themselves as most of them are "not gifted" in mathematics, and so they go along with the gang. The result is a deluge of shoddy products from which teachers cannot teach and from which students cannot learn. The professors of education who caused these shoddy products to be produced will be horrified at my pointing out that they are the cause. They demand that schools use the **constructivist approach** so that students can **discover** the mathematics they need to know. They justify this blind leap with the following statement:

> Our *premise* is that what a student learns depends to a great degree on how he or she has learned it.

This is totally false. What a student knows depends on what a student knows. The discovery method is not a sure-fire method. Many students have to practice the use of a concept every day for a very, very, long time before the concept and the skills necessary to apply the concept can be internalized. We cannot base American mathematics education on a **premise.**

We are no longer in a cold war and we cannot accept the recommendations for the constructivist approach without proof that it works in some school somewhere. Saxon Publishers has proven that an improved version of **direct instruction** works for students at every ability level. The idea that students should be encouraged to invent the mathematics they need is not valid. Students need to be led, albeit gently.

If we look at the *Standards* we see that this document articulates five general goals for students: (1) that they learn to value mathematics, (2) that they become confident in their ability to do mathematics, (3) that they become mathematical problem solvers, (4) that they learn to communicate mathematically, and (5) that they learn to reason mathematically. As Lawrence Welk would say, "Wonnerful, wonnerful, wonnerful." But how are publishers to write books that allow students to meet these goals? How are teachers to conduct their classes to meet these goals? Specifically, what does a teacher do to teach students to value mathematics, to become problem solvers, to communicate, and to reason mathematically? The *Standards* do not address these questions, and asking these questions without recommended methods that have been tested and proven is certainly not a solution.

The *Standards* consist of a listing of words that are supposed to represent everything good and nothing bad. The first four are (1) problem-solving, (2) communication, (3) reasoning, and (4) connections. Let us look at the first standard. Using mathematics to problem-solve is the art of applying the concepts of mathematics in new and unusual situations. Thus, our first task is to teach students the fundamental concepts and the skills necessary to apply those concepts. Right? No, wrong! What the authors of the *Standards* want is to teach the art of problem solving first and let the students pick up the necessary concepts and skills as they tackle real-world problems. Teachers are encouraged to place students in groups and direct them in the art of group problem solving. The authors of the *Standards* do not realize that mathematics is an individual sport. Each student must hit the ball himself or herself. When students are placed in groups and asked to perform, they will. They find a way for the smartest student to solve the problem and to make it look like a group solution.

***The Disaster in Math Education Is a Direct Result of Poor Leadership
From the Top***   It is one thing to make statements such as I have made, and it
is another thing to prove it. My associates and I have written math books that
have caused great gains at all grade levels and for students at all ability levels. Almost every high school that has used our books has been able to double the
number of seniors who take academic math courses, to triple calculus enrollment, and to raise college board scores from 20 percent in schools whose
scores are average to over 40 percent in schools whose scores are low. Best of
all, these schools have been able to reduce, by over 50 percent, the number of
students taking "dum-dum," slow-track courses such as basic math and consumer math.

At Sparta High School in Sparta, Illinois, ACT scores jumped from 15.90 to
21.55 between 1987 and 1989, and have averaged 21.43 since that time, a gain
of 34.7 percent. In four years, the average ACT scores at Maine East High school
in Park Ridge, Illinois, went from 18.9 to 22.9, a gain of 21 percent, and the calculus enrollment went from three sections to nine sections. The ACT scores at
Blackfoot High School in Blackfoot, Idaho, went from 13.1 in 1987 to 20.6 in
1993, a gain of 57 percent. Revere High School in Ovid, Colorado, reports that
of seniors who completed *Saxon's Advanced Math* book in 1992, all are still in
college, and from the class of 1993, all but one are still in college. Math teacher
Kathleen Killifer says that their ACT scores are up but that she is more proud of
the number of math students who are successful in college.

Superintendent Harold Barnett in Cartersville, Georgia, reports that his
eighth graders' ranking on the state test of basic skills went from 47th in 1988
to 53rd in 1989 (Pre-*Saxon*). The scores jumped to 9th in 1990, 12th in 1991,
and have been first in the state for the last four years. Agatha Kent is curriculum
director for the Screven County Schools in Sylvania, Georgia. She reports that
the second year Saxon math was used the enrollment in Algebra I went from 84
to 173, a gain of 106 percent. This is a 3,000-student system, 45 percent white,
located halfway between Augusta and Savannah. We have had success like this
in hundreds of schools and have compiled a booklet of about 135 reports similar to those above. . . .

We have overwhelming proof that a turnaround in math education is possible by switching from *touchy-feely* books to books that use a much improved
method of *direct instruction.* The direct instruction methods in the past have
had great flaws. Direct instruction will work well when used properly. The
NCTM's basic philosophy for thirty years has been terribly flawed. We have followed the lead of "experts" who have been unable to produce even small gains
in any school anywhere. **Can you imagine the national celebration the
NCTM would be having if they produced even one of the gains that I report in this article?** There have been no measurable gains in any school in
America for over thirty years as a result of using the NCTM's recommendations, yet this organization has announced plans to put out another set of wild
guesses!!! American parents want out. They want charter schools and vouchers. The number of students being home-schooled has increased dramatically,
and school systems are throwing up their hands and moving to site-based man-

agement because anything the teachers come up with will be better than what we have now.

Saxon Publishers has developed books that work wonderfully well. This year our promotions will emphasize our elementary math program, which produces measurable results almost immediately. We will **attempt** to give away one class set of books for grades K, 1, 2, 3, 4, and 5 to three thousand elementary schools for use in the 1996–97 school year. **We will inservice the teachers at no charge** and use our money to prove to these schools that a quick turnaround in math achievement is possible. I say that we will *attempt* to do this because people with what I call an "NCTM mentality" are doing everything they can to keep the schools from finding a better way if it is not recommended by the NCTM. What are they afraid of? They are afraid I will prove them wrong. What would you say if you were a 50- or 60-year-old "expert" in math education and someone threatened to prove that your philosophy had caused the disaster in math education in America? I like to think that I would not object because American students deserve the best. But I am not an "expert" in math education. I am a retired Air Force test pilot who has two degrees in engineering. What does John Saxon know?

Now we will find out. I have lured these people out of the forest and into the long grass, and then out of the long grass into the short grass. There is no longer any place to hide. So the battle will continue this year on a playing field that is not yet level. But, it gets more and more level every year. Direct instruction will produce results and touchy-feely math will not. The next few years will produce the evidence. Saxon Publishers will attempt to give away $10,000,000 in free math books in pilots each year for the next three years. The schools that are brave enough to let me prove my contentions will lead the way. I encourage these schools to accept free pilot books from their publishers who want to compete.

If schools are willing to test the books, they can prove to themselves which method is the best.

Panel Urges Shift of Focus for School Science Courses
The New York Times

Rather than memorizing the nomenclature of plant families, the anatomy of a frog or the periodic table, long staples of school science courses, students

SOURCE: *The New York Times*, December 7, 1995, p. A20. Reprinted with permission from *The New York Times*.

should learn to investigate and question the workings of the natural world, a national panel of teachers and scientists recommends.

Their report, a set of guidelines known as the National Science Standards, is the latest in a series of recommendations for 11 disciplines, including history, mathematics and social studies. Most have been announced; two others, English and economics are still being written.

Scientists and educators have long believed that the schools have failed to teach adequately even the most basic scientific concepts and have not done enough to make science an appealing subject.

"We've managed to turn people off of science by making it some kind of rote learning exercise," said Bruce M. Alberts, chairman of the National Research Council, which coordinated the study, and president of its scientific arm, the National Academy of Sciences. "What we're talking about here would be a revolution in science education."

The guidelines, developed over the last three years [by] teachers, scientists and school administrators, say that fourth-grade students should have a basic understanding of the properties of objects and materials, life cycles of organisms, objects in the sky and the use of science and technology in solving simple problems. By eighth grade, students should be able to model scientific inquiry and understand motions and forces, reproduction and heredity, the Earth's history and the history of science. By 12th grade, their understanding should include chemical reactions, natural resources and the nature of scientific knowledge.

Many of the same themes already appear in science curriculums being developed in about half the states, including New York, New Jersey and Connecticut, with a greater focus on the bigger ideas of science: energy, evolution, stability, change and equilibrium.

"We were doing a darn good job of training highly skilled specialists," said Eugenie C. Scott, executive director of the National Center for Science Education in El Cerrito, Calif. "But there were quite a series of sieves we would put people through to get that highly trained elite. And in the process, we lost most of the American public."

While the dense, 250-page document, released yesterday, offers state and local educators more philosophy than prescription, it calls for specific changes like making science a "core" course that students would take every year, starting in kindergarten, and providing all teachers with science training.

While many science teachers said they welcomed the national standards, some were doubtful that states and local districts would have the resources to implement many of the recommendations. For instance, the standards call for extensive teacher training and "more space and time" for classroom exercises.

"It's not good enough to tell people you have to do this," said Carole Greene, who heads the biology department at the Bronx High School of Science in New York. "You have to give them tools. It's not necessarily even the materials because clever teachers know how to keep things cheap. But the labs are extremely crowded and when you've got 34 kids in a 40-minute class, not everyone is going to have the opportunity to investigate and inquire."

The End of History
Lynne V. Cheney

Imagine an outline for the teaching of American history in which George Washington makes only a fleeting appearance and is never described as our first president. Or in which the foundings of the Sierra Club and the National Organization for Women are considered noteworthy events, but the first gathering of the U.S. Congress is not.

This is, in fact, the version of history set forth in the soon-to-be-released National Standards for United States History. If these standards are approved by the National Education Standards and Improvement Council—part of the bureaucracy created by the Clinton administration's Goals 2000 Act—students across the country, from grades five to 12, may begin to learn their history according to them.

The document setting forth the National Standards divides American history into 10 eras and establishes two to four standards for each era, for a total of 31. Each "standard" states briefly, and in general terms, what students should learn for a particular period (e.g., "Early European exploration and Colonization: The Resulting Cultural and Ecological Interaction"). Each standard is followed, in the document, by lengthy teaching recommendations (e.g., students should "construct a dialogue between an Indian leader and George Washington at the end of the [Revolutionary] war").

Paradoxical Constitution

The general drift of the document becomes apparent when one realizes that not a single one of the 31 standards mentions the Constitution. True, it does come up in the 250 pages of supporting materials. It is even described as "the culmination of the most creative era of constitutionalism in American history"—but only in the dependent clause of a sentence that has as its main point that students should "ponder the paradox that the Constitution sidetracked the movement to abolish slavery that had taken rise in the revolutionary era."

The authors tend to save their unqualified admiration for people, places and events that are politically correct. The first era, "Three Worlds Meet (Beginnings to 1620)," covers societies in the Americas, Western Europe and West Africa that began to interact significantly after 1450. To understand West Africa, students are encouraged to "analyze the achievements and grandeur of Mansa Musa's court, and the social customs and wealth of the kingdom of Mali."

What Midnight Ride?

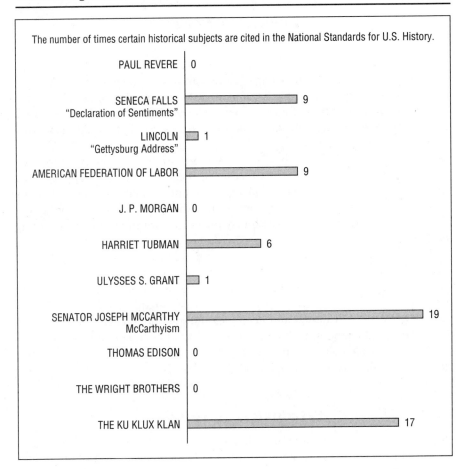

The number of times certain historical subjects are cited in the National Standards for U.S. History.

PAUL REVERE	0
SENECA FALLS "Declaration of Sentiments"	9
LINCOLN "Gettysburg Address"	1
AMERICAN FEDERATION OF LABOR	9
J. P. MORGAN	0
HARRIET TUBMAN	6
ULYSSES S. GRANT	1
SENATOR JOSEPH MCCARTHY McCarthyism	19
THOMAS EDISON	0
THE WRIGHT BROTHERS	0
THE KU KLUX KLAN	17

Such celebratory prose is rare when the document gets to American history itself. In the U.S. context, the kind of wealth that Mansa Musa commanded is not considered a good thing. When the subject of John D. Rockefeller comes up, students are instructed to conduct a trial in which he is accused of "knowingly and willfully participat[ing] in unethical and amoral business practices designed to undermine traditions of fair, open competition for personal and private aggrandizement in direct violation of the common welfare."

African and Native American societies, like all societies, had their failings, but one would hardly know it from National Standards. Students are encouraged to consider Aztec "architecture, skills, labor systems, and agriculture." But not the practice of human sacrifice.

Counting how many times different subjects are mentioned in the document yields telling results. One of the most often mentioned subjects, with 19 references, is McCarthy and McCarthyism. The Ku Klux Klan gets its fair share, too, with 17. As for individuals, Harriet Tubman, an African-American who helped rescue slaves by way of the underground railroad, is mentioned six times. Two white males who were contemporaries of Tubman, Ulysses S. Grant and Robert E. Lee, get one and zero mentions, respectively. Alexander Graham Bell, Thomas Edison, Albert Einstein, Jonas Salk and the Wright brothers make no appearance at all.

I have abundant reason to be troubled by the way that the history standards have turned out. When I was chairman of the National Endowment for the Humanities, I signed a grant that helped enable their development. In 1992, the NEH put $525,000 and the Department of Education $865,000 toward establishing standards for what students should know about both U.S. and world history. The grantee was the National Center for History in the Schools at UCLA, an organization that had produced some fine work, including a highly regarded publication called "Lessons From History" that was also an effort to set standards for the teaching of history. It was this publication, the Center for History said in its application, upon which the government-sponsored standard-setting effort would build.

But a comparison of "Lessons From History" with the National Standards shows only a distant relationship between the two. "Lessons," while rightfully including important Americans, like Sojourner Truth, who have been ignored in the past, also emphasizes major figures like George Washington, who is not only described as our first president but even pictured, as is Robert E. Lee.

"Lessons" conveys the notion that wealth has sometimes had positive cultural consequences in this country, as elsewhere. For the period between 1815 and 1850, students are asked to consider how "the rise of the cities and the accumulation of wealth by industrial capitalists brought an efflorescence of culture—classical revival architecture; the rise of the theater and the establishment of academies of art and music; the first lyceums and historical societies; and a 'communication revolution' in which book and newspaper publishing accelerated and urban dwellers came into much closer contact with the outside world."

"Lessons" is honest about the failings of the U.S., but it also regularly manages a tone of affirmation. It describes the American Revolution as part of "the long human struggle for liberty, equality, justice, and dignity." The National Standards, by contrast, concentrates on "multiple perspectives" and on how the American Revolution did or did not serve the interests of different groups.

"Lessons" emphasizes the individual greatness that has flourished within our political system and in our representative institutions. It refers—twice—to "congressional giants" like Henry Clay and Daniel Webster and the "great debates" in which they participated. The National Standards, which mentions Clay once and Webster not at all, gives no hint of their spellbinding oratory. It does, however, suggest that students analyze Pat Buchanan's speech at the 1992 Republican convention. The only congressional leader I could find actually quoted in the document was Tip O'Neill, calling Ronald Reagan "a cheerleader for selfishness."

What went wrong? One member of the National Council for History Standards (the group that oversaw the drafting of the standards) says that the 1992 presidential election unleashed the forces of political correctness. According to this person, who wishes not to be named, those who were "pursuing the revisionist agenda" no longer bothered to conceal their "great hatred for traditional history." Various political groups, such as African-American organizations and Native American groups, also complained about what they saw as omissions and distortions. As a result, says the council member, "nobody dared to cut the inclusive part," and what got left out was traditional history.

The standards for world history are also soon to be made public. By all accounts, the sessions leading to their development were even more contentious than those that produced U.S. standards. The main battle was over the emphasis that would be given to Western civilization, says a second council member. After the 1992 election, this member reports, the American Historical Association, an academic organization, became particularly aggressive in its opposition to "privileging" the West. The AHA threatened to boycott the proceedings if Western civilization was given any emphasis. From that point on, says the second council member, "the AHA hijacked standards-setting." Several council members fervently protested the diminution of the West, "but," says the second council member, "we were all iced-out."

Official Knowledge

UCLA's Center for History suggests that its document on standards be viewed as a work in progress rather than a definitive statement. But there is every reason to believe that the certification process put in place by the Clinton administration will lead to the adoption of the proposed standards more or less intact—as official knowledge—with the result that much that is significant in our past will begin to disappear from our schools.

Preventing certification will be a formidable task. Those wishing to do so will have to go up against an academic establishment that revels in the kind of politicized history that characterizes much of the National Standards. But the battle is worth taking on. We are a better people than the National Standards indicate, and our children deserve to know it.

Panel Agrees to Revise National History Standards
Karen Diegmueller

The embattled developers of the voluntary national standards for history agreed late last week to revise their documents outlining what K-12 students should know and be able to do in that subject.

The agreement followed a meeting here between leaders of the National History Standards Project and some leading critics.

After the meeting, Gary B. Nash, the co-director of the project, said he and other historians and teachers on the panel will examine and revise the three documents that make up the standards. Those revisions would include changing some of the content standards themselves.

What the changes will be and how much the panel will accede to critics, however, was not divulged.

Mr. Nash said the revised standards will be published in a basic version that will exclude the hotly debated teaching activities and in an expanded three-volume set. Both will be available sometime this spring.

Mr. Nash said his group will scrutinize the standards and the teaching activities to insure they are balanced and free of the ideological bias that critics say they have found in the documents for U.S. and world history, which were released last fall.

He said the third part of the national standards, the consolidated K-4 history document, which has been relatively free from criticism, will also be reviewed and revised.

"Not every issue is resolvable, but I think we can go a long way towards accommodating the criticisms," Mr. Nash said.

But he also said the group would not make any changes that were inconsistent with sound historical scholarship.

Friction Continues

While the large majority of participants at the session, which was closed to reporters, said they believed that progress had been made to resolve their differences, the friction had not disappeared.

In a move that seemed to take some participants by surprise, John Fonte, the executive director of the Committee to Review National Standards, an independent panel, disputed the characterization that progress had been made or

SOURCE: *Education Week, 14,* no. 17, (January 18, 1995): p. 8. Reprinted with permission from *Education Week.*

that the developers of the history standards had committed themselves to making changes.

"We believe the standards are seriously flawed. . . from start to finish," said Mr. Fonte, who represented Lynne V. Cheney, the former head of the National Endowment for the Humanities. Ms. Cheney has been both the chief benefactor of the history-standards project—through funding she provided while at the N.E.H.—and their chief critic.

"There's nothing today that would change that," said Mr. Fonte, whose group was established by Ms. Cheney to counterbalance a Congressionally mandated standards-certification panel that has yet to be named.

"There is no commitment to change," he charged.

"That's not true," replied Charles N. Quigley, the executive director of the Center for Civic Education, which brokered last week's session.

Most of the others who attended the press briefing following the session also defended the developers' commitment to improving the history standards.

But most of the standards' critics who attended, including Diane Ravitch, a former assistant secretary of education, and Albert Shanker, the president of the American Federation of Teachers, were unavailable for comment.

In the past, however, Ms. Ravitch has generally been critical of the teaching activities rather than the standards themselves.

Gilbert T. Sewall, the director of the American Textbook Council and a member of Ms. Cheney's group who has also expressed reservations about the benchmarks, portrayed the debate as open and honorable.

"The fact that we all sat down is a kind of progress after the friction and ill feelings of the last few months," he said.

History Center Shares New Set of Standards
Karen Diegmueller

Timbuktu has disappeared. Pearl Harbor has ascended. George Washington is in; Eleanor Roosevelt is out. And names and places like Joseph McCarthy and Seneca Falls, N.Y., whose prominence so irked critics the last time around, have been allotted one mention apiece in the revived national history standards that were released last week.

Students exposed to the new voluntary guidelines that spell out what they should know in grades 4, 8, and 12 also will be introduced to a more uplifting history of the United States and the West.

SOURCE: *Education Week, 15,* no. 29, (April 10, 1996): pp. 1; 14. Reprinted with permission from *Education Week.*

At the same time, though, the authors have not sugarcoated the past. Episodes such as the internment of Japanese-Americans during World War II are still expected to be studied.

"The revisions were very successful," said Diane Ravitch, who awarded funding for the project when she was an assistant U.S. secretary of education and who later became a critic of the standards. "What they have managed to do now is be nonjudgmental."

Additions and Subtraction

The National Center for History in the Schools, based at the University of California at Los Angeles, undertook the task of rewriting the standards after they became embroiled in controversy when they were released in late 1994.

Conservatives did most of the criticizing, but more moderate historians and educators also complained. They said the drafters were so concerned about telling the stories of previously neglected minority groups and women—and the unjust treatment they were subjected to—that they disregarded significant historical figures and the positive features of the United States and the West.

Some critics recommended that the entire project be scrapped. But the Washington-based Council for Basic Education, which promotes high academic standards in the schools, impaneled two groups to review the standards. The panels deemed them flawed but salvageable and suggested ways to improve them.

The recommendations are reflected in the new "basic edition." The three sets of standards—K–4, U.S. history, and world history—that totaled 663 pages the first time around have been incorporated into a single 225-page volume.

The downsizing is the result of eliminating the teaching examples, the most contentious part of the standards.

"To many people, they were exciting examples, but they made it so terribly unbalanced," said Albert Quie, a former Minnesota governor who was the chairman of the U.S. history review panel for the CBE.

Teachers, in conjunction with the history center, are preparing two stand-alone volumes for classroom use that will include revised teaching examples.

The most extensive changes are in U.S. history. Introductions to each of the 10 eras have been expanded generally with more upbeat additions. To the era on expansion and reform, for instance, has been added: "Students should study how Americans, animated by land hunger, the ideology of 'Manifest Destiny,' and the optimism that anything was possible with imagination, hard work, and the maximum freedom of the individual, flocked to the Western frontier."

The standards also address such issues as the attraction of immigrants to the United States and the opportunities available to them—subjects that were largely overlooked in the original document.

But students also are asked to learn about the difficulties the newcomers encountered.

In the standards for both U.S. and world history, white Westerners no longer seem to be portrayed as the only oppressors. Students are expected to know about gang slavery in the Middle East and the rise of racial hostility on the part of many groups in 19th-century U.S. cities.

The Cold War and the 20th century have been amplified in both subjects as well. Education, science and technology, and economics have also been beefed up. Another addition is the study of ideas, particularly as they relate to democracy.

The authors have added more than they have subtracted, but what is missing is the notion that minorities—and particularly women—were members of monolithic groups.

And while a few names, such as George Washington, have been added prominently to the standards, many more names do not appear. One standard discusses electric power and telephones, but Thomas Edison and Alexander Graham Bell, the men who are credited with inventing the incandescent electric lamp and the telephone, respectively, are still not mentioned.

"We didn't feel we were in the business of writing lists of names for kids to study," said Gary B. Nash, the UCLA history professor who directed the project. "To do that would have been catering to the bean counters," said Mr. Nash, referring to the critics who kept track of the number of times the names of lesser figures appeared and the absence of more prominent ones.

"Political Correctness" Gone

For the most part, the revised standards have been well received, especially those dealing with the United States.

"This is a much more usable and attractive and far less controversial product, and not because it's namby-pamby," said Steven Muller, the president emeritus of Johns Hopkins University in Baltimore and the chairman of the CBE'S review panel for the world history standards.

Albert Shanker, the president of the American Federation of Teachers, and Ruth Wattenberg, the union's liaison to the history-standards project, said the U.S. standards had improved substantially.

And though they are still troubled by the world history standards, the pair says that they, too, have been improved.

"The PC problem is essentially remedied," Ms. Wattenberg said, referring to charges of political correctness, "the anti-Western bias is gone, and the sense that the Cold War was nothing but a neutral competition between the United States and the Soviet Union is all remedied.

"The problem, and it's still a big problem, is there is no focus in the [world history] document."

John Fonte, the executive director of the Washington-based Committee to Review National Standards, said the standards are better overall but do not deserve to be a national model.

Lynne V. Cheney, who spearheaded the national history-standards project when she was the chairwoman of the National Endowment for the Humanities and later became one of its most vocal critics, founded the private group.

HISTORY STANDARDS: ROUND TWO

The revised standards integrate positive features of U.S. history that critics claimed were lacking. The new version includes the idea that the nation is alluring to immigrants, who were willing to unite despite their differences. It also addresses education, a topic that has been buttressed.

The Standard: Massive immigration after 1870 and how new social patterns, conflicts, and ideas of national unity developed amid growing cultural diversity.

ORIGINAL VERSION	REVISED VERSION
Students should be able to demonstrate understanding of the sources and experiences of the of the new immigrants by:	*The student understands the sources and experiences of the new immigrant. Therefore, the student is able to:*
■ Distinguishing between the "old" and "new" immigration in terms of its volume and the newcomers' ethnicity, religion, language, and place of origin. (Analyze multiple causation)	■ Distinguish between the "old" and the "new" immigration in terms of its volume and the immigrants' ethnicity, religion, language, place of origin, and motives for emigrating from their homelands. (Analyze multiple causation)
■ Tracing the patterns of immigrant settlements in different regions of the country. (Reconstruct patterns of historical succession and duration)	■ Trace patterns of immigrant settlement in different regions of the country and how new immigrants helped produce a composite American culture that transcended group boundaries. (Reconstruct patterns of historical succession and duration)
■ Analyzing the obstacles, opportunities, and contributions of different immigrant groups.	■ Assess the challenges, opportunities, and contributions of different immigrant groups. (Examine historical perspectives)
■ Evaluating how Catholic and Jewish newcomers responded to discrimination and internal divisions, in their new surroundings. (Obtain historical data)	■ Evaluate how Catholic and Jewish immigrants responded to religious discrimination. (Obtain historical data)
	■ Evaluate the role of public and parochial schools in integrating immigrants into the American mainstream. (Analyze cause-and-effect relationships)

SOURCE: National Center for History in the Schools.

While much of the offensive language and political bias has been removed, Mr. Fonte said, the standards still slight the West, display partisanship, editorialize, and contain inaccuracies.

Mr. Nash, the project director, said: "I'm very pleased there is even broader consensus than we achieved the first time around and it includes some of the major critics. This has been a long, on-going effort and a historic collaboration between teachers and historians to do something very positive about the very sad state of history education.

"My hope is it won't be political season anymore."

Where in the World Are World-Class Standards?
Lauren Resnick and Kate Nolan

A current television ad portrays a neatly dressed young girl walking into a middle school classroom, a pile of books cradled in her arms. With a pleasant voice, the teacher calls roll. The scene is genial and familiar, until we notice that there is only one long row of chairs, and that the names being called are the names of countries: "Taiwan, Korea, Switzerland. . . ." As the girl takes her place in the very last seat, the teacher intones ominously, "the United States of America."

The ad expresses our national concern over how well U.S. students are doing in school. Readers of an article on international standards typically expect a similarly gloomy perspective, buttressed with handy charts comparing students from around the world. Because the international standing of U.S. children is well-known, we will spare you another such chart. Instead, we want to look at countries known for producing high-performing students to discover why these school systems look so good on the honor roll of nations.

Documents Don't Tell the Story

At a recent forum on 21st century education, a co-panelist asked us to send him a copy of the world-class standards in education. We had to chuckle; would that it were so easy! If world-class standards were defined and available in the local library's reference section, researchers and policymakers alike would make frequent use of it. Unfortunately, no such volume exists.

SOURCE: *Educational Leadership, 52,* no. 6, (March 1995): pp. 6–10. Reprinted with permission of the Association for Supervision and Curriculum Development. Copyright © 1995 by ASCD. All rights reserved.

In 1993, when the New Standards Project at the University of Pittsburgh began its international benchmarking efforts, we hoped to collect and analyze the standards documents of other countries. We began by concentrating on mathematics, thinking it might suffer less from cultural differences than do other areas.

The countries that interested us fell into the following categories:

- those whose students perform well on international tests (for example, France),
- those whose education systems enjoy international esteem (for example, the Netherlands),
- those with a federal structure much like our own (for example, Germany), and
- those representing major economic competitors of the United States (for example, Japan).

We quickly discovered that standards are not in neat volumes on the shelves of education ministries, but instead arise out of a complex interaction of curriculums, textbooks, exams, classroom practice, and student work.

Moreover, when we sought to compile a library of materials, teachers, both at home and abroad, warned us that documents alone cannot tell the whole standards story. After all, teachers do not teach all and only what is in a textbook. They advised us to (1) find out what happens to kids who do *not* meet the standards, and (2) look at student work, which is where one really finds out what is expected of students.

We realized we had to answer six important questions to get a clear picture of world-class performance:

- What is the structure of the education systems in other countries?
- What are students expected to know and be able to do at key junctures in their schooling careers?
- What kinds of performances are used to demonstrate competence?
- What counts as "good enough" in these performances?
- What percentage of the students is meeting the standards?
- What reform efforts are under way or on the horizon?

The answers to these questions were often fascinating, and, at times, startling. For example, students in France, Japan, and the Netherlands have traditionally done very well on international mathematics tests (Educational Testing Service 1993, McKnight et al. 1987). In addition, international experts hold these systems in high esteem. At first glance, these systems differ dramatically from one another, but a closer look yields two important lessons:

- There is more than one way to help students achieve excellence.
- To successfully serve a large number and variety of students, schools must work as systems whose parts are focused on coherent, consistent, publicly articulated goals.

Let's look at mathematics education in Japan, France, and the Netherlands.

Tracking: Results Are Mixed

Historically, U.S. schools were among the first to provide secondary schooling for all students. Many argue that this is why the United States fares poorly in international comparisons: while we are committed to the education of all children, other countries practice strict ability tracking that creams off the best students. Hence, our average students are compared with their best students.

In fact, our research shows that things are no longer that simple. Other developed nations have caught up with and even surpassed us in terms of retaining students throughout the years of secondary schooling (Centre for Educational Research and Innovation 1993). Further, tracking practices do not correlate in any straightforward way with high performance internationally. In such comparisons, tracking and achievement appear to be independent of one another.

In practice, U.S. students are often tracked into classes for the gifted and talented, vocational education, and the like. On the other hand, those systems in which students outperform ours include both highly tracked and highly untracked systems.

Tracking is common in the Netherlands, where secondary school students elect one of four levels of study based on both their career goals and their past experience in school. French students are untracked through age 13; thereafter, about 85 percent of students are in a single track. In Japan, there is no tracking throughout the years of compulsory schooling.

In other words, tracking and education's availability to the whole populace cannot by themselves explain away the poor performance of U.S. students on international tests.

We have, however, learned some important lessons while examining tracking.

Japan   Japanese schools prefer heterogeneous grouping because it seems to produce higher performance all around: High performing students actually learn more, it is argued, by serving as tutors to their classmates. Further, a central focus of Japanese schools is to help form the moral and cultural character of students. High performance is valued because it contributes to the well-being of the group. In school, this means that students see their own excellence as compromised by another student's failure! One of the standards for all Japanese students, then, is to be a contributing member of an effective work group.[1]

The Netherlands   Tracking in the Netherlands is not determined by achievement tests, which are a predominant means of sorting students in the United

---

[1] For more on Japanese attitudes toward ability, effort, and grouping, see H. W. Stevenson and J. W. Stigler, (1992), *The Learning Gap*, (New York: Summit Books); K. Okamoto, (1992), *Education of the Rising Sun*, (Tokyo: Monbusho); H. W. Stevenson, C. Chen, and S. Lee, (1993), "Motivation and Achievement of Gifted Children in East Asia and the United States," *Journal for the Education of the Gifted 16*, 3: 223–250.

FIGURE 1

**Exercise From a Dutch Leaving Exam in Mathematics Designed for
16-Year-Olds Who Will Not Go on to College**

Exercise 4
A swimming pool of 16 x 50 meters has a shallow part A (depth 1 meter) and a deep part C (depth 4 meters). In between, the depth increases regularly from 1 meter to 4 meters. (See the drawing.) All measurements are given in meters. The swimming pool is filled up to the edge.

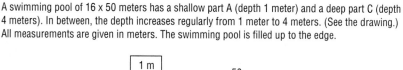
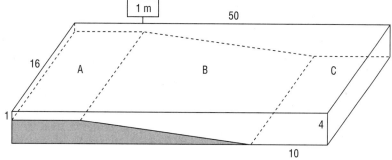

• Calculate how many m³ of water are in the swimming pool.

On the border between part A and part B is a sign that indicates the depth (see the drawing). The lifeguard wants to put another sign on the edge saying "depth 1.80 meters."
• Calculate the distance between the two signs.

SOURCE: Dutch National Institute for Educational Measurement.

States. In fact, achievement tests are not used in the Netherlands. Instead, secondary students, in consultation with parents, teachers, and—sometimes—school administrators, choose the track that is most appropriate for them.

The major factor in the student's choice of track is his or her career goals, because each of the four tracks in Dutch secondary schools leads to a broad set of careers and levels of specialization. Further, throughout the first two years of secondary school, and in some cases beyond that, students may switch tracks if their goals change. Early on, then, Dutch students have a clear sense that their studies are directly connected with life after school.

A defining characteristic of tracking in Dutch schools is that *all* students are expected to perform well. Mathematics exams at the conclusion of high school are a case in point: Although students who intend to go on to a university are asked to perform at a more sophisticated level than those who wish to enter the work force, the latter group faces very difficult exams. As Figure 1 shows, these exams involve complex applications of algebra and geometry. Students are also expected to show how they arrived at their answers; there is

FIGURE 2
Portion of a Swedish Mathematics Exam for 16-Year-Olds

Part B. For exercises 12–15, complete solutions must be given. NOTE! If you only give the answer you will get 0 points.

12. What is the price of a piece of ham weighing 6 hg if the price is 150 krona per kilogram.

13. How much is the telephone bill for a quarter of the year if it shows 300 units of use for that time? Each unit costs 23 Öre. In addition, there is a charge of 187 krona per quarter in subscription fees.

SOURCE: PRIM Group of the School Administration for the Stockholm Teacher Training Institute.

more than one right way. Dutch educators have been developing a mathematics program geared to helping all students perform well.

The Dutch approach contrasts sharply with that used in the United States today, where educators are hotly debating the relationship between tracking and achievement. Some argue that tracking results in a weak curriculum for students whose work has been weak in the past; others argue that a failure to track means holding back highly motivated students, forcing them into heterogeneous groups with a dumbed-down curriculum.

Curriculums: Common Goals Are Crucial

Many countries whose schools have achieved academic excellence have a national curriculum. Many educators maintain that a single curriculum naturally leads to high performance, but the fact that the United States values local control of schools precludes such a national curriculum. This argument would have us throw in the towel regarding raising achievement.

Our research has shown that national curriculums are a diverse group of documents. Some express the educational philosophy or traditions of the country, while others concentrate on prevailing cultural needs. Some describe teaching strategies or content considered important. Most are very sketchy. They do not detail lesson plans that mandate uniform classroom practice throughout the country.

In Japan, for example, the curriculum includes brief objectives for each grade and content level, and a few specific items that should be mastered. Teachers must and do go far beyond the guidelines. The same is true in France and in the Netherlands.

Still, a centrally articulated set of goals, even if vaguely stated, plays important roles: It organizes the development of exams and curriculums, informs textbook writing, and determines the direction of teacher training. As a result, high-stakes exams, texts, curriculums, and lesson plans do not work at cross-purposes. When all parties involved in these diverse activities have their eyes on the same set of goals, students get a consistent message about what they should know to be well educated.

France   France offers the clearest example of this convergence of goals. In texts and exams, the influence of the national curriculum is obvious. For example, a French math text for 16-year-olds begins by spelling out the national curriculum for the year so that all 16-year-olds know what they are expected to study. The book's similar table of contents shows that the text developers referred to the curriculum. Moreover, the text makes frequent references to math exams the regional school districts have given in the past. Students practice on these exams to help them prepare for the exams they will face; they know where to concentrate to meet the standard.

One could draw a tempting but fallacious inference from these examples. Can simply having a coherent system of curriculums, texts, and exams produce excellent student performance? In fact, coherence is not enough: Sweden offers the counterexample.

Sweden   As in France, the Swedish national curriculum strongly influences texts and exams, giving students a clear message about what is expected. Still, the mathematics exam for Swedish 16-year-olds shows that a clear message, too, can set a low standard (see Fig. 2). Unlike its Dutch counterpart, the Swedish exam does not ask for complex mathematical reasoning, but focuses instead on relatively low-skill computation. The lesson here: Unless coherent schooling elements set high academic standards, we can't expect student achievement to rise.

Exams: Upholding Standards

To understand how certain systems produce excellence, we also must find out how students demonstrate what they know and can do. Many countries give an exam at the end of compulsory schooling, at about age 16, and that exam often is the last measure we have of how *all* students are performing. After this point, not all students are expected to work to high standards.

France   In France, virtually all students attempt to qualify for the *Brevet* certificate at the end of middle school, and more than 75 percent succeed. This qualification is awarded on two bases: final exams in several subjects, and classroom teachers' continuous assessment during the last two years. The exams differ among the country's 27 regional school districts, but multiple choice is virtually unknown. Students must write essays, argue for positions, and solve problems while giving evidence of their reasoning. Texts and curriculums support these practices. This means that students can prepare for the *Brevet,* because it reflects the very same skills and knowledge they have been honing in school.

The Netherlands   In the Netherlands, all students take high school leaving exams. The final grade is the average of the exam's two parts: one generated nationally, the other compiled by the school. Dutch schools have four tracks and give four corresponding national exams in most subjects. As in France, multiple-choice and short-answer questions are rare.

U.S. teachers often marvel at these exams that require a lot of writing. "How are they graded?" they want to know. Obviously, with few exceptions, machine grading is impossible. By and large, teachers do it. If selected as graders, they are either freed from other duties for a time, paid a stipend, or both. To be sure grades are given fairly across regions, all scorers receive scoring guides, and auditors check a random sample of scores.

Germany   In Hessen, Germany, however, teachers both compile and grade the exam for their own students. When questioned about the possibility of teachers artificially inflating grades or helping their students cheat, one university professor seemed puzzled. "Why would they cheat," she asked us, "when they are professionals who care about their work?" This trust in and respect for teachers as professionals is common in countries whose students are noted for excellence.

What We've Learned

These shared practices and common threads among apparently very different approaches to education teach important lessons:

- Setting clear, consistent, demanding, public standards helps students perform well.
- Tracking and grouping practices must make sense in the culture of the school and for both the student's and community's future goals.
- Exams should test what students have been asked to learn, preferably in the same ways they must perform in class.
- Exams that call for complex, demanding tasks can be given to a wide range of students, perhaps to all students.
- As the front-line professionals in the education process, teachers should have much to say about what goes into exams and how they are graded.

None of these results is surprising. They represent what good teachers in good programs with hard-working students have always done. For the New Standards Project, the good news from international comparisons is that it is possible to set high standards and expect all students to work to achieve them.

One caveat is in order: The route to high performance is not necessarily to simply implement the good practices of other countries. When we aim for world-class standards, we are not aiming at a target that is standing still and waiting for us. Far from it.

Concerns about preparing students for the challenges of work and community in the 21st century are not unique to the United States. The Netherlands continues to stress the development of improved mathematics curriculums as a national priority. Around the world, schools are seeking to improve the technological abilities of all students.

Sweden and France are piloting creative means for teaching children of immigrants. All over the world, in fact, educators are working to improve school services to traditionally marginalized groups, including children from low-income families and girls of all economic classes. Issues of equity, or the performance of language, racial, and ethnic minorities are not unique to the United States.

The challenge for the United States is to create a national agenda of excellence that can raise the performance of all students without creating a national exam or curriculum. Each community must adapt the agenda in unique ways that nonetheless work in unison.

The image of a symphony comes to mind: each instrument has its own score, its own qualities, its own goals, but the scores must harmonize if a satisfying performance is to result. Just so with state and local reforms: they must and will vary in ways that make sense to local schools and communities. But they must also share a common vision of the high performance we must expect from all students.

REFERENCES

Centre for Educational Research and Innovation. (1993). *Education at a Glance: OECD Indicators.* Paris: Organisation for Economic Co-operation and Development, p. 116.

Educational Testing Service. (1993). *NAEP 1992 Mathematics Report Card for the Nation and the States,* IAEP/NAEP Cross-linking Study. Washington, D.C.: U.S. Government Printing Office.

McKnight, C., F. Crosswhite, J. Dossey, E. Kifer, S. Swafford, K. Travers, and T. Cooney. (1987). *The Underachieving Curriculum: Assessing U.S. School Mathematics from an International Perspective.* Champaign, Ill.: Stipes Publishing Company.

Longer Year, Day Proposed for Schooling
Meg Sommerfeld

If the education-reform movement is to succeed, American schools will need a longer school day and year, and should allocate at least 5½ hours daily for instruction in nine core academic subjects, the final report of a federal commission recommends.

The six-hour school day and 180-day school year "should be relegated to museums as an exhibit of our education past," the commission says in its report, released at a news conference here last week.

Established by Congress in 1991 as an independent advisory panel, the National Education Commission on Time and Learning was charged with conducting a "comprehensive review of the relationship between time and learning in the nation's schools."

Over two years, the nine commission members visited 19 schools and education programs across the country and heard from more than 150 teachers, administrators, parents, students, and others who testified at hearings. Panelists also visited schools in Japan and Germany.

"Increasingly, we Americans live in a world of fax machines, car phones, and beepers—technology that is meant to speed up our lives and make us all a little bit more productive," Secretary of Education Richard W. Riley said at the news conference. "Yet, when it comes to how we teach our children, we seem fixed on a time schedule from another era."

Although the average American school day lasts about six hours, the commission found that high school students spend only about three hours in academic classes. It called on schools to essentially double the amount of time allocated for the core subjects listed in the National Education Goals: English, mathematics, science, foreign language, civics and government, economics, arts, history, and geography.

"Protecting" Academics

The commission estimates U.S. high school students spend an average of 1,460 hours on core academic courses before graduating, less than half as much time as their counterparts in Japan, France, and Germany.

In other nations, the report says, "academic time is protected," and distinctions are made between the "academic day" and the rest of the school day. The commission urges schools to establish an academic day "devoted almost exclusively to core-academic instruction."

SOURCE: *Education Week, 13,* no. 33, (May 11, 1994): pp. 1; 12. Reprinted with permission from *Education Week.*

Other activities, it says, such as athletics, compensatory instruction, programs for the gifted and talented, and language instruction for non-native English speakers, could be offered during the remainder of a longer school day.

The commission is also calling for schools to stay open longer and for some schools in every district to offer an extended year.

More time for teachers to engage in professional development is also essential, the commission says.

In general, the report urges schools to be less rigid in how they use time, by moving away from standard 51-minute class period and adopting block scheduling or other devices that make students' and teachers' schedules more flexible.

Praise, Caution, and Blame

Several education groups moved quickly to embrace the commission's recommendations.

"Liberating pedagogy and the curriculum from time constraints enhances teaching and learning," Keith Geiger, the president of the National Education Association, said in a statement.

Gordon M. Ambach, the executive director of the Council of Chief State School Officers, called the report "on target," but he also cautioned that more time will cost more money. "Let's hope this report has better success than past efforts across the nation in persuading taxpayers of the value of longer quality learning time," he said.

But not all reaction was positive.

A longer school year is not the most cost-effective way to improve the quality of education and would have a detrimental effect on amusement parks and other seasonal tourist attractions that provide jobs for youths, argued Quinn Rasberry, a spokeswoman for the International Association of Amusement Parks and Attractions.

And Beverly LaHaye, the president of Concerned Women for America, issued a statement calling the recommendations "another attempt by the state to usurp parental authority and influence over our children." But the group said it supported the study's call for more emphasis on academic subjects.

The commission's chairman, John Hodge Jones, the superintendent of the Murfreesboro, Tenn., schools, said his district encountered some resistance several years ago when it first proposed a longer school day and year. But, he said, it allowed parents to decide whether or not to send their child to a school with the extended schedule.

"The choice which we gave our families enriched them," he said.

In his remarks last week, Secretary Riley acknowledged the anxiety created by departing from the nearly sacred character of the traditional school schedule.

"The American school day, as we have known it, has been a constant for generations of Americans; we've all grown up with it," he said. "But we may be at the point where our affection for it must yield to some new thinking about time."

CHANGING TIME AND LEARNING

In its report, the National Education Commission on Time and Learning recommends that:

- Schools be reinvented around learning, not time, in order to bring every child to world-class standards in core academic areas.
- State and local boards work with schools to redesign education so that time becomes a factor supporting learning, not a boundary marking its limits.
- Schools provide additional academic time by reclaiming the school day for academic instruction.
- Schools remain open longer during the day, and some schools in every district remain open throughout the year.
- Teachers be provided with the professional time and opportunities they need to do their jobs.
- Schools use new technologies to increase productivity, enhance student achievement, and expand learning time.
- Every district convene local leaders to develop action plans that offer different school options and encourage parents, students, and teachers to choose among them.
- All people shoulder their individual responsibilities to transform learning in America.

What School Choice Could Do in Milwaukee
George Will

The Milwaukee teachers' union cares so much for the city's students it is fighting a program that by next year would give 15 percent of them the choice of escaping from this caring. The state branch of the American Civil Liberties Union, pursuing constitutional propriety as it understands it, supports this attempt to circumscribe the liberty of thousands of Milwaukee's poorer parents and children. And now Wisconsin's Supreme Court has served the interests of the union and the ACLU by acting with a swiftness and force that suggests the court thinks Milwaukee is in danger of suffering the "establishment of religion."

SOURCE: *The Washington Post,* September 10, 1995, p. C7. Copyright © 1995, Washington Post Writers Group. Reprinted with permission.

Because of all this high-mindedness, thousands of children of low-income parents had their school year jeopardized until contributions from the Bradley Foundation and sympathetic individuals met the tuition needs of most of them. This case illustrates the tenacity of opponents of programs that extend to the poor the school choices available to most of the tenacious opponents, who are not poor.

In 1990 Wisconsin's legislature approved a voucher program for Milwaukee. The program makes children from families earning less than $26,000 eligible for vouchers worth up to $3,600 for private school tuitions. The teachers' union unsuccessfully fought the program even before there was a religious issue, on a variety of state constitutional grounds.

So did the ACLU, which argued that the program would drain money from public schools. That is hardly a civil liberties problem. And it is an odd argument coming from the ACLU, which has sued public schools more than any other organization, and is partly responsible for rulings that make it difficult to discipline disruptive students—rulings that have contributed to public school disorder and thus to the attractiveness of private schools.

And the local NAACP filed a brief in support of the union's position even though 95 percent of the children enjoying choices under this program are black or Hispanic. The local African American paper, the *Milwaukee Journal,* which supports the voucher program, reports, believably, that 88 percent of black families do, too.

In July the legislature expanded the program by making the vouchers redeemable at religious schools (Ninety-three of Milwaukee's 130 private schools are sectarian). So the ACLU and the teachers' union dashed back to court, claiming that this change violated the separation of church and state. Now the state Supreme Court has issued an injunction stopping the program until the constitutional point has been adjudicated.

But what danger justifies this disruption of a program affecting approximately 3,000 students (about 3 percent of the city's students) who were admitted to religious schools under the voucher system? What irreparable harm could come from allowing the program produced by Wisconsin's democratic institutions to proceed while the lawyers argue? Even if the court eventually comes to the preposterous conclusion that the program constitutes "establishment" of religion, disestablishment could be promptly ordered.

The "establishment" accusation is a flimsy pretext for attacking school choice (and defending union jobs). The voucher program does not have as its "primary effect" the advancement of religion (a U.S. Supreme Court test). The program, which gives vouchers to individuals, gives no direct financial assistance to religious institutions. It establishes no incentive for individuals to pick private over public schools or sectarian over nonsectarian private schools. And because state regulations affecting schools in the voucher program are minimal, the program cannot be said to involve "excessive entanglement" of government with religion.

Nine inner-city private schools report an average 88 percent graduation rate, compared with 48 percent for public high schools. Opponents of school choice say such disparities are largely explained by the fact that vouchers enable private schools to "skim the cream" from the student population, leaving public schools to cope with the rest. But a state auditor found that before students in Milwaukee's choice program entered the program they had significantly worse results on reading and math tests than the average of public school students.

In Milwaukee's public schools, at most 48 percent of students graduate, the dropout rate is more than seven times the state average, and even after substantial attrition of many of the least promising students, 79 percent of entering seniors failed a math proficiency examination required for graduation. In 11 public high schools that enroll more than three-fourths of all black students, the average grade is 1.5 on a scale of 4.0 and the failure rate in core academic subjects ranges from 26 percent to 43 percent.

Obviously public schools should not be blamed for all the consequences of inner-city life. But neither should they be allowed to treat the inner city as a plantation inhabited by captive students whose avenues of choice must be restricted to prevent escapes.

School Choice and Racial/Class Inequities
Roberta Tovey

The magnet school program in Montgomery County, Maryland, is flourishing. Begun in 1977 to further racial integration and serve a diverse student population, the program today involves almost 20 elementary and secondary schools and enrolls more than 10,000 students. Individual programs focus on computer literacy, French immersion, physically handicapped students, and the "gifted and talented."

Yet most Montgomery County parents who choose magnet schools are not motivated primarily by the school's curriculum. Nor are their preferences likely to advance integration. Instead, parents seek schools where the students' families make about the same amount of money they do, and where the kids match their own color or ethnicity.

In Milwaukee, grassroots efforts in the late 1980s led to the creation of a voucher program to allow low-income public school students to attend private school like the popular Urban Day School. Such schools receive about $2,000 in public funds for each voucher student. Parents who use these vouchers are

Source: *Education Digest*, September 1995, pp. 14–18. Condensed and reprinted with permission from *The Harvard Education Letter*, XI, no. 3, pp. 1–3. Copyright © 1995 by the President and Fellows of Harvard College. All rights reserved.

enthusiastic about the program. So are the private schools, for whom vouchers have been a financial boon.

But John Witte, of the University of Wisconsin, an independent evaluator of the Milwaukee voucher scheme, observes that "this program was not inspired by an interest in desegregation." Indeed, with one exception, the private schools taking part in the program are as segregated as or more segregated than the public schools: Urban Day's students are almost 100 percent black; the students at Bruce-Guadalupe Community School are nearly 100 percent Hispanic.

Milwaukee does have a mandatory desegregation program—Chapter 220— in which 7,000 white students are bused to city schools and 6,000 nonwhites go to the suburbs. One reason the private school voucher program is so popular, says Witte, is that "it is a way to get out of busing."

School choice was first advocated by Southern conservatives as a means of thwarting desegregation efforts in the 1960s; the new choice programs of the 1990s, if not carefully monitored, could further that same goal. Though proponents of choice often describe it as a form of voluntary desegregation, as well as an opportunity for low-income and minority students to get a better education tailored to their particular needs, recent research tells a different story.

"Choice appears to have a stratifying effect, by race, social class, and ethnicity," says Richard Elmore, of the Harvard Graduate School of Education, "even when it is explicitly designed to remedy inequalities on these dimensions."

These new studies reveal a disturbing trend: Families that participate in choice programs often choose schools on the basis of similarity in culture, location, and ethnic mix—factors that tend to perpetuate segregation. Jeffrey Henig, of George Washington University, studied the Montgomery County magnet schools and found that "race continues to play a role in shaping parental choices among schools."

White students from higher-income families were more likely to request transfers into mainly white schools in higher-income neighborhoods; students of color were more likely to request transfers into mainly nonwhite schools in lower-income areas. The reasons, Henig speculates, may be that the schools' academic programs are not as clearly differentiated as they appear to be; or simply that parents place more importance on the nonacademic qualities of schools, like proximity to home or familiarity.

Because school officials in Montgomery County are bound by racial balance requirements, the magnet program there has not actually worsened segregation. Henig believes that, "when done right," magnet programs can be used to promote integration, and can help "keep white families in town."

More Segregation

But without intervention of the sort that many choice proponents reject in the name of "downsizing" government, parents' choices would lead to more segregation, not less. "Unless aggressively regulated by authorities," says Henig, "choice may exacerbate, rather than ameliorate, racial segregation. And the choice movement today, unfortunately, seems to be turning away from managed programs."

The potential for increased racial segregation in uncontrolled choice programs is cause for concern in light of more than 30 years of research showing that students in integrated schools are more likely to complete college, get better-paying jobs, and break out of the cycle of racial isolation and poverty in which many black and Latino families are stuck.

Choice programs may intensify the gap, not just between races, but also between those who are better educated, more motivated, and better employed and those who are not. In study after study, analysts find that those families most in need are least likely to take advantage of choice programs.

San Antonio's multilingual magnet school program, designed explicitly to improve the performance of Latino students through immersion in their culture and language, is a case in point. While researcher Valerie Martinez, of the University of North Texas, found positive effects on achievement for participating students, she also found that the children most likely to participate are higher achievers, from relatively better-off families, with parents who are involved in their children's education.

A study of Detroit families' attitudes by Valerie Lee, of the University of Michigan, similarly revealed that, while many lower-income families favor choice, those in the lowest third in terms of income and education were likely to have no opinion on the subject and were least likely to participate. Moreover, Lee points out, as relatively better educated and more involved parents opt out of the public school system, the loss of their influence "can have an adverse effect on the schools and families left behind."

"When children from poor districts opt for richer districts, the result can be financially detrimental to poor districts," says Lee. "This is a case of 'the rich getting richer, the poor getting poorer'—the essence of social stratification." Because the presence of good students is known to have a "pull up" effect on other students, the skimming off of the best students in a school can further harm those who remain.

"How did the many Detroits of our nation develop the socially disastrous environments that they currently offer families?" Lee asks. "One by one, families left the cities when they were able to do so. But other families were unable to leave, whether for economic reasons, lack of motivation, or the hostility they faced in neighborhoods elsewhere." Choice, she concludes, "bears an unsettling resemblance to the very social, economic, and political processes that created the problems of urban education."

Skepticism

In light of Lee's and other scholars' research, Elmore cautions policymakers "to treat with considerable skepticism the claim that educational choice enhances equality of opportunity."

Nevertheless, many low-income parents favor choice, seeing it as a chance to give their children better schools and more opportunities. Bruce Fuller, of Harvard University, argues that school choice is "potentially a good answer to educational problems for parents who are well-motivated and who have plentiful information." In Fuller's view, choice programs pose a dilemma for policymakers. While they worsen inequities among those who don't participate, he says, there is also inequity in not allowing some parents a chance to improve their children's lives. "This is why many advocates for choice come from ethnic neighborhoods usually viewed as part of the political left."

"Should the state's role be to encourage motivated parents to move upward socially and economically?" Fuller asks. "Or should the state control choice to keep these parents where they are in the name of equalizing advantages to all? This dilemma becomes more and more bewildering in multicultural societies, where parents express diverse educational values." Fuller therefore favors so-called involuntary choice, such as the program in Cambridge, Massachusetts, where all parents have to choose their children's schools. "When all parents choose," he argues, "they must search out information and express their preferences."

Although families that send their children to private, magnet, or suburban schools through choice programs generally express satisfaction with these schools, evidence of the effect on students' academic achievement is mixed. Witte compared the test scores of students who participated in the Milwaukee voucher program with those of a random sampling of Milwaukee public school students, controlling for the influence of student background. He found that voucher students did not appear to do any better than the public school students. Witte also observed a high rate of attrition from private schools.

To complicate the picture, several studies indicate that merely being from a family that chooses to participate in a choice program has a positive effect on achievement. Researchers were able to isolate the impact of being from a choosing family by comparing achievement scores of students who wanted to attend a choice school but for one reason or another were not admitted with the scores of students who were admitted.

Even without clear evidence of academic gains for students who participate in these programs, choice remains inherently attractive to most parents: 62 percent of Americans favor school choice, according to a 1990 Gallup poll. Support for educational choice is rooted in the strong individualism of American politics and culture. Witte puts it simply: "Parents support choice because it gives them options." Perhaps the very act of choosing is empowering and is itself a benefit of choice programs.

But what about those families for whom choice programs are not empowering? The research of Lee, Witte, and Martinez points to an identifiable group of families that tend not to take part, families for whom choice programs do not offer attractive or feasible options. Several recent studies attempt to throw light on the attitudes of this "nonchoosing" group.

Amy Stuart Wells, of the University of California at Los Angeles, interviewed African-American students and parents who live in St. Louis and found that, while some students take advantage of a program that sends them to largely white suburban schools, others feel uncomfortable in these schools and opt for the familiarity of neighborhood schools. Still others deliberately reject what they perceive as a white, middle-class value system that equates better schooling with good jobs and a better life.

Bruce Fuller's analysis of preschool choices shows that Latino families are much more likely to shy away from formal preschools than black or white families, even though there is clear evidence that children who attend such preschools will do better in school later. The reason? Many Latino parents prefer to keep their children in familiar surroundings, with family members or home caretakers who share their culture and values. Elizabeth Weiser Ramirez, of the Hispanic youth organization Aspira, says that Latino families see preschools and day-care centers "as a kind of foreign turf."

Another reason parents don't participate in choice programs is that they don't know about them. Here, again, the least educated and least integrated families are most at risk. Witte found that in 1991, the first year vouchers were used in Milwaukee, 51 percent of families had not heard of the program. In Montgomery County, more than a third of families have never heard the term "magnet program," with higher proportions among minorities, especially Hispanics.

Even parents who participate in school choice programs often select schools without being well informed about them, relying on casual remarks by friends and neighbors or a vague sense that a given school "has a good reputation." Many parents and students simply assume that any school in a white or suburban area or other higher-status neighborhood is better than a mainly black school.

Critics argue that, for many parents and children, choice programs as they are currently formulated do not present viable options. Ironically, these are the families whose children, because of lower incomes and less education, stand to gain the most from choice. If these increasingly popular programs do not take into account cultural preferences, Fuller argues, "the results will be far from empowering."